Reasonable Radical?

Paula — in admiration
and appreciation for all
you do in the church
and the wider world.
God Bless,

[signature]

June 2018

Reasonable Radical?

Reading the Writings of Martyn Percy

EDITED BY
Ian S. Markham
AND
Joshua Daniel

PICKWICK *Publications* · Eugene, Oregon

REASONABLE RADICAL?
Reading the Writings of Martyn Percy

Pickwick Publications
An Imprint of Wipf and Stock Publishers
199 W. 8th Ave., Suite 3
Eugene, OR 97401

www.wipfandstock.com

PAPERBACK ISBN: 978-1-5326-1783-6
HARDCOVER ISBN: 978-1-4982-4284-4
EBOOK ISBN: 978-1-4982-4283-7

Cataloguing-in-Publication data:

Names: Markham, Ian S. | Daniel, Joshua

Title: Reasonable radical? : reading the writings of Martyn Percy / edited by Ian S. Markham and Joshua Daniel.

Description: Eugene, OR: Pickwick Publications, 2018 | Includes bibliographical references and index.

Identifiers: ISBN 978-1-5326-1783-6 (paperback) | ISBN 978-1-4982-4284-4 (hardcover) | ISBN 978-1-4982-4283-7 (ebook)

Subjects: LCSH: Percy, Martyn | Anglican Communion | Church renewal—Anglican Communion | Church of England | Christianity—21st century | Church | Clergy

Classification: BX5005 M36 2018 (print) | BX5005 (ebook)

Manufactured in the U.S.A.   01/15/18

Contents

Contributors

Kathryn D. Blanchard is Associate Professor of Religious Studies at Alma College. She is the author of *The Protestant Ethic or the Spirit of Capitalism: Christians, Freedom and Free Markets* (Cascade 2010) and co-author of *An Introduction to Christian Environmentalism* (Baylor University Press 2014).

Simon Coleman is Chancellor Jackman Professor at the Department for the Study of Religion, University of Toronto. He received his PhD in Social Anthropology from the University of Cambridge, and has also worked in the Anthropology Departments at the Universities of Durham and Sussex. He is a former editor of the *Journal of the Royal Anthropological Association*, and a current co-editor of both the journal *Religion and Society* and the book series Routledge Studies in Pilgrimage, Religious Travel and Tourism. His books include *The Globalisation of Charismatic Christianity* (Cambridge University Press 2000), *Reframing Pilgrimage* (edited with John Eade, Routledge 2004) and *The Anthropology of Global Pentecostalism and Evangelicalism* (edited with Rosalind Hackett, New York University Press 2015).

Joshua Daniel is a candidate for Holy Orders in the Diocese of Arkansas and a seminarian at Virginia Theological Seminary. He completed his PhD in Philosophy, writing a dissertation on Wittgenstein and religion, at the University of Arkansas in 2015.

Joel C. Daniels is a postdoctoral fellow at the Institute for the Biocultural Study of Religion, assisting editor of the journal *Religion, Brain & Behavior*, and an Episcopal priest at Saint Thomas Church Fifth Avenue in New York City. He is the author of the monograph *Theology, Tragedy, and Suffering in Nature: Toward a Realist Doctrine of Creation*, and articles in the *Anglican Theological Review* and the *Journal of Ecumenical Studies*.

Matt Gompels is a postgraduate student in the study of religion at the Faculty of Theology and Religion, and Keble College at the University of Oxford. Alongside a career in Education, he has spent time researching charismatic Christianity in both the United States and Britain, under the supervision of Martyn Percy. His broader research interests include the changing role of religion in public life, specifically the relationship between conceptualizations of religious identity and public policy.

Samantha R. E. Gottlich is a transitional deacon in the Episcopal Diocese of Texas and the curate at St. Mark's Episcopal Church in Houston. Her background in physiology, camping ministry, and higher education feed into her larger concern for holistic wellness and faith. She also co-authored *Faith Rules: An Episcopal Manual* (Moorehouse 2016) and *Lectionary Levity* (Church Publishing 2017) with Ian S. Markham.

Monique M. Ingalls is Assistant Professor of Music at Baylor University. She received her PhD from the University of Pennsylvania. Her work on evangelical and charismatic music and worship has been published within the fields of ethnomusicology, media studies, liturgical studies, and hymnology. She is co-founder of the Christian Congregational Music: Local and Global Perspectives conference, and a series editor for Routledge's *Congregational Music Studies* book series.

Richard Lawson is the dean of Saint John's Cathedral in Denver, Colorado. He has served as the rector of parishes in the dioceses of Alabama and West Tennessee. Richard's essays have been published in the *Anglican Theological Review* and the *Sewanee Theological Review*.

Gerard Mannion holds the Amaturo Chair in Catholic Studies at Georgetown University, where he is also a Fellow of the Berkley Center for Religion, Peace and World Affairs. He was educated at the Universities of Cambridge and Oxford. Founding Chair of the Ecclesiological Investigations International Research Network, to date he has authored, co-authored and edited some nineteen books and numerous articles and chapters elsewhere in the fields of ecclesiology and ethics, as well as in other aspects of systematic theology and philosophy.

Ian S. Markham is the Dean and President of Virginia Theological Seminary and Professor of Theology and Ethics. He is the author of *A Theology of Engagement* (Wiley 2003), *Truth and the Reality of God* (T. & T. Clark 1998), and *Plurality and Christian Ethics* (Cambridge University Press 1994). His awards include the Robertson Fellow 2006; Teape Lecturer in India 2004; Claggett Fellow attached to Washington National Cathedral in 2000; and Frank Woods Fellow at Trinity College, Melbourne in 1997, F. D. Maurice Lectures at King's College, London, 2015.

Lyndon Shakespeare, an Episcopal priest, has served parishes in Washington, DC; Virginia; New Jersey; and Long Island. From 2011–2013, Lyndon was the Director of Program and Ministry at Washington National Cathedral. As a scholar-priest, he teaches and publishes in the areas of theological anthropology and ecclesiology. His PhD thesis, written while a member of the Archbishop's Examination in Theology, has been published in the *Veritas* series of Cascade Books with the title *Being the Body of Christ in the Age of Management.* He currently serves as chair of the Society of Scholar-Priests, which fosters and supports scholarly-minded priests in their vocation to serve in parish and teaching ministries.

Daniel Warnke is a doctoral student at the University of Oxford, and currently an ordinand in the Church of England, training through St Mellitus College and serving at St Mary-le-Bow in London. His research is focused on Christianity and contemporary culture, modern ecclesiology, and practical theology. Daniel has also served as a church planter in Vineyard Churches UK and Ireland from 2005–2016.

Acknowledgments

A n endeavor of such complexity as this book is made possible by many. The Conant Grant funded the conference on the work of Martyn Percy. The participants made the conference very special. Katherine Malloy helped with some of the logistics. Benjamin Judd prepared many of the meals. Sharon Williams and Jenna Daniel compiled the index. Lesley Markham was gracious as the group took over much of her home at the Deanery. And finally, Martyn Percy took time out of his extraordinarily busy life to be present at the conference and then write responses to all the sections. We are deeply grateful to Martyn and all those involved for making the project both fascinating and great fun. The team at Pickwick was amazing. So with thanks to Robin Parry, Calvin Jaffarian, and Shannon Carter, who were professional, careful, and ensured a high quality product.

The editors also wish to thank the following publishers for permission to reproduce, in part or in whole, the following material written by Martyn Percy. Chapter 17 comes from a selection of Percy's *The Salt of the Earth: Religious Resilience in a Secular Age*, published by Sheffield Academic Press and T. & T. Clark (2002) and reissued by Bloomsbury Academic Collection (2016); chapter 18 originally appeared in *The Wisdom of the Spirit: Gospel, Church & Culture*, edited by Peter Ward, published by Ashgate (2014); chapter 19 was originally published in the *Daily Telegraph* (November 21, 2012); chapter 20 comes from Percy's *Clergy: The Origin of Species*, published by Continuum/Bloomsbury (2006); chapter 21 originally appeared in *Christian Congregational Music: Performance, Identity and Experience*, edited by Monique Ingalls, Carolyn Landau and Tom Wagner, and published by Ashgate (2013); chapter 22 comes from Percy's *Anglicanism: Confidence, Commitment and Communion*, published by Ashgate (2013); chapter 23 draws from three different works: from Percy's *Words, Wonders and Power: Understanding Contemporary Christian Fundamentalism and Revivalism*, published by SPCK (1996), from Percy's *Power and the Church: Ecclesiology in an Age of Transition*, published by Cassell (1997), and from *Theologies of Retrieval: Practices and Perspectives*, edited by Darren Sarisky, published by T. & T. Clark (2017); chapter 24 comes from two works: an article published in *Modern Believing* 55:3 (2014) and from a piece that appeared in *Church Times* (February 28, 2014); chapter 25 originally appeared in the *Anglican Theological Review* 90 (Winter 2008); chapter 26 originally appeared in *Exploring Ordinary Theology: Everyday Christian Believing and the Church*, edited by Jeff Astley and Leslie Francis, published by Ashgate (2013); chapter 27 originally appeared in *Fundamentalisms: Threats and Ideologies in the Modern World*, edited by James D. G. Dunn, published by I. B. Taurus (2016); chapter 28 originally appeared in *Practicing the Faith: The Ritual Life of Pentecostal-Charismatic Christians*, edited by Martin Lindhardt, published by Berghahn Books (2011); chapter 29 originally appeared in *Modern Church* (December 2015); chapter 30 originally appeared in *Public Faith? The State of Religious Belief and Practice in Britain*, edited by Paul Avis, published by SPCK (2003); and chapter 31 originally appeared in Percy's *The Ecclesial Canopy: Faith, Hope, Charity*, published by Ashgate (2012).

Finally, chapter 9 brings together four previously published reviews of Percy's work. Robert Carroll's review of *Words, Wonders and Power* was published in the *Anglican Theological Review*; Peter Coleman's review of *Intimate Affairs: Sexuality and Spirituality in Perspective* was published in *Crucible*; Richard H. Roberts' review of *Power and the Church: Ecclesiology in an Age of Transition* was published in *The Journal of Contemporary Religion*; and Gavin D'Costa's review of *Engaging with Contemporary Culture: Christianity, Theology and the Concrete Church* was published in *The International Journal of Public Theology*. For these publishers' permission to include this material, the editors of this book give their thanks.

Introducing Martyn Percy

To step into the world of Martyn Percy is to step into a world of faith, church, music, culture, the social sciences, and controversy. The Dean of Christ Church, Oxford, is a polymath: his corpus is vast; his interests are varied; and his positions always interesting. This book is an invitation to encounter this remarkable world.

The beginning of this book is a critical engagement with the thought of Martyn Percy. In September 2016, a group of scholars gathered at Virginia Theological Seminary to reflect on the Percy project. Perspectives were offered from a variety of disciplines, including anthropology, sociology, ecclesiology, musicology, theology (contextual, practical, and pastoral), and feminism. The contributors are drawn from universities, colleges, seminaries, and the church, reflecting the reception of Percy's work to a wide audience. As each paper was shared; a lively conversation ensued. These papers became the initial chapters of this book. But then the project evolved. We wanted the reader to have the option of returning to the primary texts of Percy, to read the original extracts from the Percy corpus that provoked much of the lively discussion. We wanted readers to understand why engaging with Percy is so important and interesting. So we have a combination: this book is a reader introduction to Percy and a critical engagement with his work.

So Why Martyn Percy?

There is in the academy a ruthless hierarchy. The pure theologian or pure biblical scholar is at the top; the practical or contextual theologian is nearer the bottom. Our models of great work are Karl Barth and Paul Tillich, not James Hopewell or Arlin J. Rothauge. We are invited to live in the realm of carefully formulated argument, often disconnected from the immediate context, that takes us to a plausible account of God and how God relates to the world. We constantly celebrate the abstract world of pure theology.

But for those of us in theological education, our theology needs to be much closer to earth. We need the theologian who is well-versed in the tradition but can connect with the church as it really is. Percy is a "contextual theologian" or even, perhaps, a "practical theologian." With the contextual theologians, Percy believes that context is both important as theological ideas emerge (so even with the Trinity at Nicaea) and for the application of theological ideas in different situations. With the practical theologian, Percy is as interested in what people do (or in the case of the charismatics—what they sing) as in what they say. What they do (or sing) is often more revealing of their theology, then the formal statement of faith found on a website.

Percy constantly deals with the real church. It is not surprising that two chapters come from priests currently serving in congregations. Percy has spent most of his life in theological education: he has been training future priests for decades. And he moves out from the congregation to offer a critique of culture, often seeing the grace of God at work in that culture. Dr. Linda Woodhead MBE (Professor of Sociology at the University of Lancaster, UK) observes that Percy's work is unusual among contextual theologians, and uncommon for those working in the arena of ecclesiological investigations:

> One of the most striking areas of originality in Martyn's work is his method. He is a latter-day essayist—unusual amongst contemporary academics—but part of a classic tradition. The medium is perfect for his message: the two are inseparable. Martyn does theology, sociology and anthropology not from the vantage point of the preacher in the pulpit or the academic in the ivory tower, but from *within* the communities of practice he is addressing—church, society and academy. He offers it *to* those communities and writes *for* them. He doesn't offer a systematic theology or grand social theory. He is part of the communities he addresses, an adroit participant observer. He picks up telling fragments from them, reflects on them and places them in a brighter setting, offering them back for further reflection. Later, he will often weave the fragments into wholes—articles become books.[1]

The center of gravity to Percy's work is a passion for the God revealed in Christ. In some respects, he is strikingly orthodox in his theology. His interest in evangelicalism

---

1. From personal correspondence with Martyn Percy, June 8, 2017.

is not as an outsider, but as one who continues to appreciate the richness of that tradition and welcomes the vitality that evangelical congregations often bring. But he is not interested in a faith that cannot recognize grace in other traditions—whether explicitly secular or in a different faith tradition. His Christian commitments are invitations to engagement with different perspectives. The God that Martyn finds in the Christian tradition is the God that is working everywhere.

This all means that he is perhaps the leading exponent of a theology that engages constructively with the social sciences. The social sciences are a tool that facilitates a reading of the world that can illuminate the theological task. He wants to push back on the propensity of many theologians (influenced, for example, by Radical Orthodoxy) who believe that theology and the social scientists are operating in opposing narratives by illustrating that, when engagement happens, the results are good. The results prove that antagonism between the social sciences and theology are inappropriate. As Linda Woodhead perceptively observes,

> Martyn realizes that truth and language is always situated, contextual. He believes that the writer should give as well as take, and that responsible scholarship is about call and answer. The method is perfectly adapted to the kind of ethnography he is skilled at, and to the Anglican tradition to which he belongs—in which lived practice has always been more important than abstract reflection or doctrinal definition. Martyn has crafted a medium which is perfectly adapted to his message, indeed it *is* his message.[2]

One last reason why we are producing this book on Martyn Percy is that he is utterly and totally Anglican. The characteristics of an Anglican are hard to define, but the list must include the following: a deep sense of the tradition, a commitment to the Incarnation as an engaged embodiment in life that we, as the church, should model, and a willingness to engage across disciplines and across ecclesial lines. The tradition matters because Anglicans have seen themselves as the *via media* between the Catholic and Reformed traditions, which was best seen in the patristic period. The Incarnation matters as a metaphor for Christian engagement with society. And the fact that Anglicans strive to take the best from other traditions captures the intrinsic commitment to such engagement. As editors, we wanted to lift up the distinctive Anglican approach. Indeed as ecclesial identities dissipate in the modern age, we appreciated the deep locatedness of Percy.

The tone of Percy's writing is something that has intrigued the contributors of this book. Percy advocates "Big Tent" ecclesiology; capacious, broad, and catholic. But it also has a reformed edge. The tone is often a subtle, sometimes-uneasy blend of the irenic and the critical. It is not passive-aggressive. But it often does combine the pastoral and the prophetic, and kindness with criticism. There is generosity and hope, but tempered with wrestling and realism.

---

2. From personal correspondence with Martyn Percy, June 8, 2017.

So, when Simon Coleman titles his chapter "Radical Reasonableness," which we, as editors, adjusted for the purpose of a title to "reasonable radical," we would want to say that this is all part of the Anglican dimension of Percy's approach. It captures a tone of the Anglican tradition.

The Audience

This text is intended to be a challenge of the academy. We want this volume to expose the limited, and often unhelpful, hierarchy of disciplines. When done well, the applied or contextual or practical theologian can illuminate the theological task in such a way that it makes a real difference to the life of the congregation and how the Church thinks of herself in the world. The academy needs models of such "contextual theology" done extremely well; those searching for such models will find this book invaluable.

Furthermore, this is a text intended for all those in theological education. There is a dearth of substantial texts that help assist the future leadership of congregations to correctly "read" the church and the society in which the church seeks to serve. Courses that focus on ministry or congregational studies will find this text helpful. It is a deep immersion into the debates, questions, and issues of applied theological education.

The last section in this text offers a distinctively Anglican take on the complex relationship of the social sciences to theology. It is an approach that is unapologetically engaged. For those in other ecclesial traditions, we trust this volume will be a conversation partner. For those in the Anglican tradition, the work of Martyn Percy is an appropriate and powerful model.

And Finally

Readers of this book will note that we have invited Percy to respond at the end of each sector. This is appropriate. There are questions asked and disagreements aired in these chapters. Percy's work characteristically lends itself to this type of conversation. Conversation characterizes his own work: he is always bringing that perspective in to engagement with another perspective; he is always finding grace in the surprising places. Perhaps the main reason for this book is that Martyn Percy's work is quite simply remarkable. His elegant prose, often memorable with hints of humor, yields us a rich encounter with the God revealed in Christ, who is active in the Church and throughout the world. In short, Martyn Percy is a substantial theological thinker and writer from whom we have much to learn.

—Ian Markham and Joshua Daniel

Part I

Methodology

1

Contextual Theologian

The Methodology of Martyn Percy

IAN S. MARKHAM

O F THE MANY CHALLENGES facing the church in the modern world, one must be the complicated relationship between the social sciences and religious truth. The argument that religion is "just" a social construct is so compelling and persuasive for many people. To provide a few illustrations: Jesus cast out demons because demons were the explanation for mental illness that premodern cultures did not yet understand; for cultures ruled by a king, it was important that the divine king had his own court, hence the belief in angels arose; and biblical prophets attributed the winning of wars and the rise of empires to providence because they didn't understand the political and social factors that really determine these things. Modernity assumes these arguments are valid. They are assumed by the "talking head" expert on the TV show. For many, the social sciences have explained away religion.[1]

In response, the temptation is some form of imperialism. This was the attraction of Radical Orthodoxy (perhaps still is, although this school of thought is less fashionable than it was). For John Milbank, he offered a narrative explaining that sociology is, itself, a story: one grounded in a particular worldview, emerging from the Enlightenment, and built on an "ontology of violence."[2] Milbank wanted to reduce the social sciences down from the role of judge and jury on the validity of religious assertions and instead depict sociology as a sibling to theology, built on a faith of unjustifiable assumptions. A different imperialism was fundamentalism—both in its Roman Catholic and Evangelical forms. Here a transcendent inerrancy was claimed for the Bible, for the church or for both. On this view, an infallible text or tradition protected the faith from the insidious attacks of the social sciences. God is the author of the Bible:

---

1. One could make the case that the threat from the social sciences is greater than the physical sciences. It is only a matter of time before we see a sociologist Richard Dawkin garner the same attention and the church will scramble to respond.

2. See John Milbank, *Theology and Social Theory*.

God does not make mistakes. Therefore, any social explanation is interesting but not a reason to reject the truth of the text.

Into this debate steps Martyn Percy. He completely rejects all forms of imperialism. The social sciences contain considerable truth: they can illuminate the faith: we can learn from the social sciences. Yet, at the same time, faith is true. Granted, the social sciences might illuminate how certain forms of the faith are unlikely to be true, but still the essential drama told by the church is true. His books are all an argument for a dance between the social sciences and theology, where God is at work in the cultural situation and where all true ideas (all false ones too, for that matter) need a cultural location. And if one recognizes this reality, then one understands a little more clearly what God is saying. He believes a certain disposition to faith emerges. One holds one's convictions with humility: one recognizes the complexity of belief. For Percy, God chose to locate truth within culture, therefore God always invites us to hold our beliefs while aware of that truth.

In this chapter, we shall explore the remarkable achievement of Percy. This chapter will begin by placing Percy in the appropriate trajectory of intellectual thought. Then, in keeping with the Percy methodology, we shall do some contextual work on his worldview by locating his thought in his own biography. Finally, I shall identify four dimensions to the application of his methodology.

Trajectories of Thought

We start by placing Percy in an appropriate intellectual trajectory. Probably the most oft-cited author is James Hopewell and his classic *Congregations: Stories and Structures*. Hopewell was puzzled why some congregations endure despite everything. In reflecting on this, he arrived at an analysis that divided congregations into four narrative types—comic (where everything has a happy ending), romantic (the transcendent and divine intervention), tragic (judgment and law are central), and ironic (rich in paradox and emphasis on the gray)—the typology actually comes from Northrop Frye. Hopewell argued that congregations tell their stories, often in unspoken and subconscious ways. A key corollary of Hopewell's book was that leadership in harmony with the narrative is much more likely to succeed than leadership in conflict with the narrative.

Hopewell, of course, needs to be read in the light of Clifford Geertz, the famous advocate of a symbolic anthropology, most elegantly expounded in his remarkable book *The Interpretation of Culture*. Although a collection of essays, it set out a distinctive approach to the social sciences. Geertz sets out his assumption when he writes, "Believing, with Max Weber, that man is an animal suspended in webs of significance he himself has spun."[3] The way to interrogate these "webs of significance" is through "thick

---

3. Geertz, *The Interpretation of Culture*, 5.

description"—a term taken from Gilbert Ryle. Geertz explains that one understands culture in a certain way that requires this thick description. He writes, "As interworked systems of construable signs . . . , culture is not a power, something to which social events, behaviors, institutions, or processes can be causally attributed; it is a context, something within which they can be intelligibly—that is, thickly—described."[4] It is in the same volume that we find Geertz's famous essay "Notes on the Balinese Cockfight." In a style that Percy (and Hopewell) emulate, Geertz starts as an anthropologist in Bali watching an illegal cockfight (and running away from the police) and moves to a detailed critique of all the aspects of the cockfight—thick description indeed.

Percy likes the Geertz/Hopewell approach for many reasons. He appreciates the iceberg approach that stresses that what is happening under the water (in the realm of assumptions and values) is more important than what is visible (in, for example, a statement of faith). He also likes the methodology. For all of Percy's conversation with the social science, he does not use the typical instruments of sociology. His books do not have charts; he does not organize massive surveys and focus groups. Hopewell, along with Bellah's *Habits of the Heart*, provides Percy's preferred methodology. A primary focus in Percy's doctorate *Words, Wonders and Power* was the informal worship of the charismatic churches. Like Hopewell, he wants to find the pre-existing clues to the underlying narrative of the congregation (what practice or place exposes what this congregation really thinks) rather than construct an artificial instrument that might or might not work. A contemporary who is similar in methodology to Percy is Nicholas Healy. It is the church as it really is that matters—the *actual* church.[5]

Perhaps the most explicit theological influence on Percy is Daniel Hardy. Percy worked with Dan Hardy while he was training for his ordination at Durham University. Percy learned from Hardy the obligation that the church was never called to be a sect or partisan group. So Hardy writes, "[T]he church is called as an apostle and witness to society as a whole on behalf of One whose work was for the whole of society, its witness being determined by Christ's achievement in securing the Kingdom of God through an ethical and spiritual victory."[6] Hardy sees Christ's work everywhere—in social structures, in the lives of non-Christians (hence his very active involvement in the Abrahamic dialogue) and in society more broadly. Percy imbibed this assumption. The establishment of the Church of England is, for Percy, generally a good thing. Percy writes, "I would argue that the function of a national Church—even one that is tied into an evolving monarchy—might still represent a viable form of Church-State relationship in a modern state. The idea of a (Christian) establishment as an essential organic and living part of national identity that still has a valuable role to play in local, regional, national and international life has plenty of life left it."[7] Of course, Percy is

4. Ibid., 14.

5. See Healy, *Church, World and the Christian Life.*

6. Hardy, "Created and Redeemed Sociality," 39.

7. Percy, "Opportunity Knocks: Church, Nationhood and Establishment," 31.

the first to admit that an established church is under some strain due to pluralism and demographic changes, but nevertheless feels that "the presence of an established religion within a reticulate and complex ecology of establishment ensures that questions of value, ethics and justice can be raised within the midst of the governance of Parliament, and in the very heart of a consumerist society."[8]

One last theologian should be mentioned as we seek to map Percy's intellectual trajectory. There are interesting similarities between David Tracy and Martyn Percy. Percy shares with Tracy an emphasis on the inevitability of interpretation in context.[9] Percy values Tracy's idea of public theology, where one is always addressing three social realities, namely, the wider society, the academy, and the church.[10] Although Percy does not explicitly use Tracy's concept of the "classic," which explains how a particular "person, text, event, melody, or symbol" points to the timeless, Percy does operate with a similar relationship between time and the divine.[11]

Percy's Own Context

Turning now to Percy's own biography, we find that central to understanding Percy is his evangelical roots. In a lovely introduction to *Previous Convictions*, Percy writes:

> Before I reached my early teens, I went forward at a Christian rally and gave my life to God. . . . Growing up evangelical, as I did, mostly, it was not unusual to give your life to Christ several times, and I was no exception to that statistic. "Dedication," "re-dedication," "affirmation," "commitment," "re-commitment," "assurance"—and in the maelstrom of teenage years, with guilt bursting into your psyche with as much frequency as the spots on your face, you could be forgiven for feeling as though you were drowning in a cauldron of your own hormones.[12]

The contextual theologian is already at work in his own analysis of his conversion. It is located in the complex processes of being a teenager. This is part of the reason why he endlessly went forward to "recommit" at evangelical rallies. Yet as he goes on to explain: there was a theological truth in all this. God was at work in his life. Although at baptism he had been "saved," God was continuing to invite him into an ever-deeper relationship with God.

It is interesting that his doctorate, published as *Word, Wonders, and Power*, shows an ex-evangelical in conversation with his evangelical past. It is a study of the impact,

---

8. Ibid., 31–32.

9. See Tracy, *Plurality and Ambiguity*.

10. See Tracy, *The Analogical Imagination*, 5.

11. But one should note that in this point Tracy is more relativist than Percy would be—see ibid., 101–7.

12. Percy, "Introduction," ix.

theology, and practices emerging from John Wimber—the creator of the Vineyard churches. Percy the contextual theologian is clearly developing his methodology. He offers a critique drawing on the texts and sermons of Wimber. Here he discovers Wimber's theology is one of power—a powerful God who heals (rarely is present in suffering), building a powerful church army, which will vanquish its foes. However, the interesting feature of this study is the way Percy focuses on the music. The temptation is to view the music as incidental—the padding that makes up much of euphoric feeling in the service. Yet for Percy, this is the key to understanding the charismatic movement. He writes:

> In examining Wimber's worship, we need to avoid the common trap of treating his songs as simply texts. The music . . . is not incidental, but integral. To ignore the theological impact of the music is surely a mistake. The melodic, harmonic and rhythmic dimensions of the music are all value-laden. Music imprints its own ideological meaning, no matter how hard this is to articulate.[13]

Here we have the essence of the Percy approach. Like many practical theologians, the "confessed" theology is less interesting than the "lived" or "practiced" theology. And the latter is often more visible in the places where almost subconsciously the real sentiments and worldview come out. The music, which is a substantial part of the service and sung while driving home in the car, is packed through with the implicit, which is the actual, theology of the group. The result is a distinctive approach: it is a critique of the charismatic movement that takes seriously the context and a key aspect that illuminates the whole.

Percy became the most well-known Anglican commentator on the charismatic movement. From time to time, he has returned to the topic and offered his own assessment. For example, when reviewing David Hilborn's edited collection of essays on *Toronto in Perspective*, Percy writes:

> [T]he "Toronto Blessing" needs to be understood in its own (postmodern) cultural context of revivalism. . . . The discreet branding of manifestations created a consumer-led market hungry for larger and more powerful spiritual epiphenomena, which might just achieve what the previous manifestation had only hinted at. Yet as this narration is beginning to suggest, weariness and routinization, the ministering Cherubim and Seraphim that accompany the Ark of Charisma wherever it may travel, eventually settle on the movement, smothering it once more with their own feathered intensity. Oddly, people became bored and disenchanted with the spectacular. Others conclude that in spirit of the premise and promise, the epiphenomena has not delivered the

---

13. Percy, *Words, Wonders and Power*, 79.

hoped-for global revival, and the much anticipated avalanche of converts. At-rophy sets in, and the movement begins to lose its momentum.[14]

This judgment was not simply accurate, but also revealing. It was accurate in that the charismatic movement is absorbed, and part of the mainline and the spectacular claims (e.g. the movement is evidence for the imminent return of Christ) for the movement are dissipating. But for our purposes, this is revealing. Percy has deep affection for his evangelical roots, but he is now resolutely Anglican. He acknowledges that the "Anglican tendency" can be characterized as dull and a little boring. Percy sees the understated emotional repertoire of Anglican polity differently. He says of the Anglican Communion that "politeness, integrity, restraint, diplomacy, patience, a willingness to listen, and above all, not to be ill-mannered—these are the things that enable the Anglican Communion to cohere."[15] It is almost as if the temperament of such Anglican polity is, for Percy, healthier. It does not promise the spectacular, but it does deliver discipleship, faithfulness, and a capacity to endure in the midst of the complex demands that living makes of us all.

Four Features of the Percy Methodology

With these preliminaries established, let us now identify four features of the Percy methodology. The first is that the basic shape of his theology is orthodox. In his *Thirty Nine New Articles: An Anglican Landscape of Faith*, Percy cites approvingly Brian McLaren's call for a "generous orthodoxy."[16] Unlike the non-realists, God really does exist; unlike the *Myth of God Incarnate* contributors, God really is triune and Jesus really is the incarnation of God. Unlike some liberal popularizers (e.g. Marcus Borg), the tomb really is empty.

But there is more to Percy. When discussing *glossalia,* he admits to a "graphic spiritual experience" at the shrine of Saint Friedeswyde "which reduced me to my knees and rooted me to the spot."[17] He describes an exorcism that he performs, where a child complains of seeing an elderly man wandering around the upstairs of the house. While admitting the "potential social, psychological, and psychotherapeutic angles that could be explored,"[18] he nevertheless sprinkles holy water, says the Lord's Prayer with appropriate collects, and then has a cup of tea with the family before going home. It appears to do the trick. It is very clear that this is not necessarily an affirmation of Saint Paul's "powers and principalities," but he is also very careful not to deny

---

14. Percy, Review of *Toronto in Perspective: Papers on the New Charismatic Wave of the Mid-1990s,* 202.

15. Percy, *Shaping the Church,* 144.

16. Percy, *Thirty Nine New Articles,* xi.

17. Ibid., 17.

18. Percy, *Clergy,* 154.

their existence.[19] Percy has a flexibility—almost an agnosticism—that inclines him to belief, while at the same time wanting to play down any certainty.

Now Percy rarely writes at any great length about traditional theological questions. So, on the Trinity, he cites approvingly the Daniel Hardy and David Ford suggestion of thinking of the Trinity as music—in particular jazz. And he approves of this analogy precisely because it does not explicate precisely what is meant by the Trinity; so he writes, "To worship the Trinity is not to understand each note or to deconstruct the score; it is to listen, learn and participate. Ultimately, all the doctrine of the Trinity is trying to do is to say something about the abundance of God. All our theology is but intellectual fumbling for truth—a matrix that eludes us."[20] Now, where precisely he stands on the Trinity is not clear: is Percy with Augustine of Hippo or Jurgen Moltmann? Interestingly, his Jazz Trinity of composer-performer-listener is preceded with a recognition that the orthodox doctrinal formulation at Nicaea was grounded in complex context. So Percy writes, "It is partly a social consensus bound by time, and partly a political settlement that attempted to bind up arguments and paradoxes to capture the essence of a mystery—something that was glimpsed in a mirror, but only dimly."[21] Truth is embodied in the doctrine, but it is hidden behind the social complexities of the Emperor Constantine and the need for unity in his empire. When he comes to the Incarnation, his reflection centers on the paradox of God as a baby and the invitation to handle the all-consuming demands of that encounter with a baby.[22]

The social context is front and central for Percy. Yet he does want to affirm the truth of the tradition. Perhaps the best way to make sense of this is that he trusts the witness of the tradition sufficiently to affirm the creeds as true, but does not want (and almost feels it is unsuitable to do so) to try and unpack them further. The focus of his energy is the church as it is now and how it can best serve the reign of God.

We turn then to the second and primary theme. Percy believes that all good theology needs to work alongside the insights we can learn from the social science. As we have already seen, this was the theme of his book *Words, Wonders and Power*. As an essayist, Percy consistently draws on the social sciences and cultural studies to shape his contextual theology. For Percy, the social sciences can illuminate, clarify, and transform a Christian analysis. Understanding the context is simply essential.

Percy is adamant that the church should be literate in both theology and the social sciences. One good illustration of this is his various critiques by the Church of England to revitalize its structures. He gets exasperated with tendencies of the church to be both theologically uninformed and sociologically uninformed. So back in 1996,

---

19. Percy writes about this experience: "it suggests a vernacular spiritual dimension to human and social existence that needs addressing by more than mere dismissal," (ibid., 155).

20. Percy, *Thirty Nine New Articles*, 4.

21. Ibid., 3.

22. Ibid., 6.

Percy complains that the so-called Turnball report (the then-Bishop of Durham, the Rt Rev Michael Turnbull chaired the committee) was theologically inept. He writes:

> In short, *Working as One Body* attempts to offer a "mechanistic" blueprint— "the rationalization of congregational process and the animation of social will to achieve results," that lacks a "symbolic," "organic," or "contextual" vision. . . . The first three chapters do not actually inform the report, and in spite of their periodic genuflection to a symbolic and organic blueprint, they are surpassingly weak in their ecclesiology.[23]

Meanwhile the Green Report of 2014 has plenty of theological defects, but is also sociologically uninformed. Percy writes,

> First, it has no point of origination in theological or spiritual wisdom. Instead, on offer is a dish of basic contemporary approaches to executive management, with a little theological garnish. A total absence of ecclesiology flows from this. The report has little depth or immersion in educational literature. A more notable absence is any self-awareness in the report: unaware of critiques of management, executive authority, and leadership which abound in academic literature, it is steeped in its own uncritical use of executive management-speak.[24]

Percy starts his response by stressing that managerial insights do have a place, but as the finest business schools now recognize how limited their insights are, and the challenge of applying those insights to a complex entity like a church is significant, we need to tread carefully.[25] This, coupled with the assumption that the church is just another organization that can be managed, makes the entire Green project deeply misguided for Percy. He was appalled by both the lack of knowledge of management literature and the complex disregard of the Biblical conception of the church as a divinely appointed entity, which is the Body of Christ, intended to usher in the reign of God. It felt too much like "church by management of works" rather than "church by divine grace."

It is clear, then, that there is a complex relationship in Percy's work between the social sciences and theology. In different places, he works in different ways. So when reflecting on the issue of establishment, he advocates a methodology that uses the analogy of refraction. Percy writes:

> In line with the practical theological approach that characterizes this volume, I prefer to "read" (with potential for reshaping) the complex culture of establishment through the analogy of *refraction*. The idea that the truth and purposes of God are "refracted"—spread, as it were, like a band of colour—is

---

23. Percy, Review of *Working as One Body*, 20.

24. Percy, "Are These the Leaders That We Really Want?", para. 4–5.

25. Peter Drucker started a trend back in 1989 which has continued in his famous article, "What Business Can Learn from Nonprofits?"

particularly compelling for the issue in hand, and complements the strands of culture that need to be assessed in considering the issues.[26]

The purpose of the analogy is to capture the complexity. It is to challenge any simplistic equation, for example, establishment means privileging the Church of England, and create a sense of meshed factors that bring light and light that changes depending on vantage point. A fascinating discussion then follows.

More common, perhaps, is to work from an illustration that is pivotal to the social context to a theological, ecclesial, or ethical insight. Let us call this the method of "reflection on an illustrative fragment." (David Tracy has made the term fragment very fashionable: and I want to amend the meaning to make it work for Percy. For Tracy, it is an idea that challenges a totality and provides an insight into the nature of God; for Percy, it is a story that helps us see the truth about the totality).[27] For Percy, the fragment needs to be illustrative: so, for example, the role music plays in the renewal and charismatic movement is a fragment that is powerfully illustrative of the worldview of charismatics.

There are many illustrations of this approach in Percy's work. So a discussion on the emergence of the Evangelical Reform movement in the Church of England from 1993 might serve as an example. The fragment chosen is an ordinand in Durham who was so passionate about the issue of "righteousness" being imputed or imparted that he punched the noticeboard and fractured his hand. From this fragment, Percy goes on to argue that a movement has emerged that knows "how to behave (both culturally and in terms of manners), [but] has also developed a decidedly aggressive side to its character."[28] Another illustration is the tale of two congregations in Atlanta, Georgia; one congregation is a Jazz Service at the Lutheran Church of the Redeemer, and the other is the New Covenant Church of Atlanta—a lesbian gay megachurch.[29] From this fragment, Percy reflects on consumerism and Christianity. It is the fact that we have choice in religion and anything "compulsory" is deeply problematic.

To make the "reflection on an illustrative fragment" work, Percy does need to give some sort of account of how and why this is justified. As one reads Percy, one finds oneself persuaded. One recognizes the fragment is illustrative of the trend that follows. Reform, as a movement, is angry; the choice of congregations in Atlanta does illustrate the opportunities one has to choose. But how does one select the representative fragment? Could someone choose a different fragment that then offers a different picture of the whole? These are questions that Percy does not really answer.

26. Percy, *The Salt of the Earth,* 106.

27. We noted earlier some of the similarities between Percy and Tracy. At this point is it important to stress a key difference. When Tracy uses the language of fragments, it is describing the fragments of insight that we have about God, not the fragments of insight that we learn about society—see Tracy, "Form and Fragment."

28. Percy, *Engaging with Contemporary Culture,* 182.

29. Ibid., 41–42.

Third, Percy is an advocate of socially progressive positions. He supported the ordination of women. A factor, as he recognizes in a footnote, is the influence of his wife, the Rev Dr. Emma Percy.[30] However, he is completely persuaded that in the end the Gospel is about inclusion. Now, although Percy values unity, he does become impatient as the Church of England prevaricated over the ordination of women Bishops. He writes:

> In respect of the ordination of women, there has already been much waiting. The earliest campaigners for women's ordination—those on the fringes of the suffragette movement, such as Maude Royden—could barely have imagined that it would have taken more than a century for women to receive equal treatment in the Church of England.[31]

Unity is a value, but now is the time for action. To have the resources of women excluded from the church is a sin. For Percy, things have to change.

He has also been equally committed to the full inclusion of lesbians and gays. Perhaps the best illustration of this was his controversial essay entitled "Sex, Sense and Non-Sense for Anglicans." It was a contribution to the deliberations of the Primates of the Anglican Communion at their January meeting in 2016. Percy draws attention to the evil of homosexual conduct being regarded as illegal in forty-one of the fifty-three countries within the British Commonwealth. He cites the data from Daniel Munoz that shows that the Global South is exaggerating their membership for political reasons. And he then writes, "Conservatives are not oppressed or criminalized for their opposition to lesbian, gay and bisexual people—ever, anywhere."[32] Percy points out that the Biblical witness can easily be used to support slavery and patriarchy. And then he writes, "Lesbian, gay and bisexual Christians will not suffer discrimination in heaven. In the Kingdom of God, as faithful Christians, all enjoy a full and equal citizenship."[33] Of everything that Percy has written, this is the essay that received the most attention.

Part of the Percy methodology, located in many of his essays, is his deep pastoral sensibility, which does take him to strange places. He must be one of only a few theologians to write "positively" about adultery. This is a good illustration of the Percy method of "reflection on an illustrative fragment." He starts with a wife of a prominent bishop confiding in him that "she couldn't understand how the average wife in a marriage with an average bishop could possibly survive without a discreet affair here and there."[34] He then writes, "I say this in all seriousness: I believe that a number of people who embark on affairs do so to keep their marriages together and to ensure the longevity of their relationship, rather than intending to betray trust or undermine their

---

30. Ibid., 111.
31. Percy, "Women Bishops: a Failure of Leadership," para. 7.
32. Percy, "Sex, Sense and Non-Sense for Anglicans", 5.
33. Ibid.
34. Percy, *The Salt of the Earth,* 214.

partner or their relationship."[35] While making it clear that it is easy for self-deception to creep in, he wants to leave open the possibility that the affair might be the best way of keeping the promise to stay together until "death do us part."

Fourth and finally, he is an incrementalist optimist. Almost all of Percy's work is hopeful. This is partly because he challenges the crude narratives of decline that often pervade sociological discourses in the study of religion (e.g., secularization theories). The contemporary problem for faith, argues Percy in a number of essays and commentaries, is not as great as many may suppose. He has a lovely discussion of James Woodforde's *Diary of a Country Parson (1758–1802)*. He writes, "A close reading of the text suggests that whatever secularization is, it is not obviously a product of the Industrial Revolution."[36] Plenty of modern priests would recognize Woodforde's experience: church is only full when there is a war or a member of the royal family is ill. On Sunday, October 17, 1758, only four parishioners were present. The picture of the past that Percy offers is one where church attendance was always low; therefore, the language of decline is—historically—completely misleading.

But change for Percy comes by working with the contours of the age. Given his deep respect for context and culture, he is not interested in a sudden revolution that creates a utopia overnight. Part of his frustration with reform proposals for the Church of England is that these assume just such a revolution. One challenges secularization with some care. One thinks imaginatively about society. One understands where we are; and one works with the forces of good in society to create a way forward.

Much as I admire his methodology, inevitable questions arise. The first is this: what exactly is this church that Percy is striving for? One complaint of Radical Orthodoxy (and to a lesser extent the work of Stanley Hauerwas) was that there is no clarity about exactly what this idealized church is. Now for Radical Orthodoxy and Hauerwas, the problem was acute. For Radical Orthodoxy, the church was supposed to be this community shaped by a narrative built on an ontology of peace. For Hauerwas, the church was supposed to be this pacifist community witnessing to the value of peace over violence. The fact that this church did not exist in real time and space was a problem. Now does Percy have the same problem? Not in the same way, perhaps. Percy constantly argues for the "real church" to be recognized as the church. But it is there in his prescriptions: when he wants the church to be different. It was David Jacobsen, in his sympathetic discussion of *The Ecclesial Canopy,* who worried that Percy is not clear on exactly what sort of church he wants. Jacobsen writes:

> At its weakest points, the perspective Percy offers reads a little like nostalgic Anglicanism. At such points in particular I would have wished for greater theological clarity—that is, if the gospel involves the church, as Percy claims, well then what is the gospel? Or is the gospel ultimately reduced to Percy's

35. Ibid., 214–15.
36. Ibid., 88.

cherished church? The question is important because of the ecclesial canopy itself. The underside of Percy's use of Berger's metaphor shows through here. It may just be that the church itself is insufficient to bear the cosmos-wide promises of God. The final eschatological vision of Revelation 21 envisions a holy city with no temple; perhaps church even at its best is not meant to bear such cosmic freight as Percy would seem to suggest.[37]

And there is real force to this question. Perhaps Percy does not really need the church in the end? Perhaps secular society, with certain values, might suffice?

The second question goes to the heart of Percy's methodology. What exactly is the relationship between the social construct and the truth?[38] The predicament that started this chapter needs a response. How and when does a social explanation for a theological concept or idea undermine the truth of that concept or idea? Percy has made significant progress. He believes that both together (the theological and the social sciences) can provide perspectives on the truth. He believes that God intended truth to be hard work. But this is still puzzling: how can Percy be so orthodox and yet so aware of the social and historical construct of the faith? What precisely is the relationship between a social construct and theological truth?

These are questions for conversation. They are questions that take us forward. The broad contours of the Percy project must be right. The social sciences are here to stay. We can try and put the clock back (the response of Radical Orthodoxy) or find a constructive coexistence. Percy has rightly opted for the latter. Instead of fear, Percy invites us to learn from the social sciences. He models this in all his writing. He does it well. And for that, we are indebted.

Bibliography

Bellah, Robert N., et al. *Habits of the Heart: Individualism and Commitment in American Life.* Berkeley: University of California Press, 1985.

37. Jacobsen, Review of *The Ecclesial Canopy*, 60.

38. Healy muses at some length on this problem. He writes, "The relation between the social sciences and theology is currently problematic. For some theologians, such as the pluralists . . . , it seems that certain of the social sciences are normative for their own theological constructions. The practical theologians contend that theology and social science should be on an equal footing. Other theologians, by contrast, view the social sciences with considerably greater suspicion. Some fear that the introduction of sociological or other empirical perspectives into ecclesiology will result in reductive, inadequately theological accounts of the church. And the more radical argument has been made that modern secular sociology is a form of inquiry based upon principles counter to those of Christianity. Fundamentally incommensurate with theology, secular sociology has nothing to add to a theological account at all; instead, the church should develop its own, theological forms of social science. These varied and often conflicting views of the function of the social sciences within theology seem to be a product not only of different conceptions of theological method, but also, in part at least, of somewhat different conceptions of social scientific method, especially as it bears upon the analysis of religion and religious bodies." Now Healy seeks to solve this problem with his: "theodramatic . . . informed by the traditioned notion of truth." See Healy, *Church, World and the Christian Life.*

Drucker, Peter. "What Business Can Learn from Nonprofits." *Harvard Business Review* 67 (1989) 88–93.

Geertz, Clifford. *The Interpretation of Culture.* New York: Basic Books, 1973.

Hardy, Daniel. "Created and Redeemed Sociality." In *On Being the Church: Essays on the Christian Community*, edited by Colin E. Gunton and Daniel W. Hardy, 21–47. Edinburgh, UK: T. & T. Clark, 1989.

Healy, Nicholas M. *Church, World and the Christian Life: Practical-Prophetic Ecclesiology.* Cambridge: Cambridge University Press, 2000.

Hick, John, ed. *The Myth of God Incarnate.* Philadelphia: Fortress, 1977.

Hopewell, James F. *Congregations: Stories and Structures.* Philadelphia: Fortress, 1987.

Jacobsen, David Schnasa. Review of *The Ecclesial Canopy: Faith, Hope, Charity*, by Martyn Percy. *Homiletic* 38 (1987) 60–61.

Milbank, John. *Theology and Social Theory: Beyond Secular Reason.* Oxford: Blackwell, 1990.

Percy, Martyn. "Are These the Leaders That We Really Want?" *Church Times.* December 12, 2014. https://www.churchtimes.co.uk/articles/2014/12-december/comment/opinion/are-these-the-leaders-that-we-really-want.

———. *Clergy: The Origins of Species.* London: T. & T. Clark International, 2006.

———. *Engaging with Contemporary Culture: Christianity, Theology and the Concrete Church.* Aldershot: Ashgate, 2005.

———. "Introduction." In *Previous Convictions: Conversion in the Present Day*, edited by Martyn Percy, ix–xviii. London: SPCK, 1987.

———. "Opportunity Knocks: Church, Nationhood and Establishment." In *The Established Church: Past, Present, and Future*, edited by Mark Chapman, Judith Maltby, and William Whyte, 26–38. London: T. & T. Clark, 2010.

———. Review of *Toronto in Perspective: Papers on the New Charismatic Wave of the Mid-1990s*, edited by David Hilborn. *Literature and Theology* 17 (2001) 201–203.

———. Review of *Working as One Body*, by the Archbishops' Council. *Religion and Theology* 3 (1996) 329–33.

———. *The Salt of the Earth: Religious Resilience in a Secular Age.* London: Sheffield Academic Press, 2001.

———. "Sex, Sense and Non-Sense for Anglicans." *Modern Church.* https://modernchurch.org.uk/downloads/send/32-articles/756-mpercy1215.

———. *Shaping the Church: The Promise of Implicit Theology.* London: Ashgate, 2010.

———. *Thirty Nine New Articles: An Anglican Landscape of Faith.* Norwich, UK: Canterbury, 2010.

———. "Women Bishops: a Failure of Leadership." *The Daily Telegraph.* http://www.telegraph.co.uk/news/religion/9693284/Women-bishops-a-failure-of-leadership.html.

———. *Words, Wonders and Power: Understanding Contemporary Christian Fundamentalism and Revivalism.* London: SPCK, 1987.

Tracy, David. *The Analogical Imagination: Christian Theology and the Culture of Pluralism.* New York: Crossroads, 1981.

———. "Form and Fragment: Recovering of the Hidden and Incomprehensible God." In *The Concept of God in Global Dialogue*, edited by Werner Jeanrond and Aasulv Lande, 98–114. Maryknoll, NY: Orbis, 2005.

———. *Plurality and Ambiguity: Hermeneutics, Religion, and Hope.* San Francisco: Harper & Row, 1987.

2

Radical Reasonableness

Ontologies and Politics of Knowledge
in the Work of Martyn Percy

Simon Coleman

"Beware lest any man spoil you through philosophy and vain deceit,
after the tradition of men, after the rudiments of the world, and not
after Christ" (Col 2:8, KJV). —Saint Paul

"Top Cleric Says Church of England Risks Becoming a
'Suburban Sect.'" *The Guardian*, August 13, 2016.[1]

Introduction: A Doctor and a Dean

I AM NOT SURE HOW often quotes from Saint Paul are juxtaposed with headlines from *The Guardian*, but I find both texts helpful in introducing my reflections on the work of Martyn Percy—reflections that are framed by my perspective as an anthropologist of Christianity.[2] To begin with Saint Paul, he appears to be warning against the limitations of merely *human* knowledge, such as the Greek philosophies of the time. The saint's words are unequivocal, and so it is not surprising that this particular verse also adorns the current website of the Institute for Creation Research,

---

1. See "https://www.theguardian.com/world/2016/aug/13/justin-welby-church-of-england-subur ban-sect."

With thanks to Joshua Daniel and Ian Markham for organizing the two-day symposium on which this volume is based; Martyn Percy for his gracious responses to the papers given; and to fellow contributors for their stimulating presentations and comments.

2. My work intersects with that of Percy in various ways: I carry out research on both pilgrimage and charismatic Christianity, have a passing interest in Christian views of evolution, currently do fieldwork in English Anglican cathedrals, and live in the Canadian city of "Toronto Blessing" fame.

framing an article called "Philosophy and Vain Deceit."[3] The author of that piece, world-famous creationist and independent Baptist Henry M. Morris, warns his readers against "a humanist devotion to man's wisdom for its own sake" on the grounds that it "derives in type from the tree of knowledge" and thus leads us to Satan.

We can consider ourselves duly warned. Both Henry Morris and Saint Paul are laying down a challenge about not just the origins, but also the ontology, of knowledge, and they seem to be coming up with a remarkably similar answer: do not trust mere human understanding, since it will lead to deceit and immorality. What is more, they present their argument in black and white terms, in language that leaves little space for response or debate. In the context of this chapter, they also pose two questions that have permeated Martyn Percy's work as both academic and clergyman, both Doctor and Dean.

First, how might the social sciences and the spiritual be reconciled, or at least speak to each other in fruitful and profitable ways? In the following, I reflect on Percy's attempts to find a *via media* between these two forms, and ontologies, of knowledge, and in doing so I place his work alongside that of recent anthropological contributions to the study of Christianity. While I comment on some of Percy's obvious connections to anthropology (for instance, in his explicit use of the work of Clifford Geertz), I also argue that it is possible to discern equally intriguing if not necessarily conscious affinities with the work of other scholars.

Second, I think the creationist and the saint raise a key question of *tone*: how does one persuade those with whom one disagrees that one's arguments are correct, or at least deserve consideration? Do you warn your opponent that they are going to hell, and leave it at that? The work of Martyn Percy suggests otherwise, and thus I am interested not only in what he says, but also in how he says it. My argument is that his *via media* between disciplines is paralleled by a particular kind of persuasive language of mediation.

The other quote comes from an article by the journalist Harriet Sherwood, and here admittedly we do see Percy's work being presented, at least in the context of a newspaper, in a more strident way. Sherwood uses Percy's book *The Future Shapes of Anglicanism* to stir an already bubbling clerical pot—summarizing Percy's opposition to the "management courses" and bureaucracy advocated by the Church of England's current strategic plan *Renewal and Reform*[4]—and reproducing his call for a "deeper ecclesial comprehension." ("Deeper," by the way, is a very Percy-esque adjective, since surfaces are often to be mistrusted, associated with the worst sides of post-modernism, and are often guilty of ignoring both historical roots and complex, entangled, implicit, motivations.) Percy is depicted as arguing that the zeal of the current Anglican

---

3. Morris, "Philosopy and Vain Deceit," para. 3, https://www.icr.org/article/8133/.

4. Sherwood, "Church of England," https://www.churchofengland.org/renewal-reform/about-rr. aspx.

reformers is likely to create a situation where "suburban sectarianism" is pitched against a "national church."

A number of things interest me about this article, though I confess I had not read Percy's book at the time of writing this contribution. While it is Percy who appears to be the polemicist, his polemics are in fact directed toward supporting an image of reconciliation rather than rupture, of both a unified national church and an ecclesial comprehension that have more depth than is currently evident. Note also how Percy's defense is rooted in spatial references and metaphors: avoiding conflict between "suburb" and "nation," gathering comprehensions around a rooted *ecclesia*, debating the very "shapes" of the church. I want to argue that—rather like anthropology—much of Percy's work is not only *about* space, but also emerges *from* a spatial sensibility in which notions of context, groundedness, institution, center, and depth play important metaphorical, epistemological, and ontological roles. Thus, what I think of as the "immanence" of his theology but also of his sociology/anthropology[5] come together in the construction of a distinct scholarly and theological voice, and one that is dedicated to constructing and playing a particular role of mediation. Percy's task, as I present it, is both challenging and not without ideological ambiguity. Thus I ask, finally: what are we to make of the politics of appeals to the mainstream, the reasonable, even to the idea of "context," when they come from a (male) Doctor and a Dean?

Anthropology, Theology, Ecclesiology

Martyn Percy is, among many other things, an ethnographer of Christianity, and from the perspective of my discipline he has been working at a time of great significance. Anthropology has turned self-consciously to Christianity only in the last twenty years or so. Many ethnographers had discussed Christian topics in earlier years, but the development of a self-conscious subfield of mutually-quoting scholars and conferences has emerged relatively recently[6] (see Cannell, "Introduction"), prompted most obviously by responses to the global spread of Protestant evangelical Christianity—the latter both a symptom and cause of wider trends of public religious resurgence, globalization, migration, urbanization, and debates about modernity that have become highly salient in the discipline since the 1990s. Various reasons for anthropology's relative lack of overt interest in Christianity in the past have been suggested, including the desire of fieldworkers to ignore Western missions and to focus on "local," more "authentic" religious practices, as well as the original emergence of anthropology as a discipline opposed to theology, anxious to carve out a separate ideological, spatial, and disciplinary identity. Fenella Cannell refers to the functioning of Christianity as the "repressed" of anthropology as the discipline formulated and developed, and thus

5. Coleman, "An Anthropological Apologetics."
6. See Cannell, "Introduction."

to its role as "a religion whose very proximity has hitherto rendered it only imperfectly perceptible."[7]

The current rapprochement between anthropologists and Christianity has revived a much older question: how might a useful dialogue be created between anthropologists and theologians? In an influential article, appropriately titled "Anthropology and Theology: An Awkward Relationship?,"[8] the anthropologist Joel Robbins suggests that anthropologists should go beyond treating theology as just another object of study and start to ask whether and how theology might actually influence anthropological thinking in more direct ways. The core of his argument is that while theologians have the ability to find radical Otherness in the world and to use that Otherness as a basis for hope as well as disciplinary commitment, anthropologists "have more and more resigned ourselves simply to serving as witnesses to the horror of the world, the pathos of our work uncut by the provision of real ontological alternatives."[9] A central issue thus becomes not so much anthropologists' "failure to theorize on the basis of a belief in God" (this is to be expected, and is disciplinarily appropriate) but rather their "inability to anymore show the world how to find hope for real change without him."[10] Thus a question about the ontology of anthropological knowledge as a basis for this-worldly action is placed at the center of Robbins's claim. In order to draw inspiration from a "committed" discipline, Robbins chooses as his theological interlocutor John Milbank, whose *Theology and Social Theory: Beyond Secular Reason* famously presents social theory as derivative, a product of a decaying theology that needs to reject secular reason, "reclaiming its right to stand as the real social science—the one that theorizes on the basis of ecclesiastical life what is most fundamental in human beings and what social life should therefore normatively be like."[11]

The provocation of Robbins' article comes in part from his selecting John Milbank, of all possible theologians, to teach a lesson to anthropology. Milbank's antagonistic approach to the social sciences and his Radical Orthodoxy also maintain a somewhat awkward relationship to what I see as Percy's *via media* in sociological, theological, ecclesiological, and rhetorical terms.[12] I would argue that while it is true that Milbank ostensibly provides the greater challenge to the social sciences, actually his approach and motivation are in certain respects so far removed from that of anthropology that he is likely to leave the latter untouched, and (*pace* Robbins) relatively unmoved. Percy's mediations are more subtle but actually have the potential to be

7. Ibid., 5.

8. Robbins is self-consciously drawing on Marilyn Strathern's classic article "An Awkward Relationship: The Case of Feminism and Anthropology."

9. Robbins, "Anthropology and Theology," 292.

10. Ibid., 292.

11. Ibid., 292. See also Coleman, "An Anthropological Apologetics."

12. Percy, in "Confirming the Rumour of God," characterizes *Theology and Social Theory* as strangely anti-liberal.

more radical, because they ask how mutual interchange might occur in ways that do not involve encompassment of one by the other, but rather involve—to change the metaphor of mutual engagement—a subtle and not always predictable alchemy.[13]

One of the clearest statements that I have read of Percy's disciplinary *via media* comes, perhaps not surprisingly, from his reflections written to honor another scholar who navigates and combines broadly similar epistemological and ontological worlds: David Martin. Percy gives his piece the subtitle "Why every church needs a sociologist," and in considering Martin's work he juxtaposes what he sees as the social realism of sociology with the idealism of religion[14]—a statement reminiscent of the anthropologist Clifford Geertz's well-known description of systems of symbols as both "models of" and "models for" reality.[15] I wonder whether both Percy and Martin derive their respective socio-theological imaginations and engagements from their both having made the journey from non-conformity to Anglicanism: after all, an inherent comparativism and a sense as well as a sensibility that things *could* be different are present in the work of both. Indeed, we might ask whether Percy is voicing Martin, or himself, or both, when he talks of the importance of developing a reflexive ecclesiology alongside a practical sociology,[16] and one that eschews the purification practices of sociology-shunning Radical Orthodoxy.[17] In the process, Percy criticizes what he sees as the Church of England's continued lack of a real research culture, leading it to "make decisions based on anecdotes and semi-educated guesses."[18]

The issues that Percy raises resonate powerfully with my experience of carrying out fieldwork in English cathedrals,[19] observing cathedral staff who are themselves trying to work out *how* to develop plans for the future based on knowledge of cathedrals' functioning in the present; but there is a wider question that is addressed more implicitly in Percy's work, and which precisely concerns the potentially convoluted and politically loaded relationship between models of and for reality. Let me explain what I mean by suggesting the salience of two further issues concerning the relationship between ecclesiological knowledge and ecclesiological strategy. One is that continued *lack* of knowledge about the church might in fact serve some strategic purposes: in other words, it is easier to (re)form the church when there is little empirical information to counteract one's plans. Alternatively, we might flip the question

13. During his response to this presentation at the symposium, Percy used the metaphor of "percolation."

14. Percy, "Confirming the Rumour of God," 177.

15. Compare also Percy's description of religion in "Adventure and Atrophy in a Charismatic Movement," as a complex cultural system and system of meaning: "a mixture of description and ascription, of deduction and induction" (157).

16. Ibid., 181.

17. Ibid., 186.

18. Ibid., 180.

19. In a team consisting of social scientists and historians, but also working with cathedral staff—see http://pilgrimageandcathedrals.ac.uk/.

around, and ask how a certain *kind* of data is likely to fit a certain kind of planning. In this vein, we might trace what is required to provide convincing evidence for, say, a "model for" reality that will look like Renewal and Reform, and then ask whether the same kind of evidence would support Percy's very different ecclesiological aspirations. After all, Percy is far from a number-cruncher: he is much more of a fieldworker and interpretative sociologist; and as every anthropologist knows, while "simple" and "clear" numbers appear to carry their own, stark authority, the translation of qualitative fieldwork into forms that anybody else will listen to and find strategically convincing is exceptionally hard.

Percy, then, is faced with the tricky problem of trying to present a broadly convincing model for his church of the *via media* while also sticking closely to his deeply qualitative sociological principles. Certainly, his considerable body of published work addresses a large number of varied audiences and readerships, across very different registers. Here, however, I focus on my theme of the *via media*, and argue that one of his methods is through what I think of as a kind of discursive subversion, by which I mean the reversal of the rupturing apart of theology and the social sciences as per Radical Orthodoxy, and its replacement by a kind of linguistic and theoretical commingling—a Radical Reasonableness, if you will. In *Words, Wonders and Power*, Percy does a fine job of analyzing the worship songs of John Wimber, asking how "the rhetoric of worship is both powerful and persuasive," and asking the "deeper question" of who is being addressed by such language.[20] Similarly, Percy often broadens, or renders ambiguous, his own mode of address through writing in social scientific, theological, and ecclesiological registers simultaneously. Below, I very briefly present three ways in which I think he achieves such commingling—no doubt an abomination for Radically Orthodox "purists"—taken fairly randomly from different parts of his work.

1. From Statement to Story

One of the most powerful messages of Percy's *Words, Wonders and Power* comes early in the text, when he critiques authors such as James Barr for reading fundamentalism "primarily in terms of its propositions"—a form of reading that allows Barr to conclude that fundamentalists are simplistic and/or anti-intellectual. Note Percy's sensitivity here to how a type of evidence leads to a certain type of conclusion; and indeed, his response is to move away from a propositional toward a phenomenological approach to gathering knowledge about revivalism. As soon as he concludes that "Fundamentalism *is* a way of relating, not just thinking,"[21] Percy not only moves its study away from purely textual analysis, he also challenges the idea that it is a unified

---

20. Percy, *Words, Wonders and Power*, 60–61; see also Percy, "Sweet Rapture," 92.

21. Percy, *Words, Wonders and Power*, 2.

and thus easily objectifiable—or dismissable—phenomenon,[22] and goes still further, stating that it crosses denominations,[23] and is present in virtually all religions.[24]

Such an argument is both subversive and mediating in the way it addresses and critiques sociological and theological reductionism simultaneously, and does so by suggesting the ubiquity of a phenomenon—which Percy sees as comparable to a cultural-linguistic system—that cannot be analyzed through one-dimensional theoretical or methodological frames. He points out that the (in-)famous fundamentalist doctrine of inerrancy does not simply exist to counter Darwinism[25]; rather, it "helps constitute a habit of mind, viable perception of reality, in short, a whole world. Stories also help constitute communities, not just propositions."[26] In this understanding of how to understand religious groups, narrative is often prior to and shapes theology rather than the other way around, leading to a story-centric approach that, tellingly, draws on both theologian James Hopewell and anthropologist Clifford Geertz (as well as literary theorist Northrop Frye) for its inspiration. Disciplines are thus commingled, even as fundamentalism is shown to be part of religions more generally, rather than a set of doctrines that can easily be isolated and ostracized. Percy's mediations have a further politics to them, for his meta-message is also that fundamentalists and revivalists are to be taken seriously—an important point to make, not only to skeptical theologians but also to anthropologists, since the book was written in the same decade as Susan Harding's influential article on the problems of representing fundamentalism to her colleagues without being accused of being fundamentalist herself.[27] In other words, many supposedly open-minded anthropologists were simply not prepared at the time to countenance that fundamentalism and evangelicalism were politically or epistemologically appropriate subjects to study. Although they may not have been in dialogue, both Harding and Percy were already demonstrating in the 1990s that such Christians were far more discursively complex—and interesting—than had previously been imagined.[28]

In his work more generally, Percy writes *about* stories but also *uses* stories to get his message across. I give two examples. One is taken from his volume *Intimate Affairs*, published about the same time as *Words, Wonders and Power*, and picking up themes of sexuality that were discussed more briefly in the book about Wimber. *Intimate Affairs* is an edited book, to be sure, but it is the method of representation that concerns me here. In the introduction, Percy explains that the volume began as a series of sermons based on film titles, constructed in a deliberate attempt to bring

22. Ibid., 8; *pace* Marty, *Religion and Republic*.

23. Percy, *Words, Wonders and Power*, 11.

24. Ibid., 6.

25. Ibid., 12.

26. Percy, *Power and the Church*, 66.

27. Harding, "The Problem of the Repugnant Cultural Other."

28. Cf. Coleman, "Borderlands."

texts of Scripture alongside everyday life, including the latter's fictional forms—its stories. We see here how narrative itself becomes mediating material, not only exploring difficult issues of sexuality but also bringing theology and social commentary, Scripture and society, into the same conversation for the reader. Percy's hope is nothing if not pious, in a socially engaged kind of way, as he suggests that both film and the Bible can help society both reflect on its values and potentially transcend itself.[29] His Afterword is also telling, mixing spirituality and sexuality, fiction and Scripture, and quoting famous Roman Catholic anthropologist and doyenne of (im)purity studies, Mary Douglas.[30]

Another example of Percy's use of stories also appeals, tellingly, to a genre that tends to bring listeners to the edge of propriety or at least normal expectations about social order: I mean, simply, that Percy likes to tell jokes. His works are full of them, and they usually take the form of narratives. Of course, they tend to be serious jokes, juxtaposing humor and moral or intellectual purpose. You can get away with quite a lot through the medium of humor. But jokes, rather like the best qualitative sociology and theologically-inflected narrative, work most effectively when they do not have to be picked apart and explained in exhaustive detail.

2. Putting Theory in Its Place

Stories are a bit like spaces: unlike abstract propositions, they require people to be placed in contact, in relation to each other, to be part of definable trajectories in space and time. Percy's spatial sensibility, like his humor, permeates his work as a whole; and, as with telling stories, he both analyzes space and presents analysis immanently *through* a framing language of spatiality. One can see my point working through his deployment of metaphor: as noted, Percy is often interested in that which is "deeper" rather than existing on surfaces, while, for instance, in a relatively recent revisiting of the Toronto Blessing, he is explicit in describing the use of ethnography to shift focus from "blueprints" about how a church or congregation could be or should be to that of a "grounded ecclesiology"—an examination of how and why Christian communities are actually put together in a localized context.[31] In this short statement of intent, he makes the rhetorical move from proposing an immediate "model for" the congregation toward an examination of how it actually is; this sense of groundedness also suggests, at least to me as an anthropologist, that Percy moves quickly away from systematic *theological* exegesis toward a meticulous and close-up *ecclesiology*. Such a stance perhaps takes piquancy from his personal as well as his scholastic journey, from a focus on the Toronto Blessing—a charismatic movement that he presents as more a

29. Percy, *Intimate Affairs*, 2.

30. Douglas, *Purity and Danger*.

31. Percy, "Adventure and Atrophy in a Charismatic Movement," 156.

site of pilgrimage than a shrine, divorced from residential locales[32]—in the direction of a spatially saturated exploration of Anglicanism, acknowledging for instance the continued salience of the parish.

The sense in which Percy writes both about and from space—again a distinctly anthropological habit as well—is illustrated powerfully in his recent *Anglicanism: Confidence, Commitment and Communion*. This is a book about Anglicanism in general, but it is also written out of a strong sense of place, and specifically *Anglican* place. Percy remarks that his reflections emerge not only from traveling around the Anglican world but also through his ten-year engagement as Principal of Ripon College, Cuddesdon. "Cuddesdon"—its buildings, its history, its community—becomes both frame and lens for many of Percy's observations, thus coming into and out of focus at various points in the book; it is a part that represents or at least flavors a whole, as well as the recipient of a gift in that Percy dedicates the book to the staff and students of the College.

Always in the background to Percy's "groundedness" is his concern with context. It is significant as a key constituent of ethnographic analysis as well as a means—spatial, historical, and cultural—for Percy to understand and guide ministry,[33] to comprehend the tactility and post-modernism of charismatic worship,[34] but also much more generally to commingle the social and the sacramental, the grounded and the immanent. Thus his seemingly skeptical remarks about the use of maps by the expansive, missionizing movement Fresh Expressions are intriguing but also consistent,[35] as he notes how its members pray for localities, "naming and claiming" whole streets, even though the inhabitants of these neighborhoods remain largely unaware of such actions. Percy's sociological and ecclesiological vision is orientated to the positionalities and indexicalities of landscape, rather than the overarching perspectives provided by cartography; storied place rather than surveyed space.

3. Magpie Metaphors

Magpies are famously intelligent birds, capable not only of recognizing themselves in mirrors but also prone, so it is said, to appropriate and feed on the eggs of songbirds, though the rumor that they like to steal shiny objects is apparently exaggerated. They are a suitable image—a helpful metaphor—for my final characterization of Percy's subversive, boundary-crossing language of mediation. I have already mentioned the permeation throughout his work of the "grounded" and the "deep," but he also has the knack for deploying and then shifting the orientation of metaphors that have been used by other writers, thus commingling with and redirecting such metaphors

---

32. Percy, *Power and the Church*, 104.
33. Percy, *Clergy*, 1.
34. Percy, *Intimate Affairs*.
35. Percy, *Anglicanism*, 126.

simultaneously. His book *Anglicanism*, for instance, includes an early discussion of the sociological concept of implicit religion—a term derived from clergyman and sociologist Edward Bailey—before shifting toward reflections concerning "implicit theology"[36] in a chapter called "Pitching Tents." The title of Percy and Ian Markham's edited volume *Why Liberal Churches are Growing* is not exactly metaphorical, but it is a riff on Dean Kelley's work on *Why Conservative Churches are Growing*, and one that is partly about bringing the reader's attention away from conservatism back to the mainline.

Above all, it is Percy's 2006 book *Clergy: The Origin of Species*, with a Foreword by David Martin, that deploys magpie metaphors to fullest effect. Martin remarks on how he and Percy are both shaped by genealogies of sociology and theology, while highlighting Percy's "situated" view of the church[37]—a view that provides an indexical, rather than absolutist, ecclesiastical perspective. In this book, the very groundedness of "situation" points not toward stasis but toward continual adaptation to context, providing a powerful exemplification of Percy's dislike of, and mediation between, both "false essence" and "acceptance of relativism and indifference."[38] The Darwinian metaphor provides a subversiveness that is multi-directional, involving the simultaneous provocation of clergy, creationists, and secularists. Percy thus attempts to rouse a degree of clerical reflexivity by shutting up evolutionary and ecclesiological theory in the same textual space and seeing what they might beget. The metaphor of evolution not only cross-fertilizes anthropology and practical theology, it also brings temporal and spatial awareness together with a model of change that, in Darwinian if not in strict social evolutionary eyes, suggests a mechanism of adaptation and self-transformation without assuming the unilinear and pre-determined direction of a blueprint. "Model of" and "model for" remain conjoined, but unpredictably so. Thus we see how metaphor, like humor, can place the already-known within new contexts of understanding that prompt, rather than dictate, the workings of the ecclesiastical imagination.

* * *

I have sketched out three exemplifications of radical reasonableness, three forms of discursive subversion, in Percy's work, and I have also allowed a Geertzean metaphor of modeling to come to the fore at various points of my analysis. However, while I certainly acknowledge Percy's productive engagement with Geertz, I think that part of the anthropological interest in his approach is that it emerged largely at the side of, and yet anticipating, the focus on broadly evangelical Christianity and especially charismatic Christianity that developed from the early 2000s. Thus we have seen how his engagement with the motivations and expressions of the Toronto Blessing partook of the same ethnographic seriousness as Harding's analysis of fundamentalism

36. Ibid., 60.
37. Percy, *Clergy*, xi.
38. Ibid., xi.

in roughly the same period. Furthermore, whether intentionally or not, Percy's work links well with other, current concerns in my discipline, ranging from discussions of ethics to debates over the cultural power of "rhetoric culture."[39] For the purposes of this chapter, I focus on a single area of resonance, and one that takes me back to my original discussion, catalyzed by Robbins's use of Milbank, of how an "immanent" scholarship—whether anthropological or theological—can remain grounded yet still provide a powerful sense of moral purpose.

In his article "Anthropology as a Moral Science of Possibilities,"[40] the anthropologist Michael Carrithers—who incidentally grew up in a Colorado Springs home under the partial influence of American evangelicalism—poses a classic philosophical, theological, and ethnographic question: how might a move away from expressing absolute moral certainty avoid falling into a moral vacuum or moral relativism? The immediate catalysts for this question are Carrithers's ruminations on how anthropologists might respond to the Iraq War begun in 2003, and he asks whether there is an ethics contained within his own discipline that might help him to move toward an answer. Carrithers discusses how fieldwork indicates that there are realms of sociality that are not fully encompassed by explicit and autonomous cultural reasonings; indeed, such grounded research both uncovers and works through an "interactive moral aesthetic"[41] that Carrithers sees as a general human trait: "Everyone, I argue, is possessed of moral agency-cum-patiency (a term which recognizes that we both do and are done by) and a moral sense which is informed by but never determined by the circumambient moral reasoning of others."[42] Thus while people often act as if they are adhering to some universal morality, their social and cultural roots lie in a much more improvisational form of social aesthetics. Given these circumstances, culture must be seen as more "a matter of persuasion, of rhetoric, than a determining software-like program" as "people use cultural tools to work on themselves and others."[43]

I am not doing Carrithers's arguments justice in this short summary, but my point is that his argument leads him precisely to the analysis of how *story* is central to cultural and moral life, acting as both form of persuasion and "thread of narrative through a skein of events."[44] Understanding the complexities of how story works clearly involves examining "the grass roots of experience upwards" rather than how abstract principles work downwards.[45] The links with Percy's emphasis on narrative, relationality, interaction, and the dynamics of persuasion seem evident to me, alongside the sense of moral purpose combined with a recognition of the ironies, inconsistencies, sociabilities, and

39. Carrithers, "Anthropology as a Moral Science of Possibilities."
40. Ibid., 434.
41. Ibid.
42. Ibid.
43. Ibid.
44. Ibid., 443.
45. Ibid., 446.

shifting moods—and humor—of life. I think we also gain an appreciation of the value of a broadly Geertzean interpretative anthropology alongside a much more dynamic understanding of how it might work. As Carrithers notes, we can perceive the possibilities "raised by a vision of people in the flow of events, peering forward anxiously to the consequences of acts, looking back to interpret the meaning of acts already committed, and seeking always to find a convincing account of events to guide them."[46] And so "model of" and "model for" themselves interact, now commingling in distinctly messy ways. Only in recognizing the presence and salience and impurity of "events" and their narratives can we hope to develop an ethics that goes beyond cartographically driven abstractions into something that both recognizes historicity and has the chance of creating an adaptive sense of identity and purpose. As model becomes moral, there is a strength in avoiding brittleness through a degree of flexibility, through an acknowledgement of the power of give-and-take.

Coda: Context as "Problem" and "Predicament"

I have presented Percy as a proponent of a form of radical reasonableness that is wary of abstraction, but does not avoid the challenges of either theorizing or attempting to articulate moral purpose and ecclesiastical strategy. A central plank of such reasonableness (not "pure reason," note) is Percy's ability to create a *via media*—mediating the social sciences and theology, model of and model for, article and sermon, different branches of the church, and so on. The notion of context is a central plank of his approach: it helps to frame observation in space and time, requires abstraction to be grounded, and builds in a sense of relationality, a recognition of what Carrithers sees as an "interactive moral aesthetic."

The idea of context, along with the comparative method, is also central to anthropology, and both have been at the background of the discipline's sense of epistemological and ethical grounding, alongside its exploration of the ontologies of different worlds. Context has something of the "reasonableness" of the *via media*, a common mistrust of absolutes that are expressed with a certainty that brooks no challenge or dialogue. Yet, it is not without its more unsettling epistemological and even political implications, at least in the ways in which it might be invoked.

Roy Dilley's examination of "the problem of context" stresses that interpretation and context are mutually implicated, so that: "To interpret is to make a connection. Context too involves making connections and, by implication, disconnections."[47] Thus, to contextualize is not simply to acknowledge something "out there," it is itself a performative and potentially strategic act, with the result that an analytical stance:

---

46. Ibid., 442.
47. Dilley, *The Problem of Context*, x.

from the vantage point of discourse, entails at least a temporary epoché, a momentary suspense of judgement, a bracketing off or a withholding of assent or dissent with regard to the truth claims of any specific form of contextualization. This suspension in the short term allows not only for the thorough examination of the discursive forms of contextualization, but also for a view of contextualization as a social practice and not as a transparent claim to truth.[48]

Such an analysis should give us at least some pause in advocating a *via media* without a degree of reflection. In particular, it points to the implications of articulating a sense of "tolerance" and "unity" from a gendered and institutional standpoint of privilege. I am sure that Percy is already acutely aware of the point, even if he has not expressed it in any detail, but it is nonetheless important to indicate the contingent, sometimes occluding, even strategic, dimensions of articulating context. It is very "reasonable" and "polite" to seek a middle path, but of course one is also implicitly deciding in the process where the "extremes" lie through which one claims to be proceeding.[49] Furthermore, the articulation of politeness, of patience, can have its own ideological implications and predicaments. The incrementalities, the concealments, the occasional obfuscations, of the church might help to keep it together and to avoid damaging confrontations; but they also favor those already in positions of authority. In his current position as Dean, Percy now occupies a role where he can speak relatively freely, and with expectations of an audience; but such freedom should presumably not be contradicted by stridency of tone. Thus the question becomes how far one should go rhetorically in defense of the *via media*.

I offer just one concrete example of the predicaments involved. There is a fascinating and very characteristic passage toward the beginning of *Anglicanism* where Percy refers to the apparent sluggishness of the church: he notes insightfully that what to outsiders looks like dithering can actually be reinterpreted as having theological and socio-anthropological purpose, not least since Christianity has a history of resolving differences through conversations, as people become socially and sacramentally bound together in what is both a meeting and a meal. Thus, it is a deeply Anglican sentiment to say "As a church, we tend to cook issues slowly" and to refer positively to the "rich time" of the church.[50] I think all of this is true. But what do we do about the people who do not want, and more importantly cannot afford, to wait?

48. Ibid., xi.

49. As anthropological work on the gendered implications of language has also shown, dialogue may require "muted groups" (see Ardener and Ardener, "Muted Groups") to speak the language of the dominant in ways that mean their arguments are always already compromised.

50. Percy, *Anglicanism*, 9.

Bibliography

Ardener, Shirley, and Edwin Ardener. "'Muted Groups': The Genesis of an Idea and its Praxis." *Women and Language* 28:2 (2005).

Cannell, Fenella. "Introduction: The Anthropology of Christianity." In *The Anthropology of Christianity*, edited by Fenella Cannell, 1–50. Durham, NC; London: Duke University Press, 2006.

Carrithers, Michael. "Anthropology as a Moral Science of Possibilities." *Current Anthropology* 46:3 (2005) 433–56.

Coleman, Simon. "An Anthropological Apologetics." *South Atlantic Quarterly* 109:4 (2010) 791–810.

———. "Borderlands: Ethics, Ethnography, and 'Repugnant Christianity.'" *HAU* 5:2 (2015) 275–300.

———. *The Globalisation of Charismatic Christianity: Spreading the Gospel of Prosperity.* Cambridge: Cambridge University Press, 2000.

———. "Locating Anglicanism: On Corridors and Shadows." In *Contemporary Issues in the Worldwide Anglican Communion Powers and Pieties*, edited by Abby Day, 213–28. Farnham, UK: Ashgate, 2016.

Dilley, Roy. *The Problem of Context.* Oxford: Berghahn, 1999.

Douglas, Mary. *Purity and Danger.* London: Routledge and Kegan Paul, 1966.

Geertz, Clifford. *The Interpretation of Cultures.* New York: Basic Books, 1973.

Harding, Susan. *The Book of Jerry Falwell: Fundamentalist Language and Politics.* Princeton: Princeton University Press, 2000.

———. "The Problem of the Repugnant Cultural Other." *Social Research* 58 (1991) 373–93.

Kelley, Dean. *Why Conservative Churches Are Growing.* New York: Harper & Row, 1972.

Martin, David. "Foreword." In *Clergy: The Origin of Species,* edited by Martyn Percy, ix–xi. London: Continuum, 2006.

Marty, Martin E. *Religion and Republic: The American Circumstance.* Boston: Beacon, 1987.

Milbank, John. *Theology and Social Theory: Beyond Secular Reason.* Oxford: Blackwell, 1990.

Morris, Henry M. "Philosophy and Vain Deceit." https://www.icr.org/article/8133/.

Percy, Martyn. "Adventure and Atrophy in a Charismatic Movement: Returning to the 'Toronto Blessing.'" In *Practicing the Faith: The Ritual Life of Pentecostal-Charismatic Christians*, edited by Martin Lindhardt, 152–78. Oxford: Berghahn, 2011.

———. "Afterword: Sexuality, Spirituality and the Future." In *Intimate Affairs: Sexuality and Spirituality in Perspective*, edited by Martyn Percy, 95–106. London: Darton, Longman & Todd, 1997.

———. *Anglicanism: Confidence, Commitment and Communion.* Farnham, UK: Ashgate, 2013.

———. *Clergy: The Origin of Species.* London: Continuum, 2006.

———. "Confirming the Rumour of God: Why Every Church Needs a Sociologist." In *Restoring the Image: Essays on Religion and Society in Honour of David Martin*, edited by Andrew Walker and Martyn Percy, 176–91. Sheffield: Sheffield Academic Press, 2001.

———. "Introduction: Spirituality and Sexuality in Perspective." In *Intimate Affairs: Sexuality and Spirituality in Perspective*, edited by Martyn Percy, 1–6. London: Darton, Longman & Todd, 1997.

———. *Power and the Church: Ecclesiology in an Age of Transition.* London: Cassell, 1998.

———. "Sweet Rapture: Subliminal Eroticism in Contemporary Charismatic Worship." *Theology & Sexuality* 3 (1997) 71–106.

————. *Words, Wonders and Power: Understanding Contemporary Christian Fundamentalism and Revivalism.* London: SPCK, 1996.

Percy, Martyn, and Ian Markham. "Introduction." In *Why Liberal Churches are Growing*, edited by Martyn Percy and Ian Markham, 1–3. London: T. & T. Clark, 2006.

Robbins, Joel. "Anthropology and Theology: An Awkward Relationship?" *Anthropological Quarterly* 79 (2006) 285–94.

Sherwood, Harriet. "Church of England." https://www.churchofengland.org/renewal-reform/about-rr.aspx.

Strathern, Marilyn. "An Awkward Relationship: The Case of Feminism and Anthropology." *Signs* 12:2 (1987) 276–92.

3

Signs and Signals

Ecclesial Life and the Cognitive
Science of Religion

Joel C. Daniels

I. Introduction

ONE OF THE GIFTS that Martin Percy has given to the study of contemporary Anglicanism is the utilization of the social sciences to study it both in his domestic context in the Church of England and internationally across the Communion. Issues in the church that provoke intense conflict are often undergirded by impressions: impressions about how the Communion is doing, or how parishes succeed or fail, or how they operate. Impressions do not make for good research, however, and Percy's proffering facts and proven theoretical frameworks for understanding these dynamics is more than just helpful; it is key to actually effecting change where change needs to be effected. To this end, Percy has produced a body of work that incorporates cutting edge anthropological and sociological theories and practices, paying close attention to the practicalities of the social lives of religious communities while never neglecting their theological foundations and implications.

Percy makes an *apologia* for sociology and related disciplines at the beginning of *Engaging with Contemporary Culture: Christianity, Theology and the Concrete Church*. Against those who would deny any place for the social sciences in the study of the church, Percy encourages a concrete study of ecclesial life, one that focuses on the "actual shape and context" in which those communities of disciples operate. Religions, including Christianity, are not solely intellectual matters. Instead, they include both beliefs and practices, which together are instantiated in bodily human lives within communities. Thus, to understand any religious community in its fullness, one should study it as thoroughly as possible, using as many tools as are available. As Percy shows, this is able to be done without falling into a reductionism that would seek to "explain away"[1] religion as nothing but the consequence of social processes.

The disciplines that can lend their voices to a holistic study of religious practices are many. In addition to sociology, contributions can also be received from anthropology, psychology, and, in more recent times, the cognitive science of religion, which utilizes the cognitive and evolutionary sciences to study religious beliefs and practices. After all, if human beings are evolved creatures, then that evolutionary origin can be expected to have many and varied consequences for social existence. What exactly those consequences are, and how they relate to cultural and other factors, remains a matter of inquiry, but there is no *prima facie* reason to reject such a perspective from which to study religious communities. Because the questions taken up by cognitive science of religion deal with groups—their development and maintenance, and their functioning around religious topics—they would seem particularly well-suited for ecclesiological use.

One place where Percy's integration of social sciences and theology occurs is in his in-depth study of the Vineyard religious movement, under the powerful leadership of John Wimber, in *Words, Wonders and Power*. In the paper that follows, I would like to expand on Percy's analysis of the Vineyard by incorporating CSR. While CSR is a broad field, I will specifically mention the implication of one theory within CSR, termed "costly signaling theory" (CST). Awareness of CSR generally, and CST in particular, can lend an additional dimension of understanding about how churches function. Finally, I will show how CSR can be engaged with when going forward, to the benefit of the church and its theologians as they seek to expand their ecclesiological toolkit.

II. Cognitive Science and Costly Signaling

a. Cognitive science of religion (CSR)

Though the name "cognitive science of religion" may be new, its underlying interest is not exploring why and how religious practices are such prominent features of human cultures. Why is it that some kind of religion, broadly defined, can be found throughout human societies across time and geography? As many answers to this question can be posited as there are imaginations to conceive them. Prominently in the modern era, the "masters of suspicion," Marx, Freud, and Nietzsche, posited that religions were, at their essences, matters of providing social comfort, or working out sexual immaturity, or acquiring power. From a different perspective, William James, in the twentieth lecture in *Varieties of Religious Experience*, was supportive of the way that religion gave people "a preponderance of loving affections" toward their neighbors, whatever its metaphysical

---

1. A reference to Pascal Boyer, *Religion Explained*. Critics of Boyer have sometimes referred to the book as "Religion explained away."

truth. Darwin himself had suspicions about the relationship of religion and evolutionary benefits, which he began to explore in *The Descent of Man* in 1871.

Contemporary cognitive science of religion investigates the potential relationship between religious practices and the success of human groups in evolutionary development. If the social phenomenon of religion is found universally, so the thinking goes, some aspect of religious practices must have been either adaptive for individuals or communities, increasing their evolutionary fitness relative to other individuals or communities, or be the byproduct of other adaptations that were advantageous. The dispute over which of these is the case, adaptation or byproduct, is the most hotly contested issue within CSR. Further, there is a minority position holding that religion is maladaptive, decreasing fitness, and evolutionary development has been made in spite of religion, far from being facilitated by it. The arguments are dense and long-standing, and do not lend themselves to the brief discussion that would be required in the present context. While the argument of this paper does not stand or fall on the outcome of that controversy, it should be acknowledged that this is far from a settled issue, but is an active one within a lively scholarly community. Entering into such controversies, and taking sides within them, is a necessary risk of interdisciplinary work. Suffice to say, it is my view that there is sufficient plausibility for the general evolutionary picture painted by CSR to justify its use by theologians interested in studying the concrete church.

b. Costly signaling theory (CST)

There are dozens of theories about the potential mechanisms by which religion has come to be ubiquitous. Many of them, however, come uncomfortably close to being the "just-so" stories that Stephen Jay Gould accused sociobiology of being: speculative antecedents of presently observable phenomenon, without evidential support or theoretical coherence. These operate in much the same way; for example, Voltaire's Pangloss held that noses had been wisely designed in order to support spectacles. Not all theories are so fanciful, however, and one of the more persuasive ones about the mechanism through which this process works is known as costly signaling theory (CST).

CST begins with the assumption that, across species, groups that cooperate better in a given environment are more likely to succeed than groups in the same environment that do not cooperate as well. Cooperation enables the achievement of goals that would not be possible otherwise. From the classic perspective of evolution by natural selection, however, cooperation is a problematic enterprise for an individual to enter into. Cooperative work is always bedeviled by the freeloader problem, the fact that an individual benefits the most if others cooperate in a way that benefits the group of which he is a member, but without his involvement. In a class setting, for example, a group may gather to study. The person who is well-prepared will contribute to the discussion to everyone's benefit. The person who is not prepared at all, however, will benefit from the discussion, but at no cost to himself. The latter person will freeload off of everyone else's work, using the time that others were studying to increase evolutionary fitness in some other way. In other words, everyone is better off if everyone cooperates rather than if nobody cooperates, but each person is even better off if everyone else does the cooperating while he accomplishes other tasks. The very possibility of freeloading can have detrimental effects on group functioning. If there is the suspicion that there are freeloaders in the group, it makes cooperation less likely, and thus an increase in group flourishing is less likely.

One way to mitigate the freeloader problem is to insist on some high barrier of entry to a group, the clearance of which would indicate that the individual is sincere about doing her part and unlikely to freeload. Costly signaling theory is the theory that the requirement of costly signals enhances cooperation in groups and thus advantages groups that have these functions over groups that do not. In the example above, a person could send a "costly signal" to prove that she wants to contribute to the group and can be depended on to participate in the cooperative activities that help the group. A study group costly signal may be something relatively benign in the grand scheme of things: advance preparatory work, or perhaps entry fees or dues to be paid. To be as efficacious as possible, however, these signals must be, as William Irons puts it, "hard to fake,"[2] thus ensuring sincerity of intentions or at least assurance about the likelihood of future cooperative activities. Thus, in other contexts the costs may be much higher. In the book *Sacred Pain*, Ariel Glucklich comments on the ubiquity of painful religious rituals, identifying dozens of religious traditions around the world in which they appear.[3] The anthropologist Richard Sosis, a leading proponent and developer of CST, has written of observations of ritual behavior by the Ilahita Arapesh of Papua New Guinea, whose boys, as a rite of passage, undergo terrifying experiences in which their penises are lacerated with stinging nettles by adult men dressed as fearsome boars.[4] From the point of view of survival of the fittest, socially ritualizing these behaviors, and other excruciating ones like them, is nonsensical. From a CST perspective, however, one can see how these actions allow the boys to prove how committed they are to the group. Therefore, the rituals increase group cohesion. This will presumably make free-loading less likely, increase bonding and trust, thus facilitating greater cooperation. In a competitive environment of limited resources, this could lead to greater success.

Sosis distinguishes three groups of costly signals that indicate commitment to the group. He calls these the "three B's": behavior, badges, and bans.

1. Behavior: for example, participation in otherwise-gratuitous rituals that take time and energy away from other activities.

---

2. Irons, "Hard-to-Fake."
3. Glucklich, *Sacred Pain*.
4. Sosis, "Religious Behaviors, Badges, and Bans," 61.

2. Badges: physical manifestations of group membership such as tattoos, ashes on the forehead, or religious garb such as turbans, saffron color robes, or yarmulkes.

3. Bans: prohibitions such as dietary laws or restrictions on time to work.

Even when they lack the violent nature of the Ilahita Arapesh, there are certain costs associated with each of these, costs for which the individual receives no direct benefit.

Several studies have identified cross-cultural evidence for these mechanisms and their cultural success. In one example, Sosis undertook research in Israel studying kibbutzim.[5] Some of these kibbutzim were religious; some were secular; others were explicitly anti-religious. Generally, over time, the religious communities flourished to a greater extent than the others: they were more successful, lasted longer, and had less debt and internal strife. When living with a group of ultra-orthodox Haredi Jews in their kibbutz, for example, Sosis observed group members lend cars and provide interest-free loans to each other, even when there was no direct social or familial connection between the participants. This was an example of cooperative behavior in which cheating could be insured against by the attestation of group membership manifested in the members' behaviors, badges, and bans.

In a different cultural context, Sosis and Bressler analyzed historical evidence regarding eighty-three utopian communes founded in the United States during the nineteenth century, a time of great interest in communal living.[6] Again, those religious communes that required more from their members, by imposing more restrictions and requiring more specific behaviors, tended to last longer. The costly signaling increased cooperation and discouraged freeloading, leading to more successful, longer-lasting communities. Sosis and others extrapolate that these benefits may have been present in prehistoric times as well, when groups were competing for resources in order to survive. While within any particular group, selfish individuals will flourish more than non-selfish individuals, within a particular environment cooperative groups will succeed more than non-cooperative groups.

Because of its theoretical consistency and reliable empirical support across disciplines, costly signaling has gained significant credibility within the scientific study of religion. This is not to say that signaling is the *only* function of religious practices. CST can exist peacefully alongside many other theories of the social functions of religion. Nor is it to hold that social cooperation, for the purposes of group success, is the sole reason that religion exists at all. On the contrary, it is perfectly clear that, even in naturalistic terms, there are multiple factors that have gone into the advent of religion and continue to influence it today. More modestly, we can think of CST as one additional way to study religious groups and help make sense of their internal functioning. In the next section, I will utilize this theory to reflect on a particular religious community, as written about by Percy: the Vineyard movement.

5. Sosis, "Ideology, Religion, and the Evolution of Cooperation."
6. Sosis and Bressler, "Cooperation and Commune Longevity."

III. The Vineyard: Signs of Signaling

Percy writes about the Vineyard in *Words, Wonders and Power*. He discerns a constant principle at work, both explicitly and implicitly, in that community: power and its usages. This is found both in its theological doctrine of the Holy Spirit, emphasizing brute supernatural force over loving cooperation, as well as the group's focus on Wimber's own forceful leadership. Costly signaling for group cohesion can be considered complementary to the guiding principle of power, adding another dimension to Percy's analysis of Wimber and the Vineyard. To be sure, the goal of the Vineyard movement was not cooperation toward a shared end; the congregations were not trying to build a better beehive to produce the most nutritious crops, or putting together a hunting party to chase down mastodons. The purposes of their group cohesion is different, importantly so. What cognitive science of religion adds to an analysis of the Vineyard movement, instead, is the claim that the psychology of human beings has evolved in such a way that costly signaling functions effectively to draw groups together, regardless of their ultimate objectives. It provides another set of terms to describe the same actions with potentially interesting and insightful results.

One of Percy's insights into fundamentalist movements overall was the recognition that to be a fundamentalist was not only to assent to this or that doctrine, or to have some specific opinion about scriptural interpretation. It is much deeper than that. As he writes, "A doctrine like inerrancy helps constitute a habit of mind, viable perceptions of reality, in short, *a whole world*."[7] And fellow citizens of a "whole world"—especially when it is specifically defined socially in opposition to a larger world around it—need to be able to recognize and trust each other. CSR would suggest that costly signaling could be one way of ensuring that security.

And indeed, that is one of the things we see at work in the Vineyard communities. In a way that perfectly correlates with the movement's emphasis on power, group membership is cemented by an individual's submission to the Spirit's power, channeled by Wimber, in ways that are public and dramatic. The types of experiences of the Spirit can be of various kinds, but they are specific to this particular "whole world": in no other social situation would shaking uncontrollably, laughing or crying, falling, or experiencing sudden heavy breathing or sweatiness, be considered anything but unhealthy, and indications of illness, either mental or physical. At the very least, it would be socially unacceptable. Here, however, it is not only acceptable, it is even a goal. It is seen as an acknowledgment of submission not only to God, but to the community, and to its leader. As Percy writes, "Whichever way . . . [being slain in the Spirit] occurs, it is always orientated towards reducing the autonomy and control of the individual, in order to ultimately empower them."[8] But empower them to do what? It appears that

---

7. Percy, *Words, Wonders and Power*, 12. Italics in original.
8. Ibid., 101.

the goal is to build up the community and grow its numbers, to increase its vitality, to justify the authority of its leader.

These dramatic episodes are clearly not only for the spiritual edification of the member, but for the purposes of group unity. This can be seen by noting how important it is for these experiences to happen in public, able to be observed by the community and its leaders. What good would a signal be if it was unable to be received? The interiority of John Wesley's strangely warmed heart, reacting silently to Luther's preface to the Epistle to the Romans, does not have a place here. The Vineyard's demonstrations of group membership must happen in a group context. This unity is affirmed in song as well: it is in a group context that the lack of distinction between the individual and the group is repeatedly affirmed by the hymnody. For example, in one hymn Percy mentions, the words "we" and "us" transition easily in subsequent verses to "I" and "me," with no other changes: "Lord, we ask that You would come right now" becomes "Lord, I ask that You would come right now."[9] Unified in voice and action, the members signal their engagement and investment in the Vineyard and its leader.

Percy observes that, as the movement grew, "fear, obedience and purity" helped maintain the boundaries that prevented group disintegration.[10] These behaviors and bans in particular ("badges" seem singularly lacking, as Percy describes the plain dress of Wimber) fit the CST model and Percy identifies the movement toward a theology of purity-as-holiness as an inevitable one for fundamentalist churches as they seek to shore up their defenses against the threat of dissolution. Personal observance of the restrictions that indicate purity signal to others that they are members of the same tribe, unified against the encroachments of enemies—in this case liberalism and modernity.

It should not be a surprise that when Wimber looks for scriptural antecedents to provide a warrant for his leadership style, he finds it in the story of Ananias and Sapphira, from the Acts of the Apostles. Such an appeal fits well with the present thesis, in that the story, as much as any other in the Bible, exhibits the divine punishment for freeloading that is mediated by the group's leader. In the fourth chapter of Acts, the writer describes the unity of the apostles. They were "of one heart and soul," and that unity was indicated by sacrificial behavior: "no one claimed private ownership of any possessions, but everything they owned was held in common" (Acts 4:32, 34).[11] A specific example is given of Joseph, named Barnabas, who "sold a field that belonged to him, then brought the money, and laid it at the apostles' feet" (4:36–37).

However, though the *ecclesia* had decided to pool its resources for the benefit of all, as Barnabas did, Ananias and Sapphira did not comply, holding back some of the proceeds they had collected from the sale of property. Upon learning of this, Peter accuses Ananias not only of being unfair to the group, but of attempting to deceive God.

9. Ibid., 63.

10. Ibid., 112.

11. All scriptural quotations from the New Revised Standard Version.

Again, the distinction between the divine and the group, especially the group leader, is blurred, and a sin against the latter is a sin against the former. "'Ananias,' Peter asked, 'why has Satan filled your heart to lie to the Holy Spirit and to keep back part of the proceeds of the land? . . . You did not lie to us but to God!'" (5:3–4). The punishment for this transgression is immediate and pitiless: "Now when Ananias heard these words, he fell down and died." This was its own signal, that freeloading would not be tolerated, and it was received: "And great fear seized all who heard of it." No doubt. Alas the lesson was not learned by Sapphira in time to save her. When she arrived three hours later, she repeated the lie her husband had told; she also died immediately, "and great fear seized the whole church and all who heard of these things." Not for nothing did Donald MacKinnon refer to Peter's confrontation with the couple as displaying "the ruthlessness which has across the ages characterized virtually every style of ecclesiastical institution. The survival of the institution . . . justifi[es] action that is none the less[sic] morally monstrous because it is presented as achieved by supernatural means."[12] Not only is self-sacrifice going to be required for group membership, but a failure to participate in this economy of signs will not be tolerated. Indeed, this is exactly the use to which Wimber's acolyte, Paul Cain, puts the story, insisting that opposition to Wimber or himself would have devastating, even fatal, consequences.[13]

While temperate Anglicans may find the religious ethos that justifies such behavior distasteful, the structure and (costly) processes of the Vineyard movement supported a flourishing community for many years. No one would doubt that the commitment signaled by Vineyard members and their enthusiasm helped the movement grow. In light of this, it is all the more interesting to observe what happened to some of the Vineyard communities in later years. Percy writes about the Toronto Airport Christian Fellowship, originally a Vineyard church at the time of its founding in 1994.[14] In the 1990s, the Toronto church became the site of extraordinary and dramatic experiences of the Spirit. These became known as the "Toronto Blessing" and attracted millions of pilgrims interested in experiencing this blessing for themselves. After peaking in the late 1990s, the Toronto Fellowship began to decline, and its worship became more routine. The Fellowship in Toronto continued to meet, however, and Percy visited them in 2002. What is remarkable, particularly in light of the "fear, obedience and purity" of the earlier movement, is the laxity—not moral laxity, but general relaxation—of the latter group, which had developed over the course of only a few years. In an illustrative anecdote at the end of the essay, Percy writes of interacting with a woman, positioned near the door of the worship space, as he attempted to leave the service unobtrusively. He describes the interaction:

"You look tired," she said.

12. MacKinnon, *The Problem of Metaphysics*, 134.

13. Percy, *Words, Wonders and Power*, 113.

14. Percy, *Engaging with Contemporary Culture*, 157–79.

"I am," I replied.

"We're all tired," she added, "and I feel the Lord is just using me to tell you that what you need to do is go home and rest. I think the Lord is telling me to tell you that. It's a word of encouragement for you. We all need rest—we all need to rest with Jesus. He'll take good care of us."[15]

This was a soft word of comfort (well-received, I imagine, by the gracious Percy) to a visiting outsider. Compare this, however, to Cheryl Forbes's account of attending, as a reporter, a conference of charismatics in the salad days of the movement. As quoted in *Words, Wonders and Power*, she writes

> Most of the attendees spoke in tongues and were convinced someone wasn't "completely" a Christian if he didn't. . . . People badgered me about speaking in tongues. . . . Others . . . upbraided me for not submitting to the Holy Spirit, for being proud and defensive. . . . They used every spiritual tactic they could think of to shame, harass, embarrass, and propel me into an experience that was for them the mark of a Christian.[16]

The contrast is dramatic. In earlier years, powerful, supernatural experiences of the Spirit were a requirement for group membership and highly valued by the community. By 2002, however, the fervor had subsided, the costs had lowered, and the requirements for group membership had mellowed. Forbes, for example, had been told that her lack of charismatic experiences was a sin. Percy, however, was encouraged to seek a respite from the demands of the world, including religious demands. At the same time, growth had stalled, group identity was hazier, and the denomination had splintered. This does not establish causation, of course. Many factors went into this change in the charismatic movement generally and the Vineyard in particular. Nonetheless, it is remarkable to see the correlation between the cessation of costly behaviors and the decline in group flourishing. The price of admission, so to speak, in earlier years, had been allowing oneself to be physically and emotionally bowled over, to lose oneself in that communal/personal upheaval. The price of admission in 2002 was rest.

IV. CST and the Church

It is the thesis of this paper that engagement with costly signaling theory in particular, and the cognitive science of religion in general, can provide helpful insights to Christian theologians engaging in ecclesiological study. Equally, the knowledge of the Christian tradition that theologians have can flesh out the theoretical structure of those engaged in cognitive science of religion in other disciplines, while providing

---

15. Ibid., 179.

16. Percy, *Words, Wonders and Power*, 22.

important nuances and a critical theological eye. In this section, I would like to mention a few places where this engagement may occur.

First, throughout *Words, Wonders and Power*, a particular theology at work in the Vineyard movement is not only described but critiqued from a particular theological perspective. The theory of costly signaling is agnostic about the content of a religion's theology and beliefs, of course: it is as easy to imagine a group bound together by a power-in-weakness theology, being served by the three B's, as anything else. There is another sense, however, in which an awareness of costly signaling as a way that groups cohere can serve as a useful corrective, helping to identify these dynamics at work in other Christian communities. In this case, one could be self-critical about asking whether one is insisting on costly signals for the benefit of the group (or its leader) itself, in a way that diverges from the mission of the Gospel. It is a good reminder of the religious tendency toward idolatry, of the group as well as any other object. The theologian will also note the Girardian critique that can and should be made of this emphasis on group unity, particularly when it requires the shedding of blood. This engagement with CST is to the benefit of the theological side of the conversation as well; for all of its strengths, one of the weaknesses of mimetic theory to date has been its paucity of empirical support.[17]

Second, it is also worth noting the ambiguous role of costly signaling in the primitive church, beyond the story of Ananias and Sapphira. In his recent work *Ritual and Christian Beginnings*, Risto Uro uses Pauline communities as a "test case" for costly signaling theory.[18] Uro observes that, in the Pauline correspondence, the apostle recounts the sacrifices he has made for the recipients as a way of establishing his trustworthiness and sincerity. He encourages their sacrificial behavior as well. As Paul has suffered imprisonment, given everything up for the sake of the gospel, engaged in constant prayer, etc., so he exhorts his readers to do the same. Like Paul, they should serve the gospel in every way, act self-sacrificially, provide material help to the poor, and so forth. However, Uro notes that, perhaps against expectations, few strict concrete demands besides the collection for the poor are made: "The general impression . . . is that [Paul] did not attempt to increase internal cohesion and solidarity by means of excessive and costly demands. On many issues he is modest rather than strict," referring to Paul's interpretations of divorce law, his permissiveness regarding eating the meat offered to idols, the lack of requirement for sexual abstinence, and the insistence that Gentile converts did not have to undergo circumcision.[19] Uro goes on to posit the relevance of a variant signaling hypothesis, Charismatic Signaling Theory, in which high-arousal emotional states, similarly hard to fake, also serve signaling functions.[20] Glossolalia, as

17. Sarah Coakley addresses this in her 2012 Gifford Lectures (in press).

18. Uro, *Ritual and Christian Beginnings*. Uro prefers the term "commitment signaling" (see 133n8).

19. Ibid., 144.

20. Uro is referring to a theory pioneered by Joseph Bulbulia; see Bulbulia, "Charismatic

well as the experiences described by Percy, would be an obvious example of this. One can immediately see how charismatic signaling, with its affective consequences for human bodies, could increase group identity.

However, it may be more theologically interesting to focus on how those Pauline communities diverge from the expectations of costly signaling theory than in finding ways to identify how they correspond to it, particularly insofar as we take those communities to be in some way paradigmatic for later Christian communal life. For, there is a costly signal that is always already inscribed at the center of the Christian story, in the self-giving offering of Christ. Regardless of the soteriological mechanism to which one subscribes, the crucifixion is the event that both indicates (signals) and effects the drawing together of all creation with itself and with God—the group coherence of all creation. The blood that was shed on the cross makes unnecessary the spilling of any other blood, whether of human sacrifices, animal sacrifices, circumcision, or however we would categorize the activities of the Ilahita Arapesh.

Instead of replicating that bloodshed, the Christian community instead remembers it in each celebration of the Eucharist, in which Christ's blood, but not the blood of the worshipers, is again made present. The costly signal transmitted from the cross was full, perfect, and sufficient. This suggests that, while costly signaling may be a valuable dynamic to diagnose, it should not be a desideratum in and of itself. Martyrdom may come, and even be welcomed, but it need not be sought. Christian group identity is, at its root, founded on the sacrifice that was made by Jesus, not by any other sacrifice, past, present, or future. Whatever other mechanisms may be at play at any particular point, they are secondary to the cross that precedes and fulfills them. In this sense, there will always be a dissonance when CST is applied to the *ecclesia*; ways in which it does apply, and ways in which it does not.

Third, there are some insights that CSR may give us that are relevant to the church of the present day. For example, there is no doubt that mechanisms that facilitate cooperation operate best within smaller, rather than larger, groups. Costly signaling is not the only mechanism for that effort, as we have already discussed, but it is an important one, and it depends on signals being able to be both sent and received. The cohesion that marks well-knit groups is tempered when the population scale moves from the local to the global. Ara Norenzayan has written about the development of "big gods" to overcome the problem of population growth, but even then the groups are culturally relatively uniform, even if the individuals are unknown to one another.[21] The exceptions to this—Mormons come up most frequently in this context[22]—are of the kind that prove the rule: the stringent requirements for Mormons, regardless of culture, far exceed the cultural flexibility that is allowed for Christians, particularly Anglican Christians. For a person who values the Anglican Communion, this

Signalling"; as well as Frean and Bulbulia, "The Evolution of Charismatic Cultures."

21. Norenzayan, "Big Gods for Big Groups," 124–25.

22. See Michael McBride, "Club Mormon."

should only highlight the fragility of such an international fellowship. With neither the immediate necessity for cooperation, nor rigorous standards for membership, nor semi-coercive leadership of Wimber's kind, the existence of a global communion at all seems not only surprising but nearly miraculous.

Finally, we are able to see how Percy's historical and sociological work nuances what might be an otherwise easy appeal to CST for those would push for a return to a pre-modern golden age of church membership, before the supposedly nefarious influences of modernism and liberalism. A seminal influence for costly signaling theory in religious studies was the work of the economist Laurence Iannaccone. In his article "Why Strict Churches Are Strong," Iannaccone produces research pointing to a simple conclusion: those churches that require the most of their members tend to be the ones that cohere the most, receive the most from their members, and be prioritized by their members more highly than other activities. "Strictness reduces freeriding," he finds. "It screens out members who lack commitment and stimulates participation among those who remain." A costly, strict, or distinctive communal identity "leads to higher levels of church attendance and church contributions, closer ties to the group, and reduced involvement in competing groups."[23]

Iannaccone's article is framed by the work of Dean Kelley. Kelley's *Why Conservative Churches Are Growing* seems to suggest that theological conservatism is the antidote to decreasing mainline attendance, and that liberalism is the problem that must be addressed.[24] However, as Iannaccone shows (and as he reports Kelley to hold as well), "strict" does not mean "theologically conservative," and "strong" does not mean "growing." Instead, these modifiers are historically and theologically variable, and bear only superficial correspondence to the social position of the church in various eras. Percy is particularly effective in demythologizing pre-modern England and its church attendance, including the charming image of a parish verger on Sunday mornings waiting outside the church, only bothering the priest if anyone actually showed up.[25] This from 1805. While nominally members of the Church of England, those early-nineteenth-century parishioners clearly did not find church attendance a priority, relative to other activities, and one finds it hard to imagine that church contribution levels were particularly high either. The church may have been dominant in the religious marketplace, but to what end is not clear. Geographic parishes may have been growing due to regular population increase and subsequent baptisms, but it does not sound like it was growing into a particularly strong religious community. (One could thus speculate that the seeds of Britain's current paganism were planted as far back as then.[26]) To counteract that moribund religious life, as Percy and Kelley agree,

23. Iannaccone, "Why Strict Churches Are Strong."

24. Kelley, *Why Conservative Churches Are Growing*.

25. Percy, *The Salt of the Earth*, 63.

26. I choose "paganism" rather than "secularism" intentionally, as my own interpretation of Percy's observations of widespread and diverse spirituality unmoored from religious traditions. See Percy,

"deep bonds of commitment" are needed.[27] This is something that some evangelical and conservative churches have been successful in doing, but there is no inherent reason that others cannot do so as well. While those communities have periodically experienced explosive growth, their permanence does not always endure; Iannaccone uses the Quakers as an example that differentiates strength and growth, permanence and popularity. Regardless, none of this indicates that looking backward is the way forward, that easing the concerns of the church today is as easy as replicating a preceding practice. The world is too complex, and it always has been.

V. Conclusion

I tend to agree with Percy that parishes and dioceses would be better off worrying about growth less, and discipleship more. That is, they should focus on depth, rather than breadth, with the expectation that depth will lead to long-term permanence, even if it lacks spectacular growth. In addition, the usage of the terms "liberal" and "conservative"—political terms with their origins in the particularities of the French Revolution—are not terribly helpful when they are applied to church life. They mask more than they reveal, and introduce connotations and valences that distract from the ecclesial issues at hand. There are plenty of divisions that exist within the church already; we need not duplicate political divisions as well.

Where I may differ from him, however, based on my reading of CST, is in his emphasis on the potential of being "radically inclusive" and marked by "openness, questioning, freedom and fellowship"[28] as a means to achieve those deep bonds of commitment, at least insofar as they encourage a tendency to de-prioritize individual piety and corporate worship. These are not necessarily mutually exclusive. However, there is no doubt that the constellation of related values that prioritizes openness and freedom also shies away from commitment. As Percy often notes, one of the most pervasive forces at work in modern culture is the emphasis on consumer choice, a principle that comes to be applied across all realms of personal and social life. To have the Christian community's emphasis be on endless choice without sacrifice—including the sacrifice of conformity to a tradition—replicates the values of the market. The church should feel free to differentiate itself from the surrounding culture when that culture's values are detrimental to human flourishing. It may be the case that a little more strictness is called for, not at the moment of introduction, certainly, but as an implication of baptism. To do otherwise is to imply that the life of the disciple is but one more lifestyle choice among others—a minimization of both the costs, and the rewards, of following Jesus.

The Salt of the Earth, in particular chapters 1–3.

27. Percy discusses the issues of liberal and conservative church growth, and Kelley specifically, in *Shaping the Church*.

28. Ibid., 94.

To be sure, any talk of strictness runs the risk of the moving the church into Wimber-like territory. That only makes the work of theologians more vital, however, as they reflect on Christian beliefs, Christian practices, and the relationship between them. Percy notes that one of the causes of the dysfunction in the Vineyard was its inadequate doctrine of the Trinity, for example.[29] One of the implications of that, as I read it, is that it is essential that theologians remain committed to studying and interacting with the "actual shape and context" of the church, and do so using all of the resources available, across disciplines, acting as both guardians and critics of the tradition, its custodians as well as its developers.

Theologians should be encouraged to do this not only for their own benefit, but for the good of the church. And it is this goal—the good of the church—that is the overarching motivation of Percy's work, and it is this emphasis that distinguishes his scholarship, through the use of any methodology that is available. We all benefit from his faithfulness and concern. The case he makes and its consequent insights bring clarity and illumination to a discourse that is too often partisan and subjective. We are indebted to him for reminding us periodically to take a look over the walls of our own guilds to see the riches that are offered outside, *pro ecclesia dei*.

Bibliography

Boyer, Pascal. *Religion Explained: The Evolutionary Origins of Religious Thought*. New York: Basic Books, 2001.

Bulbulia, Joseph. "Charismatic Signalling." *Journal for the Study of Religion, Nature and Culture* 3:4 (2010) 518–51. doi:10.1558/jsrnc.v3i4.518.

Frean, Marcus, and Joseph Bulbulia. "The Evolution of Charismatic Cultures." *Method & Theory in the Study of Religion* 22:4 (2010) 254–71. doi:10.1163/157006810X531049.

Glucklich, Ariel. *Sacred Pain: Hurting the Body for the Sake of the Soul*. New York: Oxford University Press, 2003.

Iannaccone, Laurence R. "Why Strict Churches Are Strong." *American Journal of Sociology* 99:5 (1994) 1180–211. doi:10.1086/230409.

Irons, William. "Religion as a Hard-to-Fake Sign of Commitment." In *Evolution and the Capacity for Commitment*, edited by Randolph M. Nesse, 290–309. New York: Russell Sage Foundation, 2001.

Kelley, Dean. *Why Conservative Churches Are Growing*. New York: Harper, 1986.

MacKinnon, Donald M. *The Problem of Metaphysics*. New York: Cambridge University Press, 1974.

McBride, Michael. "Club Mormon: Free-Riders, Monitoring, and Exclusion in the LDS Church." *Rationality and Society* 19:4 (2007) 395–424. doi:10.1177/1043463107083736.

Norenzayan, Ara. "Big Gods for Big Groups." In *Big Gods: How Religion Transformed Cooperation and Conflict*, 118–39. Princeton, NJ: Princeton University Press, 2013.

Percy, Martyn. *Engaging with Contemporary Culture: Christianity, Theology, and the Concrete Church*. Aldershot, UK; Burlington, VT: Ashgate, 2005.

29. Percy, *Words, Wonders and Power*, 135.

————. *Shaping the Church: The Promise of Implicit Theology*. Explorations in Practical, Pastoral and Empirical Theology. Aldershot, UK; Burlington, VT: Ashgate, 2010.

————. *The Salt of the Earth: Religious Resilience in a Secular Age*. Lincoln Studies in Religion & Society 4. London: Continuum, 2001.

————. *Words, Wonders and Power: Understanding Contemporary Christian Fundamentalism and Revivalism*. London: SPCK, 1996.

Sosis, Richard. "Ideology, Religion, and the Evolution of Cooperation: Field Experiments on Israeli Kibbutzim." *Socioeconomic Aspects of Human Behavioral Ecology* 23 (2004) 89–117. doi:10.1016/S0190-1281(04)23004-9.

————. "Religious Behaviors, Badges, and Bans: Signaling Theory and the Evolution of Religion." In *Where God and Science Meet: How Brain and Evolutionary Studies Alter Our Understanding of Religion*, edited by Patrick McNamara, 1:61–86. Westport, CT: Praeger, 2006.

Sosis, Richard, and Eric Bressler. "Cooperation and Commune Longevity: a Test of the Costly Signalling Theory of Religion." *Cross-Cultural Research* 37:3 (2003) 211–39. doi:10.1177/1069397103037002003.

Uro, Risto. *Ritual and Christian Beginnings: A Socio-Cognitive Analysis*. New York: Oxford University Press, 2016.

4

"Circuits of Power" in the Catholic Charismatic Renewal

Re-reading Martyn Percy's *Words, Wonders and Power*

Matt Gompels

In both religious folklore and popular understanding of charismatic and revivalist movements, it is perhaps unsurprising that the *wonders* and *power* predominate conversation. From the tongues that ignited the Pentecostal fire at Azusa Street[1] to the tears of laughter at the Toronto Blessing, tales of strange phenomena that telegraph the power of God understandably remain at the forefront of one's mind. And yet, the most revealing windows into the distinctive, all-encompassing worldviews of a contemporary fundamentalist or revivalist movement begin often with an analysis not of deeds, but of *words*, especially those softly or plainly spoken. It is fundamentally in the way actors intuit, interpret and explain the *power* and *wonders* of their religious conviction, that one can see the contours of the "cultural-linguistic systems"[2] that they inhabit. It is fitting then that perhaps the most revealing window I have had into the distinctive worldview of a revivalist movement came not in a church, but in the classroom. As a fresh Religious Education teaching trainee at a local Catholic school, power and control were very much aspirational qualities. Nonetheless, one particular day it seemed I could take some satisfaction from the impassioned debate ensuing in some corners of the room over the meaning and application of Matthew 7:12. Upon closer inspection however, the discussion had very little to do with the Golden Rule in Matthew's Gospel, and everything to do with heavyweight boxing. Conor, a vocal student of Irish Traveller descent, was mounting an impassioned defense of Tyson Fury's chances of success against bookies' favorite and (then) reigning world champion Wladimir Klitschko. In the face of increasing skepticism from his peers, he eventually resorted to a simple and seemingly sufficient justification: "he's

1. Cox, *Fire from Heaven*.
2. Lindbeck, *The Nature of Doctrine*.

packin' the power of God." Tyson Fury's colorful and frankly offensive views (not to mention his subsequent victory) did not fit well with the broader lesson focus, and at the behest of the teacher the discussion, reluctantly, was ended there. However, the comment was fascinating, on reflection. Whilst there was not even patchwork reference to formal creed or doctrine in the students' flatly stated defense of his prize-fighter, latent in this pupil's protestations and in Fury's own press appearances is a very particular conceptualization of the "power of God."[3] The proliferation of revivalist and Pentecostal currents in Roma and Traveller communities across Europe is one contemporary example of how powerfully counter-cultural charismatic movements are challenging (and indeed replacing) traditional associations with Catholic ecclesial structures.[4] At the heart of these movements are experientially centered theologies of the power of God, distinctive ecologies of power, constructed as part of an epistemological framework in which God's power is active in the world in very corporal and temporal ways, filling the lives of individual believers with experiences of the spirit, and in the above example, packing the punches of boxers.

It is this notion, of distinctive treatments of power in charismatic and revivalist theology and ecclesiology, that Martyn Percy takes as his interpretative task in *Words, Wonders and Power*. Percy's thesis begins as a probing attempt to uncover the latent structures and strategic agencies that underpin a religious tradition already manifestly systematized around power. Analyzing the charismatic fundamentalism of John Wimber, Percy situates fundamentalism broadly as a counter-cultural response to modernity and religious pluralism. Drawing on the work of Peter Berger,[5] Percy argues that, unconvinced by Christian propositionalism, fundamentalists choose instead to re-authenticate traditional religious truth claims about the power of God "inductively," through a demonstration of God's power in the present day.[6] The inductive method, one of three strategies for the defense of faith in Berger's rendering, stands in contrast to "deductive" attempts to reaffirm a form of neo-Orthodoxy, and "reductive" attempts to salvage a core of the tradition whilst discarding propositionalism itself.[7] What is significant here is that charismatic movements like Wimber's are engaged in a particular praxis when it comes to evidencing faith. Their conceptualization of the power of God as active in the world, received by Christians directly, experientially through "signs and wonders,"[8] stands in contrast to more hierarchical notions of God's

---

3. See both "https://www.theguardian.com/sport/2015/dec/13/tyson-fury-traveller-faith" and "http://www.belfasttelegraph.co.uk/sunday-life/tyson-fury-the-power-of-prayer-helped-me-to-beat-wladimir-klitschko-34263925.html" as examples of Tyson Fury's much-publicized statements on his Christian faith.

4. Cantón, "Gypsy Pentecostalism, Ethnopolitical Uses and Construction of Belonging in the South of Spain."

5. Berger, *The Heretical Imperative*.

6. Percy, *Words, Wonders and Power*, 44.

7. Ibid., 43–44.

8. Ibid., 15.

power as mediated through and evidenced through established traditions of exegesis and heavily stratified church hierarchy.

Conceiving of Power: Theory and Theology

Power has always been a distinctive motif in Pentecostal belief and praxis. Indeed, Baptism of the Holy Spirit, the characteristic Pentecostal initiatory rite, has been read as an experience of "power," in line with Acts 1:8, since the early tracts of influential preacher Charles Parham.[9] Actively exercised divine power occupies a central place in Pentecostal eschatology, with the restoration of the power of the Holy Spirit seen as the culmination of salvation history, heralding the imminent Parousia. For Pentecostals today, this power of the spirit is still very corporally visible, in the glossolalia of believers, in those "slain by the spirit" and in testimony of physical healings. In the lived faith of Catholic Pentecostals, we find the odd nexus of two approaches; two competing ecologies of power brought together in a tense hybridity. How does one reconcile the essential tension embodied in a renewal movement that professes to engage directly in the comprehension, distribution and thus reification of divine power, with a hierarchical ecclesial structure that privileges tradition and continuity? Mapping the negotiation of power in a Catholic Charismatic context is unsurprisingly complex. No excursus can reliably claim to "see" empirically speaking where, how, or whether divine power brings its influence to bear.

This chapter begins to explore this question, using Martyn Percy's adaptation of Clegg's framework of power as a "circuit"[10] to map how power in Catholic Pentecostalism is manifestly exhorted and described, but also latently vested in individuals and ascribed to group structures. Drawing principally on two important but divergent ethnographical analyses of the Catholic Charismatic Renewal (CCR), this chapter attempts to highlight how the mapping of power as a relational concept can illuminate, to paraphrase Clifford Geertz, the "moods and motivations" that operate latently to help formulate the "general order of existence," uniquely realistic to those it serves.[11]

In *Words, Wonders and Power,* Percy employs Clegg's idea of power as a "circuit" as a hermeneutic tool to map the ways in which the flow of power is directed through "nodal points," defined as "fundaments of belief or practice which conduct or direct forces or forms of power."[12] Power here is underpinned by the "agency" of members, who are engaged both in the production and signification of the emergent circuit of power. In turn, "strategic" agency determines the "rate and direction" in which power flows.[13] This enables Percy to identify aspects of the divine-human

9. Althouse, "Ideology of Power" 97–99.

10. Clegg, *Frameworks of Power.*

11. Geertz, *The Interpretation of Cultures,* 90.

12. Percy, *Words, Wonders and Power,* 46.

13. Ibid., 47.

"conflation" that takes place in fundamentalistic and charismatic ecclesial contexts. Often, believers are unable to distinguish between the *actual* power and authority of scripture, and that of the interpreter. Similarly, between the power of God, and "wonder-worker" (or "performer" of miracles). Power, therefore, is not an abstract quality or "essence"; conversely it "has an interrelational quality about it, and can only be understood properly by referring to the operating agents that receive, transfer, transform and communicate it."[14]

As will be outlined throughout this chapter, there are a number of specific merits of Clegg's theory as applied to revivalist movements by Martyn Percy. In a concise taxonomy of power theorizing, Keith Dowding acutely highlights the extent to which the term power is contested in a myriad of ways, defined antithetically as "necessarily conflictual" or "consensual," instrumentally as "power over" or "power to," as well as via recourse to a host of secondary terminology such as "authority, autonomy, domination, freedom, hegemony, legitimation and manipulation."[15] Power theorizing is crowded and contested conceptual field but one of vital importance in baseline analysis—whilst conceptualizations of power doubtless prove their utility in the "specific context(s) in which they are applied"[16] it is still, as Dowding argues, vital to guard against "normativity," namely, the construction of a hermeneutical apparatus of power that builds moral and ideological assumptions into our concepts themselves, thus drastically weakening our analytical purchase.[17]

Any theory of power is, after all, a "theory about organisation"[18] and as such, it is vital in an anthropological account of the flows of power not to overlay ethnographical data with a narrow understanding of how power is meant to function. Clegg's framework, of power as a relational concept, illuminated most clearly when mapped as currents in often-diffuse circuit style structures allows for both fixity and flow—neither diminishing the responsibility of individual actors, nor debating structural components of power. It is therefore a particularly efficient model for mapping how—through what and to where power flows—in ecclesial contexts.

Mapping "Circuits of Power": Two Anthropological Studies of the Catholic Charismatic Renewal

In Meredith McGuire's analysis, the CCR is operating within a distinct epistemological framework, within which God's active power is a focal concept. The immediacy of the Pentecostal experience is used to lend legitimation, vitality even, to the dogma of the Catholic church, with the institution seen by many believers as increasingly powerless

14. Ibid., 159.

15. Dowding, "Why Should We Care," 120.

16. Percy, *Words, Wonders and Power,* 45.

17. Dowding, "Why Should We Care," 119.

18. Percy, *Words, Wonders and Power,* 45.

within wider society. In her thematic excursus of common prophecy in the CCR, Mc-Guire identifies several discursive themes that, on our schema, serve as "nodal points," via which everyday practice and speech is directed and channeled. Of particular importance are the repeated emphases upon the "presence of God" as experienced by the believer, "surrender to God" as a necessary precondition of Spirit Baptism, and the "power of God" in the world, predicated on giving oneself up in complete "security and trust in God."[19] On the above schema, these key themes of prophecy are nodal points in the conceptual apparatus of Catholic Pentecostals, who as individual agents engage the production and reification of a distinctive worldview, through which a circuit of power flows. The extent to which members are engaged in production and signification is evidenced, as McGuire asserts, from the extent to which ritual themes seen in prophecy mirror the fundamental appeal of the movement, namely a reassertion of God's power in the world in response to the malaise of contemporary conditions and the declining power of traditional religious institutions.[20]

That fundaments of belief direct and reflect conceptualizations of God's power is particularly visible in McGuire's detailed analysis of disease aetiologies, in which the condition of the sick person is only the symbolic expression of a greater sickness, the illness of the world. In the distinctive worldview constructed by Catholic Pentecostals, there are two sources of pollution, internal and external. External pollution refers to the chaos of the world and evil spirits, whilst internal pollution refers to innate human weakness and inner frailty. To combat both these ills, Pentecostal Catholics harness the power of God. Self-purification through the Spirit is thus a form of group vindication and victory over the ills of the world.[21] In this way, cosmic battles are "temporalized," as "healing rituals give symbolic form to group norms" through the construction of disease aetiologies.[22]

McGuire is adept at showing how a distinctively Pentecostal worldview shapes the way in which divine power is received and channeled, its flow directed by particular nodal points of belief and practice. Yet at this stage, there is little that distinguishes the CCR from other forms of charismatic Christianity that see God's power as active in the world. As briefly rehearsed above, the distinctive factor in analyzing Catholic Pentecostalism is the way in which it marries two very different ecologies of power, combining two traditionally separate conceptualizations of how God acts in the world. For Meredith McGuire, the "most natural" expression of Pentecostal Catholicism is the prayer group meeting, which features traditional Catholic forms of reflection and prayer alongside prophecy, speaking in tongues, and witness to the faith. It is also the most acute example of controlled spontaneity, or on our explanatory schema, of how strategic agencies in a circuit of power wield control over its direction. As McGuire

19. McGuire, *Pentecostal Catholics*, 101.

20. Ibid., 101.

21. Ibid., 101.

22. Ibid., 166.

points out that the "flow of the spirit" introduces a deliberate aspect of instability into an otherwise-hierarchical Catholic structure; indeed, "every time a prophecy is spoken the group must act anew to construct, maintain a collective 'definition of the situation' the resolution of which contributes to group unity."[23] In this regard McGuire records that considerable effort is paid in supporting literature to the notion of "orthodoxy." This notion has two distinct but interrelated meanings—orthodoxy is concerned with identifying "correct" praxis and structure within the prayer meeting itself, just as members seek to reassure church authorities that their movement fits within the bounds of canonical Catholicism.[24]

In line with this concern over orthodoxy, McGuire is particularly interested to show how, as ritual practice becomes increasingly routinized in established prayer groups, leaders use a broad range of control mechanisms to mediate and direct spontaneity, controlling the volume, pace, and participation of an ostensibly spontaneous, spirit-led meeting. In a detailed taxonomy of the varied forms of prayer meeting she observed in a seven-year ethnographic study, McGuire delineates between "open" and "closed" structures, scaling meetings on these two poles to reflect the extent to which general members and other participants can actively contribute to the direction and flow of the meeting.[25] Where some meetings are open and egalitarian, others are more rigidly structured with a visible stratification of those attending, in which senior members of the prayer group occupy specialized roles. This differentiation from "open" to "closed" is palpably Weberian in McGuire's schema, a "routinization of Charisma"[26] that occurs over time as the movement consolidates. McGuire is quick to point out that this control is mostly welcomed by participants, who seek the "new framework of order . . . to replace the old undermined source."[27]

Returning to the characteristics of control, McGuire argues that it is strategic agents in circuits of power who mediate most keenly between the two competing ecologies of power described above. Some of the mechanisms of control are manifest—prominent prayer group members are ascribed the gift of "discernment," which they use to interpret and mediate prophecy by leaders.[28] In "closed systems" the period of prophecy within prayer meetings is far more circumscribed, directed, and interpreted by prominent members, with thematic and semantic emphases of prophecy already mostly limited to the particular lexicon described above. Alongside the explicit mediatory roles that prominent figures take in the prayer group, considerable attention is paid in McGuire's rendering to latent mechanisms through which power is controlled and channeled. To this end, an interesting observation

23. Ibid., 93.
24. Ibid., 93.
25. Ibid., 77.
26. Ibid., 93.
27. Ibid., 105.
28. Ibid.

is how group leaders use a particularly meaning-laden form of silence as a tool for control. As McGuire highlights, in terms of prophecy or spontaneous prayer, group silence is at times used as a tool of disapproval, to integrate impropriety in content or timing; it also directs the meetings flow—in periods of intense prayer "as long as the leader's eyes stay closed, silence continues."[29]

Thomas Csordas depth study of ritual life in the Catholic Charismatic Renewal (CCR) begins by tracing the history of the CCR from its inception at Duquesne University in the summer of 1966, through its peak popularity by the mid 1970s, and offers a comprehensive sketch of how (and why) its fortunes have waned in the United States since the early 1990s.[30] Importantly, Csordas' study also includes a detailed ethnographical of the Ann Arbour community in Michigan, a Catholic Charismatic intentional community that Csordas uses as an ethnographic miniature for a broader excursus of the CCR. The partial focus of Csordas' study in the ecclesial microclimate of the Ann Arbour community is important to the trajectory of his analysis; Csordas problematizes the notion of seeing CCR broadly as a "movement" but here he has a discrete unit for analysis, set up as a cultural micro-climate in isolation from wider society. From here, Csordas can extrapolate more general theories of negotiated power as a structure broadly onto the CCR.

Where McGuire focuses on the way in which power is exercised as control by strategic agents in prayer meetings, Csordas is interested in the first instance not in power as exercised, but in charisma as conferred. This is built upon Csordas' use of Fabian as a base to argue that religious movements are "rhetorical systems" of discourse with Charisma, in turn, rhetoric—"a mode of interpersonal efficacy: not a quality, but a collective, performative, intersubjective self-process."[31] Weber, on Csordas reading, held that Charisma was as a quality held in an individual personality, or was at least interested more in the locus of charisma that it's source. On Csordas reading however, a circuit of power is not legitimized by religious leaders, but itself creates their charisma.[32] Using adapted Weberian terminology, Csordas seeks to describe the internal dynamics of the CCR, principally via recourse to two key terms: "rhetorical involution" and "ritualization of practice."[33] The ritualization of practice in Csordas' rendering denotes how the emerging themes emanating from the renewal are actualized in everyday living. Three important psycho-cultural categories, "spontaneity, intimacy and control," operate as a discursive framework around which charismatic experience is thematized:

29. Ibid., 84.
30. Csordas, *Language, Charisma, and Creativity.*
31. Ibid., 114.
32. Ibid., 138.
33. Ibid., 138.

> Spontaneity is thematised not only as a capacity of the self that can be threatened by various types of interpersonal and spiritual bondages but also as the phenomenological criterion of the sacred that is manifest "suddenly" . . . . Intimacy is thematised as an ideal characteristic of personal relationships with the divine, one's spouse and other members of the charismatic group . . . finally both control and lack of control are thematised in positive and negative ways. One must be in control of one's behavior, but surrender control of one's affairs to the divine will.[34]

Mapping Csordas' terminology onto our already-established framework, these psycho-cultural themes, deployed rhetorically, operate as key nodal points in the conceptualization of God's power and its relationship to the world. These themes are far from static, however, as is clear from Csordas' extensive ethnographic analysis. Csordas views intentional communities like the one at Ann Arbor as the result of rhetorical involution, the process through which psycho-cultural themes are giving increasing symbolic significance alongside their actualization in everyday life. This increasing significance imputed to the discourse of charismatic leaders allows them to "avoid the process identified by Weber as the routinization of Charisma with an ever-escalated rhetoric embedded in practice and performance."[35] On this reading, the progressively more radical demands exhorted by charismatic figures in the movement lead to factionalism—for some the demands become too much—but for a strident core, the covenant community becomes the logical end to a spiraling form of charisma.

The invocation of charisma here is important, and indicative of how power must be understood as a multivalent category. Whilst the CCR cannot be said to have a single charismatic leader, Csordas identifies that there have been significant schisms within the movement around leadership figures, especially within The Word of God community in the early 1990s,[36] and thus is critical of what he views as the "parochial homogeneity"[37] of earlier studies of the CCR. To the contrary, Csordas argues that there is an inevitable, "performative generation of diversity"[38] within the movement, as "ritualization of practice sacralises everyday conditions and radicalisation of charisma suspends security in favour of a grander striving."[39] Of particular note in this vein is Csordas exposition of the controversial "Training Course," a manual for Catholic Pentecostal intentional communities written by The Word of God leader at the time, Stephen Clark, that contained "minutely explicit prescriptions for proper comportment, gender-appropriate dress, child-rearing practices, and the domestic division of labour" whilst also "identifying global threats to the community mission

---

34. Ibid., 263.
35. Ibid., 96.
36. Ibid., 96.
37. Ibid., xv.
38. Ibid., xvii.
39. Ibid., 101.

of rebuilding the kingdom of God" given initially only to coordinators and district heads and their families.[40]

The framing of everyday praxis, described as "habitus" by Csordas, as integral in rebuilding the kingdom of God fits with his broader argument that the ritualization of practice encourages spiritual metaphors and religious terminology to permeate and shape everyday life, vis-à-vis the radicalization of charisma. Here, charisma is a source of power, conferred by group structure, but exercised by individuals. Mapping this onto a circuit of power, one can see a conflation—or at least, a blurring occurs—as what is ostensibly "God's power" is actualized through a very specific set of stringent criteria, laid out programmatically by leading figures in the CCR. On Csordas' reading, then, a rhetorically conferred legitimacy allows spiritual leaders the power to manipulate nodal points in pre-existing circuits of power, using a distinctive conceptual framework already reified to channel community focus in certain directions.

Here we can see a subtle differentiation between the analysis of power in our two respective studies, parsed partially by the writers themselves. McGuire's analysis, on Csordas' terms, ensures that both "both the rank-and-file participant and the occasional charismatic figure or 'star' are subordinated to the collective force of the group" such that McGuire "defines a sort of leaderless charisma in a Durkheimian mode as 'the empowerment of individuals drawing on the collective force of the group.'"[41] This criticism can be sustained in part. McGuire is clearly interested in how effective agency of prayer group leaders controls and directs power to allow Pentecostal ritual and practice to intricately fuse with a Catholic ecclesial structure. On this schema, "closed" meetings—run increasingly in liaison with church officials or by charismatic clergy—ensure that the spontaneity inherent in Pentecostal praxis is shaped in such a way that it can resemble "orthodoxy."[42] In a more limited study of Pentecostal Catholic prayer groups, however, McGuire understandably has less focus on how exactly the doctrine and impetus of the movement has changed over time.

Csordas' analysis takes a slightly different tack, using language of rhetorical involution to argue that when mediating power, group leaders are already working with a conceptual apparatus that includes both positive and negative portrayal of creativity and control—"Spontaneity is thematized not only as a category of the self that can be threatened by various types of interpersonal and spiritual 'bondages' but also as a phenomenological criterion of the sacred that manifests 'suddenly' or 'out of the blue.'"[43] It is this existing dialectic tension between creativity and control, couched in language of bondage, temptation, purity, and salvation, that allows Catholic Pentecostals to harmonize two competing ecologies of power. The limiting and/or directing of Pentecostal spontaneity toward Catholic orthodoxy is justified with recourse to the

40. Ibid., 87.

41. McGuire, *Pentecostal Catholics*, 45.

42. Ibid., 45.

43. Csordas, *Language, Charisma, and Creativity*, 263.

importance of discernment in an epistemological framework in which both the power of God and the power of evil are real forces of power acting in the world.

Power Analyzed: The Enduring Analytical Value of Seeing "Circuits" of Power

Here then, we can attempt to map our divergent conceptualizations of power onto the complex circuitry of power that underlies the CCR. Pentecostal Catholics combine traditional Catholic doctrines and ecclesial structures with a Pentecostal conceptualization of God's power as active in the world. Despite receiving cautious encouragement by the church hierarchy, there is without doubt a tension, as pre-existing nodal points orientating Catholic spirituality are brought into contact with a new religious framework that posits a sense of eschatological urgency, and claims to receive new prophecy and untrammeled divine intervention outside of the church's more formal ecclesial structures. Catholic Pentecostals see this as renewing and revitalizing their faith, but also must seek to negotiate and reconcile these two ostensibly competing circuits of power.

Within an adapted, but nonetheless "orthodox," fashion, questions of control—namely, how power is mediated and directed—come to the fore. Meredith McGuire's analysis highlights how, within the setting of the Pentecostal Catholic prayer meeting, established figures in the prayer groups exercise tacit as well as explicit control over the direction, rate, and flow of power, consciously or otherwise ensuring that spontaneity and creativity conform to a pattern that coheres to group norms with an aspiration to "orthodoxy." These figures operate as something of an inert backstop, to ensure that lived experience of the spirit, where possible, conforms within an already-reified circuit of power. Csordas' broad excursus of the CCR over more than twenty years adds a further dimension to this rendering, examining how the rhetorical emphases of the CCR seem specifically designed to hold together in dialectical tension the movement's coterminous desire for creativity and control. The positive and negative valence of both these terms in the epistemological framework of Catholic Pentecostals is channeled by effective agents within the CCR to direct flows of power in a myriad of ways.

In his (forthcoming) reflection upon the varied contours of Anglican polity and social practice, Percy employs a new and intriguing analytical term, the concept of "obliquity,"[44] to sketch the distinctive appeal of "broad church" Anglicanism. Using the definition of John Kay, with obliquity described as "the process of achieving complex objectives *indirectly*,"[45] the concept of obliquity has a positive valence in Percy's text; it is a useful descriptor, not only of broad church Anglicanism, but also of contemporary notions of membership and belonging. Obliquity describes a form of spiritual affiliation that is complex, transient, and negotiatory in character, emblematic in Percy's

44. Percy, "The Household of Faith."

45. Kay, *Obliquity*, 3.

rendering of a millennial generation that are self-inscriptively "spiritual-but-not-religious." Further, obliquity is a multivalent concept already contained within the ecologies of the Anglican church, both in its public function—the church as a broad and inclusive institution that many participate in without being obvious members—and its ecclesiological tensions—broad church obliquity has an negotiatory character—in a picture increasingly colored by narrowly prescribed and circumscribed images of "high" or "low" church.

An analog of obliquity is clearly visible in contemporary analyses of the CCR, with Cleary arguing that scholarly language of the "many Catholicisms" of Latin America is itself emblematic of the "vibrant and confusing surface of contemporary religion."[46] As an analytical term, "obliquity" (whether or not one retains the positive valence furnished Percy's rendering) can lend further clarity to our analysis here of power circuitry. In the previously-discussed explanatory schema, obliquity works within distinctive epistemological frameworks, like those of Catholic Pentecostals, as a useful descriptor for the space between the manifest function of ritual, rite, or sociality and the latent outcome that emerges, forming and shaping religious discourse and practice. Whilst the overarching power structure of the church offers contours of "clarity" to Catholic Pentecostals, it is this negotiatory space, this obliquity in the structure that allows believers to negotiate across two otherwise-competing ecologies of power, harmonizing "spontaneity and control" to borrow Csordas terminology again. It is in this tension between obliquity and clarity, retained in Percy's adaption of Clegg's conceptual framework, that we see the operative value of power conceived as a "circuit," as distinct from the analysis of Steven Lukes in which power is so characterized by latency that its import is impossible to quantify, and from earlier accounts that placed undue emphasis on power as the near-unique causal prerogative of agents themselves.[47]

On the schema laid out above, power as a relational concept still affords sufficient explanatory purpose to human agency, the ability of actors to exercise power "over" one another or "against" interest of others, but does not situate power as inextricably tied to such forces. Agency itself on Clegg's rendering is positioned within a broader circuit of "nodal points" that condition it, such that power can be just as easily vested in an individual by the institutional context as in a series of ritual practices.[48] It is the characteristic combination of fixity and flow, of obliquity and clarity in this analytical framework that makes it a particularly compelling tool with which to illuminate textual and ethnographic accounts of fundamentalism and revivalism.

46. Clearly, *Rise of Charismatic Catholicism,* 2.

47. Lukes, *Power.*

48. Clegg, *Frameworks of Power.*

Some Concluding Thoughts

This essay has attempted to show that Clegg's notion of power as a "circuit," advanced distinctively by Percy in *Words, Wonders and Power* is particularly useful in illuminating distinctive flows of power in the lived experience of Catholic Pentecostals. Whilst the fortunes of the CCR in the United States have waned somewhat in the new millennium, the movement continues to be of vital importance in the religious demography of Latin America, claiming an estimated seventy-three million adherents across the region.[49] As Cleary's analysis shows, it seems to be characterized by many similar organizational features (small prayer groups and covenant communities) that characterized the concurrent movement in the United States. Drawing principally on two in-depth ethnographic studies of the CCR, it has been argued that Catholic Pentecostals bring together to ordinarily antithetical ecologies of power together in a tense and intense hybridity. Catholic Pentecostals negotiate across this field using a distinctive conceptualization of power that serve as "nodal points" in their epistemological framework, using strategic agents to mediate God's power and channel flows of creativity with control.

In *Words, Wonders and Power* Percy examined fundamentalism as a dynamic, restless force, one that used an inductive form of reasoning to reassert a very particular conceptualization of God's power, thematized around omnipotence in defiance of (post)modernity. The text itself does not set out to present a causal or closed theory of power that can explain away fundamentalism, or seek to advance a catchall expansive typology of it. Instead, its enduring offer to us is a framework for analysis, a way to pattern, through which vibrant religious traditions that shift and change can be thematized and understood through their ecclesiological structures and theological emphases. In his introduction to this volume, Martyn Percy reiterates a commitment to the "role and vitality of the implicit" if and as one seeks to "comprehend the depth, density, identity and shaping of faith communities."

Words, Wonders and Power is a starting point in this endeavor. As a text, it offered a deeper and more complete understanding of the "all-encompassing wordview" of a fundamentalist movement, looking beyond the loud articulation of power performed to see that, mirrored in a conceptualization of the divine, were some very human "virtues, vices, characters and mood."[50] In both its tools and its tone, it remains a useful touchstone for contemporary analyses of fundamentalism and revivalism.

49. Cleary, *Rise of Charismatic*, 1.
50. Percy, *Words, Wonders and Power*, 162.

Bibliography

Althouse, Peter. "The Ideology of Power in Early American Pentecostalism." *Journal of Pentecostal Theology* 13:1 (2004) 97–115. doi: 10.1177/096673690401300106.

Berger, Peter L. *The Heretical Imperative: Contemporary Possibilities of Religious Affirmation.* London: Collins, 1980.

Cantón, Manuela. "Gypsy Pentecostalism, Ethnopolitical Uses and Construction of Belonging in the South of Spain." *Social Compass* 57:2 (2010) 253–67. doi: 10.1177/0037768610362418.

Cleary, Edward L. *The Rise of Charismatic Catholicism in Latin America.* Gainesville, FL: University Press of Florida, 2011.

Clegg, Stewart. *Frameworks of Power.* London: Sage, 1989.

Cox, Harvey. *Fire from Heaven: the Rise of Pentecostal Spirituality and the Reshaping of Religion in the Twenty-First Century.* Wokingham, UK: Addison-Wesley, 1995.

Csordas, Thomas J. *Language, Charisma, and Creativity: Ritual Life in the Catholic Charismatic Renewal.* Basingstoke, UK: Palgrave Macmillan, 2012.

Dowding, Keith. 2012. "Why Should We Care About the Definition of Power?" *Journal of Political Power* 5:1 (2012) 119–35. doi: 10.1080/2158379X.2012.661917.

Geertz, Clifford. *The Interpretation of Cultures.* New York: Basic Books, 1973.

John, Kay. *Obliquity: Why Our Goals Are Best Achieved Indirectly.* London: Profile, 2011.

Lindbeck, George A. *The Nature of Doctrine: Religion and Theology in a Postliberal Age.* London: SPCK, 1984.

Lukes, Steven. *Power: A Radical View.* 2nd ed. New York: Palgrave Macmillan, 2005.

McGuire, Meredith B. *Pentecostal Catholics: Power, Charisma, and Order in a Religious Movement.* Philadelphia: Temple University Press, 1982.

Percy, Martyn. "The Household of Faith: Anglican Obliquity and the Lambeth Conference." In *The Lambeth Conference and the Anglican Communion,* edited by Paul Avis, 316–40. London: T. & T. Clark, 2017.

———. *Words, Wonders and Power: Understanding Contemporary Christian Fundamentalism and Revivalism.* London: SPCK, 1996.

5

Response to Part I

On the Vocation of the Contextual Theologian

MARTYN PERCY

CONTEXT MATTERS. ALL THEOLOGY is some kind of attempt to confer intelligibility on God's ways with the world. So the study of that same world is part and parcel of what it means to be a contextual theologian. So, contextual theology, and for that matter "grounded" ecclesiology (i.e., the study of the "real" church as it is encountered, rather than "ideal" constructions of its reality), is an enterprise undertaken in a very particular kind of way—it is done dialogically with faith and tradition in mutual intercourse with the world as it is encountered in the present. So there are three essential characteristics to contextual theology that we should note, and which can be located in the infinite variety of contextual theologies.

First, contextual theologies tend to be sympathetic and syncretic to applying their knowledge and insights to particular situations. This requires on the one hand respect for revelation, texts, and traditions; yet at the same time making sure that the hermeneutical methods are praxis-based and relevant. Gay, black liberation, and political theologies tend, by and large, to be infused with an open, textured, and liberal spirit; at the base of their method lies a relative freedom in the exposition of the material of Christianity.

Second, contextual theologies often tend to stress that Christianity will have behavioral, social, ethical, and political implications. Contextual theologians are not usually content with Christianity being positioned as a purely propositional religion, concerned with correct dogma and simply holding fast to the creeds. Contextual theologians believe that Christianity is an integration of the relational and environmental, and is therefore fundamentally about *how* religion adapts within society, and how society adapts to religion. Yet the excavation and exposition of such theology will always need to be done with humility and patience, recognizing that the tightly linked compounds of religion-society and church-culture cannot easily be separated—as though they were curds and whey.

Third, contextual theology is inherently receptive to contemporary culture, science and the arts. It is concerned with freedom, is first and foremost concerned with pursuing wisdom and the truth wherever it is to be found. So there is therefore no fundamental or absolute discontinuity between the truth that is out there and the truth of Christianity. Contextual theology will generally shun barriers that create neat doctrinal categories, and will usually immerse itself in the messy contingencies and miscibility of lived faith, rather than "ideal" theological constructions of reality. Contextual theologians typically believe that truth emerges not only in revelation, but also in dialogue with experience, reason, culture, and broader histories. Confessional monologues addressed to the world, or derived from allegedly pure sources of revelation, are therefore seen as weak, defensive and unengaging. Characteristically, contextual theologians are suspicious of dogmatism, and are open to counter-truths from a range of disciplines and methods, or alternative insights that belong to other ranges of reference and spheres of knowledge.

Now, there are many threads I could draw on in this first section that both illustrate and illuminate the kind of methodology I have sought to develop in writings during the last twenty-five years. The characteristic way of describing this might be to speak of a kind of weaving—a tapestry, if you will—where the threads come together to create both image and texture. The spatial imagery that Simon Coleman's essay is attentive to, picks up on precisely this point. To do theology is to identify space, critique that space, and then to re-imagine the space. Theology is the making of maps and the charting of territory and activity. It is aesthetic and archi-techtonic in character. Similarly, Joel Daniels's essay sees an assortment of signs and signals as indicators of ecclesial life, and notes how important the social sciences are for shaping holistic theology. Matt Gompels's essay draws attention to how power functions within the "ecclesial grid" (so to speak). There are latent and manifest dimensions to power; formal and operant; implicit and explicit. More often than not, there is a process of conflation at work, with the believer, for example, unable to distinguish between the authority of scripture and that of the interpreter.

Ian Markham's essay, it seems to me, set out the most ambitious chart of all: public theology, spiritual experience, faith and its relation to ethics, contextual theology, cultural-linguistic readings of congregational life, practical theology, and pastoral theology. Markham picks out the representative threads from the tapestry, examining each with careful singularity. Toward the end of his chapter, he notes a "deep pastoral sensibility, which does take him [Percy] to strange places . . . he must be one of the few theologians to write positively about adultery."[1] I am not sure about the "positively" here, but will perhaps affirm "exposition-ally and empathetically."

---

1. See page 12 of this book. See also Percy, *The Salt of the Earth*, 214.

There are three caveats to mention before explaining more. First, I do think that the doctrine of sin needs more attention from the churches, and that contemporary culture has eroded Christianity's important and valuable sense of sinfulness.[2] Second, sin needs to be understood in context. I don't mean by this that one simply capitulates to some lazy liberal and vapid relativism. But what is important here is distinguishing between absolute and relative standards. Murder is murder. But modesty and immodesty is, well, relative and culturally variable across histories and peoples. Third, there is a pastoral dimension to any practical and contextual theology, and Markham's essay, not unreasonably, picks up on how much I am indebted to the work of Nicholas Healy,[3] amongst others, for constantly returning theology to the issue of "grounded ecclesiology," so that we understand the church in the cultural-complexity of the particular (its past and present), rather than the ornate-aesthetic of more abstract theological metanarratives.

So, an issue like adultery calls for discernment, compassion, judgment, empathy, pastoral care, practical theology, and a capacity to see the issue within some wider contexts.[4] So let me offer this small example of why clergy might leave ministry by subliminally engineering deliberate breakdowns in their marital relationships. James Scott's work is illuminating here, in helping to identify the "hidden transcript" in organizations, which he says, can cause people to live with unbearable tensions, such that they can only psychologically or emotionally self-harm, in order to qualify for some kind of evacuation.[5]

Hoge and Wenger concur, and suggest that clerical extra-marital affairs might be a kind of cry for help: "a sick way of relieving stress . . . to shoot yourself in the foot is the only way to get out of a terribly stressful situation . . . 'I can't handle this, but I can't say that' [so] . . . " (to those in authority above who have been deaf to the growing stress).[6] For some this may appear to be a way of transferring blame, but in the light of James Scott's observations, we can perhaps begin to see how "petty acts of rebellion" in ministry (or other organizations) are really attempts to reify resistance to a dominant script. Small acts of resistance may begin to accumulate and occur when clergy feel that they are no longer themselves; that they have become "lost" in the expectations, demands, projections, desires, and routines of others.

Although I have reflected at greater length in a closing essay on methodology, there are a few comments to make at this juncture in relation to the broader picture on ecclesiology. My work tends not to be constrained by the present or the past, and can be playfully experimental in attempting to illuminate themes and issues in

2. See Percy, "Falling Far Short: Taking Sin Seriously."

3. See Healy, *Church, World and the Christian Life.*

4. See Tomlinson, "Clergy, Culture and Ministry."

5. Scott, *The Art of Resistance: Hidden Transcripts*, 18.

6. Hoge and Wenger, *Pastors in Transition*, 130ff.

studying the church.[7] Here, I draw on the legacy of James Hopewell especially, who was unafraid and innovative in his readings of congregational life, combining theories of myth, literary criticism, sociology, and anthropology to help us make sense of how congregations are behavioral and performative "households" that are shaped ("storied dwellings") by beliefs and practices locked, long ago in the cultures from within which churches emerge.[8]

Hopewell was therefore able to call upon Max Weber, Clifford Geertz, Northrop Frye and others, all in a single essay. To deploy a Hopewellian analytical framework is to extend our knowledge of ecclesiology beyond congregations, and to explore movements within the church, and to also examine the life and character of a denomination. But it is exactly this kind of contextual mutation that is taking place in religious life within contemporary culture that means that the task of hospitable and interdisciplinary methods in ecclesiology is more urgent than ever, both for the academy and for the church as a whole.

Some will still dispute this approach to ecclesiology, arguing it is for "pure" theology and ecclesial discourse to self-explain the church. I disagree. I don't think the social sciences subtract from, pollute, or dilute the study of the church, but rather, skillfully blended, can only add to our stock of knowledge. I don't assume that social sciences work from a position of privilege over the subject. Social sciences are unusually open to hybridity in method, and well-used to engaging respectfully with other disciplines. I would add that,

> . . . all doctrine is pastoral, biblical and applied. All theology is contextual. All of it is historical, ideological, philosophical and to some extent sociological. Theology refuses to be neatly organized. It cannot be coaxed into neat silos.[9]

As readers will discover, the subtext of many of the chapters in this book is that, concurring with Lewis Mudge, "ecclesiology itself is a kind of *social theory*" (emphasis mine).[10] Ecclesiology, based on (or understood as) social theory can read and interpret the stories of the people of God, who are themselves reading the story of God through their tradition, even as they are performed by it. Some understanding of concrete social and ecclesial existence is therefore vital if the churches are to truly engage with the cultures which are their contexts.

Correspondingly, I hold (along with Nicholas Healy and Lewis Mudge, and many others)[11] that ecclesiology must make fuller use of non-theological methods and insights, which will help the church to think of itself as an organization, as well as a "text"

---

7. See, for example, Percy, *Clergy: the Origin of Species*; Percy, *The Future Shapes of Anglicanism*.

8. Hopewell, *Congregation*.

9. Percy, "Theological Education and Formation for an Uncommon Occupation," 232.

10. Mudge, *Rethinking the Beloved Community*, 12, emphasis added.

11. See for example Scharen, *Explorations in Ecclesiology and Ethnography*; Paas, *Church Planting in the Secular West*; Ormerod, *Re-Visioning the Church*.

that is read and expressed. Thus, the underlying thread of the argument in my work is for an anthropologically-attuned and sociologically-informed theology (which is, per se, an ecclesiology), and for a cultural-linguistic understanding of Christianity (following George Lindbeck)[12] that pays attention to the grounded reality of the church and the cultures that congregations inhabit. Some of the basic tools comprise ethnography, fieldwork, interviews, textual analysis, and the like.

It is this the type of approach that allows us to study apparently simple things, such as a funeral tea?[13] Can we ask basic questions, such as where is the theology of this group located? Is it in their creeds and articles of faith? Or is it in their habits, customs, rituals and stories? And if the latter, how do we best discover and study them? And once we have discovered them, how do we read and interpret them? And finally, what are the implications of such studies for the academy, with its methodologies and present understandings?

The key to good methodology and successful researching in religion lies in establishing that the knowledge we have is inadequate and insufficient, or even quite wrong, in spite of appearances to the contrary (e.g., what we thought we once knew about churches and church-going). It lies in identifying new knowledge, or how existing, reinterpreted knowledge might change the way we look at a specific topic or field. It leads us into a situation where we can begin to say something entirely new about the apparently familiar. Rather like Catherine Bell's work, we look for large patterns and ask big questions.[14] We connect a parish tea that might be for the many, to perhaps just the few taking part in the parish Eucharist later that week.[15] We notice those things that hide in plain sight: flowers, humor, smells, hospitality, and what ordinary folk about to worship decide to wear to church, to name but a few.[16] We find pleasure in creativity. Perhaps amazingly, and for an institution that has existed for some two thousand years, there is always something new to say.

Bibliography

Bell, Catherine. *Ritual Theory, Ritual Practice*. Oxford: Oxford University Press, 1992.

Clark, David. *Between Pulpit and Pew: Folk Religion in a North Yorkshire Fishing Village*. Cambridge: Cambridge University Press, 1982.

Day, Abby. *The Religious Lives of Older Women: The Last Active Anglican Generation*. Oxford: Oxford University Press, 2017.

Healy, Nicholas M. *Church, World and the Christian Life: Practical-Prophetic Ecclesiology*. Cambridge: Cambridge University Press, 2000.

12. Lindbeck, *The Nature of Doctrine*.

13. See Clark, *Between Pulpit and Pew*.

14. Bell, *Ritual Theory, Ritual Practice*.

15. Percy, "Identity, Character and Practices in Rural Anglican Congregation."

16. For further discussion, readers are referred to the excellent anthropological work in this sphere by Abby Day. See Day, *The Religious Lives of Older Women*.

Hoge, Dean R. and J. E. Wenger. *Pastors in Transition: Why Clergy Leave Local Church Ministry*. Grand Rapids, MI: Eerdmans, 2005.

Hopewell, James. *Congregation; Stories and Structures*. London: SCM Press, 1987.

Lindbeck, George. *The Nature of Doctrine: Religion and Theology in a Postliberal Age*. London: SPCK, 1984.

Mudge, Lewis. *Rethinking the Beloved Community: Ecclesiology, Hermeneutics, Social Theory*. Lanham, MY: University Press of America, 2001.

Ormerod, Neil. *Re-Visioning the Church: An Experiment in Systematic Historical Ecclesiology*. Minneapolis: Fortress, 2014.

Paas, Stefan. *Church Planting in the Secular West*. Grand Rapids, MI: Eerdmans, 2016.

Percy, Martyn. *Clergy: The Origin of Species*. London: Continuum, 2006.

———. "Falling Far Short: Taking Sin Seriously." *Reinhold Niebuhr and Contemporary Politics*, edited by R. Harries and S. Platten, 116–28. Oxford: Oxford University Press, 2010.

———. *The Future Shapes of Anglicanism: Currents, Contours, Charts*. London: Routledge, 2017.

———. "Identity, Character and Practices in Rural Anglican Congregation." In *Theologically-Engaged Anthropology*, edited by Derrick Lemmons. Oxford: Oxford University Press, 2017.

———. "Theological Education and Formation for an Uncommon Occupation." In *Contemporary Issues in the Worldwide Anglican Communion: Powers and Pieties*, edited by Abby Day, 229–44. Farnham, UK: Ashgate, 2016.

Scharen, Christian B., ed. *Explorations in Ecclesiology and Ethnography*. Grand Rapids, MI: Eerdmans, 2012.

Scott, James C. *The Art of Resistance: Hidden Transcripts*. New Haven: Yale University Press, 1990.

Tomlinson, Ian. "Clergy, Culture and Ministry: The Dynamics of Roles and Relations." In *Church and Society*, edited by Martyn Percy. London: SCM, 2017.

Part II

Ecclesiology

6

Three Sketches of Symbols and Sacraments

An Appreciation of Martyn Percy's Perspective and Tone

RICHARD LAWSON

VEDA REED IS A landscape painter and professor emerita at the Memphis College of Art. In Reed's landscapes, the horizon is a common theme. Describing what the horizon means to her personally, Reed says, "Being able to see where the sky meets the land has always made me feel safe."[1]

Reed's art entered a new phase, however, when she began painting the sky without the horizon. Her 2011 painting *King of Clouds (Cumulonimbus Incus with Mamma)* signals a dramatic turn from the horizon. The painting is a horizontal view of a mollusk-like cloud formation. At first, the viewer is intrigued. At some point, the viewer is disoriented by this perspective, as if flying through the sky in a dream.

These two themes—the horizon and the difference perspective makes—are found in the very different medium of theology, especially Martyn Percy's. Percy describes a horizon where God meets humanity. Yet Percy's metaphysical horizon does not blind him to other, less dramatic horizons, such as the way the "sacred" and the "secular" mingle in life, so much so that it is unwise to try and separate what is religious from what is not.

Like an artist, this theologian understands perspective. The same view—even of God's ways—can evoke different and even conflicting emotions and reactions. The place where perspective meets reality is a kind of horizon.

In the essay "Baptism: Belief, Practice and Culture," Percy cites the influence of photography on his approach:

> Looking at photographs, the literary critic Roland Barthes made a distinction between what he called the *Studium* and *Punctum*. The *Studium* is the photograph's overt agenda, which might include a view, the person, an event

---

1. Veda Reed spoke these words during a "Question and Answer" at the opening of the exhibit "Veda Reed: Day into Night" at the Memphis Brooks Museum of Art, Memphis, June 19, 2016.

or a drama. This will be the reason why the photograph was taken: to catch an event and preserve it for others to see. But photography cannot control all the images it captures; the eye of the camera is indiscriminate, and may include things in the detail that the photographer never intended to capture in the final image. Quite often, something strange or unfamiliar will slip in, disturbing the *Studium*. Whatever it may be, it is often something that the photographer was not looking to include, but then becomes part of the focus of the viewer; it can become a transfixing point. Often the *Punctum* of a photograph can convey a message, which, if read and interpreted, gives a completely different slant to the *Studium*.[2]

This distinction illuminates Percy's picture of baptism. The *Studium* of baptismal preparation includes formal beliefs and parish policies, such as the expectation that baptisms take place in the public liturgy on Sunday morning.[3] This expectation is linked with others, such as "appropriate interviews and courses that establish a level of understanding about what the nature of the rite is, and what it confers."[4]

There is more to the picture of baptism, though. Baptism is not only about formal expectations or even God. Percy quotes Carl Jung's letter to a pastor:

> Every event of our biological life has a numinous character: birth, puberty, marriage, illness . . . this is a natural fact demanding recognition, a question waiting for an answer. It is a need that should be satisfied with a solemn act, characterizing the numinous moment with a combination of words and gestures of an archetypal, symbolic nature. Rites give satisfaction to the collective and numinous aspects of the moment, beyond their purely personal significance . . . to unite the present with the historical and mythological past.[5]

Jung's insight is one reason why Percy argues for "an 'open' policy, even to the extent of conducting the majority of the rites 'privately' (i.e., not within the context of a normal church service)."[6] This open or flexible approach to baptism is not merely a technique designed to increase numbers. This open approach is theological, for Percy appreciates the connection between the meaning of baptism and "local customs, implicit theology and 'folk religion.'"[7]

Percy's picture of baptism is complex, making it difficult to separate what is primary (Christ's unconditional love?) from what is secondary (the numinous? the comfort of ritual?). Baptism is layered with meaning.

---

2. Percy, *Shaping the Church*, 20.

3. Ibid., 21.

4. Ibid., 26–27.

5. Ibid., 32.

6. Ibid., 32.

7. Ibid., 31.

Percy's theology, then, is evocative, like a nuanced photograph. This artistic approach is in part the result of his ordination as a priest in the Church of England, where a diocese is a geographical boundary and thus a map of actual places where God and humanity meet. The origin of the word *diocese* in fact predates its religious use: "Before the church adopted the word it had a long secular usage. It was originally used in the Roman Empire for an administrative subdivision."[8] This notion of place shapes Percy's theology, which is detailed and dense, resisting abstraction.

Tone of Voice

Tone of voice implies something about human awareness of the divine. Percy's voice is conversational, curious, honest, and generous. It is as easy to imagine Percy in a pub as much as in a pulpit.[9]

Percy's tone of voice is not a means to an end, however. It is not a tool for evangelism or for church growth. Tone of voice can be imagined as a theological echo of God's tone. For example, one of Percy's theological disagreements with John Milbank concerns tone of voice: "Whilst I find the tone (and therefore the ethos) of his argument to be rather insistent (hectoring, even)."[10] He also criticizes the tone of other theologians associated with Milbank: "Put another way, a theology that is uninformed by the social sciences may turn out to be very clever and erudite in some sense, but it may also be ultimately 'unreal.'"[11] This sentence is dense, but Percy's point is so succinct it could be spoken from a bar stool.

Percy has a sense of humor, too. Once, after illustrating at some length, with data and anecdotes, England's ambivalence regarding church attendance, Percy senses his reader's wariness and concludes with a line from one churchman, drawn from another age, "'I cannot consider myself to be a pillar of the church, for I never go. But I am a buttress—insofar as I support it from the outside.'"[12] His soft irenic humor emerges in the title of his essay about bishops: "Herding Cats? Leading the Church (of England) in a New Age."[13]

There is something intrinsically Anglican about Percy's tone of voice. For Percy, Anglicanism is—in part—perspective and tone. Its "peculiar genius is *not* to have solved the problem of its own identity—although that looks increasingly ragged as a

---

8. Armentrout and Slocum, *An Episcopal Dictionary of the Church*, 146.

9. In *Clergy*, Percy describes his work as honorary chaplain for a professional rugby club, work which took him from pitch to pub: "Yet the most demanding aspect of being a rugby club chaplain was sitting with my fellow supporters. Inevitably, in all the fracas and fury of a game, it was the name of God that was frequently invoked by all who watched. ('Say one for us, Padre . . .' was the classic vernacular request)" (Percy, *Clergy*, 157).

10. Percy, *The Ecclesial Canopy*, 5.

11. Percy, *Engaging with Contemporary Culture*, 67.

12. Percy, *Shaping the Church*, 61.

13. Ibid., 113.

virtue, at present. Anglicanism is episcopal, yet synodical; Catholic, yet Protestant—the *via media*.[14] Anglicanism is scripturally engaged but not in a narrow way. Likewise, Percy's voice is rarely preachy or prescriptive, although scriptural imagery and stories influence how he sees the world.[15]

The tone of Percy's voice, then, is a part of his method. He is curious about real people, empirical but not dry, sacramental in the broadest sense, and usually conversational. Percy describes his method as a "sketch":

> A sketch, in contrast, is a work in progress. It is an intentional approach to its subject: a piece of work that recognizes that the living, breathing church—this social skin of the world—can support a form of commentary that is neither systematic nor dogmatic in outlook, but is rather provisional and speculative in nature.[16]

After fifteen years as a parish priest, when I read Percy I think about a world of stories and experiences. I can best engage with Percy's theology by sketching some of these experiences that raise larger questions about the look and feel of God's relationship with actual people. The only problem is the criteria for selection: there is so much material. What stories should be chosen as particularly symbolic and evocative of larger themes?

God the Creator is active in all of parish life and—vitally—in all of life. For this reason, I have long been fascinated by the ancient saying, "God is a circle whose center is everywhere and whose circumference is nowhere."[17] Therefore, my selection of certain stories or experiences as particularly significant could be complemented by the selection of others that are equally, if not more, significant.

With this caveat in mind, I have chosen three stories that relate to important themes in Percy's own work, namely, death, resurrection, and emotion.[18] All three stories raise questions about the broader context of sacraments. Since sacraments are "outward and visible signs of inward and spiritual grace," they are inseparable from nature and human imagination in general.[19] For this reason, the Catechism of the 1979 *Book of Common Prayer* notes that "God does not limit himself to these [sacramental] rites; they are patterns of countless ways by which God uses material things

14. Percy, *Engaging with Contemporary Culture*, 68.

15. For a good example of Percy's engagement with scripture, see "Part One: A Catholic Faith" and his sermons in *Thirty Nine New Articles*.

16. Percy, *The Ecclesial Canopy*, 5. For a good example of how Percy sketches a subject, see "Formation and Embodiment: Sketches on Sacred Space" in *The Ecclesial Canopy* (55–70).

17. I have seen this quote used by pagan writers, Saint Bonaventure, Carl Jung, and an Episcopal priest.

18. For death and resurrection, see Percy's section "The Spiritual, Spatial Turn" in *The Ecclesial Canopy* (10–16); for emotion, see his essay "Feeling for the Church: Emotion and Anger in Ecclesial Polity" in *Shaping the Church* (143–57).

19. This definition of sacraments is found in the 1662 *Book of Common Prayer* and in the current Prayer Book of the Episcopal Church.

to reach out to us."[20] Thus, sacraments should not be imagined as exceptions, but as patterns that are recognizable in a variety of places.

A Sketch of One Death

St. John's Episcopal Church in Decatur, Alabama, is downtown. The church is inseparable from its neighborhood. The block north of the parish includes the bus stop, the block south includes a public elementary school, the block west includes retail, and the block east is residential.[21] Roads and sidewalks connect all of these places.

St. John's original architectural style was "carpenter gothic," a nineteenth century style common in the Episcopal Church. By building in wood and using locally sourced materials, churches could affordably replicate gothic architecture. In the twentieth century, St. John's added a limestone facade to the wooden church and built a limestone bell tower. The limestone and bell tower physically connect the parish to the ground and to the sky.

During my tenure, the church built an outdoor limestone amphitheater and extended the lawn, which added a new dimension to the feel of the church. The amphitheater and the lawn are not gated, thus creating a sense of openness and invitation.

On a Saturday morning in 2009, I receive a phone call from the organist. The organist works part-time at the church and regularly practices on Saturday mornings. This organist also has a sense of humor and enjoys practical jokes. Therefore, when he calls and says, "Richard, there is a dead woman in the church parking lot," I do not believe him.

When I drive to the parish, however, I see police and a naked woman lying a few feet from the amphitheater. A car is parked beside her body, but I do not recognize the woman or the car. She is caucasian. The police interview me, and I learn from the police that the woman is thirty-one years old and a resident of the town.

On Sunday morning, I begin each liturgy with an announcement about what has happened and a prayer for the nameless woman, saying, "May her soul and the souls of all the departed rest in peace."

The local paper reports the woman's name and states she was the mother of a thirteen-year-old daughter. I contact a member of the woman's family, introduce myself, and offer the church for a burial service and the memorial garden for a final resting place. The family member thanks me for reaching out and lets me know that they have a minister and plans for a service.

In the meantime, the Alabama Department of Forensic Sciences performs an autopsy, which reveals no signs of foul play or assault. The toxicology report is positive, and a police officer explains to me that the woman overdosed on a drug that makes the body become dangerously hot, which explains why she was naked when she died.

20. Episcopal Church, *The Book of Common Prayer*, 861.

21. The bus stop moved out of this block in the early 2000s.

I never discover any personal connections between the woman and the parish or the Episcopal Church. In one sense, though, she and the parish are deeply connected. It is possible that she came to the stone church in order to die in a sacred place, even if she was not conscious of exactly where she was or exactly what she was doing. No one will ever know her final thoughts or motives, of course, but the location of her death implies a final search for transcendence.[22] Her death is also reminiscent of baptism and the early church's custom whereby candidates were naked when baptized in a font or in a body of water. As Paul Tillich notes in his *Systematic Theology*, ordinary life is the material of the symbolic or sacramental: "For every religious term is a symbol using material from ordinary experience, and the symbol itself cannot be understood without an understanding of the symbolic material."[23]

The young woman's penultimate resting place, then, is symbolic. As Percy notes, the church building itself "is a sacrament—stone, glass, and other materials, not to mention people—ordinary profane materials that God nevertheless blesses, imbues with his grace, beauty and holiness, and allows to be an outward sign that points to a spiritual and inward grace."[24] In this sense, the church's architecture is part of the public imagination, which is the wider context of sacraments.

Death is a public symbol: each person faces his or her own death in the death of another person. Death is also a universal rite of passage. Building on the work of anthropologists Arnold van Gennep, Margaret Mead, and Victor Turner, Urban Holmes notes that a symbol such as death places human beings in a liminal position alongside all other human beings:

> In a liminal existence those things in the structures that define life are left behind. By this I mean anything from job descriptions, signs of rank, or bureaucratic organizational charts to formal, operational logic, rubrics, and canon law. There exists here an undifferentiated, homogenous, human kindness, as Turner puts it.[25]

In *A Dictionary of Symbols*, the poet and scholar J. E. Cirlot compares the universality of symbols with music: "Though transmuted to another plane of reality, it consists of the essential relationship between one process and another, between one object and another, an intimate relationship which has been defined as rhythm."[26] I have been told by a musician that every culture has percussion. We know every culture includes

---

22. I could be wrong, of course. The location of her death may have been chosen because it was an open parking lot.

23. Tillich, *Systematic Theology*, 22.

24. Percy, *Shaping the Church*, 63.

25. Holmes, "Liminality and Liturgy," 389. Holmes is a fairly important resource for Percy. For example, Percy's *Shaping the Church* notes Holmes's understanding of Anglican ethos (8, 131), and his book *Clergy* builds upon Holmes's observations about priesthood (19–20, 22, 23–25, 161–62, 182).

26. Cirlot, *A Dictionary of Symbols*, xxxii.

death. Perhaps death should be thought of as the down beat of culture, with heartbeat providing a welcome contrast and a softer rhythm.

A Sketch of Easter

On Easter Day in the parish, after the appointed Gospel (John 20:1–10), I begin my sermon with a story and an invitation to see resurrection in the familiar:

> The baked bread during communion a few Sundays ago was perfect: it smelled delicious, felt warm, and tasted so good. So, at the altar rail, a little boy tasted the bread and responded not with the traditional "amen" but with the similar and equally appropriate word, "mmm." "Mmm" is not a word, of course, but it is the perfect sound to make in response to something really good.
>
> Some linguists and philosophers believe these sounds are an essential part of language's meaning, that is, the very sounds that words make mean something. And this idea explains why we sing, and why we raise our voices with a shout or lower them in a whisper.
>
> At the tomb, Mary Magdalene does not recognize the risen Christ, at least not at first. She does not recognize Christ until she hears Christ speak her name, "Mariam." It is interesting to imagine Christ's tone of voice, speaking from the other side of death. Did Christ speak in a whisper or with a raised voice? Tone of voice in this moment is part of what Mariam hears and feels.
>
> In the educational world, a distinction is made between experiential learners and abstract learners. The resurrection in John's Gospel is for experiential learners, for people who will not believe it until they see it and feel it.
>
> "While it was still dark," Mary Magdalene goes to the tomb. We know about darkness. Darkness is familiar. Literally, every night we experience it. At some point in our life, we experience metaphorical darkness. All of us who are old enough go to dark places, places where artificial light would not help us see any more clearly.

On Easter Monday, I receive a call on my cell phone. (My cell phone is found on the out-of-office message of my office phone.) I am at home, dozing in and out of sleep, and thinking unreligious thoughts after a sublime Holy Week.

The voice I hear on my phone is hysterical and incomprehensible. My first thought is that someone has died tragically. Once the person calms down, I learn that no one has died, at least not recently. The person on the phone is a parishioner whom I do not know well.

She references my Easter sermon and the part about Mary Magdalene going to the tomb "while it was still dark." She goes on to tell me several stories. When she was a teenager, her younger brother died in a tragic accident at home. Her own children are close to the age of her brother when he died.[27] She recounts a recent dream that

---

27. I have received this parishioner's permission to include these details from her personal life.

felt like "a premonition" of the death of one of her children. Then, she recalls a recent experience in which a child—and the child of family friends—had been in a coma in the hospital, almost died, survived, and reported a conversation in heaven with my parishioner's deceased brother.

During the phone call, my parishioner mentions her "therapist's take." I affirm that therapists and psychologists can help in these situations. She replies that she wants a "Christian and Episcopal" view of what she is experiencing, especially the "premonition." Throughout the phone call, I listen, ask a few clarifying questions, thank her for her trust in me, say a prayer, and ask if she could meet with me in person. I schedule our meeting a few days after her next appointment with the therapist.

A week later, we meet in the parish's lounge, a comfortable and quiet place that is similar to a living room in a home. The parishioner is intelligent, professional, and self-aware. Our conversation proceeds for well over one hour, during which she covers many different topics and stories in great detail, all of which fit together coherently.

She also shares with me that she had been raped during college. I listen to her story without asking too many questions, having the sense that for this parishioner I represent God's healing presence and the larger community more than I represent a professional or psychological view.

At some point near the end of our conversation, she speaks movingly of the love of her husband, family, friends, and therapist. Without being prompted to do so, she also talks about her trust that God will take care of her and of her children in life and in death, "no matter what happens."

I say a prayer at the end of our meeting, although I do not remember exactly what I said, only that I prayed for my parishioner and for her family, mentioning something about "God's hope and love in Christ meeting with our real fears."

The subjects of a child's death and a rape raise the question of evil. What is the relationship between the symbolic and that which threatens to destroy or disintegrate human identity? The symbol of sexuality is mysterious, but in the wrong hands it can be manipulative and violent, in the same way the symbol of death can be. Urban Holmes underlines this point in *Ministry and Imagination*: "It is essential that we have a sense of diabolical meaning as well as symbolic meaning if we are going to avoid an unrealistic optimism in regard to the imagination."[28] In other words, the symbolic has the power to make human beings whole, but evil can manipulate and destroy human identity with these same symbols.

Holmes describes two contradictory views of evil. First, evil is the product of human choice or sin. Second, evil is the result of something demonic and otherworldly. Holmes argues that these two views are actually complementary: "Somehow it is necessary to combine the strengths of both views of evil—as both the product of man's ungraceful living and as the result of an other-than-human experience—without

---

28. Holmes, *Ministry and Imagination*, 128.

succumbing to the weaknesses of either."[29] Holmes's view leaves room for a variety of pastoral approaches. For example, a person struggling with addiction needs the presence and the wisdom of a recovery group in order to resist destructive behavior. In other cases, however, the response to "evil" needs to include prayer for God to act in the ways that God alone can act, both in this life and in the life to come. For example, people who have experienced abuse or violence cannot be completely healed by a support group or by therapy alone. Furthermore, some people who suffer from trauma may not be able to experience even modest healing or wholeness within the timespan of ordinary life.[30]

Evil, then, is one context for resurrection. Resurrection entails resistance to deadly powers as much as resistance to the futility of death. Thus, resurrection should be imagined as an earthly and a heavenly reality, although human beings know much more about earth than heaven.

Percy understands these complex, ambiguous settings for God's presence. In *Clergy: The Origin of Species*, he tells the story of a young couple with a two-year-old son, all of whom had recently moved into a house. "But after a while," Percy writes, "the child had started to complain about 'seeing things' and had started to become disturbed and frightened. The boy reported seeing an elderly man wandering around the upstairs of the house, although no one else could see this."[31] This family lives in Percy's parish and asks for a visit from him so that he can perform an "exorcism."[32]

During the visit, Percy concludes "that there were no obvious reasons for what one might call 'a lingering, disturbing and unexplained presence.' There were, for example, no deaths in the house reported by the previous occupants."[33] So, in the rooms where there had been problems, Percy sprinkles holy water and says the Lord's Prayer and some collects. Afterward, he has a cup of tea with the family and plays with the child. Two weeks later, the mother tells Percy that the child is sleeping well. "Fine," Percy says to the mother, "and thanks for the tea."[34]

Percy concludes,

> So what does the encounter mean? Of course, I don't know what it means. But in my view, the encounter, and others like it that I have been part of, points in two contrary ways. First, it suggests a vernacular spiritual dimension to human and social existence that needs addressing by more than mere dismissal. Second, it suggests that the grace of God, operative in imaginative *pastoralia*, elicits faith and trust, and creates a new environment of hope in which the

29. Holmes, *Ministry and Imagination*, 30.

30. For an Anglican theological treatment of abuse, violence, and other forms of evil, see Marilyn McCord Adams's *Horrendous Evils and the Goodness of God*.

31. Percy, *Clergy*, 154.

32. Ibid., 154.

33. Ibid., 154.

34. Ibid., 155.

presence of God, mediated through words and symbols, speaks in fresh ways to reassure and reconfigure.[35]

Percy's exorcism is not the same as the pastoral conversations I had with my parishioner. However, Percy's response is similar to my own. These very personal and often emotional pastoral experiences are the real context in which God is—if not experienced—at least sought.

A Quick Sketch of Grief

During premarital counseling, I talk with couples about how family history influences every couple's expectations for their own marriage. Then, I ask the couple to spend some time—preferably, several weeks—thinking about two questions. How did one's parents and grandparents deal with conflict or crisis? And how did one's parents and grandparents show affection in their own marriages?

In response to these two questions, a woman told her fiancé and me a story about her own mother's first marriage, which ended in divorce:

> After my mother's divorce, my grandmother, who was very religious, stern, and lived on a farm, she actually took my mom's white wedding dress and burned it in her backyard. This was a really out of character thing for her to do. She was not known for showing emotions or doing anything unusual or dramatic.

At first glance, this odd incident may not seem theological at all. But Percy's theology is "absorbed with the apparently tangential and tacit; with the seemingly oblique and obtuse. For underneath this lurks a conviction; namely that what is natural, given, and ordinary is also imbued with meaning and value that is a form of theological currency."[36] Nothing is more ordinary than disappointment and grief, and a burned wedding dress certainly counts as oblique and obtuse.

The white dress is also a formal symbol, and—like all symbols—it is associated with a range of feelings and thoughts. Holmes writes that symbols "represent a 'fan' of denotations and connotations and they evoke emotions that are sometimes quite in conflict; which is to say, they are ambiguous and incongruous. This is their attraction."[37] During the wedding, the bride's dress is beautiful and mysterious; after the divorce, the dress reflects the grandmother's anger and grief.

Holmes notes that symbols "always engage us first as feeling."[38] Similarly, Cirlot cites a Hindu philosopher who writes that symbolism is "the art of thinking in

35. Ibid., 155.
36. Percy, *Shaping the Church*, 2–3.
37. Holmes, "Liturgy and Liminality," 390.
38. Ibid., 390.

images," which explains why the grandmother burned her daughter's wedding dress.[39] She had to feel what she was thinking.

Sketching the Human Experience of God: Percy's Vision for the Parish Church

Theologian David Brown understands that symbols are the broader context of God's sacramental presence, and for this reason Brown's theology complements Percy's.[40] Both theologians are empirical, Anglican, and fascinated by God's presence in the world beyond the church. Although their methods are similar, these two theologians usually cover different subjects. On the whole, Brown focuses on art and music, whereas Percy focuses on human experience and culture.[41] Although Brown and Percy respect doctrine and liturgy, they emphasize that God's presence is not limited to the religious sphere.

With regard to the vexing question of what the experience of God actually feels like and looks like, Brown makes three observations. First, God's presence is experienced emotionally, not just intellectually or spiritually: "Being embodied creatures we are just as likely to respond emotionally and indeed physically."[42] The validity of this point is implied in my three sketches, all of which depict the body and hence emotions as a site for God's activity.

Second, Brown observes that the whole of God's presence is never experienced: "As I wrote in *God and Grace of Body*, 'the fact that God in his totality cannot be experienced does not mean that the divine may not be experienced in part.'"[43] This observation is realistic. Human experience of the divine is always limited and often obscure. Furthermore, experience of God is not the same as knowledge of God. In my third sketch, for example, the grandmother who burned her daughter's wedding dress may have experienced catharsis and release with God even though she may not have come to a better grasp of divine compassion for divorcees.

Third, and most unusually, Brown argues that symbolic experiences of God do not necessarily lead to moral transformation: "[One theologian] seems to require that, if the word "experience" is to be used of God at all, then the experience must be wholly transformative. I disagree profoundly. God has made a wonderful world and so part of the point of such experience may sometimes be just to see the world

---

39. Cirlot, *A Dictionary of Symbols*, xxix.

40. Percy notes in *Engaging with Contemporary Culture* that Brown's approach to biblical interpretation "resonates" with his own (38).

41. See Brown's trilogy: *God and Enchantment of Place*; *God and Grace of Body*; and *God and Mystery in Words*.

42. Brown, "Experience, Symbol, and Revelation," 270.

43. Ibid., 272. In this same essay, Brown makes a similar point about art, noting that the criteria for art should not be set in advance by theology and that the meaning of art should not therefore be limited by "what might be labeled instrumentalism and dogmatism" (276).

as it really is."[44] In other words, Brown believes that the experience of God might not make a person better.

I also observe that the personal experience of God *in and of itself* does not necessarily lead to moral transformation, whether in the moment of experiencing God or after the experience. Of my three sketches, the parishioner who called me on Easter Monday is the only sketch that raises the question of ethics and human resistance to evil. In my other two sketches, ethics do not really enter the picture, although I believe both persons—especially the woman who died beside the stone church—experienced the divine.

I want to raise one possibility that Brown does not consider, however. If one symbolic experience becomes the prelude to another, it makes sense to imagine that *over time* moral transformation or resistance to evil will enter the picture as a person—or community—experiences more and more of the divine presence. The experience of divine mystery, for example, may be followed at a later point by the experience of divine goodness. One experience of God prepares a person for another, perhaps deeper, experience of God. Within this range of experiences, it is reasonable to expect that divine goodness will eventually make its mark upon a person's moral life. Therefore, the range of human experiences of the divine corresponds to the range and depth of divine attributes (mysterious, compassionate, creative, sacrificial, and so on). Nevertheless, Brown's point still stands: an isolated sacramental or symbolic experience of God does not encompass the whole of God's nature.

My three sketches show that the actual look and feel of different kinds of experiences of God deserve attention and discernment. These experiences of the divine are not uncommon, even if the stories about them are not told as coherently or as publicly as they could be. These kinds of experiences and stories are what give shape and color to Percy's vision for the church, especially parishes bound to place and people. Percy envisions the parish as a curator of these experiences in an age that is not secular:

> In short, the statistics for church attendance, if read crudely, relate one of the great lies of the modern age. For the statistics tell us little about the faith of the nation; believing and belonging should not be confused. Very few people choose not to relate at all to the church, or to mainstream religion. In any secular age, there is space and demand for religion, faith and spirituality. So, rather than cursing the alleged darkness of secularization, churches should perhaps ponder the virtues of striking the odd match, and begin to start pointing to the discreet, contestable and ambiguous signs of religious life—millions of them—that thrive beyond the tightly controlled margins of the church. These signs are not competition for organized religion, but are rather an indication that the hunger for spiritual illumination will never really disappear. And in

---

44. Brown, "Experience, Symbol, and Revelation," 272. The theologian in question is Ben Quash.

the midst of these disparate signs, the sacraments are among the brightest lights the church offers, yet how often they are hidden.[45]

In Percy's vision, the difference between religion and culture is less clear than once thought, but the world itself is perhaps more interesting: a world that is complex and yet enchanted, symbolic and sacramental.

Bibliography

Adams, Marilyn McCord. *Horrendous Evils and the Goodness of God*. Ithaca, NY: Cornell University Press, 1999.

Armentrout, Don, and Robert Slocum, eds. *An Episcopal Dictionary of the Church: A User-Friendly Reference for Episcopalians*. New York: Church Publishing, 2010.

Brown, David. *God and Enchantment of Place: Reclaiming Human Experience*. Oxford: Oxford University Press, 2004.

———. *God and Grace of Body: Sacrament in Ordinary*. Oxford: Oxford University Press, 2007.

———. *God and Mystery in Words: Experience Through Metaphor and Drama*. Oxford: Oxford University Press, 2008.

———. "Experience, Symbol, and Revelation: Continuing the Conversation." In *Theology, Aesthetics, & Culture*, edited by Robert MacSwain and Taylor Worley, 265–96. Oxford: Oxford University Press, 2012.

Cirlot, J. E. *A Dictionary of Symbols*. New York: Philosophical Library, 1971.

Episcopal Church. *The Book of Common Prayer*. New York: Church Hymnal Corp, 1979.

Holmes, Urban. "Liminality and Liturgy." *Worship* 7:7 (1973) 386–87.

———. *Ministry and Imagination*. New York: The Seabury Press, 1976.

Percy, Martyn. *Clergy: The Origins of Species*. London: Continuum International, 2006.

———. *The Ecclesial Canopy: Faith, Hope, Charity*. Burlington: Ashgate, 2012.

———. *Engaging with Contemporary Culture: Christianity, Theology and the Concrete Church*. Aldershot: Ashgate, 2005.

———. *Shaping the Church: The Promise of Implicit Theology*. London: Ashgate, 2010.

———. *Thirty Nine Articles: An Anglican Landscape of Faith*. Norwich, UK: Canterbury, 2010.

Tillich, Paul. *Systematic Theology: Three Volumes in One*. Chicago: The University of Chicago Press, 1967.

45. Percy, *Shaping the Church*, 62.

7

Time for an Anglican Ecclesiological Revolution?

Martyn Percy's Ecclesiological Realism

GERARD MANNION

I AM MOST GRATEFUL TO Ian Markham and Joshua Daniel for extending the kind invitation to be part of the splendid gathering at Virginia Theological Seminary from which this volume originated. Despite his considerable success in an ecclesiastical and academic career alike over the past few decades, Martyn Percy has remained grounded in humility, humor, and faith throughout. It is a pleasure and a privilege to know him, to be inspired by his writings and to call him a friend. But he has also been grounded in a thoroughgoing ecclesiological realism and, in this chapter, I wish to say a bit more about what that has entailed.

I. Getting Real in Ecclesiology

In recent years, a distinctive approach to ecclesiological questions has been emerging and growing in diverse church contexts around the globe. I think it is also the approach one can say helps characterize the many, many contributions of Martyn Percy to the study and applied outcomes of ecclesiology. I have termed this approach *ecclesiological realism* and have spent a good deal of time exploring differing forms of this approach. Lest anyone doubt its applicability to the work of Martyn Percy, then a headline from *The Guardian* will perhaps place that suggestion into sharp relief. On August 13th, 2016 the newspaper ran a story which featured several key statements from Martyn under the banner "Top Cleric Says Church of England Risks Becoming a 'Suburban Sect.'"[1] If that does not constitute ecclesiological realism, then it is hard to know what might!

---

1. Sherwood, "Top Cleric Says Church of England Risks Becoming a 'Suburban Sect.'" The story featured some of the more challenging conclusions from Percy, *The Future Shapes of Anglicanism.*

I think this term proves complementary to those other descriptors that other contributors to this volume have employed to characterize Martyn's approach to theology in general, and especially to the church. That is to say, complementary rather than trying to say this is the only category that can capture his ecclesiology accurately.

First, let me explain what I mean by ecclesiological realism in more-detailed, yet general, terms before turning to make the case for why I think this describes Martyn Percy's own approach to certain questions and challenges in ecclesiology in general, providing but a few examples along the way. I will then turn to illustrate how he is in good contemporary company by adopting such an approach followed by some concluding remarks.

The church[2] will always gain so much to its benefit from more existentially oriented and humble (both in existential and epistemological terms) accounts of what the church is and what the church exists for. Such ecclesiological approaches can therefore help influence and improve understanding and exercise of specific ecclesial structures and practices complementary to this.[3]

In emphasizing here the need to further develop and encourage what I call ecclesiological realism, I do not mean the type of realism encountered in, for example, Augustine of Hippo's pragmatic realism in relation to the Donatist crisis, nor the somewhat pessimistic Christian realism outlined in Reinhold Niebuhr's mid-twentieth century writings; nor should what I refer to as realism still be mistaken for *realpolitik*. Rather, the ecclesiological realism I have in mind will be in the service of constructive and liberative ways of doing ecclesiology that are aspirational and transformative rather than primarily reductive or pragmatic in character.

Therefore, this realism is an approach that deals with reality as it is, with people and communities as they are and in a world that contains all the joys as well as the sufferings that it does. It is a realism that does not become trapped in impossible ideals and notions of a perfect church or society, but it also does not resign itself to accepting that the way things are is simply how they must or even will be. Rather, the realism is aimed toward enhancing our communities and societies and the lives of all within them for such is what the gospel calls us to do. In fact, the New Testament itself is charged with a thoroughgoing realism across the gospels and epistles alike.

In what follows, I assume and build upon earlier work I have done on engaging in a comparative approach to ecclesiology, particularly affirming those understandings of the church shaped and informed by perspectives "from below" as opposed

2. When I employ the term church here and throughout this paper, I mean Christianity in general unless the context makes clear I am referring to a specific branch or community within the wider Christian family.

3. Here and in the following section of this chapter, I draw upon some of my writings elsewhere, particularly materials from a lecture delivered at the "Ecclesiology in the Trenches" conference at the University of Uppsala in November 2015 and further materials that will be published in the near future including, in particular; Mannion, *The Art of Magisterium*. See also Mannion, "Time, Space and Magisterium."

to idealistic, even totalizing ecclesiologies presumed to be uniform and normative whether pronounced from hierarchical structures of authority among church leadership or by no-less-hierarchical assumptions on the part of particular academic schools of thought and the perspectives and styles of certain scholars. I believe Martyn Percy is very much a kindred spirit in terms of such an approach.

II. Ecclesiology in Wider Interdisciplinary Contexts

What many of the most realistic and fruitful ecclesiological approaches share in common is a commitment to honesty and frankness, alongside an embrace of interdisciplinary approaches to understanding the church. The tools of the social sciences, such as historical consciousness, organizational analysis, philosophical (and particularly epistemological) frameworks, can all be—and have been—employed to fruitful ends. I also strongly believe, as does Martyn Percy, that the discernment offered by ethics in particular needs to play a major role in any exploration of the church.[4] In the other chapters of this volume, as well as in the Ashgate Series in Contemporary Ecclesiology that Percy launched and co-edits, we find further rich food for thought on differing approaches.

While some voices in theology in recent decades have appeared perturbed by and opposed to inter-disciplinary contributions,[5] this ignores a reality that has always been with the church—and this across different Christian denominations. Such opposition frequently goes hand in hand with a more world-renouncing ecclesiological perspective.

In the final decades of the twentieth century and beyond, there emerged more aggressively unapologetic forms of "apologetics" that came to the fore in theological circles across differing churches increasingly throughout the 1990s and into our own century.[6] In many such approaches the Christian narrative is perceived as the only narrative in town that matters—all other attempts at explaining reality, social or otherwise, fall short by comparison.

But a unidirectional understanding of positive influence between church and world is a fictional and ecclesiological realism informed by interdisciplinary perspectives can both help challenge this fiction and counter other negative effects that have followed from the type of ecclesiological idealism one can abundantly find elsewhere—and not simply in the works of particular theologians, but also even in the official teachings of differing churches themselves.

---

4. See Mannion, "The Point of Ecclesiology." See, also, Mannion, *The Art of Magisterium*.

5. Fearing that such interdisciplinarity results in theological reductivism, see the discussion in Mannion, "Postmodern Ecclesiologies."

6. For a discussion of these developments, see, again; Mannion, "Postmodern Ecclesiologies," particularly at 134–35, 136–42.

Nor should the relationship between ecclesiology and other disciplines, human cultures and perspectives ever be understood in a uni-directional fashion, as if official church teaching can inform and help change the world but the opposite is never the case. Indeed, speaking generally, we often build barriers and fences between academic disciplines in artificial forms. There is certainly no reductivism entailed by such an interdisciplinary approach, for the church has always, from the earliest times, drawn upon and learned from wider cultural and intellectual gifts in order to assist it in its process of discerning the truth that God has graciously self-communicated to the world that is his own creation.[7] If we take the latter word seriously, those gifts from philosophy[8] and the social sciences,[9] as well as a myriad of other sources, need to be perceived as potentially being gifts from God. As the Dominican Thomas O'Meara has stated, thereby illustrating the ubiquity of inter-disciplinary and wider socio-cultural and intellectual factors in ecclesiology in general, "The study of the influence of metaphysical, sociological or political frameworks in the history of the church is as large as the history of ecclesiology."[10]

Now we see through a glass darkly, but many lanterns along the journey help illuminate our way. Without Hellenistic philosophy, the articulation of the core Christological doctrines of the church would have proved very different indeed. Without an analogical application of a particular social "theory," so, also, would the doctrine of the Trinity. Theology—that is, discourse—by humans, about God and about God's own word, in response to divine "discourse," so to speak, proceeds in and through dialogue. Indeed, many forms of understanding and practicing church teaching, authority, and governance throughout history have borrowed variously from the social and political theories and practices in wider society. And this has been carried out in order to explicate and facilitate the practice of wider ecclesial mindsets, structures and practices alike, especially in relation to teaching authority and ecclesial governance alike. Obviously, sometimes this has been fruitful; sometimes those "borrowings" have not been from the most morally and socially good elements of wider society.

So, seeking to broaden our perspectives with the aid of a variety of methods and tools is a fruitful and well-established ecclesial undertaking. It is also necessary because wider social and cultural factors—including religious belief systems,

---

7. C.f. Vatican II's Dogmatic Constitutuion on the Church, *Lumen Gentium*, chapter I, §§1–8.

8. An incisive study here is the following source: O'Meara, "Philosophical Models in Ecclesiology." In still broader and interdisciplinary terms, c.f. the discussion in Bevans, *Models of Contextual Theology*, esp. 28–35.

9. Two exhaustive, albeit differing, approaches to the study of the church that seek to employ historical and social scientific perspectives in the service of ecclesiology throughout are found in Haight, *Christian Community in History*, and Ormerod, *Re-envisioning the Church*. One useful introductory survey of the wider contextual settings of the church is Cadorette, *Catholicism in Social and Historical Contexts*. As we shall see in later chapters, the more explicitly political sciences have also been fruitfully employed in the study of ecclesiology and with specific application to that of magisterium.

10. O'Meara, "Philosophical Models in Ecclesiology," 20.

along with their attendant moral and value systems, obviously have an impact on human individual lives and communities. These social and cultural factors themselves obviously undergo ongoing change (including due to religious and axiological factors)—with both differing contexts and the passage of time having an enormous impact upon such change.[11]

Therefore, while we can take as a given the importance of the theological backdrop to and implications of any understanding of the church—both in theory and practice—for the day-to-day life of Christian communities of these times and of the future, it is equally important to acknowledge that theology—and therefore also ecclesiology—never takes place in a vacuum.

Differing ways of conceiving what the church is entail very differing ways of practicing ecclesiology, and therefore qualitatively different social and ethical consequences both within the church and in the wider world, and different ways of understanding the church, are inseparably bound up with cultural contexts. This remains true—indeed, it is often demonstrated to be so, even when those who hold to such ways seek to assert that they transcend such contexts and have a universal reach and relevance across time and geographical space alike.

In addition to the need to be attentive to historical consciousness as well as to philosophical and particularly epistemological approaches, I particularly wish to elaborate upon how vitally important it is that due attentiveness be given to the social and political contexts of ecclesiology, including those approaches illuminated by ethnographic approaches. Indeed, these differing perspectives can often be combined and are complementary. As Michael Lawler has stated, "The social sciences and theology are not isolated from, but inseparably bound to, one another, in as much as they derive from the same socio-historical matrix."[12] I do so not least of all because we find such approaches combined in an exemplary fashion in the works of Martyn Percy.

So many scholars have embraced and openly utilized the social sciences in various fruitful and constructive ways.[13] Critical social analysis is necessitated by

---

11. Obviously, the understanding of shared social being and practices, as well as of the norms and mores valued collectively, will undergo periods of transformation, development and change just as much. Systems of beliefs and values are rarely neatly demarcated in the story of human communities. Indeed, the sense of there even being a systematic form and character often only comes much further down their developmental line, and is usually artificially imposed for the sake of greater understanding and engagement with the most important "ingredients" that are brought together to build such a system.

12. Lawler, *What is and What Ought to Be*, 61.

13. In particular, there have been various applications made of social constructionism in the church, and theologians such as Gregory Baum have made great use of this and other sociological theories in seeking to make sense of the church. See, for example, his *Essays in Critical Theology*—Baum blends critical social theory and liberation theology in an especially thoughtful and practically fruitful manner. A further example of direct relevance to our discussion topics here is that by Lawler himself, *What is and What Ought to Be*, where he discusses the "Sociology of Knowledge and Theology" in particular at 44–67. There have also been many attempts to apply such social scientific theories to scholarship concerning the Bible and the history of the early church, just as there have been various

the theological (and particularly eschatological) need to make sense of the sin and death from which the good news saves. The social structures of sin must be analyzed: "Thus theology itself calls for critical social analysis. Sociology here enters into the very constitution of theology."[14]

In an approach to ecclesiology that is attentive to realism, we embark upon an attempt to consider certain implications of the social construction of ecclesial reality and, in turn, the ecclesially-informed and shaped social construction of significant aspects of our wider shared reality.[15] By the first of these categories, I mean ways and means of interacting, along with the accompanying discourse, conceptual frameworks and knowledge that impact how we perceive, and therefore how we actually relate to and live out ecclesial life. By the second category, I refer to the ways in which our ecclesial modes of being and our beliefs impact our wider being in the world and our belonging (or otherwise) to additional social groups and communities. This approach can, of course, be applied to wider ecclesiological viewpoints and modes of ecclesial being. Hence the realism generated by such reflective engagement is twofold.

III. Martyn Percy's Ecclesiological Realism

As alluded to above, the 1980s and much of the 1990s could be said to be a time (although not an age) of ecclesiological "idealism," with sweeping ecclesiologies, such as those of communion, regularly rolled out as privileged official and normative understanding of the church in different parts of the world. Even some emergent forms of public theology and theologies that placed their remit firmly "in the public square" were prone to such ecclesiological idealism, overtly emphasizing what the church could teach wider society and the world in general, as opposed to a vice-versa or two-way relationship. The Vatican offered hardened forms of such ecclesiologies from above and applied these at most levels of ecclesiastical administration. Even the World Council of Churches fell prone to such trends in many of the theological perspectives it chose to privilege in a number of its own official documents and statements. Anglicanism's similar struggles and divisions throughout this era are well-known and considered in more detail elsewhere in this work and in so many of Martyn Percy's own writings.

Yet others challenged such idealism and spoke of a disparity between the reality of Christian communities and these ecclesiologies handed down "from above," so

applications of these theories to later periods of church history, particularly the modern and contemporary periods. The late Presbyterian scholar and noted ecumenist, Lewis S. Mudge, offers a further example of a fruitful and inter-disciplinary approach to ecclesiological questions. See, for example, his *The Sense of a People* and *Rethinking the Beloved Community*. See, again, Roger Haight, *Christian Community in History*, and Neil Ormerod, *Re-envisioning the Church*.

14. Baum, "Sociology and Salvation," 742; realism informed by a liberationist perspective.

15. The classic work is by Peter L. Berger and Thomas Luckmann, *The Social Construction of Reality*.

to speak, including liberationist and contextual perspectives as well as those who blended social scientific research with explorations of the church in theological terms too). Such ecclesiologies, then, spoke of the need to begin "from below," from reality. So ecclesiological realism, which has increasingly come to shape and has informed many approaches to ecclesiology in the new century, has been part of this shift toward ecclesiology being done "from below" and being attentive to differing contexts and needs and aspirations in churches, as opposed to a one-size-fits-all ecclesiology predominating.

Martyn Percy was, of course, cutting his ecclesiological teeth in this era. And he literally did the heavy lifting necessary to develop an ecclesiological realism through his doctoral research into the Toronto blessing[16] and the empirical and social scientific approaches he developed there have continued to inform all he says and does about the church and in the church. He has expressed his dissatisfaction with blueprint and normative ecclesiologies, and particularly with the privileging of an ecclesiology of communion and the often-attendant notion of communion at all costs in multiple venues over the years.[17] Percy's ecclesiological realism is revealed in how he is attentive to grassroots realities and societal shifts and trends, as well as to sources and norms for understanding the church coming from surprising and non-traditional places. He states the following: "Because it is never easy to say, precisely, where the church begins and ends—let alone Christian beliefs and practices—a proper attention to informal, apparently innocuous and innocent forces that shape ecclesial life is always bound to have significant repercussions for the field and disciplines of theology." Furthermore, he continues, "the dynamics of ecclesial life are often shaped and delimited by operant, grounded, unarticulated and habitual processes, which whilst laced with theological significance, do not of themselves usually count as explicit religious discourse, or are valued as "official" practice.[18] He therefore charges professional theologians and church leaders with overlooking such sources in favor of "sanctioned sources and authorized traditions," which equally means they overlook theologies and practices and beliefs growing out of the church as grassroots levels and non-official sources.[19] In what can be seen to be perhaps an older and more authentically traditional approach, Percy wants to re-encourage ecclesiology to appreciate how both the sacred and the secular give rise to Christian theology, belief, and practices. 'Twas ever thus. Taking us back to our earlier reflections on social constructivism, Percy therefore suggests that a very different form of "natural theology" arises at every level of the church in surprising places. Therefore, "Because the church is a body, grounded in a context and

16. Percy, *The Toronto Blessing*.

17. E.g. Percy, "Saving the Roman Catholic Church?"; Martyn Percy, "A Blessed Rage for Order: Exploring the Rise of 'Reform' in the Church of England." Both so published as book chapters.

18. Percy, *Shaping the Church*, 159.

19. Ibid., 159.

social construction of reality, it always reflects and sacralizes values that have yet to be fully processed and comprehended."[20]

Not every ecclesial-cultural fusion will prove to be good for the church[21]—and we know history teaches us that in so many ways, not least of all in multiple examples that can be furnished from just the Church of England and wider Anglican family of churches themselves. For Percy, this is one of the reasons why ecclesiology has something distinctive to offer the church—in making sense of how the church and world, church culture, interact[22] And Percy has employed his own development of ecclesiological realism toward highly critical ends with regard to his assessments of particular trends, new forms of being church and new forms of ecclesial oversight in a multitude of writing to date. The critical-ecclesiological consciousness can therefore, and indeed must, work both ways.

This leads him to shape his ecclesiological researches via a hermeneutics both of retrieval and suspicion: two further essential hallmarks, I suggest, of ecclesiological realism. So, for example, in 2000, he concluded a particularly strident assessment of the state at the time of the Charismatic Renewal movement in his own church, in the following utterly realistic and uncompromising fashion:

> For a Western world that is increasingly privatised and individualistic, a post-modem, enthusiastically-driven religion may be the one that proves to be the most popular at the dawn of a new millennium: yet that is no guarantee of ultimate longevity. Charismatic religion is often a fashion full of fads, a populist, culturally-relative and relevant phenomena. We should learn to read the signs: the charismatic crazes of today are often only destined to become tomorrow's footnote in the history of revivalism. In my view, the bright and beautiful colours that once made up Charismatic Renewal are fading fast. A healthy and vibrant body of belief with a once lustrous skin is now showing signs of age: wrinkles, worry-lines, and some middle-age sagging have set-in. But perhaps growing up isn't all bad? Ecclesial maturation and ultimately denominational inculcation may yet be the greatest achievement of British Charismatic Renewal.[23]

And, to take a more recent example, Percy cautions against abandoning tried and tested (and indeed, cherished) forms of ecclesial life and structure and a rush to allow a "post-institutional structure" to dictate present and future policies—for example as advocated by the Fresh Expressions movement.[24]

20. Percy, *Shaping the Church*, 160.

21. Ibid., 160.

22. Ibid., 160. See also Percy, *Engaging with Contemporary Culture*.

23. Among the many others writings discussed by other contributors to this symposium and the publications cited here, see, for example, the particularly focused critique in Percy, "All Things Bright and Beautiful," 41.

24. Percy, *Anglicanism*, 133.

But it is not simply new movements and trends that Percy aims his hermeneutic of suspicion toward. Over the course of his career, Percy's ecclesiological realism has sought to address more and more levels of the church and, in a recent increasing sense, to be applied to the structures and governance, the very polity of the Church of England and wider Anglican communion itself. Percy has never been afraid to speak truth to power long before the somewhat sensationalist headline-makers of the *Guardian* reminded us of this fact. So, for example, his study from 1998, *Power and the Church: Ecclesiology in an Age of Transition*,[25] and many other works on questions of authority and governance—publications informed not least of all by his own considerable experience in church-linked positions of leadership—so further mined at the "coalface," so to speak. Writing in 2004, his realism here came very much to the fore:

> In the 21st century, many (perhaps most?) types of authority are now subjected to renewed interrogation. The survival of authority will to some extent depend on an imaginative and reflexive response to such questions, and a deep willingness to engage in patient dialogue. To be sure, authority will be transformed by this interactive process. But there is nothing to be feared here. What authorities cannot afford to do is remain aloof from dialogue, and merely invest in reassertion and institutional deafness. Good arguments must be reciprocal, and it is only in such contexts that any authority discovers itself to be "true," rather than merely privileged or dominant. So, let the conversations begin.[26]

More recently, he has lamented the shift in missionary priorities in his own church and stated that "Quality may need to be valued more than quantity. Pace, solidarity and connectedness more than haste, energy and apparent achievement. . . . Presence and deep relational engagement may have a greater missiological impact than overt evangelistic schema and initiatives."[27] Elsewhere, he states that, "We need to be free of our distraction dependency, and of being satisfied with anything that sates the quantification of expectation, and our neuralgic yearning for conformity and control. We need more emphasis on wisdom and depth, and less dependency on orientating our life (and happiness?) by pursuing bigger and better numbers."[28]

And yet, despite the negative connotations that can sometimes be attached to the term "realism," Percy is no doom monger—again, despite that headline of that *Guardian* story. In fact, he is quite the reverse. Martyn's vision for the future of the church is one that is hope-filled and constructive but only because of his thoroughgoing realism. So, for example, secularism need not prove fatal to the church at all.[29] The

---

25. Percy, *Power and the Church.*

26. Percy, "Editorial."

27. Percy, *Anglicanism.* See also similar sentiments in Percy, "Growth and Management," esp. 261–62.

28. Percy, "Growth and Managemen,t" 269.

29. See Percy, *Anglicanism*, and Percy, *Salt of the Earth.*

obsessions with declining numbers and simultaneously with managerialism can be overcome.[30] And while his church, at present, is too "over-managed" as well as being too "theologically under-led,"[31] so, also, does he offer many constructive suggestions in relation to the exercise of episcopacy for today's Anglican Church.[32] Once again with stark realism and pulling no punches, he concludes the following:

> As a church, we are now management-led, albeit with an added emphasis on mission. We tend not to choose leaders with rough edges, or who might not fit the mould. The managerially led process delivers what the managers say the church wants: growth, organization and management. So, predictability is preferred to prophecy. More alarmingly, consistency and compliance are mistaken for catholicity. As a church we have now confused management and leadership to such an extent that our system of preferment is geared up for the evisceration of truly creative theological leadership. But there is a further problem here. The managers driving such processes believe and act as though they are leading the church.[33]

Simultaneously critical and constructive (thanks to his realism), Percy explains why the two things—management and leadership—are far from being the same (here, as in many writings, Percy draws upon organizational and business theory to make his case convincingly). He continues: "Most key policy areas in the church today are governed not by theological leadership and vision, but by management."[34] This confusion and supplanting of one by the other has negatively impacted the church in multiple ways, including in terms of ministerial training, theological education, and pastoral and missional priorities.[35]

Percy also advocates for an inclusive church but not an amorphous one. Yet intra-ecclesial dialogue is vitally important to maintain, above all else. In a telling phrase, a point he has repeated in a few scenarios, Percy reminds us that "the early church fathers, when faced with a choice of living with heresy or schism, always chose the former."[36] It is thus that Percy constantly argues for the virtue of patience to be fostered and valued in Anglican Church polity.[37] Further ecclesial virtues he

---

30. See, for example, Evans and Percy, *Managing the Church?* and Percy, "Growth and Management."

31. Percy, "Growth and Management," 262, 267.

32. See for example, Percy, "Emergent Archiepiscopal Leadership within the Anglican Communion," 46–70.

33. Percy, "Growth and Management," 263.

34. Ibid., 264.

35. Ibid., 267.

36. Percy, *Anglicanism*, 158. In answer to the occasional questioning of the accuracy of this remark, we can qualify it by stating it does apply to a significant number of those who remained the most influential early church fathers.

37. Percy, *Shaping the Church*, 167, "Engagement, Diversity and Distinctiveness"; and Slocum, *A Point of Balance,* 13–27.

commends include generosity,[38] "holding" (referring specifically to holding together church unity in the face of "increasingly held competing convictions"[39]), and even "the gift of our 'undecidability.'"[40]

And his commitment to dialogue has been longstanding—not simply within the Church of England and wider Anglican Communion in the ongoing and deepening divisions over sexual ethics and global structures of governance in recent decades. He has also been deeply committed to dialogue with other churches, as I know personally from many years of collaboration thanks to his support for and ongoing involvement with the Ecclesiological Investigations International Research Network, and so, also, has Percy been a firm advocate and facilitator of inter-faith dialogue and dialogue between the church and wider society.

Percy's works have also applied his realism to some surprising and seemingly more settled ecclesiological concepts, too. These includes collegiality and catholicity—two areas requiring attention which are generated not only by his grappling with the dilemmas and divisions facing his own church and wider communion in recent times, but also his ongoing commitment to ecumenical engagement.[41]

Furthermore this, alongside his commitment to dialogue and learning from differing contexts and realities, has taken him all over the world to visit, spend time with, and often engage in teaching assignments with Anglican communities on almost every continent. This realism, then, is not only preached, it is practiced. Such visits and encounters have further informed and deepened his ecclesiological realism.

In a further demonstration of his ecclesiological realism, Percy suggests that the Church of England's approach to moral (and therefore social) issues should be attentive to social realities and where people find themselves at in life today (a key parallel with Pope Francis, as we shall see), as opposed to lofty principles and stern obligations issued from on high that few can hope to live up to. Sometimes, the church cannot reach certitude on particular issues and that's just fine.[42] It is thus that his many contributions on the future of Anglicanism are perhaps among the most realistic of all his writings.[43]

Percy is also realistic when it comes to being attentive to the wider societal and ecclesiological sources of what has come be termed *social* or *structural* sin. In this he echoes much of what the late Gregory Baum, another great ecclesiological realist steeped in interdisciplinary researches in Christian communities at the grassroots and official level alike, wrote some time ago,

38. E.g., Percy, "Generous Liberalism."

39. Percy, "Engagement, Diversity and Distinctiveness," 26. See also Percy, "Holding Together in the Eye of the Storm."

40. Ibid.

41. For example, his writings on the marks of the church and his recent book, *39 New Articles*.

42. Percy, *Anglicanism*, 19, 114.

43. *39 New Articles* and multiple other books, stretching back to the 1990s.

Since theologians of this orientation follow an eschatological perspective, hear God's word first as divine judgment on the world, and are deeply impressed by the message of Jesus, "Repent, for the reign of God is at hand," they are compelled to analyze the structures of sin in which their society finds itself. They cannot speak of Jesus unless they specify the sin and the death from which Jesus saves us. Thus theology itself calls for critical social analysis. Sociology here enters into the very constitution of theology.[44]

Baum then goes on to articulate the implications of all this and obligations *for* theology in recent times,

To announce the gospel authentically, one must articulate God's judgment on the given society. While personal sins also build the prison in which society is caught, they cannot be properly understood unless their relation to structural sins is clarified. The crimes of the poor in the ghetto cannot be understood apart from the structures of the consistent and sometimes violent marginalization inflicted on them. The notion of structural or social sin, until recently controversial in Catholic theology, . . . [was] taken up and developed in John Paul II's *Sollicitudo rei socialis*. The orientation towards death of our civilization—world hunger, nuclear self-destruction, and ecological disaster—is here not blamed on individual sins; it is related to structural causes, to the powerful impact of economic and political institutions that are named— an impact that could be resisted but in fact is not. Personal sin enters this equation principally as nonresistance to the powerful. The theological teaching on sin and redemption contained in this encyclical has integrated the outline of a global social analysis from a particular sociological perspective, the option for the poor.[45]

And Baum rightly pointed out that we find such approaches in even older approaches to ecclesiology and ecclesial practice in the church—particularly in the theologies of liberation and related political theologies. In this we find further parallels with the perspectives of Martyn Percy.

Lest we forget, in previous incarnations Martyn Percy was the founding Director of the Lincoln Theological Institute for the Study of Religion and Society. Keeping that in mind alongside Baum's words, as well as his published admiration for Paulo Freire, especially the method developed his famous *Pedagogy of the Oppressed*,[46] I now turn to illustrate how, in his theological realism, Martyn Percy is in very good company, and I reflect first upon one prominent approach to ecclesiology that has also consistently taken onboard such a multi-disciplinary approach to understanding and shaping the life of ecclesial communities and, in doing so, has embraced a thoroughgoing ecclesiological realism.

44. Baum, "Sociology and Salvation," 742.

45. Ibid., 743.

46. See Percy, *Engaging with Contemporary Culture*.

IV. The Realism of Liberation Ecclesiology

Elsewhere, I have suggested that, in looking for additional particular methodological approaches that might help us to further develop ecclesiological realism for our times, we do not have to delve especially far back into the past at all.[47] A thoroughgoing realism permeates the very foundations of this approach, which has deep-rooted origins in Latin America, whose Catholic bishops, in 1968, addressed "First world" abuses and tackled head-on the issue of institutionalized violence, while in 1979 they announced that famous call "for conversion on the part of the whole church to a preferential option for the poor, an option aimed at their integral liberation."[48]

But liberation theology was to offer not just a critique of society, however, but also of the church and of the power structures and oppression within it. Indeed that 1979 statement from Puebla is one charged with an ecclesiological vision and one assertive of ecclesiological priorities.

Let us briefly consider some of the core themes in liberation ecclesiology in order to help appreciate its influence upon a more recent vision for the church. In doing so, we find surprising parallels at every turn. T. Howland Sanks and Brian Smith summarize the key components of such an approach to ecclesiology as follows:

> The main characteristics of the ecclesiology of liberation theology are (1) the affirmation of the universal salvific will, (2) the consequent "uncentering" of the Church in the work of salvation-liberation, (3) understanding the Church as the reflectively conscious part of humanity, whose function is to be a sign to the rest of humanity, (4) the specification of this function always in terms of the concrete historical realities in which the Church finds itself, and hence (5) the necessity for an analysis of the society's socio-political-economic situation.[49]

It is an approach to understanding and empowering the church that does not focus on hierarchical categories or older symbols that accentuate the power and authority of the institutional church and its key leaders. Again, in all this we see clear parallels with the works of Percy.

Sanks and Smith sum up how realism is such a very significant methodological feature of liberation ecclesiology in the following terms:

47. See Mannion, "Francis' Ecclesiological Revolution." In the consideration here of the ecclesiological realism of liberation theology and of Pope Francis alike, I draw upon material discussed in that chapter.

48. CELAM III (1979). It is generally agreed that the singlemost significant event for the emergence of liberation theology was that earlier 1968 assembly of the Latin American Roman Catholic Bishops' Conference—*Conferencia Episcopal Latinoamericana* (CELAM)—at Medellín, Columbia, in 1968.

49. Sanks and Smith, "Liberation Ecclesiology," 15.

Influenced by Paulo Freiré, [leading proponents of liberation theology such as Juan Luis] Segundo and [Gustavo] Gutiérrez begin with the social situation in which the Church finds itself existentially. Instead of beginning with magisterial statements or documents from the tradition and coming to some essentialist understanding of the Church's nature, they begin with an analysis of the needs of the society, the political, economic, and cultural setting, and from this move to the structures and procedures the Church should follow in such a context. The Church is a function of the society, not some entity from another culture, time, or place."[50]

All in all, notwithstanding very differing formative ecclesial and societal contexts, there are many striking parallels here between the ecclesiological realism of liberation theology and that of Martyn Percy—not least of all owing to similar influences such as Freiré and the social sciences, and concerns for grassroots to ecclesial contexts and concrete issues facing Christians today. But the similarities between Martyn and others in good company do not end there. For, I suggest a similar ecclesiological realism can be seen to permeate the ecclesiological vision and priorities of approach of a much more recent major figure in the story of global Christianity. It is to that more recent ecclesiological vision and figure I now turn.

V. The Ecclesiological Realism of Pope Francis

Roman Catholicism offers another pertinent example that is unfolding before our very eyes, for those words just cited reflect what are now self-evident ecclesiological truths that seem to have been embraced clearly by a certain Jorge Bergoglio, and regardless at what stage of his own ministry such an embrace took place, it nonetheless took place. Now, as Pope Francis, they are also clearly ecclesiological truths and guiding principles that have left a deep imprint on his major teachings to date.

Indeed, a refreshing ecclesiological realism is a vital characteristic of the ecclesiological vision of Pope Francis. This pope clearly does not hold an idealist vision of a pure church free of blemishes. Far from it. He is astonishingly refreshing in acknowledging just how much of a mess the church is in—including, especially, its central offices and leadership. There is no pretense that somehow the church itself and the messy fallible humans who constitute its people can somehow be separated. He knows drastic structural and existential change is necessary. And he has set about implementing such (this is something he has brought with him from the lessons learned during his episcopal ministry in Argentina—an episcopal ministry that overlaps in many respects with the decades and events prominent when Martyn Percy was cutting his ecclesiological teeth).

50. Sanks and Smith, "Liberation Ecclesiology," 38.

If we consider the roots of Pope Francis's ecclesiological realism, we are drawn back to the surprising enduring value of that theological approach that some critics had long dismissed as passé. For it is in the theology of liberation that we find the roots of Francis's ecclesiological realism. And in liberation ecclesiology, we find an approach by which default encourages not only interdisciplinarity in our attempts to understand the church, but also the most thoroughgoing, down-to-earth approach of an ecclesiology from below. All of us working in ecclesiology may actually find here further refreshing resources long into the future.

So, within just months of his election as Bishop of Rome, Francis released the Apostolic Exhortation, *Evangelii Gaudium*[51]—effectively his manifesto for the church in our times. In it, Francis clearly acknowledges that the church is a social entity and that its institutional forms and practices can be deficient (points made also in many of his frequent homilies, audiences, interviews and other addresses). Francis states that "There are ecclesial structures which can hamper efforts at evangelization, yet even good structures are only helpful when there is a life constantly driving, sustaining and assessing them."[52]

Church doctrines, structures, organization, ministries, and offices exist to serve the gospel and the world, not the other way around. Francis's realism is further illustrated when he frankly acknowledges that, if people are leaving the church, that suggests a fault on the part of the church, and therefore on the part of its shepherds and leaders.[53]

In *Evangelii Gaudium*, Francis warns against a "spiritual worldliness" and speaks of how "to avoid it by making the Church constantly go out from herself, keeping her mission focused on Jesus Christ, and her commitment to the poor."[54] Likewise, he warns against "a nostalgia for structures and customs which are no longer life-giving in today's world."[55] Everything must be understood not in the framework of rigid doctrine and canon law, but rather in terms of a "missionary key."[56] Here, once more, we can draw parallels with Martyn Percy's perspectives on the Church of England and Anglicanism in general.

Francis's ecclesiological realism is yet further developed in how he acknowledges the reality of the messiness of the church (alongside its gifts and charisms as well).

---

51. Pope Francis, "Apostolic Exhortation, *Evangelii Gaudium*."

52. Ibid., §26.

53. For example: "We must recognize that if part of our baptized people lack a sense of belonging to the Church, this is also due to certain structures and the occasionally unwelcoming atmosphere of some of our parishes and communities, or to a bureaucratic way of dealing with problems, be they simple or complex, in the lives of our people. In many places an administrative approach prevails over a pastoral approach, as does a concentration on administering the sacraments apart from other forms of evangelization" (ibid., §63).

54. Ibid., §97.

55. Ibid., §108.

56. Ibid., §§33–34.

Francis has apologized for an enormous range of failings on the church's part, from its handling of the abuse crisis to its exploitation of indigenous peoples;[57] from its involvement in the persecution of Waldensians, to that of Pentecostals in 1930s Italy, and he has further apologized to members of other churches and faiths for the Roman Catholic Church's failings toward them also. He has further outlined how his church must share its part of the blame for why ecumenism has not made greater progress. Ecclesiological realism, then, as well as frankness and honesty at every turn, a realism best epitomized in one of the most evocative passages from *Evangelii Gaudium* of all,

> I prefer a Church which is bruised, hurting and dirty because it has been out on the streets, rather than a Church which is unhealthy from being confined and from clinging to its own security. I do not want a Church concerned with being at the centre and which then ends by being caught up in a web of obsessions and procedures. If something should rightly disturb us and trouble our consciences, it is the fact that so many of our brothers and sisters are living without the strength, light and consolation born of friendship with Jesus Christ, without a community of faith to support them, without meaning and a goal in life. More than by fear of going astray, my hope is that we will be moved by the fear of remaining shut up within structures which give us a false sense of security, within rules which make us harsh judges, within habits which make us feel safe, while at our door people are starving and Jesus does not tire of saying to us: "Give them something to eat" (Mark 6:37).[58]

VI. Concluding Remarks: Realism Driving Ecclesiological Revolution

All three of our examples of ecclesiological realism have a further characteristic in common: they are clearly advocating no less than an ecclesiological revolution in multiple ways.

My good friend and colleague, Peter Phan, has previously written about a "Copernican revolution in ecclesiology"—a revolution brought about by the churches of the global south, and one which he warned must be embraced by those of the global "north" if they are not to drastically decline further.[59] This is a revolution that shifts from a core focus on the institutional church—an ecclesiocentric vision—to one that focuses on the kingdom, with the church in the service of building the reign of God on earth. Perhaps the word revolution raises fear and uncertainty among some in the

57. See, for example, http://www.independent.co.uk/news/world/americas/pope-francis-apolo gises-for-catholic-crimes-against-indigenous-peoples-during-the-colonisation-of-the-ameri cas-10380319.html, http://www.cruxnow.com/church/2015/07/09/pope-francis-apologizes-for-explo itation-of-native-peoples-calls-for-economic-justice/.

58. Ibid., §49.

59. Phan, "A New Way of Being Church." See also Phan, *Christianity With an Asian Face.*

church, and yet it need not do so. In *Evangelii Gaudium,* Pope Francis spoke of the incarnation as a "revolution of tenderness." A new way of being church has already been set in motion. And Martyn Percy, cumulatively in his many ecclesiological writings and especially in his 2016 work, *The Future Shape of Anglicanism,* is also offering no less than a manifesto for ecclesiological revolution in Anglicanism and the Church of England especially. And yet, in Martyn Percy's writings we see a firm refusal to try and bury or ignore the genuine and painful differences and divisions in his own church and wider communion. Rather, the realism is deep rooted, even when painful. Yet it is always there to serve constructive and hope-filled ends.

And I further suggest that the work of Martyn Percy also helps to demonstrate in so very many ways what ecclesiological realism has to offer the Christian Church in general, ecumenical discourse across churches, and, of course, his own Anglican tradition. In fact, taken collectively, we might say that Martyn's work constitutes a call to an ecclesiological revolution within Anglicanism that is utterly realistic at the same time as being bold, pragmatic, and yet grounded in some of the surest fruits of his own theoretical and empirical researches just as it is grounded in distinctive Anglican and wider ecumenical resources old and new. *The Future Shape of Anglicanism,* will hopefully come to be seen to epitomize all this, and his ecclesiological realism most of all.

Yes, the test for the fruits of ecclesiological realism will quite rightly involve the assessment of what substantial and long-term changes are forthcoming in any particular ecclesial culture and structures once ecclesiological realism has been embraced. And I hope and believe we can rediscover the courage to own doubts openly in the church today and long into the future. Such courage will facilitate all the more those constructive visions that seek to prioritize the pastorally and socially oriented visions for being church. Ecclesiological realism is an essential prerequisite for this to happen. It's time for ecclesiology to get real. And the works of Martyn Percy have long been pointing the way forward to how this can be achieved.

Bibliography

Baum, Gregory. *Essays in Critical Theology.* Kansas, MO: Sheed and Ward, 1994.
———. "Sociology and Salvation." *Theological Studies* (1989) 719–43.
Berger, Peter L., and Thomas Luckmann. *The Social Construction of Reality: A Treatise in the Sociology of Knowledge.* Garden City, NY: Anchor, 1966.
Bevans, Stephen B. *Models of Contextual Theology.* Maryknoll, NY: Orbis Books, 1992.
Cadorette, Curt. *Catholicism in Social and Historical Contexts: an Introduction.* Maryknoll, NY: Orbis Books, 2009.
Evans, G. R., and Martyn Percy, eds. *Managing the Church? Order and Organization in a Secular Age.* New York: Sheffield Academic Press, 2000.
Haight, Roger. *Christian Community in History.* 3 vols. New York and London: Continuum, 2004–2008
Lawler, Michael G. *What is and What Ought to Be: the Dialectic of Experience, Theology and Church.* New York and London: Continuum, 2005.

Mannion, Gerard. *The Art of Magisterium: A Teaching Church That Learns*. Collegeville, MN: Liturgical Press, 2015.

———. "Francis' Ecclesiological Revolution: A New Way of Being Church, a New Way of Being Pope." In *Pope Francis and the Future of Catholicism: Evangelii Gaudium and the Papal Agenda*, edited by Gerard Mannion, 93–124. Cambridge: Cambridge University Press, 2017.

———. "The Point of Ecclesiology." In *Ecclesiology in the Trenches: Theory and Method under Construction*, edited by Sune Fahlgren and Jonas Ideström, ix–xiv. Eugene, OR: Pickwick Press, 2015.

———. "Postmodern Ecclesiologies." In *The Routledge Companion to the Christian Church*, edited by Gerard Mannion and Lewis S. Mudge, 127–52. London and New York: Routledge, 2007.

———. "Time, Space and Magisterium." *Australian eJournal of Theology* 21:3 (2014) 197–211.

Mudge, Lewis S. *Rethinking the Beloved Community; Ecclesiology, Hermeneutics, Social Theory*. Geneva, Switzerland: University Press of America, 2001.

———. *The Sense of a People: Toward a Church for the Human Future*. Philadelphia: Trinity Press International, 1992.

O'Meara, Thomas F. "Philosophical Models in Ecclesiology." *Theological Studies* 39:1 (1978) 3–21.

Ormerod, Neil. *Re-envisioning the Church: An Experiment in Systematic-Historical Ecclesiology*. New York: Fortress, 2014.

Percy, Martyn. *39 New Articles: an Anglican Landscape of Faith*. Norwich: Canterbury, 2013.

———. "All Things Bright and Beautiful: A Theological Response," *Journal of Empirical Theology* 13:1 (2000) 35–41.

———. *Anglicanism: Confidence, Commitment, and Communion*. Farnham: Ashgate, 2013.

———. "A Blessed Rage for Order: Exploring the Rise of 'Reform" in the Church of England." *Journal of Anglican Studies* 3:1 (2005) 33–52.

———. "Editorial." *Modern Believing* 45:4 (2004) 2–4.

———. "Emergent Archiepiscopal Leadership within the Anglican Communion." *Journal of Anglican Studies* 14:1 (2015) 46–70.

———. "Engagement, Diversity and Distinctiveness: Anglicanism in Contemporary Culture." In *A Point of Balance: the Weight and Measure of Anglicanism*, edited by Martyn Percy and Robert Boak Slocum, 13–27. New York: Canterbury, 2012.

———. *Engaging with Contemporary Culture: Christianity, Theology and the Concrete Church*. Aldershot: Ashgate, 2005.

———. *The Future Shapes of Anglicanism: Currents, Contours, Charts*. London: Routledge, 2016.

———. "Generous Liberalism: A Search For Our Spiritual Soul." *Modern Believing* 56:3 (2015) 259–72.

———. "Growth and Management in the Church of England: Some Comments." *Modern Believing* 55:3 (2014) 257–70.

———. "Holding Together in the Eye of the Storm: Responding to Barney Hawkins and Ian Markham." *Modern Believing* 49:4 (2008) 62–70.

———. *Power and the Church: Ecclesiology in an Age of Transition*. London: Cassell, 1998.

———. *Salt of the Earth: Religious Resilience in a Secular Age*. New York: Sheffield Academic, 2001.

————. "Saving the Roman Catholic Church?" *Conversations in Religion and Theology* vol. 1:1 (2003) 79–95.

————. *Shaping the Church: The Promise of Implicit Theology*. London: Ashgate, 2010.

————. *The Toronto Blessing*. London: Latimer Trust, 1996.

Phan, Peter C. *Christianity With an Asian Face: American Theology in the Making*. Maryknoll, NY: Orbis Books, 2003.

————. "A New Way of Being Church: Perspectives from Asia." *Governance, Accountability and the Future of the Church*, edited by Francis Oakley and Bruce Russet, 178–90. New York: Continuum, 2003.

Pope Francis. "Apostolic Exhortation, *Evangelii Gaudium*." http://w2.vatican.va/content /francesco/en/apost_exhortations/documents/papa-francesco_esortazione-ap_2013 1124_evangelii-gaudium.html.

Sanks, T. Howland, and Brian H. Smith. "Liberation Ecclesiology: Praxis, Theory, Praxis." *Theological Studies* 38:1 (March 1977) 3–38.

Sherwood, Harriet. "Top Cleric Says Church of England Risks Becoming a 'Suburban Sect.'" *The Guardian*. https://www.theguardian.com/world/2016/aug/13/justin-welby-church-of-england-suburban-sect.

8

The Prudent Priest

Exercising "Good Sense" for
the Good of the Church

Lyndon Shakespeare

I BEGIN WITH SOME ANECDOTAL reflections from the world of transition ministry. In the Episcopal Church (TEC), when a parish is receiving names for a rector or the like, it is common for the Transition Ministers from the Diocese of the parish and the candidate to have what is called, a "red flag" chat. As the title suggest, the chat pertains to anything about the candidate that could be an issue or concern for the parish under consideration. From speaking with a number of Transition Ministers, I learned that the questions range from issues of canonical standing and clerical temperament, to whether or not the priest is a "team player" when it comes to colleagues, including the Bishop.

This process is designed to weed out candidates who might be "trouble" or simply unqualified for the post. It is not foolproof, of course. As one Transition Minister noted, there exists such a range of opinions on what counts as "leadership" that the red flag check is often no more helpful than simply searching for the priest online. A conversation designed to help a search process can be little more than answering questions like, has the priest in question broken a canon or destroyed a parish? It is fair to say that this is a surprisingly low bar when it comes to identifying suitable candidates.

The question of candidate suitability for a particular position fits within a larger framework of questions on leadership, a subject that for several decades has been a cottage industry for books, workshops, articles, and seminary courses.[1] In parallel to the red flag process, the range of theories and practices associated with pastoral

---

1. Examples are legion. From my own reading, some representative examples include: Thomas G. Bandy, *Mission Mover*; Jennifer R. Strawbridge, "The Word of the Cross"; Mervyn Davies and Graham Dodds, *Leadership in the Church*; Thomas Edward Frank, "Leadership and Administration"; "Non-Profit Management and Leadership."

leadership have contributed to a landscape where what constitutes *good* leadership seems just out of reach, as if one horizon too far removed. It is not surprising that at the conclusion of a recent survey on leadership training in business, a majority of leading CEOs stated a lack of confidence in leadership-training programs.[2] Yet, the programs and workshops continue unabated.

The church, like any social body, requires a level of leadership and organization that sets the conditions for how the community operates in terms of worship, outreach, and care, in addition to scheduling, personnel, finances, and governance. While some church leadership discourse portrays a disturbing and uncritical adoption of the latest "management principles,"[3] the work of Martyn Percy seeks to ground the *being* and *doing* of clergy in a nonreductive and nonreactive register.

Throughout a number of recent studies, Percy gives attention to the ambiguity and fragmentation faced by clergy in the present age. Living in a mobile, transient, and compressed world, the notion of "community," "church," and "ministry" is under increasing pressure to fit the ever-shifting "professional" norms that privilege the entrepreneur and innovator.[4] The shape of clerical leadership, Percy notes, is becoming less and less clear. In response, Percy investigates and develops an approach to clergy life through focusing on the social and historical context of ministry, the critical role of clergy *formation* over ministry development, and by means of a constructive vision for pastoral leadership shaped by the virtues of holiness, charity, hope, faith, and deep spiritual joy.[5]

These themes of Percy's work on pastoral leadership attend to the core questions this paper is exploring: mainly, what constitutes good pastoral leadership, and where does "leadership" as a concept fit within the ecclesial landscape? The strength of Percy's approach to these and related questions lies in his sociological insights that, combined with theological acumen, resist reductionistic accounts of the ministry while positing a form of critical realism that take seriously the lived experience of clergy and the conversations and debates that shape average parish life.

This approach, helpful and hopeful as it might be, carries certain risks. In particular, there is a tendency for Percy to rely on sociological categorizations of the church that promote a flattened notion of what it means for the church to be a particular social body, the body of Christ. In addition, while Percy addresses pastoral leadership in terms of *character*, there remains room for a more developed account of virtue to help resist the pressure of defining ministry by what ministers *produce*, in terms of results. Finally, Percy's overall vision can be augmented through attending to pastoral leadership as a form of *prudentia*, which is the virtue of deliberating, choosing, and

---

2. Claudio Feser et al., "Decoding Leadership."

3. See Shakespeare, *Being the Body of Christ*. See also Percy, "On Not Rearranging the Deckchairs."

4. Percy, *Clergy*, 80. Also, Percy, "Can Church Leaders Learn to Be Leaders Again?"

5. Percy, "18th October: Proper 24: Mark 10:35–45," 605.

exercising decisions well.[6] The benefit of approaching pastoral leadership as a form of *prudentia* or "good sense" is that it is the virtue that assumes the connection between choice and character, principles and context, and purposes and ends.

In this paper, I will briefly examine the core themes of Percy's account of pastoral leadership, explore how certain Thomistic leitmotifs can help strengthen Percy's overall account, and finally provide a sketch of pastoral leadership as the possessing of "good sense" for the good of the church.

Thinking with Percy on Pastoral Leadership

What Percy refers to as "implicit theology" provides a good starting point (and core hermeneutic) to the topic of pastoral leadership across his publications. Unsatisfied with the assumptions of so-called "blueprint" ecclesiologies,[7] Percy engages the study of the church through examining the implicit aspects of ecclesial life. It is a journey, he states, into the basic-but-nascent theological habits, such as language, culture, and practice, which more properly account for the daily life of congregations and denominations. In addition, to seek implicit understanding means focusing in on the often-hidden structures and practices that shape the density and integrity of the church, in ways that are not plainly observable and expressed. In adopting the notion of implicit theology, Percy contends, matters of style (not just substance) become theologically significant.[8]

A central tenet of an implicit theology is the "ecclesial terroir" that defines and shapes church communities. *Terroir*, a term usually reserved for the viticulture, refers to the combination of factors (e.g. soil variety, altitude, and microclimate) that make one wine from one region different from other wines from other regions. When applied to the church, the *terroir* defines the history and ethos of a church, its stories, buildings, forms of organization, and ecclesial and theological accents. Like the nuances between wines of the same region, one parish might be composed through all manner of stories, buildings, forms of organization, and ecclesial and theological accents; in an adjacent church, the ethos might be entirely different. "The 'ecclesial *terroir*'," Percy notes, "is something that a minister needs to be able to read sensitively and deeply if they are to cultivate congregational life and offer connected parochial ministry."[9] Referencing what this sensitivity means for clergy, Percy argues that ministerial formation needs to promote "deeper forms of discernment that enable ministers

6. I keep the Latin *prudentia* rather than the usual translation of "prudence" to avoid the contemporary caricature of prudence as the disposition of the overly cautious, pragmatic, and emotionally distant person. See *Oxford Dictionaries*, s.v. "prudence," http://www.oxforddictionaries.com/definition/english/prudence.

7. See the discussion on "blueprint ecclesiologies" in chapter two of Healy, *Church, World and the Christian Life*.

8. Percy, *Shaping the Church*, 2–4.

9. Ibid., 103.

to move beyond the surface or presenting task of demand-led organization, and make time and space to read each congregation and parish as a semi-discrete, but related, locally distinctive expression of Christian faith."[10] The kind of contextual awareness of the ecclesial *terroir* is not, Percy notes, an emptying of clerical identity into the tide of cultural relativism. Rather, such awareness forms the basis of acknowledging how environmental factors prompt, cue, and prod the church in her reflection and action in a way that does not diminish the authority of tradition and revelation.[11] What this arrangement provides is a more complex and honest picture of how clergy exercise their craft by means of an "organic structuring" of skills, rituals, and knowledge that are tested, practiced, and reformed within concrete communities. This picture makes clear the benefit for clergy in having a form of "deep literacy" that rejects the binary of church/society in service to a vocation that is both distinct yet diffusive in its location and focus in the way the salt in Jesus' parables is understood as both an agent of purification and preservation.[12]

A vocation of deep literacy requires an approach to clerical training that must, Percy contends, involve more than the equipping of the individual cleric with techniques for *doing* ministry. What is required is engaging deeply with the complex institutional issues that invariably shape or even determine the particular *terroir* in which the cleric must operate. The particulars of clerical tasks and functions are important, but only as secondary to the formation in the values of character, compassion, and wisdom that are critical to understanding what constitutes pastoral leadership.[13]

As terms go, "formation" is as conceptually vague as "leadership." Drawing on the work of Philip Selznick and Simon Western, Percy argues that, as an institution, the church is a "natural community" which has historic roots that are embedded in the fabric of society.[14] Whereas organizations exist as a "no-nonsense system of consciously coordinated activities" that are engineered to fulfil a task that require the oversight of *managers*, the church as an institution is an "adaptive organism" that by means of the concrete realities of buildings, people, and programs incorporates various modes of operating that require a generous amount of "moral leadership."[15] Pastoral leadership, therefore, cannot rest on the formation associated with management, such as the developing of existing or new competencies; rather, as *embedded*, what the church requires is the cultivation of "heightened ecclesial intelligence, and its visionary application." It is a mode of leadership that displays the charisms and skills of ecological sensitivity, inter-dependence, and the capacity to "learn from the middle."[16]

10. Ibid., 103.

11. Percy, *Clergy*, 76.

12. Percy, *Shaping the Church*, 106.

13. Ibid., 114; Percy, "Emergent Archiepiscopal Leadership," 53.

14. Percy, *Shaping the Church*, 114.

15. Percy, "Emergent Archiepiscopal Leadership," 53.

16. Ibid., 56–57. Percy here draws on and adapts Simon Western's notion of "eco-leadership." See

As Christian, the leadership needed for the church demonstrates an authenticity—the "stamp" of character—that displays the indelible mark of God's presence and leading that point back to their source. As embedded and adaptive, pastoral leading requires both informal and formal processes of formation that learn, reflect, and apply as members of the social body of the church, as participants in the council of colleagues and related church structures, and as citizens of a particular political community. Where things go awry in the church, Percy concludes, is when the kind of leadership marketed and deployed displays the kind of crude instrumentality of "organizations" where performance-based metrics and universalized strategies and tools replace the more faithful and difficult work of "paying attention to the implicit" as the site where the church is truly animated by the agency of the Holy Spirit.[17]

In sum, pastoral leadership for Percy is fundamentally centered on role and identity rather than any particular outcome. Though clergy have identifiable tasks and purposes that can be described and measured at some level, clergy "occupy that strange hinterland between the secular and the sacred, the temporal and the eternal, acting as interpreters and mediators, embodying and signifying faith, hope, and love."[18] As such, there is a character to pastoral leadership that resists reduction to the logic of contemporary leadership techniques or programs. In place of initiatives designed to align those who serve in ministry with their peers in business or finance, the character of the office to which they have been ordained should determine the character of clergy.[19] Pastoral leadership is more than the deployment of tools and tactics; inasmuch as it is fostered and formed by the ecclesial *terroir*, the church and her clergy exercise a vocational integrity that is fundamentally embodied and grace-filled.

Reading the (Implicit) Body of Christ

In his recent essay on the *Reform and Renewal* program of the Church of England, Percy flags the importance of how the church is to be read as a kind of social body. He asks the following question: is the church a failing member-based organization in need of a new business plan, or a support-based institution that needs nourishing and deepening community connections? It should be clear from the above analysis that Percy favors the later. In his critique of *Reform and Renewal,* Percy sees in its DNA the outline for a "zombie church" that, by means of a superficial missional gloss and titles that are meant to impress entrepreneurs, is nevertheless a soulless corpse that will never be a body to inspire and cherish.[20]

---

chapter 12 in Western, *Leadership*.

17. Percy, *Shaping the Church*, 129.

18. Percy, *Clergy*, 188.

19. Hauerwas, "Clerical Character," 183.

20. Percy, "On Not Rearranging the Deckchairs."

In this second part of the paper, I will take up Percy's concern for a reading of the church as a body,[21] and show how a vision of the church that begins with the implicit nature of Christ's body informs an understanding of pastoral leadership as the developed disposition of "good sense" (*prudentia*). Such a reading is an exercise in an "implicit theology" that assumes the connection between choice and character, principles and context, and purposes and ends. As such, it is a critical engagement with Percy's more sociological analysis while augmenting his theological insights on the place and role of leadership in the ecclesial landscape.

In his writing on the church as the body of Christ, Thomas Aquinas offers a theologically rigorous and metaphysically sophisticated account of ecclesiology, and Christian life and practice.[22] In similar vein to Percy, for Aquinas, the church is more than simply an organization that reflects in speech and action particular beliefs about God and the world. Aquinas comes to the social body of the church with an organic, theologically derived imagery of the "body" in mind. We see this in two principles Aquinas holds in relation to human life and human community. First, Aquinas believes human bodily life to be the means by which our desire to be a real human community is made possible. The kind of bodies we are—as meaning-making and symbol-sharing embodied souls—allows us to become *more* of what it means to be human, the more we are present to each other.[23]

Second, Aquinas argues that, although we form one human race because our bodies are linked with those of our common ancestors, our destiny and proper end is to belong to the new human race through our bodies being linked with the risen body of Christ.[24] To be linked with Christ, to be the body of Christ is not, for Aquinas, simply a "brand" or "slogan" used to denote the unique identity of the church among other institutions. The church, in a very literal sense, is the body of Christ, enacted and made material through the sacrament of the Eucharist.[25] The sacraments, for Aquinas, are regarded as mysteries of human community symbolizing the union in the Holy Spirit between people. The sacraments are our living contact with the humanity of

21. I am following the lead of Mary Douglas and others who argue for a clear link between how a human body is perceived and understood, and how an organization or institution operating as an analogous body is perceived and understood. See Douglas, *Natural Symbols*, 66–70; Dale and Burrell, "What Shape Are We In?", 15.

22. To draw on Aquinas as an authority in present matters is to make the explicit claim that his thinking offers a continued resource and measure for the larger Christian tradition. To put a finer point on it, Thomas's descriptive method of engaging questions of human life with and towards God displays an internal consistency that avails his work to ongoing consideration and use. His is the work of a thirteenth-century theologian that has shown a remarkable buoyancy for contemporary retrieval and application.

23. Aquinas, *Summa Theologiae* 1a2æ.4.5 and 8 (*ST* from here on).

24. *ST* 3a.61.1.

25. The notion that the Eucharist is the basis for the church is exemplified in the past century by the theology of Henri de Lubac, in particular, *Corpus Mysticum*, chapter 4; and more recently in the work of Paul McPartlan, particularly his *The Eucharist Makes the Church*.

Christ through which alone we share in divine life.[26] To speak of the *body of Christ*, as does the Apostle Paul and, following him, Aquinas, is to speak of a body like no other, whose life is sourced in the resurrected and glorified body of Christ by the power of the Holy Spirit and in union with God the Father. The sacraments make that body present to us and make us present as that body.

The church as the body of Christ is like a "natural body," in that it is one living reality made up of many living members. However, unlike a natural body, it is supernatural; that is, Christ, as the Head of the Body, enlivens it through the divine life of his Holy Spirit and so, simultaneously, through the same Spirit, makes it one living reality in union with himself. The church, posits Herbert McCabe, is not present merely because her members are together in one room. "It is not their bodily presence to each other that fundamentally links them, but their common bodily presence to the risen body of Christ."[27] The Eucharist and the sacraments in general make Christ present, but they do this in the act of making the church present. Thus, while the Body of Christ differs from a natural body, it equally must not be thought of as simply an accidental or merely constructed body—a group of loosely knit individuals united by some common purpose. For Aquinas, the unity of the mystical body of Christ that is the church is nothing less than *caritas*, the love that is a sharing *into* the Holy Spirit. To speak of the purpose of the church, therefore, is not to address first its functionality;[28] rather, it is to address that to which the church is ordered, namely, the joy of God.

In Aquinas's theological vision, the church is treated as the site of membership and union with the living God, an ecclesial body unified by the love and grace of the Holy Spirit. This vision stands in contrast to the "zombie church," where secular reasoning and business-think seek to provide a kind of rational order that presumes as normal the goals of expansion and specialization via increased organizational structure and bureaucracy. For the acolytes of performance-based metrics and universalized strategies and tools, social bodies, whether the church or a bank, are an amalgam of individual positions arranged in numerous ways to perform particular tasks. This social arrangement is presented as value-free.[29] Such organization, proponents suggest, is simply a means to coordinate the allocation of resources. For the managed church, what matters is that all the right parts are placed in the right order so a particular outcome can be reached, one shaped by the principles of efficiency, calculability, predictability, and control. The church, therefore, is little more than a functional body, organized as bits and pieces, and lacking the complex unity and purposefulness true

---

26. As Aquinas states in *Summa Theologica* 3a.26.1.*ad*.1, "The sacraments mediate the divine power, but only by virtue of the perfect mediation of the assumed humanity of the Word."

27. McCabe, *The New Creation*, 83.

28. See Sabra, *Thomas Aquinas' Vision*, 115–21.

29. Don Browning refers to the apparent value or theory-free assumptions in the practice and theory of modern modes in inquiry like managerialism as an illusion. See Browning, *A Fundamental Practical Theology*.

of human bodies and through the animating life of the Spirit, equally and profoundly true of the body of Christ.

As a social body that has its beginning and end within God's divine economy of grace, the church is ordered and oriented to an end (*telos*) suitable to the kind of body it is. It is the community that sacramentally foreshadows the life for which God has destined humanity. Consequently, the church is not fundamentally an example of a social body in an environment of other organizations and institutions; as the body of Christ, the church has an *implicit* identity that informs her proper end and the purposes and activities that order the church to this end.[30] As the social body animated by Christ's life through the indwelling of the Holy Spirit, the church is not organized by means of some general aspect of social production, nor principally the result of the contextual *terroir*, but has its end in terms of grace. Moreover, since the church is informed by the living presence of Christ, it is organized along an alternative logic to that of modern organization or institution. The church, in Aquinas's theological project, is a dynamic and animated entity, which as an *inclusive* and *incorporating* body welcomes members to share in the life and benefits of Christ through her sacramental life that orders the entire body to the joy of God.[31]

The shape and order of the church as the sacramental community whose life anticipates the consummation of God's kingdom requires a form of pastoral leadership that is non-managerial in orientation. In Thomistic thought, the virtue of *prudentia* as "right practical reason" provides an alternative basis and logic to the reductive and instrumentalizing habits associated with the emergence of a church shaped by "a combination of anxiety, displaced nostalgia, pragmatism, managerial hubris, and a desire for tangible signs of success."[32] As a virtue exercised with a view to the ultimate goal of human beings, *prudentia* names a way of being and acting in the world that assumes the connection between choice and character, principles and context, and purposes and ends. As such, it is a disposition suitable to the identity and formation of pastoral leaders who are ordered and oriented to wise deliberation and action that has its basis in what the church is, and what the church is for.

The Prudent Priest: Exercising "Good Sense" for the Good of the Church

For Aquinas, *prudentia* is not some quality that is brought to deliberations in order to deploy particular law-like generalizations or to accomplish predetermined goals in

30. This follows one of Aquinas's metaphysical principles; namely, what something is *essentially* provides the logic for how the thing in question operates and provides the goals for the good order of the thing. Thomas applies this to living things, artifacts, social structures, and even the mystery of God.

31. Sabra notes that for Aquinas, the "mark" of the church that occupied him the most was the question of unity. See Sabra, *Thomas Aquinas' Vision*, 70.

32. Percy, "On Not Rearranging the Deckchairs on the Titanic."

the most effective way. It is not a technique or strategy that is theorized to have universal applicability regardless of context.[33] What Aquinas had in mind (and took from Aristotle) was a virtue or developed ability which enables a person to make and carry out good decisions and to do so as the kind of person who would engage such activity.[34] *Prudentia*, like all the virtues, is concerned with character, in that a virtue is that which makes its possessor good, and the work, likewise, good.[35] In Thomistic theory, the exercise of *prudentia* or "right practical reason" is the developed ability to choose the right means that are appropriate to the goal sought, to make decisions, to consider other possibilities when necessary, and to put the decision correctly into action.[36] It is, according to Herbert McCabe, the possessing and exercise of *good sense*.[37]

The rationale for where *prudentia* fits within an understanding of human identity and purpose is presented by Aquinas in *Summa Theologica* 1a2ae.57.5. In the body of the article, Aquinas outlines the way the application of "good sense" contributes to the perfection and purposefulness of human beings as a particular kind of ensouled body. As rational animals, the interplay of intellect and will contributes to the ability of the human agent to see actions in relationship to a goal. A rational agent is able to see the connection between the goal and actions which may not be attractive at all in themselves (such as undergoing surgery), and willingly choose them for the purpose they achieve. For instance, the woman who wants to become an expert on Russian affairs chooses to spend her time on the tedium of learning Russian verbs, while the man who desires to excel on the playing field may willingly spend hours jogging and lifting weights.[38] For Aquinas, all human actions are a product of a choice that is the result of a judgment of reason.

The choosing of a course of action, notes Aquinas, requires an understanding of what constitutes a good goal or end and what means are suitable for attaining that

33. Recent attempts to apply Thomistic *prudentia* (or Aristotelian, *phronesis*) to managerial practices tend to use it as a new "tool" for improving managerial effectiveness. See Kinsella and Pitman, *Phronesis as Professional Knowledge.* In an attempt to align insights from Aquinas with management practice, Wolfgang Grassl, though less tempted to simply apply *prudentia,* nevertheless creates a hybrid account of the managed organization whereby the structure of action that Aquinas uses to define "good sense" becomes a "model" for how managers can reach decisions. See Grassl, "Aquinas on Management"; Grassl, "Mission, Vision, Strategy."

34. It is important to keep in mind the difference between a skill or technique, and a virtue. The former is directed to the excellence of the thing produced, a virtue is directed to the excellence of the producer (the development of good or bad dispositions of this kind, virtues or vices, is the development of a self). See McCabe, *On Aquinas,* 57.

35. *ST* 2a2ae.47.4. The connection between virtue and goodness is summarized nicely by John Milbank and Adrian Pabst, when they speak of virtue "as an everyday matter of performing your job well, being a good lover, spouse, parent, friend, colleague and citizen, or even enjoying a game or trip" (Milbank and Pabst, *The Politics of Virtue,* 5). For the Thomistic tradition, goodness is what it means for something to live fully into the *nature* of what it is.

36. Westberg, *Right Practical Reason,* 187.

37. McCabe, "Aquinas on Good Sense," 419.

38. Westberg, *Right Practical Reason,* 74.

due end. Consequently, he notes, "an intellectual virtue is needed in the reason, to perfect the reason, and make it suitably affected toward things ordained to the end; and this virtue is *prudentia*. Consequently, *prudentia* is a virtue necessary to lead a good life."[39] The application of *prudentia* means that a person operates with a deep sense of what is needed in a particular situation to reach a goal, and with a flexibility to discern in new situations the means to reach the desired goal. For Aquinas, "good sense" is as concerned with the overall goal of an action as it is with the particular circumstances within which deliberation and choice is exercised. It is not true, therefore, that ends justify the means, for *prudentia* operates in light of the perfecting inclinations implicit to the entire human person, mainly human happiness (*felicitas*) and through divine grace, beatitude.[40] In sum, while "good sense" is operative in everything from taking a walk to learning the Russian language, the actualizing of the judgment, deliberation, and execution associated with *prudentia* is constituent to the goal-directedness of human life, and in particular the goal, actualized by *caritas*, to share in the divine friendship of God.

Another benefit of the exercise of *prudentia* is that the good of the community is assessed in terms of the means to a proper end, not simply the benefit of the individual person whose role it is to make a decision. The concern, in other words, is not simply with "leadership development" as a skill, but with the inhabiting of good sense by leaders who recognize the larger good in relation to the goal. Aquinas recognized that those who inhabit "good sense" are doing so as members and participants of communities. In *Summa Theologica* 2a2ae.47.10, Aquinas speaks of *prudentia* as pertaining to "not only the private good of the individual, but also the common good of the multitude," since right reason "judges the common good to be better than the good of the individual."[41] In other words, and keeping with his general metaphysical outlook, Aquinas maintains that the good disposition of the parts depends on their relation to the whole. It is the identity and purpose of the whole that shapes what is appropriate for the activity of the parts.

The connection between means and ends, and individual and communal, is further clarified by Aquinas when he considers the implications of the lack of *prudentia*. *Astutia* (that is, the careful rational pursuit of a bad or inappropriate end[42]) employs most of the same characteristics of "good sense," with the exception that the goal sought is "good not in truth but in appearance."[43] The goal may seem worthy and indeed it

---

39. *ST* 1a2ae.57.5.

40. For Aquinas, there is a connection between *prudentia* and divine *providentia* (providence). As he notes in *Summa Theologica* 1.22.1, it belongs to *prudentia* to direct other things toward an end whether in regard to oneself or in regard to others subject to that person. Aquinas contends that *prudentia* is suitably attributed to God, and given that the God is the last end, the ordering in things toward an end in God is called *providentia*.

41. *ST* 2a2ae.47.10.

42. *ST* 2a2ae.55.3. Modern English translations render *astutia* as craftiness or cunning.

43. *ST* 2a2ae.55.3c.

might be worthy (growing the church, for example);, however, to assume that the *results* of an action is all that matters is assume that the identity and purpose of the community in question requires the imposing of goals rather than the judgment, deliberation, and execution of actions that seek to address or fulfill the implicit purpose and goals of the particular kind of community. Again, for Aquinas, different kinds of communities have different ends, so it is to risk *astutia* to assume that the goals of one kind of community (e.g., a business) are appropriate to another (e.g., a parish).

What, then, is the shape *prudentia* takes in relation to pastoral leadership? The possessing and exercise of "good sense" is shaped by the church being a social body animated by the indwelling of Christ's life through the grace of the Holy Spirit.[44] In this body, the sacraments are the effective signs of living contact with the humanity of Christ, through which people share in divine life. The church, therefore, is understood as a community of graced people who form the body of Christ: a body that is strengthened and transformed by the sacraments; in particular, baptism and the Eucharist. Given this, the notion that a church leader is a person who efficiently leads by way of a rationalized and results-oriented strategy is proven inadequate and incoherent. Leadership, under these rationalized conditions, is the exercise of law-like precepts that have universal applicability, limited to judicial functions. Yet, leadership in the church, specifically in the clergy, requires a closer relationship with what the church is, and what the church is for, in order for it to be *pastoral* leadership. The possession and exercise of "right practical reason" in relation to the identity and purpose of the church places pastoral leadership on a more solid foundation. In particular, there are three criteria of pastoral leadership that serve to help order and orient the members of Christ's body to their proper end of salvation and joy.

The first criterion is that of *good service*. The exercise of "good sense" church leadership is understood in terms of its operation or function, "whereby the good of our neighbor is intended."[45] Its function is its principal and final goal of divine joy, and that function is always oriented to serving others. Aquinas gives the example of bishops. The perfection of the episcopal state, he argues, is grounded in the love of God that binds a person to work for the salvation of their neighbor.[46] The vocation of service in reference to ordained leadership is present in Aquinas's use of *utilitas* ("good service"). Ordained leaders are there for the *utilitas*, the "good of their subjects," the "good of the church," and the "good of their neighbor."[47] Such service is not the pragmatic utility of practical usefulness that is oriented principally to efficient and effective means to completing tasks and functions. What *utilitas* defines is the exercise of practical wisdom that is oriented to the goal of the church as the site of the unifying

44. *ST* 1a.92.3.

45. *ST* 2a2ae.185.1.

46. *ST* 2a2ae.185.4.

47. A few examples of this use are found in *Summa Theologica* 2a2ae.63.2, 147.3, and 185.3.

and salvific good for all human beings.[48] As such, the service in question is no less *practical* than managerial-inspired activity in that it seeks to accomplish actions, and do them well. The difference resides in the relationship of the means of service (i.e., its inner logic) to its proper end. For pastoral leaders, the ultimate and defining end for the church is always the supernatural gift of unity in Christ.

The second criterion of pastoral leadership as an exercise of "good sense" is leadership as an *instrumentum* ("good tool or instrument"). Aquinas considered ordained leadership as an *extrinsic* instrument; that is, when church leaders perform tasks or make decisions, they act as specific agents in service to, and as an instrument of, the *intrinsic* activity of God in and through the ministry of the entire church. As *animate* instruments, leaders play an active role in bringing about a specific result in what they do, but the primary agency by which the purposes of the church are obtained belongs to God.[49] Aquinas has in mind here the role of ordained leaders in reference to the administration of the sacraments. In 3a.64.8, for example, he notes how washing with water can be done for the purpose of bodily cleanliness and even amusement. When it comes to washing with water for the purpose of baptism, "it needs to be determined to one purpose, i.e. the sacramental effect, by the intention of him who washes."[50] The water itself as an inanimate instrument is not implicitly intended toward a particular effect; rather, it is the motion and intent of the priest or bishop to subject themselves as an *instrumentum* to the goal and action of the principal agent of the sacramental activity; that is, Christ. In so doing, the ordained leader serves for the purpose of effecting a result that is oriented toward the final goal, the unity of people as the body of Christ.

The leader as *instrumentum* problematizes the rationalized goals of efficiency and effectiveness of more managerial-shaped leadership in re-ordering the goals of the church to reflect clearly the final reality of the sacraments; that is, the life of grace. The effect of good leadership, therefore, is measured principally in how and by what means the leader of the community acts to promote and assist in orienting the community to unity in Christ. Not every action is meant to be a sacramental action, yet in that the sacraments are the principal means to share in God's life, the general movement expressed in actions and decisions small and large is oriented to, and as an instrument of, the agency of Christ in effecting human wholeness and unity. Since the *instrumentum* of the ordained leadership is ordered to be the final goal of the church, the ministry and activity of the church itself can be construed as a "healing instrument."[51]

A third criterion when considering leadership in the church is that of *ministerium* (having a specific office). Whereas *utilitas* and *instrumentum* outline how leadership

48. Sabra, *Thomas Aquinas' Vision*, 117.

49. *ST* 3a.64.3.

50. *ST* 3a.64.8.

51. Sabra, *Thomas Aquinas' Vision*, 119.

is exercised, the use of *ministerium* in relation to leaders acknowledges that, in the life of the church, there are specific roles or offices occupied by individuals. What is notable to Aquinas's understanding of these roles is that he places far greater emphasis on these offices as relating to, and receiving coherence from, the sacramental life of worship and service, more than the formalistic and procedural responsibilities allied with these roles (for example, the administration of committees or parish buildings and grounds). As was discussed above, leadership in the church is specific to the kind of social body the church is. Hence, to emphasize the sacramental over the procedural is to acknowledge that participation in the sacraments conveys a spiritual power or ability that affects those participating in a manner that is fundamentally ordered to the true and ultimate end of human life. The administration of sacraments are, for Aquinas, immovable (*immobiles*) as to their nature and effect, whereas the functional operations are of a "lower power", in that associated actions lack *immobiles* because functional operations are more determined by circumstance and context.[52] Appropriate church leadership is principally the exercise of activity that is "natural" to the kind of social body where the leadership is manifest. For there is nothing more natural for the church than the participation and reception of the gifts of grace and love received through sacramental actions.

Leadership as *ministerium* averts the dualisms of spiritual/temporal or visible/invisible that might be assigned to particular parts of ordained office by maintaining a strongly realist position when it comes to how the church and the sacramental life are fitting to the nature of human beings and their graced final end. We can see in this position the grounds for a rationale for the church as a social body whose life is properly sourced in that of the Incarnate Word as the first and universal cause of salvation. It is fitting, therefore, that the instruments of salvation (i.e., the sacraments and those who administer them) should possess a certain similitude to their first cause. Thus, the role of pastoral leader is not established by means of comparison to leadership in other kinds of social bodies, but through a certain similitude to Christ, who, as the invisible Word that operates through the visible signs in the sacraments, orders and orients the good sense and person of church leaders to himself.[53] There is no greater orientation for pastoral leaders than being the instruments of service whose purpose and activity is determined by the immovable grace of God as received in the sacraments.

Leaders in the church, therefore, participate as a member of the body of which Christ is the head, and through their service, instrumentality, and office, they preserve the unity signified and effected in the sacraments, and orient the community in the day-to-day matters of the church to modes of human wholeness that are enacted through the presence and activity of the Holy Spirit. Such leadership cannot reflect the law-like imposition of goals that seek managerial efficiency or prescribed methods of planning that seek to define the church principally by its procedural modes of

52. *Summa Theologica* 2a2ae.39.3

53. Sabra, *Thomas Aquinas' Vision*, 112.

organization. As is appropriate to the kind of social body the church is, leadership is the exercise of good sense that engages in the execution of wise action that at all times is shaped by sacramental unity and oriented to divine happiness.

What *prudentia* brings to the discussion of pastoral leadership is not additional technical ordering or the efficient realignment of resources. In the place of pragmatic conditions that privilege results over personal character, the *prudent priest* is one who lives from and into an identity and orientation shaped by the life of the church and her proper identity and orientation as the body of Christ. The prudent priest is not a generic leader who happens to have training and skills in understanding parish systems or implementing ecclesial change. She will be committed to a *deep literacy* of the church and its *terroir* through deliberation and judgment that result in actions and behaviors that display the ecclesial integrity of the church as a particular social body, the body of Christ, and the political integrity of the parish as a concrete, embedded community.[54]

While not "measurable" with the kind of metrics associated with a certain organizational logic, in that *prudentia* is about the goodness and vitality of the leader and their community, when it comes to observable benefits, both leader and people will display a form of life governed by the associated virtues of justice, temperance, and fortitude. Above all, the divine gift of *caritas* (loving-kindness) will be evident through patterns of thanksgiving, forgiveness, and hospitality to friend and stranger. Though varying in time and place, the prudent priest and parish will seek to deepen their life together through prayer, worship, and new ways of showing love to other people. The activities characteristic of ordinary human life will not change *per se*, because they have their own goodness and finality, but they will change in relation to a firmly held conviction of God as the true final end of human living.[55] In the end, the customary measures of growth, financial status, and even vocational "success" are overshadowed by personal and spiritual maturity, and through confidence in the implicit identity and purposefulness of the church as the inclusive and incorporating body of Christ.

Leading Where?

Percy's approach to understanding pastoral leadership and clerical identity is, by his own definition, an exercise in "natural history." Wanting to avoid the blueprint ecclesiologies that posit a divine imprimatur on the shape of parish life and structure, Percy appeals to the implicit character of clergy and churches as they have developed over time, in places, and within cultures. As an example of an implicit

---

54. Bushlack, *Politics for a Pilgrim Church*, 125. Bushlack shows how for Aquinas, leaders in the church cultivate *prudentia* by being oriented and ordered to the theological aims of the church as a site of preaching, thanksgiving, and service, rather than to the hierarchical and institutional structures themselves.

55. Westberg, *Right Practical Reason*, 256.

theology, Percy's understanding of pastoral theology avoids an overly pragmatic and instrumentalized vision of the church that would reduce ministry to metrics, and argues for a richly variegated landscape in which leadership displays the charisms and skills of ecological sensitivity, inter-dependence, and the capacity to "learn from the middle."[56] It is a vision that, while compelling, is made more theologically robust by a Thomistic account of the church as the body of Christ and *prudentia* as the model virtue for ecclesial leadership.

Conceptually, leading is always "leading of" and "leading to," and never simply "leading for" (efficiency, for example). Percy's work gestures to the *order* and *orientation* of pastoral leadership, but seems hesitant to state a theological rationale for the kind of leading appropriate to the church. By way of conclusion, I would like to focus on how taking account of the church as a particular social body, and *prudentia* as a suitable way of understanding pastoral leadership, provides depth and clarity to Percy's own account.

First, it is through giving priority to the proper *telos* of pastoral leadership as sourced in the implicit identity and nature of the church that resists the functionalism aligned with the contemporary focus on leadership. Equipped with mythic qualities, today's leaders assume to be engaged in something that is coherent, systematic, and justifiable, as well as effective and value-free. As purveyors of organizational power, leader's effect and control change, and do so with law-like generalizations that possess strong predictive powers.[57] Such order is designed to reduce all social bodies to sites requiring greater and greater modes of coordination and control. The flattening of form and purpose dissolves any difference and benefit between one social body and another.[58]

This approach to leadership is rejected by Percy, and his position augmented by a focus on how the character of the office to which clergy have been ordained should determine the character of those serving in ministry. In other words, there is a connection between the sacramental character of the church and the moral character of those who serve.[59] To give undue preference to the mythic qualities of the modern leader over the *end* of what ministry is for and how it is defined, is to risk reducing what constitutes good pastoral leadership to whatever counts as effective. It is essentially to unmoor clerical identity and character from its source, and assume that the latest organizational or management technique is sufficient to orient the church to fulfill her eschatological objective.

Second, as a social body oriented and ordered to human unity in God, the concrete life of the church resists reduction to novelty and cliché, for what animates the church and forms her members is the Holy Spirit, who rests eternally on the body of

56. Percy, "Emergent Archiepiscopal Leadership," 56–57.

57. Parker, *Against Management*, 9.

58. Grey, "'We Are All Managers Now'; 'We Always Were,'" 562.

59. Hauerwas, "Clerical Character," 183.

the Son.[60] In the particular ecclesial *terroir* where clergy live and work, leadership is exercised through the actualizing of the judgment, deliberation, and execution associated with *prudentia,* which is the constituent virtue to the goal-directedness of human life, and in particular the goal (actualized by *caritas*) to share in the divine friendship of God. The judgments and outcomes of such a mode of leading will undoubtedly bear resemblance to the context of the parish and the gifts and charisms of the individual clergy. Where similitude exists is the degree to which the judgments and outcomes display (or not) the order and orientation appropriate to the kind of body that is "natural" to a community that sacramentally anticipates heaven. Under these conditions, the only leadership suitable is that which inhabits "good sense" for the good of the church.

Finally, retrieving *prudentia* and reorienting the church to her proper end as a particular social body will not mark the end of practices like the red flag check used by Transitions Ministers. As Aquinas cautions, *astutia,* as the mere appearance of "good sense," will continue to animate clergy who operate more by means of technical or managerial understanding of what the church needs. Shaped by a vision of leading that seeks to meet the legitimation criteria of measurement and optimization, these clergy will be rewarded with positions and status, especially in a climate where what *works* is privileged over what is *true.*

The naked pragmatism of *effectiveness-oriented* approaches to leadership is based in a rational ordering that presumes as normal the fixed goals of expansion and specialization via increased organizational structure and bureaucracy. It creates the conditions for a privileging of technical training[61] over the often-slow process of discernment and formation in the company of mentors and colleagues. As *embedded,* what the church requires in her leaders is the cultivation of what Percy calls a "heightened ecclesial intelligence, and its visionary application." Such formation promotes a search for shared and common ends that are concerned with the overall flourishing of the church. In contrast to an understanding of *common good* as little more than the aggregate of personal opinions, the exercise of "good sense" contributes to an ethos of mutuality that gives priority to discernment and action that orients clergy and parish to a life of wholeness and unity that anticipates heaven.[62]

60. See Rogers, *After the Spirit.*

61. While I'm hesitant to make a blanket statement, I do worry how DMin programs can be positioned to attract clergy seeking forms of professional legitimatization through a "doctorate" aimed at help them attain new competencies and be more effective. The language of "reflective practitioners" and "praxis-centered learning" is certainly attractive as education goals, but I question if this is even possible given the privileging of effectiveness and an instrumentalizing of ministry that occurs due to the shaping of the vocation into a "profession" that deploys constituent metrics for measurement and evaluation. The following represent efforts to clarify how DMin programs can be more formational in their methods, and less oriented to pragmatic ends: Conniry, "Reducing the Identity Crisis in Doctor of Ministry Education"; Sbanotto and Welch, "Core Components of Successful Doctor of Ministry Program."

62. Milbank and Pabst, *The Politics of Virtue,* 70.

To ground formation in anything else is to risk reshaping the church into the kind of "zombie church" that Percy critiques and about which church members and leaders ought to have serious concerns.

To conclude, what this paper has offered, in conversation with Martyn Percy and Thomas Aquinas, is an argument for a revaluation of what constitutes good pastoral leadership in light of the current ecclesial and cultural climate. While not providing precise steps or strategies for forming good leaders, it has sought to emphasize where such formation ought to be focused: mainly, on helping priests to "read" the church as the kind of social body it is, and to base deliberation, decision, and execution of actions that are ordered and oriented to our proper end in divine joy. Clergy who are fostered and formed by this ecclesial *terroir* will display in their varied contexts and ministries a vocational integrity that is fundamentally embodied and grace-filled. They will be, in other words, the pastoral leaders most attuned to the call of Jesus: to be ministers for a particular place and time; but also ambassadors of the joy of heaven.[63]

Bibliography

Aquinas, Thomas. *Summa Theologiae*. 61 vols. Cambridge: Cambridge University Press, 2006.

Bandy, Thomas G. *Mission Mover: Beyond Education for Church Leadership*. Nashville: Abingdon, 2004.

Browning, Don S. *A Fundamental Practical Theology: Descriptive and Strategic Proposals*. Minneapolis, MN: Fortress, 1991.

Bushlack, Thomas J. *Politics for a Pilgrim Church: A Thomistic Theory of Civic Virtue*. Grand Rapids, MI: Eerdmans, 2015.

Conniry, Charles J. "Reducing the Identity Crisis in Doctor of Ministry Education." *Theological Education* 40:1 (2004) 137–52.

Dale, Karen, and Gibson Burrell. "What Shape Are We In? Organization Theory and the Organized Body." In *Body and Organization*, edited by John Hassard, Ruth Holliday, and Hugh Willmott, 15–30. London: SAGE, 2000.

Davies, Mervyn, and Graham Dodds. *Leadership in the Church for a People of Hope*. New York: T. & T. Clark, 2011.

Douglas, Mary. *Natural Symbols: Explorations in Cosmology*. London: Routledge, 1996.

Feser, Claudio, et al. "Decoding Leadership: What Really Matters." *McKinsey Quarterly* 4 (December 2014) 88–91.

Frank, Thomas Edward. "Leadership and Administration: An Emerging Field in Practical Theology." *International Journal of Practical Theology* 10:1 (2006) 113–36.

———. "Non-Profit Management and Leadership." *Courses, Summer 2015*. http://www.bexleyseabury.edu/non-profit-management-and-leadership/.

Grassl, Wolfgang. "Aquinas on Management and Its Development." *The Journal of Management Development* 29:7/8 (2010) 706–15.

———. "Mission, Vision, Strategy: Discernment in Catholic Business Education." *Journal of Catholic Higher Education* 31:2 (2012) 213–32.

---

63. Percy, *Clergy*, 188.

Grey, Christopher. "'We Are All Managers Now'; 'We Always Were': On the Development and Demise of Management." *Journal of Management Studies* 36:5 (1999).

Hauerwas, Stanley. "Clerical Character: Reflecting on Ministerial Morality." *Word & World* 6:2 (1986) 183.

Healy, Nicholas M. *Church, World and the Christian Life: Practical-Prophetic Ecclesiology.* New York: Cambridge University Press, 2000.

Kinsella, Elizabeth Anne, and Allan Pitman, eds. *Phronesis as Professional Knowledge: Practical Wisdom in the Professions.* Boston: Sense Publishers, 2012.

Lubac, Henri de. *Corpus Mysticum: The Eucharist and the Church in the Middle Ages.* Translated by Gemma Simmonds. South Bend, IN: University of Notre Dame Press, 2007.

McCabe, Herbert. "Aquinas on Good Sense." *New Blackfriars* 67:798 (October 1, 1986) 419.

———. *On Aquinas.* London: Burns & Oates, 2008.

———. *The New Creation: Studies on Living in the Church.* London: Sheed and Ward, 1964.

McPartlan, Paul. *The Eucharist Makes the Church.* 2nd edition. Fairfax, VA: Eastern Christian, 2006.

Milbank, John, and Adrian Pabst. *The Politics of Virtue: Post-Liberalism and the Human Future.* Lanham: Rowman & Littlefield, 2016.

Parker, Martin. *Against Management: Organization in the Age of Managerialism.* Cambridge: Blackwell Publishing, 2002.

Percy, Martyn. "18th October: Proper 24: Mark 10:35–45." *The Expository Times* 120:12 (September 1, 2009) 605.

———. "Can Church Leaders Learn to Be Leaders Again?" In *Creative Church Leadership*, edited by John Eric Adair and John Nelson, 48–61. Norwich: Canterbury, 2004.

———. *Clergy: The Origin of Species.* London: Continuum, 2006.

———. "Emergent Archiepiscopal Leadership within the Anglican Communion." *Journal of Anglican Studies* 14:1 (2015) 53.

———. "On Not Rearranging the Deckchairs on the Titanic: A Commentary on Reform and Renewal in the Church of England." *Modern Church* (Febrary 2016). https://modernchurch.org.uk/downloads/send/32-articles/768-on-not-rearranging-the-deckchairs-on-the-titanic.

———. *Shaping the Church: The Promise of Implicit Theology.* Farnham, UK: Ashgate, 2010.

Rogers, Eugene F. *After the Spirit.* Grand Rapids, MI: Eerdmans, 2005.

Sabra, George. *Thomas Aquinas' Vision of the Church: Fundamentals of an Ecumenical Ecclesiology.* Mainz, Germany: Matthias-Grünewald-Verlag, 1987.

Sbanotto, Elizabeth Nesbit, and Ronald D. Welch. "Core Components of Successful Doctor of Ministry Program." *Theological Education* 50:1 (2015) 13–32.

Shakespeare, Lyndon. *Being the Body of Christ in the Age of Management.* Eugene, OR: Cascade Books, 2016.

Strawbridge, Jennifer R. "The Word of the Cross: Mission, Power, and the Theology of Leadership." *Anglican Theological Review* 91:1 (2009) 61–79.

Westberg, Daniel. *Right Practical Reason: Aristotle, Action, and Prudence in Aquinas.* Oxford: Oxford University Press, 1994.

Western, Simon. *Leadership: A Critical Text.* London: SAGE, 2013.

9

Ecclesial Engagements

Some Reviews and Responses

*WITH ROBERT CARROLL, PETER COLEMAN,
RICHARD ROBERTS, AND GAVIN D'COSTA*

MARTYN PERCY'S EARLY EXPLORATIONS in ecclesiology tended to focus on pathologies and problems for established denominations and other kinds of specific ecclesial communities. His work has examined themes of leadership, governance and polity, as well as more specific issues such as the negotiations churches made in arenas such as sexuality, the uses and abuses of power, and the contours of moral and ecclesial authority. In this chapter, we sample three brief book reviews that addressed Percy's publications from the 1990s—on fundamentalism (Robert Carroll), sexuality (Peter Coleman) and power (Richard Roberts)—and then invited Percy to comment on the subsequent developments in the ecclesial landscape during the early years of the twenty-first century. The chapter concludes with his response to Gavin D'Costa's review of Percy's *Engaging Contemporary Culture*, and a reflection on the "inward turn" of Anglicanism, moving away from a confident public theology and institutional body to becoming a more private spiritual realm member-based organization.

Past-Present: *Fundamentalism, Sexuality and Power*

Robert Carroll's review of *Words, Wonders and Power*[1]

As the second millennium of the Common Era nears its end, we hear more and more of raucous New Age religions and of the religious fundamentalisms which typify this kind of reliance on the dogma of experience in religion. In a short but convincing book, Martyn Percy offers a very perceptive analysis of specific kinds of contemporary Christian revivalistic fundamentalism. Focusing on the Vineyard Ministries

1. This review originally appeared in the *Anglican Theological Review*. Robert Carroll (1941–2000) was Professor of Hebrew and Semitic Studies at the University of Glasgow.

International movement associated with the Californian ecclesiastical leader John Wimber and his churches, Percy examines in close detail the phenomenology of these churches (including some pertinent observations about "the Toronto Blessing") where power is the dominant value and belief in signs and miracles is rampant. The scrutiny is merciless and devastating in its exposure of a power-crazed movement intent on the rigid control of its followers and on the planting (growth) of churches. The account of such conformistic, coercive obsessions with power and certainty, combined with such a mechanistic language of "tools," conjures up a terrifying scene of ecclesiastical chaos masquerading as some kind of imagined repetition of the biblical legend of the Day of Pentecost. It all sounds like a bad day out with Scientologists!

Percy's analysis is a most conscientious, careful and responsible scrutiny of fundamentalistic churches which have been Wimberized, and of the ideology behind their practices. Adding to the analyses of fundamentalism already provided by the writings of James Barr and Kathleen Boone, Percy provides a devastating Christian critique of such manipulative, power-obsessed groups, and a most insightful theological examination of their narrow and defective understandings of the rich diversity of Christian traditions. Authority, power, and certainty seem to be what these Wimberized churches crave and therefore acquire—no sense here of uncertain knowledge, proffered grace, negotiated neighborliness, or questing love—which inevitably means that the human authority figure (Wimber, and other church leaders) takes the place of God and rules over the group with a rod of iron, backed up by warrants derived from sensationalistic miracle-mongering and defective interpretations of scripture. While the accounts of the behavior of Wimberized churches struck me as bordering on the carnivalesque, I daresay control freaks would love such places of rigid authority and enforced experience. Percy takes these churches very seriously, and his analysis of the ideology of the Wimberization of churches as reflecting "a theology of power" seems to me to be a very careful, responsible reading of the dynamics of such ecclesiastical communities.

I recommend his book because it should contribute to a more sophisticated understanding of certain aspects of religious fundamentalism and because it is so focused on the ideology and praxis of specific churches. He ends by citing Donald Davie's poem "Ordinary God," and this makes a fine counterweight to the depictions of such manipulative obsessions with power and control characteristic of the churches described in his book. So much emphasis on control, so much obsession with power; whatever became of gentleness, grace, seeing through a glass darkly, and love? For that matter whatever happened to the apostolic counsel to think on such things which are true, honorable, just, pure, lovely, gracious, excellent? Percy's critique is irresistible because he speaks out of Christian concern about groups which overvalue power at the expense of love, and thereby represent a very defective understanding and practice of the Gospel.

Peter Coleman's Review of *Intimate Affairs:*
Sexuality and Spirituality in Perspective[2]

One wonders what the undergraduates at Christ's College Cambridge made of this series of eight sermons, designed by their Chaplain, Martyn Percy, to reflect on the sexual revolution of the past seventy years. Each sermon focused on a film of the period between 1922 *(Forbidden Fruit)* and 1992 *(Peter's Friends)*. Obviously, few of the congregation would have seen some of these films except in a cinema club, as part of celluloid history, but Percy chose them because cinema reflects changes of perspective in society and "many people derive such knowledge about sexuality through television or film: drama and story teach and influence us more about ourselves then many of us would like to admit."[3]

To be sure, the list of preachers was impressive: a bishop from Wales, several professors and authors, and a BBC producer—all of them expert in this difficult task of relating Christian sexual ethics to contemporary lifestyles. So did they defend orthodox Christian morality against secular attack, and argue that the best (if not only proper) use of sexual intercourse is between married partners of different gender? If so, the sermons would only be interesting if they offered fresh arguments to justify old truths.

Or did the preachers start de *nova w*ith the mores of our times, recorded by these films, looking for anything good a Christian thinker could find in them? Could they conclude that modern convictions about sexual relationships were actually good in themselves? Thus, intercourse expresses the joy and pain of relating, even temporarily—it is not just for procreation; adult sex requires genuine friendship and equality between partners and flexible role models; our concepts of masculinity and femininity need to be reworked, etc. Each conviction might express some elements of responsible love in God's design.

Percy chose his preachers wisely—three men and five women, to avoid an either-or approach. He notes that Christians "are united in our desire to explore sexuality and spirituality in a way that makes sense in contemporary society, yet it is not uncritical of it either, since we are rooted in a faith in God that is constantly embarking on a new culture the Kingdom of God."[4] So what we have here in book form is a set of snapshots by very competent photographers, each focusing on a particular subject in the foreground, but standing near enough for every picture to have an obviously common background.

The original setting was Evensong, and the spiritual perspective was set by carefully chosen lessons and relevant psalms. In the first sermon, *(The Graduate,* 1967)

2. This review originally appeared in the *Crucible.* Peter Coleman (1928–2001), a former Bishop of Crediton, taught Christian ethics at the University of Bristol in 1983–1984, where Percy was an undergraduate.

3. Percy, *Intimate Affairs*, 2.

4. Ibid., 4.

Percy sets the revolution in historical context. He looks at the archidiaconal records of 1578 and found pages of reports on adultery, illegitimacy, whoredom, and general sexual licence. He also warns against seeing the nineteenth century through sanitized Victorian eyes.

Rowan Williams (*Forbidden Fruit*, 1922) looks at the Fall and the Fourth Gospel story about the woman taken in adultery, and stresses that Jesus and Saint Paul were not answering our questions about sexuality. They knew about marriage as a complicated bundle of economic arrangements. Sex for early Christians was regarded as vulgar and messy—best not to bother about it as you waited for God's Kingdom. But positively, he goes on: "I cannot see that the New Testament easily allows any *straightforwardly* positive evaluation of sexual intimacy outside a relationship that is publicly committed; but it does not suggest that the essential text of Christian orthodoxy lies in a willingness to treat all other relationships as incapable of sharing in the Love of God."

Grace Jantzen, as a Quaker, reflects on the story of a man who tests HIV-positive (*Peter's Friends*, 1992) and then works his way toward a dignity and maturity which helps him discern what to be ashamed of and what not. Angela Tilby (*When Harry Met Sally*, 1989) affirms the erotic because God "trusts us to love and be loved, without jealousy, or, as Bonhoeffer once put it, "it is bad taste to yearn for the infinite when you are in the arms of your spouse." Margie Tolstoy *(Blow Up*, 1966) reckons that the harm of pornography is that treating others as objects of pleasure is exploitation, a dehumanizing process, and Elizabeth Stuart argues against homophobia *(A Walk on the Wild Side*, 1962). Anthony Dyson's call for a reassessment of Masculinity (Carnal Knowledge, 1974) and the balancing study of femininity by Mary Grey (*All about Eve*, 1950) are among the two most searching theological pieces in the series, and Percy sums up. Incidentally, there are two extremely funny clean sex jokes: the Vicar whose hat blew off (p. 9) and the Monk's Champagne (p. 48).

Albeit mostly sermons, but with useful introductions and appendices, this book could well be used as a standard introduction to sexual ethics courses for theological colleges and courses.

Richard H. Roberts's Review of *Power and the Church:* *Ecclesiology in an Age of Transition*[5]

Martyn Percy describes this book as "a preliminary set of essays that sets out to discuss the diversity and digressions of power from a theoretical and applied perspective in terms of their relation to theology and religious studies" (p. vii). This is an honest description, for these papers are indeed in many ways preparatory. The reader is best served by taking each paper on its own merit and using the contents

5. This review originally appeared in *The Journal of Contemporary Religion*. Richard H. Roberts is the former Professor of Religious Studies at the University of Lancaster.

of the collection as a resource. Read in this way, *Power and the Church* is provocative and stimulating.

The first paper considers models of power. Against a background of what Percy calls "modernism," a number of basic issues are opened up concerning the nature of the power of God in the context of ecclesiology. Percy is clearly a Christian theologian, and summarizes his perspective in the following terms:

> In choosing to use sociology and theology together, the book is essentially an offering of ecclesiology that is concerned with the knowledge of and use of divine and human power. For behind the reality of power lies a very different reality that is grounded in love and truth, and is willing to be made known in weakness-and even death. (p. 16)

Percy's book offers rapid explorations of issues such as fundamentalism, violence, theories of exchange, bureaucratic ideology, spiritual eroticism, and the absence of theology in contemporary experiential Christianity. There is a brief conclusion in which Percy considers the future of the power of God in a post-foundational world. This presents the reader with a set of further questions, which we hope will be explored more fully in future.

The most productive feature of *Power and the Church* is to be found in the sheer range of allusion which crowds into the text and is further supplemented by footnotes that never cease to inform and entertain the reader. We await with anticipation further work which might present us with a fuller, more consistently developed argument from a writer who undoubtedly possesses one of the liveliest and most energetic minds in contemporary English theology.

Comment by Martyn Percy

Writing in the 1990s (the forces of fundamentalism, power, and authority, and of the challenges posed to churches in relation to increasingly progressive views on issues such as sexuality), I had made a number of assumptions. First, that the millennium would cause a "blip"—a kind of "power surge," if you will—in some intense and novel forms of religious expression, such as was witnessed in the "Toronto Blessing." Second, that denominations would continue to be challenged by developments in contemporary western culture, such as the rise of consumerism as a factor *within* religion. Third, that the early years of the twenty-first century would neither be secular nor (traditionally) sacred, but rather "spiritual-but-not-religious." In suggesting this, I had in mind a continuity of interest and appetite for transcendent reference points in the lives of individuals and communities. However, such transcendence would not necessarily be rooted in traditional institutions and purveyed as "formal religion," as had been hitherto understood.

To an extent, these trajectories were correct; but with some important qualifiers. First, the power of global fundamentalism—and one thinks here especially of the events surrounding and following September 11th, 2001—indicated a new arrival, namely that of "furious religion," as Gilles Kepel has termed it. The power of that fury—often extending to areas such as gender and sexuality, and directed inwards against believers, as much as it is projected into the wider world—has highlighted a marked change in the "mood" of churches and denominations. The phenomenon of highly acrimonious, bitter, and divisive internalized disputes is now a relatively common spectacle in most mainline denominations, is proving to be a drain on resources and the natural resources of governance and polity, and is tending toward the schismatic. "Blessed are the peacemakers" (Matt 5:9) has always been true, but increasingly, these peacemakers need be workers of miracles within denominations where warring factions would rather divorce and divide than see themselves as children of one covenant and in a common communion.

Second, the consumerism present within religion—a feature arguably present since emergent guarantees of religious freedom in the seventeenth century—has placed extraordinary pressures on coherence, resources, and polity, as the search for more distinctive and bespoke forms of spiritual identity intensify. Generally, it is a mistake to assume that issues of purity and power are for small and kraal-like religious groups. Such issues stalk Christian groups and all churches, and fundamentalism, as one subject of study, is simply a concentration of a "problem" that affects many different faiths, including all forms of Christianity—those that espouse liberalism or openness, traditionalism or innovation. Boundaries of definition can quickly become borders marking territory and, ultimately, barriers. The relatively rapid emergence of phenomena such as "fresh expressions," alongside the rising number of new churches, has continued to loosen the grip and monopoly of established denominations, and created new markets and choices for religious consumers. This has, in turn, forced established denominations to adapt their identities as they compete for new members in the spiritual marketplace.

Third, the emergence of fundamentalism as a major force within world religion is now well into its second century. The term "fundamentalism" has successfully migrated and evolved from referring to a specific group of Christians in the early twentieth century, to defining more generic behavioral and ideological positions within other established religious traditions. Invariably, such positions involve hostility toward secular modernity, and to any (allegedly) compromised religious tradition. This has a significant impact on the conduct and form of debates in denominations on issues such as gender and sexuality. More "traditionalist" outlooks have become indicative: characterized, often, by a sense of fury, resistance, (re-)assertive power, and the advocacy of "theocracy." The resilience, vibrancy, and adaptability of "retro-traditionalist" religious expressions in modernity suggest that scholars may need to take the cultural complexity of such movements more seriously. There is no sign that modernity will gradually dissolve emergent fundamentalisms and neo-traditionalists. Indeed, some indications seem to point in the opposite direction.

Present-Future: A Public and Engaged Church

Gavin D'Costa's review of *Engaging with Contemporary Culture:*
Christianity, Theology and the Concrete Church[6]

Martyn Percy is a seasoned insider, well-read, urbane, witty, and eclectic. For a snapshot of a particular flavor of English Anglicanism, this is the picture to send to friends. Percy focuses on the question of the relationship of theology and the church to culture. His book is also at the same time a plea for an Anglican public theology; that is, a theological voice and practice deeply shaped by the complex interdisciplinary culture which constitutes both modernity and postmodernity. Rather than speaking from an insulated worldview with ideal church and ideal gospel in place, such as Percy finds in certain Roman Catholic writers and Anglo-Catholics like John Milbank, Percy instead argues that the church and gospel are always rich and plural cultures themselves, so that cultural analysis is the therapy of theology, and leads to good health in the church. His interdisciplinary approach is evinced in his sources, and particularly in a most fruitful and novel use of the ethnographical work of James Hopewell that marks the final part of the book.

Percy develops his argument over nine wide ranging chapters, covering engagement of theology, religious studies, missiology, and ecclesiology within contemporary culture (in pt 1), exploring the nature of practical theology and theological education (pt 2) and employing ethnography to explore congregations, movements and denominations (pt 3). This is a rich fare and difficult to summarize as it is so broad ranging; although focusing on a couple of chapters may give readers a flavor of Percy.

In chapter one, for example, Percy explores questions of ecclesial authority and credibility using the test case of United States Catholicism and four Catholic theologians reflecting upon their church (Francis Buckley, Anthony Gittins, John Fuellenbach, and Nicholas Healey). He is most sympathetic to Healey's criticisms of "blueprint ecclesiology," whereby authoritative super-models of what the church is guide theological thinking on the church with little or no reference to what is actually happening in ecclesial communities which constitute that "church." This type of approach undermines the actual struggle of church membership, its pulls and pushes, strains and creaks, such that it gains less and less credibility. Its authority is thus undermined. Cardinal Bernard Law's handling of sex scandals in Boston is paraded as a typical example of this approach; this type of thing should not happen in the church, so its implications and its reality are suppressed. Percy certainly has a point, but perhaps goes too far in claiming

---

6. This review originally appeared in *The International Journal of Public Theology*. Gavin D'Costa is Professor of Theology at the University of Bristol.

that Law was "scowling at the black female judge" (p. 23) during the trial, because he did not believe he was answerable to a black woman, let alone a secular court of law. No evidence is cited except Law's facial expression.

Authority and credibility are in effect gained, according to Percy, through collaborative, contextual, and communal theologizing, reflecting on actual and diverse practices with the help of all possible disciplines, not just theology, and with the active engagement of the laity. Percy's hero in this chapter is Paulo Freire, author of *Pedagogy of the Oppressed.* To the criticism that authority evaporates and relativity enters, Percy responds that authority ultimately resides with Christ, and this reminds "the church that it does not possess the truth; it is, instead, possessed by the Truth, which is not the same" (p. 38). Agreed, but is it not a possession of a truth to claim to be possessed by the truth, and a profession that then requires proper explication? Percy gives it, but with insufficient thick description, stating that "the authority of the church depends primarily on an authentic discipleship that manifests the love of God for the human race and for the whole of the created order" (p. 40). It is difficult to understand the public (idealized?) voice of this statement without it being tested and discerned against multiple examples of its praxis. And interestingly, in his formulation, it falls back into a mono-theological expressivism criticized by Percy in other contexts. I am not calling into question the virtues of listening, humility and openness extolled by Percy; indeed, they are central to an intellectually alert church, but they might not be quite as opposed to dogmatic truth as Percy so often implies.

In another chapter, Percy reflects on the nature of Anglicanism. For a practical theologian writing in the midst of possible schism and the collapse of the Anglican Communion, we would expect no less than the direct addressing of what constitutes Anglican unity. There is a serene, committed and ironic cast to Percy's writing. He is aware of the different models of Anglicanism jostling for center-stage: doctrinal and theological priorities in Skyes, Avis, Booty, and Wright; ambiguity and aesthetics in Pickering and Cupitt; a sacralized system of manners, which is Percy's own preferred "core." The latter signifies "a cultural ecclesiology" that is "mild, temperate, given to measured humour, but also anticipative of the ultimacy of a sacramental resolution to all serious forms of dispute and the threat of schism" (p. 212). While some might argue that this reflects old-style middle-class England imbued with Shakespeare (which is not a bad thing), how it relates to a form of "discipleship" that might entail martyrdom is difficult to see (which also might not be a bad thing). Percy realistically extols amicable divorce in the Anglican Communion, living as "friends and neighbours—at least for the sake of its children" (p. 228).

This metaphor is exemplary of Percy's method and theology; it makes the best of living in a messy world, with humor, faith, hope, and intelligence.

Comment by Martyn Percy

I am grateful to Gavin D'Costa's reading of my ecclesial outlook, one where churches exist not for themselves and their own sake, but rather as "agents" within society that transform culture through responsible and dialogical engagement (and so yes, are also themselves transformed in the process), and as agencies of moral, spiritual, and social capital.

However, the early years of the twenty-first century have seen a retreat from this socio-cultural vision, and a collapse into congregational anxieties, often internally re-narrated (mistakenly) as "missional" or "evangelistic." The seeds of this situation have been gestating for several decades. In the Church of England, the current ascendency of neo-conservative Anglicanism has presided over a remarkable change in the "mental map" that the average Anglican carries around inside her or his head. It used to be a simple type of triptych: High, Middle, or Low. The High Church party had a distinctive theology, vocabulary, liturgical aesthetic—and even, for clergy, modes of dress. The Low Church party was just as easy to identify, yet quite different. And in the middle was the Broad Church—neither High nor Low, and capable of blending and infusing the best elements of either wing—it was passionately committed to holding the centerground.

The Broad Church was, at its best, a vehicle that conveyed generous, orthodox, inclusive Anglicanism. It was not Laodicean—a tepid compromise of warm, balmy Catholicism with the chilly climes of Calvinism. The Broad Church was simply warm—but also reflective, cool, and capacious. It was an embodiment of the faith in the church as an open, non-membership-based institution, in which "low-threshold entry" (e.g., open, inclusive baptism, wedding, or funeral policies) were normal. Such polity eschewed sectarianism, and sought, above all, to serve the *mass* of society. It was temperate and mild—and so perfectly suited to the pastoral climates it served. It was public.

The neo-conservative revolution of the last fifty years—the last three decades of the twentieth century, and the first two decades of the twenty-first century—have seen both the Higher (Anglo-Catholic) and Lower (Evangelical) wings of Anglicanism entirely out-narrate the middle ground (i.e., Broad Church), and rebrand it as "liberal." And, in turn, this has been followed swiftly by the term "liberal" being allotted a consistently negative value in ecclesial climes. For Catholic conservatives, and a handful of conservative Evangelicals, this began with Gender Wars (i.e., the debate on the ordination of women). The vast majority of clergy and laity who desired (and eventually voted for) women priests found themselves repositioned as "liberals." On sexuality, a gradual acceptance of lesbian and gay Christians, and an eventual (still growing) acceptance of same-sex marriages has also led to the Broad Church and middle ground being labelled, once again, negatively, as "liberal."

What is intriguing in all of this is that this Broad Church element within Anglicanism merely holds sensible views on gender, and progressive (note, not radical) views on sexuality. The Broad Church, such as it is, tends to be entirely orthodox on creeds, doctrines (e.g., the physical resurrection of Jesus), articles of faith, liturgical proclivities, church polity, Christian practice, and canon law. They practice what I call "generous orthodoxy". These Broad Church elements within Anglicanism tend to be, if anything, theologically orthodox. And they view the High and Low elements of the church as rather more sectarian—and inclined toward "membership-speak"—than the more inclusive, "public" ministry that they would seek to embody and practice.

The shift from High-Middle-Low to a much cruder Liberal-Conservative dialectic has been one of the ecclesial great confidence tricks of the last fifty years within Anglican polity. But like all such tricks, it had a purpose. It has been an attempt to persuade people who inhabit the wings (whether high or low, catholic or evangelical) that the *true church* and *real faith* is only to be found in their own more intense, sectarian expression that they represent. And that the middle-ground—which is largely where the population as whole resides, with their innate spiritual proclivities—are in fact starved of "real" religion and faith, and now need evangelizing or catechizing. Indeed, secularization, and the failure of evangelization or catechization, is often (still) blamed on the centerground of the Broad Church.

The Dutch ecclesiologist Mady Thung, in her prescient and prophetic book *The Precarious Organisation: Sociological Explorations of the Church's Mission and Structure* (The Hague, the Netherlands: Mouton & Co., 1976), suggests that national churches in northern Europe have come under increasing pressure in the post-war years to become "organizations"—"nervous activity and hectic programmes . . . constantly try(ing) to engage" members in an attempt to reach "non-members." She contrasts the "organizational" model and its frenetic activism with the "institutional" model of the church—the latter instead offering contemplative, aesthetic, and liturgical frameworks that take longer to grow and are often latent for significant periods of time, but which she argues may be more culturally resilient and conducive than those of the activist-organizational model. She concludes her book by suggesting that the model being adopted by many national churches—a kind of missional "organization-activist" approach—is what drives the population away. It leads, eventually, to sectarianism.

What we need now is a conversation about the Church of England, and for whom it is for? If it is for a small, depleting group of activist members, who simply want to go on perpetual recruitment drives, than it will be a kind of suburban sectarianism. But if there is another vision of the church—broader—this might significantly impact our public persona, and also our leadership. As Terry Eagleton notes, "religion is not effective because it is otherworldly, but because it incarnates this otherworldliness in a practical form of life . . . a link between absolute values and daily life" (T. Eagleton, *The Idea of Culture*, Oxford: Blackwell, 2000, p. 38).

In so doing, churches should be able to attend to whole areas of human experience and understanding that are normally neglected by society. But such a move requires a risk; namely, churches ceasing to operate as a private club for members, and instead to take their place as distinctive bodies of beliefs and practices that seek to serve their contexts.

Churches should not permit themselves to collapse into modes of practice or reflection that means they can be easily placed at the margins of culture. Churches need to engage in contemporary culture, thereby claiming their full citizenship as a member of the social contexts they seek to serve and shape. Spiritual particularity and public religion are not opposed. An ecclesiology rooted in incarnational engagement and wisdom can still sincerely seek to be empathetically participative within contemporary culture, and as a servant-leader, can still yet make a distinct contribution to our public life.

10

Response to Part II

"Savoring the Social-Sacred":
Reading the "Real Church"

Martyn Percy

H OW DO WE LEARN to discern the distinctiveness of faith communities, churches, congregations and denominations? One fertile notion that comes from the vocabulary of sommeliers might be helpful here. "Terroir" is a Gallic word for which there is no English-language equivalent.[1] The term refers to the combination of factors that might make one wine slightly different from another, even when they are geographically proximate in origin. Sunshine and temperature; north or south facing, and the amount of rainfall; the height of the land (and the drainage, the type and acidity of the soil); the types and subtypes of grape, and their progeny; local know-how and human skill; the amount of time permitted for a wine to mature, and the types of barrels chosen: all combine to make wines taste different.

This accounts for why one burgundy tastes quite different from another, even though they might be from the same village. And this analogy has something to teach theologians as they reflect on the composition of local ecclesial identity. On one level, one might say church is church, just as wine is wine. For some, there are only really four kinds of wine: red, white, rose and fizzy. Yet to the refined palate, the manifold differences are detectable and telling. So, like dividing the Christian world up into a fourfold typology—Catholic, Protestant, Orthodox and "other"—it can be done, but it serves little useful purpose for the deeper study of historical or contemporary Christianity. Scholarship always seeks to get beyond labels and categorizations: how the field is organized tells you a lot about the organizer, usually—but not that much about the field.

Thus, the ecclesial history and ethos of one given rural church might be composed through all manner of stories, buildings, forms of organization, ecclesial and

1. See Lyndon Shakespeare's earlier essay.

theological accents; and in an adjacent church, in an apparently similar context, turn out to be entirely different. And arguably, it is only through deep and patient immersion and reflection—the refining of the palate, in effect—that good ecclesial comprehension can be developed. Reading the church—discerning the social-sacred in any given context—requires experience, sampling, expertise, comparisons, and patience. And also instinct, too, coupled to a capacity to "richly word" what we taste and see, such that the aesthetics themselves receive appropriate aesthetic description, whether critical or affirmative. Just as some wines might be described as "nutty, with a hint of citrus," or "deeply flavored with intense notes of honey and berries," so are some churches "sour, with a dry, cerebral atmosphere"; "warm and mellow, with an informal-yet-smart feel"; or "sweet and light."

The "ecclesial terroir," in other words, is something that scholars need to be able to read sensitively and deeply if they are to understand the dynamics of congregational life. Moreover, if any scholar is reading and analyzing, say, several locally-clustered rural churches, their emerging singular organizational purpose will seldom disguise the fact that, although roughly proximate, each congregation will have a slightly different feel, flavor, history, and dialect. Rather, as in anthropological terms, neighboring tribes in a given place can feel and behave very different. Indeed, the surfacing and expression of such differences is what makes distinctive identity possible.

The essays from Richard Lawson, Gerard Mannion, and Lyndon Shakespeare focus on a common concern; namely, how to read the "real" church, as lived and encountered in the real world. This might, on one level, seem like a mundane task. After all, could there be any possible significance, worthy of our gaze and attention, to the ordinary business of church-going? The answer must be "yes." Anthropology—the study of human behavior, the practice of everyday life, social bonding and organization, community and civic life, ritual and symbol—can help point us to other frames of reference that may be rooted in notions of the sacred or transcendent. The ordinary material of humanity—shared moods and emotions, the sacred and profane, virtues and vices, pollution and taboo, purity and defilement, how dead bodies are treated, how the bereaved are cared for, what groups do with humor—these are the concerns of those who study the church or congregation, as much as with any tribe or society.

This is all fairly logical, if one steps back and gazes at the field of study the church provides. The data is overwhelming: human interaction, aesthetics, performance, ritual, symbol, culture, ascription—to say nothing of power, authority, and charisma. And we have not even mentioned doctrine in this list. To study the church is to encounter the phenomenon of the "ethnographic dazzle": sights, sounds, taste, touch—a veritable sensory overload of the social-sacred. So "reading" the church faithfully and analogically can be an important way forward for us here. This agenda has been a constant concern in my ecclesiological explorations, and the four brief book reviews and commentary (see chapter 8) all coalesce around a common desire: to understand the church within the context of contemporary culture.

Because churches are essentially "households of faith," in that telling biblical phrase (Gal 6:10) adopted by James Hopewell,[2] the making of homes is a profound analogical and literal reference to the function of faith. Making safe spaces of nourishment, well-being, maturity, diversity, and individuation. Our "faith homes" (or households—*oikos*) are places both of open hospitality and security. Yet churches rarely, self-consciously, understand and process their identity in this way. Indeed, much of what they offer is implicit rather than explicit; latent, rather than manifest; and rather than being formal and expressive in terms of their inner life, churches tend more toward being customary and relaxed. Indeed, there is a lot invested in what we might term "ecclesial obliquity"—with obliquity here, according to John Kay, describing a simple process; namely, that of achieving complex objectives indirectly.[3]

Thus, through a simple ministry of "deep hanging out"[4] with the people we serve, attentiveness, hospitality, care, and celebration, ministers often do more good for the parishes, communities, and institutions they serve than they can ever know. This may simply be through the offering of some regular lunches, simple acts of visiting, or open house for tea and coffee at any time. These are plannable events with manifest intentions. But the potency of the gestures and practices lies more in their latency, and is significant for ministry: namely, kindly presence and engagement, much as Jesus' ministry was simply walking from place to place.[5]

If my own work in the field of ecclesiology can sometimes appear to be eclectic, it is only because life itself is serendipitous. So what exactly are the forces, currents, practices, and ideas that shape the church? How does a congregation or a denomination understand its identity, on the one hand, in relation to the providence and revelation of God, and on the other, in relation to the context and culture in which ecclesial composition inexorably occurs? What is the relationship between the acknowledged propositional truths that order ecclesial identity, and the more hidden and mellifluous currents that might shape the life of the church? How do churches embrace and resist "secular" forms of organization that introduce metrics and modes of evaluation that, to some, are welcome in the cause of mission, but to others, alienating in terms of identity? One does not need to be a sociologist to understand that class, ethnicity, gender, age, and aesthetics all exercise powerful influences on the theological construction of reality that comprise ecclesial cosmologies. The late James Hopewell, in his modest yet prescient study of local ecclesiology, notes that,

> As slight and predictable as the language of a congregation might seem on casual inspection, it actually reflects a complex process of human imagination.

2. Hopewell, *Congregation*.

3. Kay, *Obliquity*.

4. A phrase purloined from Clifford Geertz, describing the work of the anthropologist. I concur. Much ecclesial research, like ministry, is pursued through "deep hanging out." But the minister and the researcher have quite different purposes, of course.

5. Percy, "Theological Education and Formation for an Uncommon Occupation," 232.

Each is a negotiation of metaphors, a field of tales and histories and meanings that identify its life, its world, and God. Word, gesture, and artefact form local language—a system of construable signs that Clifford Geertz, following Weber, calls a "web of significance." Even a plain church on a pale day catches one in a deep current of narrative interpretation and representation by which people give sense and order to their lives. Most of this creative stream is unconscious and involuntary, drawing in part upon images lodged long ago in the human struggle for meaning. Thus, a congregation is held together by much more than creeds, governing structures and programs. At a deeper level, it is implicated in the symbols and signals of the world, gathering and surrounding them in the congregation's own idiom.[6]

Here, Hopewell (following Clifford Geertz) is more than hinting at the implicit forces that shape ecclesial life. He is extending a rather novel invitation to theologians: to explore far more than the (set) propositional texts that churches appeal to in order to construct and justify their identity, and to consider the apparently benign and insignificant peripheries and artefacts of ecclesial life. Essentially, my own work in the field of ecclesiology is a series of responses to that invitation, namely to ponder the *implicit aspects of ecclesial life*, and thereby explore the composition of congregations and denominations in a new light.

In committing ourselves to reading the "real" church, therefore, we are embarking on something of a journey. On the one hand, it is examining the basic-but-nascent theological habits (e.g., language, culture, worship, practice, etc.) that more properly account for the daily life of churches, congregations, and denominations. On the other, it is guessing at the hidden meanings in structures and practices that, on the surface, appear to be benign and innocent. Fundamentally, the invitation to engage in the exploration of implicit theology is centered on the premise that not everything that shapes the church can be or is plainly expressed. There is something natural about the implicit too; premises rest on authorities or sources that are rarely surfaced or challenged. Credulity, and a degree of faith in any ecclesial body, depend, to some extent, on the implicit being present and yet unquestioned. Dress codes in any church, for example, even amongst the laity, carry and convey unspoken messages about the ethos of worship—the extent to which it is formal or informal, perhaps—that are seldom articulated. James Nieman offers an example of this in his essay, "Attending Locally":

Consider a dispute in a church council about how to conduct business. One group relishes long meetings with extensive discussions of details, while another group insists on brief meetings only as needed, trusting members to carry out assigned duties between times. Simply to reduce such a situation to questions of managerial style can completely miss the serious theological claims by each group about the nature of the church and the commitment to it. The former sees the church in terms of familiar associations, so that

6. Hopewell, *Congregation*, 11.

commitment requires shared time. The latter sees the church in terms of operations, so that commitment is shown by productivity. Deeper still, both groups *implicitly assert a view of God* through how they want to conduct church business. Failure to recognize this not only does violence to the situation but also subverts the chance for both groups to discern what is mutually at stake for them in being church.[7]

Correspondingly, when the concept of implicit theology is understood and valued as part of the heritage of Christianity, theology itself can be reconceived as commonplace—an everyday performance and practice (so yes, linguistic),[8] and not merely discipline reserved for a select few. Thus, Ellen Clark King's work[9] draws attention to the "natural" ways in which women speak about God on deprived working class estates in the northeast of England, demonstrating admirably the theological prescience of vernacular and lay spiritual language. So, central to any reading of the social-sacred is the recognition that practices shape beliefs and beliefs also shape practice. As Kathryn Tanner notes,

> religious beliefs are a form of culture, inextricably implicated in the material practices of daily social living on the part of those who hold them . . . in the concrete circumstances in which beliefs are lived . . . actions, attitudes, and interests are likely to be as much infiltrated and informed by the beliefs one holds as beliefs are to be influenced by actions, attitudes and interests.[10]

Here, doctrines are "dramatic scripts" which Christians perform and by which they are performed. Doctrines "provide a scripted code for the motions of a Christian's life in much the same way that broader cultural codes and linguistic patterns structure the self": "practices are what we become as we are set in motion in the space of doctrine."[11] In this sense, we are once again close to Lindbeck's theory of theology—its performative dimension as something that is "cultural-linguistic": it "gains power and meaning insofar as it is embodied in the total *gestalt* of community life and action."[12] There is the irony for the theologian, and for the church. For in gaining an understanding of how the world might imagine beliefs and practice to cohere, one begins to develop a deeper sense—that they may not, in fact, neatly mesh at all.

---

7. Nieman, "Attending Locally," 202, emphasis added.

8. Lindbeck, *The Nature of Doctrine*.

9. Clark-King, *Theology By Heart*.

10. Tanner, *Theories of Culture*, 9.

11. Volf and Bass, *Practicing Theology*, 75.

12. Lindbeck, *The Nature of Doctrine*, 36.

Bibliography

Clark-King, Ellen. *Theology By Heart: Women, the Church and God.* Peterborough, UK: Epworth, 2004.

Hopewell, James. *Congregation: Stories and Strictures.* London: SCM, 1987.

Kay, John. *Obliquity.* London: Profile, 2011.

Lindbeck, George. *The Nature of Doctrine: Religion and Theology in a Postliberal Age.* London: SPCK, 1984.

Nieman, James. "Attending Locally: Theologies in Congregations." *International Journal of Practical Theology* 6:2 (2002) 198–252.

Percy, Martyn. "Theological Education and Formation for an Uncommon Occupation." In *Contemporary Issues in the Worldwide Anglican Communion: Powers and Pieties*, edited by Abby Day, 229–44. Farnham, UK: Ashgate, 2016.

Tanner, Kathryn. *Theories of Culture: A New Agenda for Theology.* Minneapolis, MN: Fortress, 1997.

Volf, Miroslav, and Dorothy C. Bass. *Practicing Theology: Beliefs and Practices in the Church.* Grand Rapids, MI: Eerdmans, 2002.

Part III

Applications

11

"Secondary Indicators of Emphasis"

Sexuality and Gender in Martyn Percy's Writings

KATHRYN D. BLANCHARD

I'M NOT SURE WHETHER it is true that the Anglican Communion's "public mission and ministry is perpetually blighted" by fights over sex, but it is not difficult to believe that Anglicans are as "dog-tired of debating sex and sexuality" as are Christians in other denominations.[1] The exhaustion among Christians comes from talking past each other completely; those who fight for full acceptance of multiple sexualities and those who fight for traditional heterosexual norms have retrenched into almost entirely separate conversations, each calling the other "shrill" when they dare to make an impassioned argument. "Inclusive has come to mean liberal and progressive," writes Percy, bemoaning this state of affairs; "exclusive has come to mean conservative and traditionalist; and orthodoxy [is] now claimed by all. So there is no escaping the need for some serious theological work in moving the Communion forward."[2]

The serious theological work Percy would like to see is the type that would allow for the full inclusion of LGBTQ+ Christians in the life of the Anglican Church, without sending the church into schism. While this is a worthy goal, it is unclear whether Percy himself offers the kind of sustained argument that might help convert the hearts and minds of his opponents. To be sure, he discusses many topics that might, if deeply explored, open up new paths through the fighting. He calls the church, for example, to a radical inclusivity that expresses "nothing less than the mad, passionate, all-embracing, far-reaching love of God."[3] For the most part, however, he avoids the non-negotiable concerns that more traditional Christians hold most dear, thus making it likely that his arguments will fall on deaf ears, except among those who already agree with him. The non-negotiables for evangelicals and traditional-

1. Percy, "Sex, Sense and Non-Sense for Anglicans," 1.
2. Percy, "Sexuality and the Citizenship of Heaven," 4.
3. Percy, "Generous Liberalism," 261.

ists are generally threefold and work in a particular order. Scripture comes first and foremost, and it forbids same-sex intercourse in no uncertain terms; there simply is no persuasive textual or historical evidence suggesting that any biblical author or editor wanted to leave room for women to have sex with women, or men to have sex with men.[4] Tradition takes a close second place in their arguments; Christian tradition has always, until very recently, approved of sex only in monogamous, heterosexual marriage (and that was itself a concession; early church fathers questioned the need for sex at all). Finally, when scripture and tradition fail, a third argument often comes into play: nature. Sometimes paired with heterosexual experience of "instinct" and a bit of Genesis chapter 2 thrown in for good measure, "nature" is said to declare that sex is primarily, if not exclusively, for procreation, and therefore only makes sense between a married woman and man.

Any serious theological work in arguments over gender and sexuality must then engage such arguments head-on, but instead of engaging, Martyn Percy seems to walk through the midst of them.[5] He highlights the importance of the "quadrilateral" of sources that shape Anglican theology: "The fourfold relationship between scripture, tradition, reason and experience (or culture) is sacred to the ecology of Anglican identity."[6] And he notes that a preference for each piece corresponds to certain factions: evangelicals, catholics, liberals, and charismatics respectively.[7] But rather than tackle these aspects individually, he takes refuge in the quadrilateral as a whole, which he finds pleasantly liberal in its leanings because it, "by definition, invites a plurality of belief, interpretation and response."[8] Dr. Percy's embrace of the social sciences means that reason and experience (or, as he says, culture) take precedence in his argumentation, while Anglican tolerance is the tradition he loves best.[9]

In what follows, I offer an overview of Martyn Percy's arguments on sexuality while also noting opportunities for future theological engagement with his opponents—if he cares to engage. In general, his arguments in favor of Christian sexual inclusion tend to rely on what he considers common-sense arguments (reason), the history of Anglicans' unwillingness to break up over matters of marginal importance like sex (tradition), and a theology of Jesus as a model of all-inclusive love (scripture).

---

4. Scholars may and do argue this point (see for example Rogers's Barthian account, *Sexuality and the Christian Body* or Farley's Roman Catholic account, *Just Love*), but not in any way that is yet persuasive to those of a literalist bent.

5. In Monique Ingalls's chapter in this volume, she suggests that Percy points toward engagement and provides space for it as a patron of sorts, while ultimately leaving it to others to determine the specifics of any engagement.

6. Percy, *Power and the Church*, 125.

7. Ibid., 175.

8. Ibid., 176.

9. See Ian Markham's article in this volume on Percy's socio-scientific methodology as "contextual" and anti-systematic.

Reason and Experience, Nature and Culture

Percy's arguments in favor of sexual inclusion often rely on reason, which might be grouped together with experience. In his short piece, "Sex, Sense and Non-Sense for Anglicans," as well as elsewhere, the main reason he gives for full acceptance of LGBTQ+ persons in the Anglican Communion is not strictly theological but legislative: discrimination against "lesbian, gay and bisexual people . . . runs contrary to the spirit of the 2010 Equality Act in the UK."[10] Moreover, "a massive majority in the House of Commons, the House of Lords and in wider society, are in favour of affirming the love and desires of those seeking lifelong legal union for same-sex couples."[11] English people—especially the younger ones—want inclusion, so the Church of England should reflect this. "A theologically conservative church is not an attractive proposition to the emerging generation," he says; "A non-inclusive church is an evangelistic dead-duck."[12] In other words, the Church of England is *of England* and should mirror the society in which it dwells (as opposed to some other society, such as Nigeria, that discriminates based on sexual orientation).

Percy also appeals to what he sees as a common-sense reading of the natural world. LGBTQ+ people are so common as to be considered "'natural' and 'normal';" moreover, they are analogous to other mammals like "apes and llamas" who engage in same-sex activities, and are "therefore part of God's created order."[13] As a persistent minority, the presence of people with non-traditional sexualities is simply a fact of life: "lesbian, gay and bisexual Christians are now an inescapable part of the Anglican Communion," so we might as well trust God's created order and incorporate rather than exclude them.[14]

He insists that it is only a small number of "traditionalists and conservatives" who reject equality and that, as a minority, they should not hold the entire Anglican Communion hostage to their narrow view.[15] Bracketing the question of who has better data, any such appeals will fail to persuade those who see Christian discipleship as a call to be strange or distinctive. As Percy himself notes in other works, following Jesus may make the church very unpopular; it is "a costly calling, involving self-denial,

10. Percy, "Sex, Sense and Non-Sense," 2.

11. Percy, "Generous Liberalism," 2.

12. Percy, "Sex, Sense and Non-Sense," 6–7. He reiterates this elsewhere: "attitudes among church-goers have now shifted significantly towards a more liberal and tolerant mindset;" and the churches actions against LGBT+ equality "merely looks like petty discrimination to the wider world," which has "turned its face towards justice, integrity and equality" (Percy, "I am Spartacus," 5). And, "I fear for a generation of lost youth who do not understand, or no longer believe in, a church that clearly practices discrimination" (Percy, "Sexuality and the Citizenship of Heaven," 2).

13. Percy, "Sex, Sense and Non-Sense," 5.

14. Ibid., 8.

15. He offers a study to back up the claim that liberals have numbers on their side, over against the "myth" that churches in the global south are growing while churches in the secularizing north are shrinking (ibid., 3–4).

depletion and death" and "may not lead us to any numerical growth."[16] This, of course, is precisely what his opponents will say about why they must hold fast to traditional sexual mores in the face of (what they see as) libertinism. "If all leaders must now make obeisance before the altar of numerical church growth," they might quip, "we will erode our character and mute our mission."[17]

Theology in the twenty-first century must grapple with many varieties of "reason" in the human universe, none of which can easily claim to be the right one, any more than there is one tradition or interpretation of scripture. The style of reason that Percy prizes most is that of liberal, tolerant, and conflict-averse British folk, rather than that of schismatic purists, those with "post-colonial guilt," or the less-than "highly advanced" in the developing world.[18] Percy's variety of reason takes it as a given that a "good relationship" is anything that is "mutual and open to the other(s)," while "some relationships are invariably wrong: those that are abusive, selfish and exploitative."[19] While this makes sense among moderns steeped in the doctrines of choice and consent, it will not seem as plainly reasonable to those who place greater stock in ancient revealed tradition. The gospel, after all, is promised to appear as foolishness before the wisdom of this world.

It is thus difficult to imagine any evangelical purists being swayed by Percy's "reasonable" approach to LGBTQ+ inclusion. They are likely to read it instead as a facile, "everybody's doing it" argument, designed either to bully conservatives into submission or sweep disagreements under the rug. Appeals to nature won't help either; even if scientists could prove that being LGBTQ+ is genetic, traditionalists will simply remind us that all creation is fallen and must still be subject to scripture (and traditional interpretations thereof). As people who worship a crucified criminal, in a church seeded by the blood of martyrs, Christians who want to take an unpopular stand have ample precedent. Worldly reason is simply not up to the task of uniting Christians on divisive matters.[20]

Scripture

Scripture takes first place among evangelicals, conservatives, and traditionalists, and the New Testament is at least somewhat essential to what makes Christians distinctively "Christian." Percy believes scripture is important, but he argues it must be read

16. Percy, "It's Not Just About the Numbers."

17. Percy, "Growth and Management," 261.

18. South Africans, he thinks, are "highly advanced" and should serve as an example to Nigerians, or serve at least to assuage the post-colonial guilt of the English (Percy, "Sex, Sense and Non-Sense," 10).

19. Percy, *Ecclesial Canopy*, 97.

20. See Shakespeare's article in this volume, "The Prudent Priest," about potential risks of using secular reason as leverage in Christian arguments.

"intelligently, and with compassion" so as to relativize it in changing times.[21] He notes, for example, that even Bible-thumpers don't hold fast to all of scriptures tastes and taboos: "There will be few candidates today, even amongst the most ardent of Bible-believing communities, to rise up and condemn mortgages, wearing clothes of mixed weave or the eating of black pudding, all of which are condemned in scripture."[22] It would seem to follow analogically that sexual differences may be easily accommodated, either because sexuality is a matter of roughly equal importance as eating, or because the Bible simply has nothing useful to say about it. "Concepts of revelation are ill-equipped to cope with what we know about sexual orientation," he writes elsewhere; "Serious theology in the presence of sexuality prevents the Church from being 'holier than thou,' and from becoming too fond of its own imagined purity."[23] But if the Bible provides no apparent specifics about holiness, evangelical critics are bound to wonder if Percy thinks anything goes when it comes to sex.

It's not that Percy rejects the Bible—he does want it to "speak afresh to issues of sexuality"[24]—but his canon-within-the-canon is quite small. The textual examples he offers are few and not always fleshed out or deeply investigated. Galatians 3:28 shows up in several articles as a kind of shorthand, either by name or implication, for Christian inclusivity: e.g., "The gospel of Christ is radically inclusive: Jew, Greek, Gentile , slave, free—all shall be welcome in the Kingdom of God. . . . All are equal. Class, race, gender and age are all transcended."[25] While this has clear implications for women's ordination, he does not thoroughly make the connection to sexual orientation or marriage equality, which opponents will be quick to define as a "sin" rather than merely a race or social status. Another oft-repeated passage is "thy kingdom come . . . on earth as it is in heaven," a passage that backs up his conviction that, "Lesbian, gay and bisexual Christians will not suffer discrimination in heaven" but will enjoy "equal citizenship."[26] This angle has potential, but he again neglects to spell out whether, if there is to be no exclusion whatsoever, the church needs a sexual ethic of any kind.

His strongest arguments—at least for purposes of preaching *outside* the choir—emerge when he dips his toe into more sustained biblical exegesis. These passages are also perhaps the best examples of the kind of "inspiring" theological teaching and leadership he craves. He interprets, for example, the story in Mark about Jesus' paired healings of Jairus's twelve-year-old daughter and the woman with a twelve-year-long hemorrhage. In this story, Jesus "acts as an alternative boundary keeper in a way that

21. Percy, "Sex, Sense and Non-Sense," 8.

22. Percy, *Ecclesial Canopy*, 91.

23. Percy, "After Lambeth—Where Next?", 175.

24. Percy, *Intimate Affairs*, 2.

25. Percy, "I am Spartacus," 3. See also Percy, "Sexuality and the Citizenship of Heaven," 5.

26. Percy, "Sexuality and the Citizenship of Heaven," 8. He further accuses of "semi-Pelagianism" those who would imply that gay and lesbian Christians cannot get into heaven without maintaining lifelong celibacy.

is religiously and ritually subversive to the customs of society. Jesus disrupts and undermines the social order that declares such people outcasts."[27] If one is reading the Bible "intelligently and with compassion," one cannot fail to make the connection to LGBTQ+ Christians who dare to touch the hem of Jesus' garment, though crowds of church people would conspire to keep them away.

Within scripture, he has a special fondness for parables, which are "inherently liberal,"[28] and many of which "get right under the skin of the *real motivation* for being part of the Church, and following Jesus."[29] For Percy, inclusivity is the whole point. The parables of Jesus consistently question the idea that heaven is only for the good; instead, the kingdom of God favors the unworthy—the prodigal son (or the prodigal father, as the case may be[30]), the late-comers in the vineyard, the weeds among the tares. Jesus treats them all as equal, or even preferable, to the ritually pure. "God is loving enough to tell us lots of counter-cultural stories about numbers: going after one, and leaving the ninety-nine, for example."[31] Moreover, these stories will grate on people who imagine themselves to be good, because God's "magnanimous generosity comes at a price, paid by others."[32] It is not only Jesus who bears the cost of God's love of the unworthy; anyone who is "worthy" may also end up subsidizing those who are less worthy. While I am not certain LGBTQ+ Christians will appreciate being analogized to the unworthy characters in the gospels, Percy's appeal to New Testament parables represents the beginnings of a *distinctively Christian* sexual ethic that might help foster fruitful dialogue among Christians, conservative and liberal.

One important scripture passage I did not come across in Percy's writings—notable for its absence because it usually represents the heart of the conservative argument—is the creation story in Genesis 2. Adam's ecstatic song about "bone of my bone and flesh of my flesh," and the narrator's commentary about a man euphemistically "cleaving" to his wife and becoming "one flesh," are usually taken by traditionalists as proof that heterosexuality and procreation are the "natural," as well as revealed, order of creation. Other favorite passages come from the New Testament epistles (e.g., Rom 1; 1 Cor 6; 1 Tim 1). If Percy's goal were seriously to engage and counteract anti-LGBTQ+ sentiment, he would need to tackle his opponents' canonical texts.

Strangely, though, Percy appeals instead to "the true non-sense of poetry."[33] Such a choice seems to indicate some reluctance or even unwillingness to speak directly to his opponents, who crave nothing more than biblical debate. As one critic writes,

27. Percy, "I am Spartacus," 8.

28. Percy, "Generous Liberalism," 259.

29. Percy, "Wheat and tares and labourers in vineyards," 2. Emphasis added.

30. Percy, "Generous Liberalism," 261.

31. Percy, "Growth and Management," 260.

32. Percy, "Generous Liberalism," 264.

33. Ibid., 14. See also Richard Lawson's article in this volume about "sketches" and "symbols" in Percy's theology.

"Martyn Percy has given us an approach to thinking about the future of Anglicanism that does not start from scripture and which does not hang together as an argument."[34] Another notes that his "attempt to address scripture is really disappointing, as it shows that he does not seem to be interested in this crucial aspect of the debate."[35] If Percy wishes to persuade anyone of the importance of sexual inclusivity in the church, he will need to deal with scripture more robustly, even more systematically.

Tradition

Unlike scripture, the Anglican tradition is a matter upon which Percy speaks frequently and even somewhat vehemently. He writes that the Church of England "has never considered itself to be a sect or denomination originating in the sixteenth century. It considers itself to be both catholic and reformed, and with no special doctrines of its own."[36] But where conservatives discussing sexual questions might stress explicitly *sexual* Anglican teachings (usually excerpted from scripture), Percy stresses instead the Anglican tradition of *putting up with supposedly minor disagreements for the sake of unity.* Sexual morals, he argues, are not part of the "substance of faith that ultimately unites Anglicans;" what really matters are "the creeds, doctrine and the essentials of the faith."[37] However unpleasant it might be to disagree, Anglicans must agree to do so; when it comes to non-essentials it is "patience, forbearance, catholicity, moderation—and a genuine love for the reticulate blend of diversity and unity that forms so much of the richness for Anglican life."[38]

For example, on the matter of women bishops he wrote in 2012, "The Church lives constantly in the tension between patience and faithful reform," always looking for the sweet spot between holding fast to Christianity's "given nature" while also adapting, with the help of the Holy Spirit, to the tastes and values of each new generation.[39] This tension in Anglican life is, according to Percy, an inescapable part of its identity; the church must always focus on "maintaining religion as something that is public, accessible and extensive, whilst also being distinct, intensive, and mysterious."[40] The very resilience of the Anglican tradition comes from its combination of "resistance and accommodation," from being both practical and prophetic.[41] But while "revolutionary

34. Davie, "I Wouldn't Start From Here."

35. Symes, "Martyn Percy on Sex and the Anglican Communion."

36. Percy, *Ecclesial Canopy*, 132.

37. Percy, "Sex, Sense and Non-Sense," 9.

38. Percy, *Ecclesial Canopy*, 134.

39. Percy, "Women Bishops."

40. Percy, *Why Liberal Churches Are Growing*, 3.

41. Percy, *Salt of the Earth*, 57.

patience"[42]—or "agreeable disagreement" or "radical reasonableness"[43] or "tense diversity"[44] or "bold hesitancy"[45]—are opportunities for learning, Percy admits they cannot last forever; there eventually comes a time when "pointless waiting is merely prevarication posturing as discernment."[46] In the case of women's ordination, for example, he believes the past century represents quite enough waiting. Some Anglicans "will never change their minds, and it is because of this that the duty of our Church leaders not to be too patient now comes more sharply into focus."[47]

At the same time, though, he is fiercely opposed to those who would break away from the Anglican Communion over non-essential matters. He suggests that "gender, sexuality and polity" are "secondary indicators of emphasis" that do not demand agreement; they should rather be "subjugated" to the most important thing: unity. "The right to express and practise particularity is too often preferred to the self-imposed restraint that is hinted at by a deeper catholicity;" it doesn't work for the "branches" to try to "define the vine."[48] In other words, for a congregation or diocese to break away over, or act unilaterally on, matters as "secondary" as women's ordination or same-sex marriage, is an inexcusable offense against the spirit of Anglicanism.[49] He accuses the See of New Hampshire, for example, of "impatience and intolerance" in its election of Gene Robinson, a gay bishop; it is "an example of one small Episcopalian diocese asserting its individualism; and cloaking that decision in the rhetoric of progression, justice and inalienable rights" while displaying a "lack of regard for a wider catholicity, and the attendant responsibility this carries."[50]

It is unclear when or whether Percy might find it appropriate to stop prevaricating and simply do what one feels called to do. For him Anglicanism seems to be, above all else, a cleaving to a community of "mild"[51] tradition—"like the English weather itself"—whose center of gravity happens to be in England, rather than in Rome or in the local congregation. It "is about *these* people, at *this* time under *these* conditions."[52] The church "exists to glorify God and follow Jesus Christ";[53] it "lives to communicate

42. Percy, "Growth and Management," 268.

43. See Simon Coleman's article in this volume on Percy's "radically reasonable" approach.

44. Percy, *Shaping the Church*, 174.

45. Percy, "Generous Liberalism," 271.

46. Percy, "Women Bishops," 2.

47. Ibid., 3.

48. Percy, "After Lambeth," 184.

49. "There seems to be little understanding that an unfettered claim to act freely can actually become anti-social, or even unethical. Great freedom comes with great responsibility" (ibid., 184). He calls churches "to act with restraint, with provinces thinking more about the 'catholic' implications of their preferred local practice" (ibid., 185).

50. Percy, *Shaping the Church*, 171.

51. Percy, *Salt of the Earth*, 374.

52. Percy, "Growth and Management," 259, emphasis original.

53. Ibid., 258.

the love of God" and to "re-tell the oldest story of all."[54] It is not, he thinks, worth splitting up over matters of sexuality.

Although these supposedly secondary matters around sexuality have been the topic of a good deal of discussion over the years, I did not find any writings in which Percy addressed the sexual teachings of the Anglican Church directly. This seems a missed opportunity, especially since these teachings have not changed significantly since the late days of the Roman Empire. In its official documents, the Anglican Communion has affirmed repeatedly (and was generally unified in this until recently) that its sexual ethics come from scripture as interpreted by early church fathers. In 1930 the Lambeth Conference reaffirmed that "marriage is a life-long and indissoluble union, for better or worse, of one man with one woman, to the exclusion of all others"; that parenthood is "the glory of married life" and "the primary purpose for which marriage exists"; and that intercourse additionally, almost as a side benefit, "enhances" marital love.[55] Sex before or outside of heterosexual marriage, meanwhile, is "a grievous sin" because "illicit and irregular unions . . . offend against the true nature of love, they compromise the future happiness of married life, they are antagonistic to the welfare of the community, and, above all, they are contrary to the revealed will of God."[56] These are strong objections to more modern understandings of good sex that revolve around consent, mutuality, and personal responsibility. Perhaps a better place to begin would be with Paul's affirmation that "it is better to marry than to burn" (1 Cor 7:8–9), or with the bishops' own statement about marriage as training ground: "Without the practice and disciplines of marriage, our love will be exhausted and fail us, perhaps very harmfully to ourselves and others. When publicly and lawfully we enter into marriage, we commit ourselves to live and grow together in this love."[57] Surely the discipline of marriage—if discipline is the point—is worthwhile for all people, not only those of apparently different genders.

For those who, like Percy, would generally rather avoid quibbling about sex and gender, there is the elegantly simple approach taken by Rowan Williams: baptism. "The most substantial argument for the ordination of women," he writes, "is the simple one that connects with baptism. If women cannot be ordained, then baptised women relate differently to Jesus from baptized men—not a doctrine easily reconcilable with the New Testament."[58] To be baptized is to receive "the gift of being in Christ, speaking with Christ, acting for Christ, as a community representing the new creation."[59] This

---

54. Percy, Review of *Media Portrayals of Religion and the Secular Sacred*, *Modern Believing*.

55. *The Lambeth Conference: Resolutions Archive from 1930*, http://www.anglicancommunion.org/media/127734/1930.pdf (Resolutions 11, 14, and 13, respectively).

56. Lambeth Conference, "The Life and Witness of the Christian Community—Marriage," (Resolutions 18 and 9, respectively), 1930. Online: www.anglicancommunion.org/resources/document-library/lambeth-conference/1930/.

57. Church of England Archbishops' Council, "Marriage: A Teaching Document."

58. Williams, "Epilogue," 213.

59. Ibid., 214.

argument may easily be extended to LGBTQ+ Christians. However, it will again fail to persuade those who see same-sex intercourse as inherently sinful. (All of us are sinful, they will say, but "by no means" does baptism mean that we are to embrace and celebrate our sins.) Thus, while the irenic approach Percy and Williams demonstrate has admirable intentions, I fear there is no avoiding head-on conflict, and even church break-ups, for those who are serious about developing a thoroughly *Christian* sexual ethic. For those now being excluded from the church's marriage rites, it is a serious and urgent issue indeed.

Can an Anglican Dean Be Radically Christian?

I deeply appreciate Dr. Percy's desire to err on the side of vulnerability and inclusion. He nods to others' fears of libertinism when he acknowledges, "this 'blueprint' for a new sexual revolution is a risky strategy: the world can abuse a Church that is too open in its morality, as much as it can ignore one that is too closed."[60] Not being Anglican and having been trained to think of "church" as an alternate culture that exists in opposition to "the world," I also find it refreshing that Percy embraces the Church of England's mission to be *of England*—an unabashedly national church that exists for all people, holding the truth in trust rather than rationing it out stingily to the few who think they've earned it. "God's love is broader and deeper than anything we can conceive of," he writes, "And so we offer a church for all, because God's kingdom is for all."[61] I likewise share his dismay at the fact that so many church people seem to view the church as "God's Immigration Control or Border Police," in charge of keeping people out, "when all we have been asked to do is issue invitations and open the frontiers."[62]

At the same time, I can't help but find a bit of irony in his musings, coming as they do from someone who has doubtless jumped through multiple hoops to achieve a prominent position of authority in the church. What is an institutional church, after all, if not the representative border of God's kingdom? What is baptism if not an entry ticket? What is ordination but a rationing of the license to baptize into the Anglican Communion? It is difficult (at least for this non-Anglican American) to see how a commitment to the Anglican tradition can square with a desire for radical openness and vulnerability. If God's love is so entirely indiscriminate, what is the need for any kind of official, institutional, bureaucratic "church" at all? Why not go back to informal house churches with no central authority? Percy seems to detest the idea that Christian bodies should try "to return to a kind of (mythic) primitive and intimate fellowship that, it is held, the New Testament primarily advocates as the 'model' for

60. Percy, "The Graduate," 20. He further writes, "the new sexual freedom brings responsibility, which is not always handled well by individuals or society," (ibid., 14).

61. Percy, "Wheat and Tares," 4.

62. Ibid., 3.

the church,"[63] but wasn't this pre-institutional model precisely when the church was most radically open?

Dr. Percy's reluctance to engage in debate over sexual ethics may be a matter of priority: his is to keep the Anglican Communion together, and connected to England as a nation and a culture. "God," he says, "may be speaking to the church through society" when society (in this case the United Kingdom) is more tolerant than the church.[64] He does not see this as a compromise with secularism, as most evangelicals and conservatives would; on the contrary, he argues that British-style liberalism *is* the church's true nature—though the church has forgotten. "Liberalism has deep and profound roots in progressive, orthodox Christianity, which are found in the teachings of Jesus and his disciples—equality, justice and liberation being just some of the values that the early church embodied, and sought to extend to wider society."[65] Percy, as dean, is trying to build the largest possible tent, even if it pushes disgruntled conservative factions to the margins.

I cannot help thinking that a vision of easy tolerance, while winsome, is the special privilege of those who find themselves in the comfortable center of the tent. I am not sure whether Christians who feel excluded—whether women, LGBTQ+, evangelicals, or Nigerians—can afford to be so patient. Such groups may have good reason to feel that the Anglican Communion has had more than enough time to bring them into the fold. They do not wish to be merely tolerated but *celebrated*, in the same way that married English men have always seen themselves celebrated in the church. It is a luxury to be casual about things that some find deeply offensive. Anglicans in Sydney, Percy notes, "don't have much time for women; and no time at all for women priests,"[66] but rather than expel them from the Anglican Communion, these Sydney congregations "are catered for; even permitted to self-cater . . . no-one is asked to dine elsewhere, so to speak."[67] Is not this tolerance a slap in the face of Anglican women? Likewise, the idea that some churches should be allowed to discriminate against gay and lesbian Christians without consequence is a stumbling block; why is their full personhood not "essential" to Anglican tradition? Why should the church make "reasonable allowance" for misogyny or heteronormativity, any more than it should have made allowance for slavery?[68] Why not simply say good riddance?

63. Percy, *Shaping the Church*, 70. Reiterated in "Old Tricks For New Dogs?," 28.

64. Percy, *Intimate Affairs*, 104.

65. Percy, "I am Spartacus," 6. In *Why Liberal Churches Are Growing*, Percy makes another implicit reference to Galatians 3:28: "from the very beginning of Christianity, its assemblies were radically inclusive;" the Jewish men who normally worshipped alone found themselves with women and children, gentiles and slaves in their midst (ibid., 9).

66. Ibid., 10.

67. Ibid., 3.

68. "Some of the more catholic-inclined clergy and congregations already exercise their liberty of conscience on women priests and women bishops. They've opted out, and reasonable (some would say overly generous) provision is made for them" (ibid., 3).

In the end, despite his personal position of tolerance, it is difficult to discern whether Percy cares as dogmatically about sexual justice as he does about keeping the church together. "It does seem as though indelible Anglican habits such as toleration, diversity and debate have been challenged in late modernity," he writes; "Assertion and confrontation play a much bigger role in the Church of England's polity, and opposing views that used to coexist in flux and harmony now seem to harden positions and alienate the very concept of being in communion."[69] While certainly togetherness is much to be desired, if he genuinely wishes to see Anglicans develop a more progressive sexual theology, he will need to join the fray in earnest. This means, at the very least, calling out flawed theological reasoning, bad biblical exegesis, or poor understanding of Anglican tradition. If he goes further, it might mean going on the offense, reclaiming scripture and tradition—the creation stories in Genesis, the words and parables of Jesus, and the letters of Paul. More radically, it might mean suffering persecution, starting with demotion.[70] To paraphrase Laurel Thatcher Ulrich, "Well behaved clergy seldom make history."

But this would go against Percy's desire to avoid schism. He sadly longs for a past when the Anglican Communion was marked by "patience, forbearance, catholicity, moderation—and a genuine love for the reticulate blend of diversity and unity that forms so much of the richness for Anglican Life."[71] It is fine, he says, to be "tense and unresolved," because this is the very stuff that catholicity is made of.[72] In echoes of Bishop Sadoleto's sixteenth-century letter to Geneva, Percy argues that without the traditional, institutional church, "all we'll have left is multi-choice spirituality, individualism and innovation."[73] He saves the strongest criticism for those who would divide the church over their pet demands: "Belonging together in a body with higher purposes places demands on individuals and groups, including those of duty and service: this is discipleship. Demand-led groups, in contrast, may just service people's desires for more meaning and fulfillment, whilst vesting this in the language of purpose, connection, and even sacrifice."[74]

69. Percy, *Power and the Church*, 164.

70. Some clergy have been willing to suffer for disagreeing with their denominations over sex. E.g., Villegas, "A Letter to MC USA Delegates."

71. Percy, "After Lambeth," 172.

72. Ibid., 174.

73. Percy, "Old Tricks for New Dogs," 39. In 1539 Sadoleto wrote, "For this the Catholic Church always labors, for this she strives, viz., our concord and unity in the same Spirit, that all men, however divided by space or time, and so incapable of coming together as one body, may yet be both cherished and ruled by one Spirit, who is always and everywhere the same. To this Catholic Church and Holy Spirit those, on the contrary, are professed adversaries who attempt to break unity, to introduce various spirits, to dissolve consent, and banish concord from the Christian religion, attempting this, with an eagerness and a zeal, by machinations and arts, which no language can sufficiently express" (Calvin and Sadoleto, "A Reformation Date," 41).

74. Percy, "Old Tricks for New Dogs," 31.

But again, it's easier for some of us to be disciplined and duty-bound than others. Those of us whose identity has been approved of by the church, century after century, can afford to be magnanimous. Those who have been historically, systematically disrespected—such as female would-be priests and bishops, or lay Christians seeking same-sex marriage in the church—may be ready to break out on their own. Likewise, those who feel marginalized by their faithfulness to ancient and medieval church traditions may also wish to break away. Of course—as in the sixteenth century—each side will undoubtedly hurl accusations of "schism" against the other, while claiming for their own part that they "can do no other."[75]

The fact remains that radical change, like radical love, is hard to come by. It would seem difficult for a church founded by a patriarchal king, who needed a patriarchal divorce for the sake of a patriarchal heir, to offer a radically inclusive gospel to people whose "secondary indicators of emphasis" exclude them from established tradition. Percy says himself that the "chance of a genuinely radical woman being appointed [as bishop] remains remote;" the church will continue to favor those who promise stability rather than prophetic critique.[76] Christian tradition bears layer after layer of patriarchy and heteronormativity that make it almost impossible to discern a "core" or "essence" of a gospel that is untainted by the assumption of heterosexual, male superiority—prodigal sons and fathers, vineyard owners, sinners casting the first stone. So while I concur with Percy that Jesus came for the good of *all* creation and not merely a select portion of it, I am much more skeptical than he about the ability of an institutionalized church to express that radical message consistently and persuasively. Even if the Church of England were only secondarily and not "essentially" hierarchical, the presence of hierarchy makes it much more difficult to *appear* to offer radically inclusive love—whether across divides of gender and sexuality, or of nationality, class, and ethnicity.

At a very important level, Martyn Percy's is a fearless theology. It is "governed by a passionate heart and a real empathy" with most people.[77] It does not seek to make sure that the church includes only the worthy. It isn't worried about free-riders getting away with things while the good folks do all the heavy lifting.[78] It isn't trying to protect its turf. It doesn't see anything to be gained from excluding anyone from its

75. In his "Letter," Sadoleto accused Calvin of leading Geneva into schism; Calvin's "Reply" retorted: "great the difference is between schism from the Church, and studying to correct the faults by which the Church herself was contaminated" (82–83). As for Luther, he might or might not have said to his inquisitors regarding why he was forced to depart from their doctrines, "Here I stand; I can do no other" (Kauffman, "What Luther Said").

76. "Growth and Management," 266. Also quoted in Woodhead, "Yes Vote For Women Bishops Challenges the Church of England to Embed Equality."

77. Percy, *Intimate Affairs*, 11. He writes, "the deliverance from fear is a highly desirable goal if Christian love is to be fostered," (ibid., 18).

78. See Joel Daniels's article in this volume, "Signs and Signals," about "low thresholds" and costly signaling theory.

conversation. This, indeed, may be the only reasonable response to the reality that the church cannot build an ideal world.[79]

And yet, this fearlessness may camouflage a different kind of fear—the fear of being *too* disagreeable. The fear of being shrill. The fear of making a mountain out of a molehill—of staking one's faith on, and disturbing the peace over, something that is of only secondary importance. This is a fear that women and people on the margins know all too well—always being told to calm down, to be patient, to wait just a little longer. Eventually they, too, may come to a place of fearlessness, but unlike Percy's it is the fearlessness of those with nothing left to lose. I would encourage a well-placed leader like Percy to engage the schismatics fearlessly, not only with tolerant love but also genuine and direct conversation—however unpleasant, un-mild, and un-English that conversation may get.

Bibliography

Calvin, John, and Jacopo Sadoleto. *A Reformation Debate*. Edited by John C. Olin. New York: Fordham, 1539.

Church of England Archbishops's Council. "Marriage: A Teaching Document." www.churchofengland.org/media/45645/marriage.pdf.

Davie, Martin. "I Wouldn't Start From Here—a Response to Martyn Percy." *Reflections of an Anglican Theologian*. https://mbarrattdavie.wordpress.com/2016/01/03/i-wouldnt-start-from-here-a-response-to-martyn-percy/.

Farley, Margaret. *Just Love*. New York: Continuum, 2006.

Kauffman, Elesha. "What Luther Said." *Christianity Today: Christian History*. http://www.christianitytoday.com/history/2008/august/what-luther-said.html.

The Lambeth Conference. "The Life and Witness of the Christian Community—Marriage." www.anglicancommunion.org/resources/document-library/lambeth-conference/1930/.

———. *Resolutions Archive from 1930*. London: Anglican Communion Office, 2005. http://www.anglicancommunion.org/media/127734/1930.pdf.

Percy, Martyn. "After Lambeth—Where Next?" In *Christ and Culture*, edited by Martyn Percy, Mark Chapman, Ian Markham, and Barney Hawkins, 183–93. London: Canterbury, 2010.

———. *The Ecclesial Canopy: Faith, Hope, Charity*. London: Routledge, 2012.

———. "Generous Liberalism." *Modern Believing* 56:3 (January 2015) 259–72.

———. "Growth and Management in the Church of England: Some Comments," *Modern Believing* 55:3 (2014) 257–70.

———. "I am Spartacus: Address to LGCM's 40th Birthday Service." *One Body One Faith*. http://www.lgcm.org.uk/news/i-am-spartacus-martyn-percys-address-to-lgcms-40th-birthday-service-may-2016/.

———. "It's Not Just About the Numbers." *Church Times*, February 28, 2014. https://www.churchtimes.co.uk/articles/2014/28-february/features/features/it-s-not-just-about-the-numbers.

---

79. See Gerard Mannion's chapter comparing Percy's humble and aspirational approach to that of Pope Francis I.

———. "Old Tricks For New Dogs? Evaluating Fresh Expressions." In *Evaluating Fresh Expressions,* edited by Louise Nelstrop and Martyn Percy, 27–39, 204–6. London: Canterbury, 2008.

———. *Power and the Church: Ecclesiology in an Age of Transition.* London: Continuum, 1998.

———. Review of *Media Portrayals of Religion and the Secular Sacred,* edited by Knott et al. *Modern Believing* 55:2 (2014) 179–82.

———. *The Salt of the Earth: Religious Resilience in a Secular Age.* London: Sheffield Academic Press, 2001.

———. "Sex, Sense and Non-Sense for Anglicans." *Modern Church* (December 2015). https://modernchurch.org.uk/downloads/send/32-articles/756-mpercy1215.

———. "Sexuality and the Citizenship of Heaven." *Modern Church* (January 2016). http://modernchurch.org.uk/january-2016/906-sexuality-and-the-citizenship-of-heaven.

———. *Shaping the Church: The Promise of Implicit Theology.* London: Ashgate, 2010.

———. "Wheat and Tares and Labourers in Vineyards." *Modern Church* (January 2016). http://modernchurch.org.uk/january-2016/909-wheat-and-tares-and-labourers-in-vineyards.

———. *Why Liberal Churches Are Growing.* London: T. & T. Clark, 2006.

———. "Women Bishops: a Failure of Leadership." *The Telegraph,* November 21, 2012. www.telegraph.co.uk/news/religion/9693284/women-bishops-a-failure-of-leadership.html.

Percy, Martyn, ed. *Intimate Affairs: Sexuality & Spirituality in Perspective.* London: Darton, Longman and Todd, 1997.

Rogers, Eugene F. *Sexuality and the Christian Body.* Malden, MA: Blackwell, 1999.

Symes, Andrew, "Martyn Percy on Sex and the Anglican Communion: 20 Holes in His Argument." *Anglican Mainstream.* anglicanmainstream.org/martyn-percy-on-sex-and-the-anglican-communion-20-holes-in-his-argument/.

Villegas, Isaac. "A Letter to MC USA Delegates." *The Mennonite.* https://themennonite.org/opinion/isaac-villegas-letter-mc-usa-delegates/.

Williams, Rowan. "Epilogue." In *Voices of This Calling: Experiences of the First Generation of Women Priests,* edited by Christina Rees. Norwich, UK: Canterbury, 2002.

Woodhead, Linda. "Yes Vote For Women Bishops Challenges the Church of England to Embed Equality." *The Conversation.* https://theconversation.com/yes-vote-for-women-bishops-challenges-the-church-of-england-to-embed-equality-29226.

12

Learning to Take Note

Martyn Percy's Engagement with Music and Worship

Monique M. Ingalls

W HAT DOES (OR SHOULD) the church *look* like? Theological and ecclesiological reflection has given us many images of the present and ideal church; when considering the church's past, present, and future shape, these reflections have provided a stock set of images—from salvific boats, to weed-ridden grain fields, to imposing edifices constructed on abandoned stones—for us to scroll through in our minds. Fewer theologians are asking, what does (or should) the church *sound* like? How might sound as a metaphor and music as an embodied social practice provide us with new perspectives on the church's life, health, and future?

Approaching these questions as an ethnomusicologist and fellow student of the contemporary church, I have found Martyn Percy to be one of the few contemporary theologians to address these questions by engaging with music and worship as social practices; that is, by exploring music-making as it is embedded within ecclesial contexts rather than abstracting it from them and treating it in isolation. Over the course of the twenty-plus years of musical and liturgical reflections, Martyn Percy has engaged music within worship as a theological statement, an ideological apparatus, a performative practice, and a formative metaphor. And, in both his writings on music and behind-the-scenes work, Percy has engaged in interdisciplinary dialogue with characteristic generosity, carving out a place for musicological insight within his own work and welcoming music studies[1] perspectives to the table of ecclesiological reflection.

This chapter addresses the place of both music and worship in Martyn Percy's thought, rather than focusing on one to the exclusion of the other. The strands of music and worship are often tightly interwoven; indeed, the majority of Percy's musical

---

1. Following Nicholas Cook, I use "music studies" here to refer to the overarching, interdisciplinary field that encompasses the disciplines of musicology, ethnomusicology, and music theory. Cook, "We're All Ethnomusicologists Now."

reflections are centered on music within the context of worship and as a means of shaping the church. While "church music" might at first seem a fitting category, Percy's work also examines styles including jazz, bossa nova, and eclectic musical fusions that fall outside this category. Many of Percy's reflections on non-liturgical music nonetheless have direct bearing on ecclesial and social matters. While treating the whole of Martyn Percy's work on worship and liturgy as beyond this chapter's scope, it proved difficult to discuss Percy's insights on music-making without taking into account the shaping role and function of the worship context. Though the formulation "music and worship" may seem unwieldy, I have chosen to treat these activities as separate yet interwoven themes in my analysis of Percy's work, demonstrating the myriad ways in which they overlap and yet remain distinct.

Implicit Theology and Contextual Engagement: Martyn Percy's Musical Method

Before discussing the central insights into music, worship, and the church that characterize Martyn Percy's work, it is instructive to highlight two aspects of his approach to music and worship. First, his approach is grounded in—and perhaps has also contributed to—his model of implicit theology as method for ecclesiological reflection. Music and worship form part of the "theological habits . . . that account for the daily life of churches, congregations, and denominations"; the task of implicit theology is "looking for hidden meanings in overlooked structures and practices" like these.[2] The goals of Percy's project dovetail with the growing ranks of social scientists who research their own cultural contexts: "making the familiar strange" by elevating commonplace practices often rendered invisible. Musical style and genres, sung lyrics, and sonic aesthetics are no longer regarded as "surface" concerns peripheral to doctrinal or creedal "substance." Rather, as elements that communicate and act upon the body, they are indispensable to processes of ecclesial formation and meaning-making. As Percy writes, "the type of music a congregation chooses, how it moves (or doesn't!) to that music, dress codes, manners, the moderation of the collective emotional temperature—all have a bearing on the emerging vision of God within each congregation and denomination."[3]

Second, Martyn Percy's approach to music is richly contextual. Percy considers various aspects of musical performance, including not only lyrics and sounds but also accompanying gestures, forms of musical mediation, and the "mood" or "atmosphere" established by the soundscape, within a given ecclesial and cultural context. Scholars of Christian congregational music-making have sometimes criticized theological engagement with music for its selective reading of certain textual or musical features in the abstract. Theological engagement with music sometimes addresses lyrics without

2. Percy, *Shaping the Church*, 2.

3. Percy, "Afterword: Theology and Music in Conversation," 218.

addressing musical elements or genre; when musical sound is examined, it is often rendered as a text to be read, rather than a performance to be observed, listened to, and felt within a given context. For Percy, music is not a raw material to be extracted from its ecclesial contexts and examined in abstraction; rather, it is one key component in a complex liturgical whole that comprises much more than the sum of its parts.

The Ecclesial Work of Music and Worship: Martyn Percy's Perspective on Socio-Musical Processes

What do music and worship *do* within the church? How is congregational music-making both meaningful and performative? In other words, how do sung utterances not only convey meaning, but actually affect what they say? Martyn Percy's work addresses these questions by describing the social functions of worship and the cultural and theological work that worship does, particularly within revivalist Christian groups and contemporary Anglicanism. Emerging from Percy's work on music and worship are five interrelated processes in which worshipping and music-making are both intimately involved: first, in forming ideology; second, in serving as a means of spiritual formation; third, in providing social cohesion and structure; fourth, in providing a vehicle for the rapid spread of practice and discourse; and finally, in providing a model for the shape of the church.

First, worship—and particularly, the shared practice of congregational singing within worship—can inculcate an ideology.[4] In his early work, focused on Vineyard leader John Wimber and charismatic revival gatherings, Percy shows that music and worship act as ways to generate and shore up power. Here, worship constructs even as it reflects the particular unstated ideology that reinforces charismatic authority. In *Power and the Church*, he poses the methodological problem: "How might we locate an ideology, particularly if it is subliminal?"[5] If an ideological apparatus is not made explicit within creeds or doctrinal statements—indeed, if it is not even present to consciousness—then, Percy reasons, the analyst must focus on "the actual religious experience itself."[6] Within the charismatic communities at the center of Percy's study, the central religious experience is generated during times of musical worship. So, to distill charismatic ideology and assess its implications, Percy parses the liturgical structure, interpreting key performance practices, themes, and metaphors for God within charismatic congregational song lyrics, and setting these elements within their broader cultural milieu. Examining "Lord" and "You," two of the most common ways

4. For Percy's work on charismatic worship and music-making in relationship to ideology, see "Chapter 4: Power and Ideology" in Percy, *Words, Wonders and Power*; Percy, "Charismatic Hymnody," in *Canterbury Dictionary of Hymnology*; "Chapter 8: Erotic Ideology in Experiential Religion" in Percy, *Power and the Church: Ecclesiology in an Age of Transition*; and Percy, "The Morphology of Pilgrimage in the 'Toronto Blessing.'"

5. Percy, *Power and the Church*, 150.

6. Ibid, 151.

to reference God within the Vineyard worship songs, Percy argues that addressing God in this way promotes a posture of "submission to power in order to gain fulfilment and power."[7] This orientation toward God—and, by extension, earthly leaders as well—characterized by "passionate passivity" is key to what Percy calls the grammar of assent within charismatic worship. He concludes that, in these settings, worship songs function as ideology in that they generate and maintain asymmetrical power relations among charismatic leaders and congregants.

While worship can be a powerful tool for inculcating ideology and maintaining control, it can also be marshalled toward more ethical forms of transformation. This leads to a second emphasis in Percy's work: worship as a mode of spiritual formation. In an essay exploring the mothering metaphor of theological education, Percy draws from the work of Jeff Astley (1996) to show how worship is more than merely reflective or expressive; rather, it is transformative. Within worship, "certain words, images, kinds of music, activities and aesthetics" are capable of evoking particular "attitudes, experiences, and affections" in worshipers.[8] In other words, "worship can school, shape, teach and enculturate participants at some of the deepest levels possible."[9] As such, it functions as an important mode of spiritual formation both for laypeople in their congregations and in settings of formal theological education. Further, worship is tied up with Christian ethics and eschatological hope: "worship," he writes, "becomes a mode of discourse and behaviour in which learning about the way the world *ought* to be is regularly remembered and celebrated."[10]

A third ecclesial process that Percy's work addresses is how corporate worship creates social cohesion and structure. Worship shapes the church, both through drawing together the corporate body and by forming the individuals within it. So, how does participating in the music of congregational worship help to make a congregation out of a group of individuals? Here, Percy's observations run parallel to those of his sociological and musicological contemporaries interested in music's role in social formation in congregational settings. In *Words, Wonders, and Power*, Percy notes that songs "represent strategies for solving problems about the relations between human beings to each other and to the spiritual forces or beings of their universe."[11] Understanding music and liturgy as a strategy for solving particular social problems parallels one of the key central insights of sociologist Mark Chaves's work on liturgical repertoires within American congregations.[12] Chaves, writing a decade after Percy, builds from Ann Swidler's notion of a social repertoire of action as a "tool kit" for collective action

---

7. Percy, *Words, Wonders and Power*, 67.

8. Percy, *Engaging with Contemporary Culture*, 125.

9. Ibid., 124.

10. Ibid., 125.

11. Percy, *Words, Wonders and Power*, 62.

12. Chaves, *Congregations in America*.

that is drawn upon to solve specific social problems.[13] Chaves notes that individual congregations do not choose the elements of their worship repertoire "at random or in wholly voluntary fashion"[14]; rather, local social contexts and institutional histories structure their selection. Worship styles are formed from particular constellations of elements, which then spread across ecclesial networks, like the Vineyard gatherings that form Percy's focus.

Percy's work on charismatic songs also points to the importance of mind and body, idea and emotion, and the way that music works in concert with other aspects of church life and on multiple levels simultaneously. Percy draws from the psychological notion of *qualia*, internal perceptions arising from individual but shared sensory experiences that form our knowledge of the world. Within these gatherings, "worship . . . leads to particular forms of embodiment and somatic experience."[15] Worship forms community by acting on the body through sensory experience and emotional arousal, and by inundating the mind with a stock series of metaphors for God. As an affect-inducing component of worship, music is one of many aspects that "teaches" and forms, not in a formal sense, but through the shared, embodied experience it produces.[16] Here, Percy's ideas about musical and liturgical formation echo sociologist of music Tia De Nora's critical observation about musical efficacy:

> Music is not merely a "meaningful" or "communicative" medium. It does much more than convey signification through non-verbal means. At the level of daily life, music has power . . . It may influence how people compose their bodies, how they conduct themselves, how they experience the passage of time, how they feel about themselves, about others, about situations.[17]

Worship creates group cohesion and structure by drawing participants into what Percy describes as a "community of feeling." In the context of charismatic worship, Percy writes that, by encouraging collective participation in singing, the songs "invite the audience to become a congregation, sharing in the general description of the world encountered in the text"; this world aims to transcend the social domain, "raising participants above the lesser subjects and objects of this world, so that they may actually touch God, and he them."[18] Here, individuals gather to sing songs imbued with erotic metaphors, and in doing so together, submit to a common religious experience that forms the basis for this united community of feeling.[19] The power of collective music-making to engender such collectives is a parallel theme in the musicological

13. Ibid., 130.
14. Ibid., 130.
15. Percy, *Power and the Church*, 141.
16. Percy, *Shaping the Church*, 176.
17. De Nora, *Music in Everyday Life*, 17.
18. Percy, *Words, Wonders and Power*, 62.
19. Ibid., 62.

analysis of pop ballads—not incidentally, the very musical genre on which intimate Vineyard worship songs are modelled. Peter Manuel writes that in the pop ballad "the only factors involved are the emotions of the two individuals"; the pop ballad "rigorously avoids reference to any social contexts or constraints, portraying instead an amorphous, 'virtual' world of the emotions."[20] And like the charismatic worship songs described by Percy, romantic pop ballads draw their power from the "articulation of private feeling as public emotion," functioning to "unify an audience into an emotional community."[21]

The charismatic "community of feeling" produced in great part by singing affective worship songs is not limited to a particular locale; rather, it has shown itself capable of reproducing quickly across geographical and cultural space. This observation leads us to consider a fourth process in Martyn Percy's work: music and worship shape the church by serving as an embodied means for the rapid spread of practice and discourse. Writing in 1998 when the Toronto Blessing revival was near its height, Percy observes that the songs of the charismatic renewal movement "have affected styles and concepts in worship that have touched virtually every denomination in every corner of the globe."[22] The widespread influence of Pentecostal and charismatic practices—particularly related to worship and music—is even more apparent nearly two decades later. Many evangelical denominations, within and outside North America, for instance, have gone through the process of "charismaticization."[23] (I find it telling that many of my predominantly Baptist college students grew up on an exclusive diet of Vineyard-style contemporary worship songs and cannot remember a time before the arrival of a charismatic service structure and practices like hand-raising in their churches.) Then, of course, there is the rapid spread of pentecostal and neo-pentecostal groups and the "pentecostalization" of Catholic and Anglican congregations, endemic within but by no means limited to the Global South. Considering how and why charismatic music and worship practices travel, then, is crucial for understanding the contours of faith not only in contemporary revivalist gatherings, but also a large number of institutional churches.

Percy's work on the Toronto Blessing demonstrates that worship and music are two of the most significant "portable practices," to use Thomas Csordas's term, used to unite and spread communities of feeling.[24] Drawing from Simon Coleman's and others' work on Christian pilgrimage, Percy explores how worship is involved in processes of social and religious reproduction of the Toronto Blessing. He writes that

20. Manuel, "Popular Music."

21. Frith, "Pop Music."

22. Percy, *Power and the Church*, 142.

23. For essays describing "charismaticization" or "Pentecostalization" of Protestant and Catholic Christianity, see Spittler, "Are Pentecostals and Charismatics Fundamentalists?"; and Stiller, *Evangelicals Around the World.*

24. Csordas, *Transnational Transcendance*, 8.

the experiences produced by worship in revivals like this can be considered a type of "charismatic shrine"; in other words, it is the powerful affective experience that is generated within worship—I would add, most particularly in collective singing—that forms the center of mass pilgrimages to such revival sites. Percy demonstrates that the "sacred center" of charismatic pilgrimage comprises not specific places or physical objects, but rather a collection of portable practices that shape the self by "impart[ing] a particular type of religious experience . . . that is then transferable back into more localized ecclesial contexts."[25]

Finally, in Percy's work, worship and music can also serve as generative metaphors to promote an ecclesial ideal. Though Percy employs musical metaphors for the church on occasion throughout his writings, his most extended treatment comes in his two essays in the volume *Christian Congregational Music: Performance, Identity, and Experience.*[26] In both of these, he is fascinated with musical hybrids, those dynamic musical genres that confound any listener attempting to locate stylistic or geographical purity. He examines these hybrid genres—generally from the "secular," commercial sphere rather than from sacred music—to paint a picture of the church's polity and how musicological scholarship might be marshalled to explore themes in ecclesiology. In his essay "Jazz and Anglican Spirituality," Percy's exploration of music as an ecclesial ideal takes us out of the music of the church proper. He begins by noting David Ford's and Daniel Hardy's earlier use of jazz as a metaphor for the Trinity,[27] then argues that jazz can also serve as a fitting metaphor for the life of the church. Specifically, Percy chooses bossa nova, the mid-twentieth century Brazilian fusion of jazz and samba, as his metaphor for Anglican polity. For Percy, bossa nova and Anglicanism share an "effortless, understated composure" as well as a similar mood: a "passionate coolness" deriving from the unresolved tension between the Christian virtues of temperance and passion.[28] Percy is not content to leave temperance and passion as they are typically understood, but redefines them through an ethical lens. For Percy, "temperance is not about control from without. It is, rather, the deep spiritual exercise of restraint for the sake of the self and the other. It is a spiritual discipline and a virtue that can only be exercised in proportion to the energy and passion that wells up from the same source."[29] And passion is not just about the "expulsion of energy . . . it is also the "absorption of pain, sacrifice, and suffering."[30] Like bossa nova, Percy sees Anglicanism as a fusion of opposites that is best able to hold paradoxical virtues in productive tension as they are collectively improvised within the life of the Christian community.

25. Percy, "Morphology of Pilgrimage," 284.

26. Percy, "Jazz and Anglican Spirituality?"; Percy, "Afterword."

27. Ford and Hardy, *Jubilate.*

28. Percy, "Jazz and Anglican Spirituality," 74.

29. Ibid., 77.

30. Ibid., 77.

Try as he might,[31] in this essay, Percy cannot seem to limit his musical metaphor to bossa nova, or even to jazz. His musical passion spills over with an abundance of other examples of musical fusion, including an experimental juxtaposition of jazz saxophone and Gregorian chant; fusions of South Indian classical music with Western pop; and with the celebrated hybrid of African American gospel music, with its blend of spirituals and hymns with the blues. His two essays in *Christian Congregational Music* fleshing out more fully his reflection on hybridity in the concluding section of *Shaping the Church*. There, he writes forcefully against the imposition of "purity": "the miscible nature of the church—which is to say that the many sources that form its life, including aesthetic, institutional habits, organizational assumptions and practices, context and so forth—suggest that its hope rests in its hybridity rather than its assumed purity."[32] In *Shaping the Church*, Percy exalts the humble alloy, the "impure" compound, as the most fitting ecclesial metaphor for Anglican polity in the face of revivalist and restorationist movements that have "long attempted to remake the church as a singular element."[33] He rejects the notion that the church should (or even can) be like a "pure" element untainted by engagement with the world, arguing instead that alloys and compounds are stronger and more durable. Percy's reflections on musical fusions add an aesthetic caveat to his earlier observations: not only can the hybrid be functional, it can also be beautiful.

Encouraging Musicological and Ecclesiological Dialogue: Martyn Percy as Advocate and Patron of Congregational Music Studies

In this final section, the focus shifts from Martyn Percy's own work on music, worship, and the church to other significant ways he has encouraged broader and deeper reflection on these subjects. In doing so, I'll recount a moment from my first engagement with Percy's work a decade ago. When reading his chapter on charismatic worship from *Words, Wonders and Power*, I encountered the following statement:

> In examining Wimber's worship, we need to avoid the common trap of treating his songs as simply texts. The music, as has been suggested previously, is not incidental, but integral. To ignore the theological impact of music is surely a mistake. The melodic, harmonic and rhythmic dimensions of music are all value-laden. Music imprints its own ideological meaning, no matter how hard this is to articulate. Moreover, in a song, the words and music bear upon each other: they interact in subtle and profound ways. In the case of Wimber, the

31. Or, perhaps more accurately, "try as *his editors* might." We could not seem to contain him to one style of music.

32. Percy, *Shaping the Church*, 159.

33. Ibid., 163.

combination of 'soft contemporary rock' and 'romantic/intimate' tunes clearly help 'carry' the textual ideology of the songs.[34]

Having skimmed a number of theological works on evangelicalism and charismaticism that ignored music entirely, I felt as if I had found a rare kindred spirit within theology. In this concise quote, Percy elaborates many of the reasons I believed attention to music was so crucial for understanding contemporary evangelical and charismatic faith and practice. Percy here emphasized the importance of assessing the impact of musical rhetoric on the belief of a community; of parsing the meaning and values communicated by worship music's "melodic, harmonic, and rhythmic dimensions"; of deriving meaning from worship music's placement within broader stylistic and genre conventions; and of expounding upon the ways that lyrics and music interacted within the context of performance. As I finished reading Percy's statement on the importance of music for the first time, I looked forward to a section featuring close analysis of musical sound that would logically follow such a paragraph.

Somewhat frustratingly, Percy's discussion moved straight to ideological implications without doing any of the musicological analysis that the above excerpt seems to call for so clearly. But in several of his other early pieces on charismatic Christianity, Martyn Percy points toward the need to engage sonic processes and structures like style and genre, as well the need to attend to intermedial relations between lyrics and music; however, this work largely avoids discussion of specific sonic elements (for example, characteristics of melody, harmony, rhythm, vocal timbre, instrumental arrangement, style, or genre). In his recent reflections on musical hybrids and the shape of the church, Percy has started to incorporate some of the sonic analysis called for in this passage. Though his own engagement with musical sound has been modest, he continues to gesture emphatically toward a need for the musicological lens. What's more, he maintains that the view through this lens is crucial not only for scholars, but for church leaders as well, because the study of music-making enables a deeper understanding of social and ecclesial dynamics. "By tuning into what musicology can teach churches," Percy writes, "the Christian witness may become more self-aware, helpfully self-critical, and ideally more outwardly-orientated."[35] Yet, he has largely left it to others to put on the lens and describe what they see. His deferral has opened wide a space for music scholars to enter the conversation.

But Percy hasn't sat idly by, merely hoping that other scholars would enter the conversation. Rather, he has proactively encouraged and shaped the current musicological and ecclesiological dialogue. It is perhaps through the "entrepreneurial generosity"[36] that characterizes his administrative work that Martyn Percy has been

34. Percy, *Words, Wonders and Power*, 79.

35. Percy, "Afterword," 221.

36. Dettmar uses this memorable phrase to describe the cardinal virtue of the academic administrator who sees his or her duties as a calling: "Academe secretly runs on . . . the gift of service provided by those who recognize that they have been given much, and find they have much to give back. It's

most influential in spurring ecclesiological reflection on music and musicological reflection on the church. He has advocated for other scholars engaging in these kinds of reflections and, what's more, he has been a patron who provided the social capital and the institutional resources for the conversations to occur. These conversations have culminated in a biennial international conference, a book series, and a fledgling field of study. To demonstrate, Percy's influence in each of these related endeavors, a brief genealogy is traced below.

Percy's work as advocate for and patron of interdisciplinary reflection on music and worship in the church is most clearly evidenced in his work with the Christian Congregational Music conference, beginning in 2010 when he was the principal at Ripon College Cuddesdon. That he was willing, in the first instance, to partner with a motley crew of early career music scholars speaks volumes about his generosity and unassumingness (and perhaps also his sense of adventure?). At the time, I and the other three co-organizers besides Percy were all in our mid-to-late-twenties with no permanent academic positions and barely any publications to our names. What we brought to the table was enthusiasm and a desire to broaden the conversation about music and the church from what we felt were stale formulations within our respective academic silos. We envisioned bringing together the wayward theologians interested in understanding music in its social and cultural context; music scholars who studied the myriad musical expressions of Christian communities worldwide; and the lonely social scientists whose colleagues questioned their career prospects for writing about Christianity or music at all.

Percy offered to host the gathering at Ripon College Cuddesdon, so together we sketched themes for a small symposium where it was hoped that we could drum up two dozen participants. Interest in the symposium dramatically surpassed our expectations: a call for papers, issued late in the academic year, elicited over seventy paper proposals from twelve different countries. The conference's theme had clearly struck a chord. After the first conference, filled to the college's sixty-participant capacity with many more on the waiting list, we decided to plan another conference to meet two years later. Amid planning for our 2013 conference, Percy again guided this crew of junior scholars with little publishing experience to secure a contract with Ashgate for the edited book *Christian Congregational Music: Performance, Identity and Experience*, along with a music-themed special issue of the journal *Ecclesial Practices*. For these two outlets, we invited presenters from our 2011 and 2013 conferences to submit expanded versions of their papers. (Martyn Percy contributed an essay on theology and jazz as well as an afterword calling for a closer dialogue between musicology and theology to the edited volume.) The success of the *Christian Congregational Music* volume spurred the creation of the *Congregational Music Studies* book series with Ashgate (now Routledge Press) in 2014. Along with myself and Zoe Sherinian, Martyn Percy serves as an

---

fueled by a kind of entrepreneurial generosity—a professional liberality actively in search of colleagues in whom to invest" (Dettmar, "Don't Cry for Me, Academia!").

editor for the series. By the summer of 2018, the series will have released a total of five books with another two volumes in the planning stages.

For the fledgling field of Congregational Music Studies,[37] it was Martyn Percy who provided the plot of land, the water, and a good number of the seeds. Or, to use a musical metaphor, he provided the manuscript paper and helped to improvise a tune that was then picked up and embellished by an international, interdisciplinary audience. Percy's willingness to devote his time, energy, and social capital to this cause has encouraged a wide-ranging dialogue about music, worship, and the church, bringing together scholars within the church invested in its life and health as well as scholars writing from a critical, distanced perspective. The early success of Congregational Music Studies in bringing together musicology, the social sciences, and theology to improvise around a set of common themes for the good of the academe and the church is heavily indebted to the advocacy of Martyn Percy.

* * *

By examining Martyn Percy's work on music, worship, and the church, we see a commitment to synthesize multiple perspectives and to point the way forward for others. In his use of contextually engaged analysis to explore how pagemusic shapes and is shaped by the church, he models a critical yet hopeful stance. He is critical of how music and worship is used in some Christian circles as an ideological tool, but he remains optimistic that music can provide an aural model for the way the church could and should be. Like the strains of jazz, the church's paradoxical orientation of "passionate coolness" can appeal to aficionados and novices alike, engaging contemporary culture while shaping the church into the likeness of Christ. Participation in worship—particularly, in congregational music-making—is at the center of this formative experience. In Percy's words, "[music] is not merely an accompaniment to faith, but rather, an actual expression of it."[38] If we want to improve our vision, he reminds us that sometimes the best thing to do is to close our eyes and listen. Sometimes theologians or church leaders might need help articulating what it is that they are hearing, what it means to the community from which it arises, and how it acts upon its hearers. For that, they need look no further than to their musicological sisters and brothers who are asking many of the same questions about music, worship, and the church. As Percy observes, "To somehow miss or ignore the place of music in religious life is to overlook a whole dimension to how worship works, and how faith is fully formed. Musicology can help us to take note."[39]

37. See Porter, "The Developing Field of Congregational Music Studies."

38. Martyn Percy, "Passionate Coolness: Exploring Mood and Character in a Local Rural Anglican Church," forthcoming.

39. Percy, "Afterword," 222.

Bibliography

Blumhofer, Edith L., et al. *Pentecostal Currents in American Protestantism.* Chicago: University of Illinois Press, 1999.

Chaves, Mark. *Congregations in America.* Cambridge, MA: Harvard, 2004.

Cook, Nicholas. "We're All Ethnomusicologists Now." In *The New (Ethno)Musicologies,* edited by Henry Stobart, 48–70. London: Scarecrow, 2008.

Csordas, Thomas J. *Transnational Transcendance: Essays on Religion and Globalization.* Berkeley: University of California Press, 2009.

De Nora, Tia. *Music in Everyday Life.* Cambridge: Cambridge University Press, 2000.

Dettmar, Kevin. "Don't Cry for Me, Academia!" *The Chronicle of Higher Education,* June 27, 2016. http://www.chronicle.com/article/Don-t-Cry-for-Me-Academia-/236931?cid=rc_right.

Ford, David, and Daniel Hardy. *Jubilate: Theology in Praise.* London: Darton, Longman and Todd, 1984.

Frith, Simon. "Pop Music." In *The Cambridge Companion to Pop and Rock,* edited by Will Straw et al., 93–108. Cambridge: Cambridge University Press, 2001.

Manuel, Peter. "Popular Music." *Oxford Music Online.* http://oxfordmusiconline.com.

Percy, Martyn. "Afterword: Theology and Music in Conversation." In *Christian Congregational Music: Performance, Identity and Experience,* edited by Monique M. Ingalls et al., 217–22. Farnham: Ashgate, 2013.

———. "Charismatic Hymnody." In *Canterbury Dictionary of Hymnology.* Norwich, UK: Canterbury, 2013.

———. *Engaging with Contemporary Culture: Christianity, Theology and the Concrete Church.* Aldershot, UK: Ashgate, 2005.

———. "Jazz and Anglican Spirituality?: Some Notes on Connections." In *Christian Congregational Music: Performance, Identity and Experience,* edited by Monique M. Ingalls et al., 67–82. Farnham, UK: Ashgate, 2013.

———. "The Morphology of Pilgrimage in the 'Toronto Blessing.'" *Religion* 28 (1998) 281–88.

———. *Power and the Church: Ecclesiology in an Age of Transition.* London: Cassell, 1998.

———. *Shaping the Church: The Promise of Implicit Theology.* Farnham, UK: Ashgate, 2010.

———. *Words, Wonders and Power: Understanding Contemporary Christian Fundamentalism and Revivalism.* London: SPCK, 1996.

Porter, Mark. "The Developing Field of Congregational Music Studies." *Ecclesial Practices* 2:1 (2014).

Spittler, Russell P. "Are Pentecostals and Charismatics Fundamentalists?" In *Charismatic Christianity as Global Culture,* edited by Karla Poewe. Columbia: University of South Carolina Press, 1995.

Stiller, Brian, ed., *Evangelicals Around the World: A Global Handbook for the 21st Century.* Nashville: Thomas Nelson, 2015.

13

Practically Priests

Privileging the Lived in Ministerial Training

Daniel Warnke

How does one become a priest? For that matter, who gets to decide what being a priest really means, let alone what it would take to train someone toward this particular end? Is it merely a career choice made by the more holy (or pious) amongst us, or does it instead require the type of decision only possible in submission to being "called"? More specifically, what determines the training of clergy, and, to what extent does this take into account the lives from which people are called? This paper seeks to explore Martyn Percy's pedagogy in the context of vocations within the Anglican Communion as it relates to adult-led education. Given the significant developments of a theologically informed anthropology within Percy's work, which takes seriously the context and concrete experience of the church, this paper argues that continued use of the term *pedagogy* (child-leading) can generate something of a "blind-spot" (or at worst an infantilization) limiting the rich life experiences that adult learners offer through a potential educational reciprocity. By reading Percy in view of recent developments of *andragogy* (adult-leading), we will explore how these insights might better shape future clergy toward the kind of collegiality that sustains unity in the face of disagreements and the ensuing ecclesial dispositions.

When considering their vocation, it is worth remembering that priests are trained for the church. While this may seem like an obvious statement, it begs the more search-ing question: what type of church are they trained for? Far from being normative, or developed from a distinct ecclesial blueprint, the church is multifarious, with as many variants as it has locations. Paying attention to the particular people, context, and grounded reality of the local church reveals that training priests is subsequently far from a simple transferal of skills and knowledge. Further to this is the need for what Percy highlights (through the work of Dan Hardy) as an *a posteriori* understanding of the church and ministry in real-time. Rather than devise generic training courses to output clergy, attention should be given from the outset to the nature of the body being served. Equipping clergy in this way engenders the kind of reflexivity necessary to discern the "pastoral priorities and ecclesial proclivities" operant within local congregations and across the breadth of the Anglican Communion.[1]

Throughout Percy's publications on theological education, vocations, and the training of clergy, the common thread of character formation emerges, particularly drawing our attention toward a virtue-ethic of ministry fit for the contemporary church. Percy contends that this shaping of character is unlike the notion of simply preparing priests for a professional career, pointing out that their "role is not work, strictly speaking, in the way the world might understand the concept," but is uniquely "beyond the normal vocabulary for defining work."[2] Searching for this vocabulary, Percy guides us toward the notion of "occupation" as suitably narrating priests who are to be wholly "occupied with God, and then to be pre-occupied with all the people, places and parishes that are given by God into our care."[3] Yet what remains problematic for training is defining the kind of curriculum and character formation necessary for this sort of being occupied. As we will now observe, the variety of priorities and tensions that arise from a "party-like" propensity across the spectrum of the Anglican Communion is something that in turn continues to polarize theological education.

To train clergy there needs to be an educational institution, but institutions are not neutral. As Percy keenly observes: "Nearly all residential colleges across the Communion were and have been formed as part of the internal debates within the church."[4] Charting these debates from the early nineteenth century, he identifies a range of new colleges, which in their establishment continued to divide, rather than unify, the theology and ethos of Anglican polity, concluding:

> It is ironic that seminaries and colleges have mostly developed out of tensions and disputes in contending for Anglican identity. Many institutions emerge because of their sense of needing to provide a distinctive mode and ethos of formation that was rooted in particular theological and ecclesial "party" vision.[5]

The challenge, it would seem, lies in addressing:

> Prior ecclesial and pedagogical characteristics: a reticulate blend of the instrumental, formational, organizational, and institutional visions of the church that are all contained within expressions of the Anglican polity.[6]

---

1. Percy, "Context, Character, and Challenges: The Shaping of Ordination Training," 492.

2. Percy, "Theological Education and Formation for an Uncommon Occupation," 230.

3. Ibid., 242. Percy also makes this same point in a particularly pastoral lecture; "Understanding the Ministry of the Church Today," given at the funeral of friend and former student in November 2016.

4. Percy, "Context, Character, and Challenges," 499.

5. Ibid., 499.

6. Ibid., 496.

In summary, the educational ethos engendered throughout ministerial training holds something of a key toward greater unity and catholicity within Anglican identity. To explore this further we shall now turn our attention toward the "pedagogical characteristics" within Percy's work as a means to unlocking this potential.

Percy's Pedagogy

In the discourse of educational philosophy, or systems of learning, *pedagogy* is frequently the catchall term used to elucidate the science and methodology of teaching. Within Percy's writings, this is certainly the case. However, whilst use of the term has become normative within higher education, it is by no means sufficient in articulating a distinct vision of adult education. In homage to Percy's own method: a simple etymological study of the word *pedagogy* reveals its origins (*paidagogue*) as being rooted in the care of a child. Michael J. Smith points out that use of this term by Paul in Galatians actually infers a "child-tender," or what we might consider a modern-day *au pair*.[7] The immediate tension with the teaching of adults is self-evident. Whilst Percy's use is not literal, with no clear indication of an educational philosophy oriented toward the child, the implicit allusion with pedagogic praxis remains. It should also be noted that Percy advocates a more theological reading of pedagogy, lamenting the "management-led" and "secular shaping of pedagogy" creeping into ministerial training.[8]

If, as we have seen so far, Percy's view of theological education and training is then grounded in a keen attention to context, how then do we best understand his philosophy of formation in light of this use of the term "pedagogy"? Far from being a matter of semantics, it appears this might be a minor oversight in Percy's work, and one that we shall now explore, particularly as the term fails to encapsulate Percy's educational philosophy more broadly. However, it should be noted from the outset that whilst explicit use of the term is minimal, an implicit framework of pedagogy can be drawn from Percy's ranging publications and work within education.

The use of vignettes, metaphors, and poetry populates the way in which Percy writes about the occupation and life of a priest. His method of reflection is frequently pastoral in tone, affectionately tracing the contours, characteristics, and challenges of ministry life. Whilst potentially abstract, these insights bring into sharp focus the intensity and pressures of ministry life. With first-hand understanding of parish life, as a priest, Percy recognizes that preparing clergy is often varied and challenging, particularly given that "ministry remains difficult to *define*, and the roles increasingly hard to articulate. And therefore, by extension, it is hard to define the training, education, and formation ministry *requires*."[9] As we have already noted, Percy highlights that being trained for ministry is dependent on more than simply developing a particular set of

7. Smith, "The Role of the Pedagogue in Galatians," 198.
8. Percy, "Theological Education and Formation for an Uncommon Occupation."
9. Ibid., 229–30.

skills and knowledge (as is the case for education more broadly). Critically, becoming a priest incorporates a third strand, and one that holds a key to the distinctive nature of priestly activity. As Percy illustrates:

> A trainee doctor who has failed medical school will probably not make a good doctor; an accountant or lawyer that fails their professional exams is unlikely to proceed in that line of work. But a person who is perhaps not a good theologian or fine preacher may, nonetheless, be an excellent priest.[10]

If this is true, that being a priest is not reliant on high marks, or displaying a particular set of skills, then what is the "secret ingredient" eclipsing these curricula norms? Having drawn our attention to the benchmarks of skill and knowledge, both guiding the nature and equipping of ministry, Percy points out that what remains unique to the training of clergy is the development of character and virtue (often referred to simply as "formation"). In other words, *who* you are is as important as *what* you know or are capable of doing. But as noted earlier, the propensity of each ecclesial tradition to hold onto their distinct proto-formational values remains fervent.

It might be safe to assume that what we have been discussing thus far, in search of bridging the divide between traditions, is somewhat theoretical, or potentially naive. After all, unity is something far easier said than done. Yet as principal of Ripon College Cuddesdon in Oxford, Percy impacted the life and ethos of what had become known as a liberal-catholic "club," transforming it to one of generosity and inclusion across traditions. Students with a range of ecclesial backgrounds; from charismatics to evangelicals, alongside an increased number of women ordinands, were amongst some of the developments during Percy's tenure. Rather than understand this through the lens of pragmatic change theory, this institutional evolution flows from a distinct outworking of a practical theology grounded in the concrete church and informed by the social sciences. Commenting on this desire for diversity, Percy states:

> [O]ur treasure lies in our very breadth of expression, and our refusal to become tribal or too closely identified with any single party; that the College is at its best when it is serving the church by being faithful to its middle, open way, which welcomes and affirms diversity as much as it promotes unity.[11]

This "breadth of expression" is what Percy advocates through this uniquely informed practical theology, not as a hypothetical position or theological posturing, but as an adaptive praxis for the training institution, capable of responding to the needs of the local church. In short, this methodology (or pedagogy as Percy would see it) is as much about who we are, as what we know. Unity, in this sense, is not then a call for uniformity, but rather a desire for mediation between divergent proclivities, wherein the college becomes something of a superhighway, connecting people across a rolling,

10. Percy, "Context, Character, and Challenges," 491.
11. Percy, *Anglicanism*, 24.

sweeping landscape of traditions. By experiencing this diversity through ministerial training, Percy intends for clergy to become "broad in outlook," "genuinely hospitable," "intelligent and theologically curious learners" who continue developing this in the life of their parish.[12] How this desire comes to bear on his pedagogy within the training process is a matter of attending to the principle role of formation. As Percy clarifies, "formation, as a process, refers both to the character and virtues of the individual, and to the nature of the institution that helps to infuse individuals with formational values. More often than not, such values are implicit rather than explicit."[13] Characteristically, Percy highlights the role of the institution within this schema. It is not enough to say that people are to be shaped, without asking direct and fundamental questions of the institution doing the shaping. Attention should be given to the shared life and implicit expectations embedded within the training college, or seminary, if we are to better understand the possible theological permutations, capabilities and character of graduating students. Percy contends that how the training institution acts as a body, through eating, learning, and worshiping together, is as important as the development of curricula content. Or to put it another way: the practices and realities of the college reveal the implicit theology beyond the curriculum.[14] On this basis, the program of learning becomes infused with pedagogic principles that ground formation as an end in itself, rather than instrumentalizing learning toward institutional goals: "[Theological education] needs to be orientated toward wisdom, and the cultivation of character and virtue. It should not be concerned with 'missiological measurable results,' no matter how well intended this may be."[15] Percy is also clear that ministry, whilst being a calling and vocation, is not a career choice, stating that "It is not 'work,' or a 'profession,' as such, but rather a sacred calling in which character and virtues matter as much as, and perhaps more than, aims, objectives, and outcomes."[16] Instead, as noted earlier, the calling of a priest is an occupation: with God (through worship), with what God occupies (the people called church), and with what occupies God (his love and care for the world). This could all too easily sound ideological, or at best romantic, but the reclaiming of a term such as "occupation" over and above the operant nature of managerial methodology is at the heart of Percy's concern with character formation in ministerial training and education. In short, the shape of our pedagogy determines the shape of our priests. Managerial methods beget managerial ministers, but clergy of character and virtue are necessarily prepared for priestly occupation.

Percy is also clear in his reservations of an economic model of the church, which seeks to reify the activity of God through managerial and measurable methods, yet mistakenly "managing the transcendence of God" through a desire to see predictable

12. Percy, "Context, Character, and Challenges," 25.
13. Ibid., 491.
14. Ibid., 491.
15. Percy, "Theological Education and Formation," 242.
16. Percy, *The Future Shapes of Anglicanism*, 37.

results and numerical growth.[17] With this in mind, Percy welcomes the development of assessment in more recent years, shifting the focus from outcomes to competencies, which "allows for the integrity of local theologies and the ministry needs of different social and cultural contexts."[18] Context and grounded learning clearly remain at the heart of Percy's pedagogy.

However, despite this concession, Percy is not convinced about the "appropriateness of primarily evaluating ministerial formation through this lens." David Heywood would agree, pointing out that knowledge acquisition in the context of formation remains susceptible to becoming a "disembedded technical rationality" insufficient for the training of ministers. Heywood contends:

> This task requires a focus on the type of knowledge required for reflective practice: *phronesis* or practical wisdom, the skills by which theology becomes a means of interpreting experience. Integral to the acquisition of theology as *phronesis* is the development of Christian character. In fact, as we have seen, a theological *habitus* might be defined as a virtue ethic for discipleship and ministry.[19]

Heywood's virtue ethic in this instance is reliant upon David Ford's development of Pierre Bourdieu's notion of *habitus,* accounting for the kind of "training not preoccupied with the cultivation of self but with being responsive to Jesus Christ and other people and coping with their responses in turn."[20] This responsiveness reveals itself in Percy's pedagogy, looking beyond training, and toward the local church: "ministries need to self-consciously contemplate, critically reflect upon and imagine their occurrence in relation to their context and environment, over and against the typical sense of development that is normally conveyed by theology and or ecclesiology."[21] Rather than assume a set of prior formulations, clergy should be trained with the capacity to re-narrate, or re-energize the ecclesial landscape often scarred by "party" fractions and proclivities. Through this approach, Percy invites us to consider a broad and embracing ecclesiology, which requires nothing less than "a new theory of ministry."[22] However, by "new" this does not imply anything new at all, but rather, in Percy's own words, all that is really needed for ministry are some "old tricks for new dogs."

As we have seen thus far, a reading of Percy's educational philosophy as it relates to theological education, assessment, and training ordinands, reveals a consistent use of the language, if not always the term, of "pedagogy." When used, it appears to be with generalist intent, because the actual thrust of his educational philosophy elicits an

---

17. Ibid., 13.
18. Percy, "Context, Character, and Challenges," 499.
19. Heywood, "Educating Ministers of Character," 22.
20. Ford, *Self and Salvation,* 165.
21. Percy, *Clergy,* 1.
22. Ibid., 1.

understanding of the interrelatedness between the life of the adult learner, the training college, and the local church. The role of character and virtue (who the person is, and is becoming) takes center stage, yet orientates away from the mode of self-discovery, toward one of faithful response in Christ. Coupled with Percy's theologically informed anthropology *vis-à-vis* the grounded reality of the church, this attentiveness to context, practical wisdom, and formation pushes the vocabulary of pedagogy beyond its usual elasticity. Continued use only risks impoverishing the potential of Percy's educational philosophy. If this is true, then a new language is required, and one that will avoid the proverbial wine splitting the skin. It is this new language of adult learners that we shall now explore.

Andragogy and Privileging the Lived

Adult education is generally understood to involve those in post-secondary level learning, aged twenty-five and over. In many higher educational settings this demographic is on the rise and quickly becoming the majority.[23] To accommodate this development, institutions have become increasingly adaptable, adjusting curricula and support in recognition of prior learning experience. Through a range of assessment methodologies, this more reflexive approach seeks not only to attribute prior learning for the pragmatics of course credit, but also as a means of synthesizing new learning within prior experience. In the context of theological education, this can be particularly fruitful, as Laura Foote highlights: "Asking students to critically reflect upon the past and consider ways they might reframe and make meaning of past experiences can be particularly useful as a means of integrating faith and learning within Christian higher education."[24] This meaning making is central to the set of assumptions that Tara Fenwick and Mark Tennant propose when considering adult learners. They point out that, due to the wide-ranging variety of experiences amongst adults, there can be no "ideal type" or essentialized adult learner. Further, they acknowledge that learning does not take place in a vacuum; it is dynamic within an active and variable context. And finally, they note that the relationship between "learner" and "educator" is not neutral. As such, the positionality of the educator influences learners, and should itself be subject to an ongoing self-reflection.[25] Oliver O'Donovan points out that this kind of reflexive self-awareness is not "only a change in how we see ourselves . . . but in the way we see the world as a result of finding ourselves located within it."[26] Clearly there is a difference between acquiring knowledge, and the subsequent understanding of its application. O'Donovan is keen to emphasize that this knowing of the self can only occur

23. Foote, "Re-Storying Life as a Means of Critical Reflection," 117. For more detailed statistical analysis see HESA, "Summary of UK Performance Indicators 2014/15."

24. Foote, "Re-Storying Life as a Means of Critical Reflection," 18.

25. Fenwick and Tennant, "Understanding Adult Learners," 55.

26. O'Donovan, *Finding and Seeking*, 55.

through "the gaze of others," in a mode of "equality and reciprocity" bound within our being known by God.[27] This equality and reciprocity is therefore not simply a case of collegiality, but rather, cooperation between people bound in Christ. This resonates well with the language of "discernment," which is replete within formational training, and one that Percy himself identifies as a prayerful cooperative process, involving "the institution, together with the sponsoring or receiving bishop."[28]

Further to this, Percy highlights the same age trend found in higher education institutions noted above as being reflected in the increased age of ordinands presented for training. In the 1970s, around two-thirds of those training were under the age of thirty. By early 2000, this same majority now comprised those within the thirty-to-fifty age range. Whilst the direct pathway from school to seminary has clearly diminished, Percy notes the positive aspect of this shift reveals that "wisdom, maturity and life experience are more present in the arena of formation than might have been the case even twenty years ago."[29] These trends indicate that attention toward the particular needs of adult learners is of pressing importance. Yet this focus is by no means anything new.

Citing the work of Yugoslavian adult educator Dusan Savicevic, Sharan Merriam and Laura Bierema remind us that Plato's Academy and Aristotle's Lyceum were places of adult education, using "dialogue, parables, and what today we would call problem-based learning activities with adults." Interestingly, they also point out that it was "not until monasteries in the seventh century established schools for children that the term "pedagogy" came into use."[30] The irony is self-evident. The church, having pioneered an accessible form of education geared toward the child, found itself caught on a "conveyor-belt" model designed around students dependency, where autonomy becomes the end goal, and not a dynamic of the curriculum. This autonomy is precisely the dimension of formation and training that risks being overlooked through a pedagogical framework, missing the rich life experience that adult learners bring into the classroom.

As a counteractive model, *andragogy* (literally: man-leading) is increasingly being developed within the field of adult learning theories as a framework incorporating prior experience as the basis of all learning. One of the central assumptions of andragogy is that because adults are self-directing in their work, family, and community lives, they will in turn be self-directing in their learning.

The term "andragogy" was first used by Eduard Lindeman in 1926, when devising a "situation approach" to the burgeoning field of adult education, whereby "the curriculum is built around the students needs and interests" embedded in "his work, his recreation, his family life, his community life."[31] Despite the advancement of this

27. Ibid., 54.

28. Percy, "Context, Character, and Challenges," 491.

29. Percy, *Clergy*, 161.

30. Merriam and Bierema, *Adult Learning*, 44.

31. Lindeman, *The Meaning of Adult Education in the United States*, 8–9.

theory, adult education remained broadly in the margins, struggling for legitimacy in the academy. It was not until the work of Malcolm Knowles in the 1950s and 1960s, defining andragogy as "the art and science of helping adults learn" and contrasting it with pedagogy (the art and science of teaching children), that use of the term became more popular, along with the elevated status of adult education more broadly. Rather than introduce a polemic, Knowles saw andragogy and pedagogy along a spectrum of strategies to learning. However, Knowles conception of andragogy is not without its faults. Focusing on Knowles's most influential work, *The Modern Practice of Adult Education*, Derek Briton critiques its seemingly coterminous nature with institutional interests, and the practices of human resources development. Briton contends that this was a byproduct of adult education more broadly as it sought to consolidate its position amongst competing economic and academic interests, drawing on the science of behaviorism, elevating terms such as "self directed," "goal-orientated" and "facilitated" within learning practices.[32] Despite these propensities, further development of the theory continues to yield benefit to adult education. Sharan Merriman highlights the five enduring assumptions underlying andragogy, which she states:

> Describe the adult learner as someone who (1) has an independent self-concept and who can direct his or her own learning, (2) has accumulated a reservoir of life experiences that is a rich resource for learning, (3) has learning needs closely related to changing social roles, (4) is problem-centered and interested in immediate application of knowledge, and (5) is motivated to learn by internal rather than external factors.[33]

With these tenets in mind, it is worth noting that Lindeman's earlier work remains prescient to our focus on the training of priests, given that its "primary goal is not vocational. Its aim is not to teach people how to make a living but rather how to live. It offers no ulterior reward . . . Life is its fundamental subject matter."[34] Whilst priests are formed for a vocation, their being precedes their doing. Further application of andragogy can be drawn from Pete Ward, who observes that theology students entering the classroom "carry their ministerial experience and theological commitment with them when they come to study."[35] This vital experience is something Ward refers to as "enactment," which has the capacity to transcend "both the clerical, and the academic paradigms, by privileging the lived."[36] It is this "privileging the lived" that andragogy seeks to foster, and could hold the key to further development of Percy's approach to education and the training of ordinands. As Ward continues: "One of the ways that we might overcome these problems is by paying attention to the embodied and the lived

32. Briton, *The Modern Practice of Adult Education*, 20.

33. Merriam, "Andragogy and Self-Directed Learning," 5.

34. Lindeman, "The Meaning of Adult Learning," 37.

35. Ward, "Hermeneutical and Epistemological Significance," 57.

36. Ibid., 57.

theological perspectives that students bring with them into the classroom."[37] Heywood appears to agree with this oversight, asserting the value of synthesizing lived knowledge into new learning. He frames this within the notion of a "schema of understanding," borrowing from Michael Polanyi's conception of "tacit knowledge" to integrate theology learned in a classroom with the enacted theology of real-life. As Heywood states: "A course on ecclesiology therefore needs to engage with students' existing experience and beliefs about the Church."[38] Further, he states:

> To equip students as competent reflective practitioners requires theological educators to work with the grain of the way people learn naturally. The change required is to cease to see formal theological understanding as complete in itself, but rather to see it as an element in the development of ministerial character.[39]

This working "with the grain," or *a posteriori* attention to the concrete reality of the church, is precisely the type of reflexivity that Percy augments within his anthropologically informed ecclesiology. The convergence with andragogy at this point is clear, and increasingly highlights the incongruent language of pedagogy within this line of thought. Michael DeLashmutt shares this view, and as an academic involved in educating lay and ordained ministers (particularly in the Church of England), he critiques the current framework for ministry formation as one that "devalues the role of academic theology."[40] His concern orients toward the disconnection between the epistemological and transformational dimension of theology, asserting that: "the church views HE[higher education] theology purely as an instrument for the acquisition of knowledge." This view accords with Heywood's observation of the Preface in the Church of England's "Common Awards" scheme, which ideologically seeks to integrate theory and practice. However, whilst the Preface vies for a changed educational methodology with a more distinctly Christian root, Heywood contends this remains to be seen. Both DeLashmutt and Heywood would agree that, due to the nature of contemporary higher education courses, this divide is only upheld within current ministerial training.

For Heywood, any change to the *status quo* hinges on fostering this "tacit knowledge" through a curriculum that recognizes character formation as an integral, and essential, part of the training process. This, he contends, is necessary in the face of "an education system, which to a significant extent lacks the facility to discern and promote the formation and qualities of character."[41]

37. Ward, "Hermeneutical and Epistemological Significance," 58.

38. Heywood, "Educating Ministers of Character," 18.

39. Ibid., 16.

40. Delashmutt, "Exploring Formation for Ministry," 211.

41. Heywood, "Educating Ministers of Character," 7.

This returns our thoughts to Percy's educational philosophy, contending that character and virtue sit at the heart of training priests. But the lament of both Heywood and DeLashmutt continues: The potential divide between the epistemological and transformational dimensions of theology remains. In response to this challenge, it would seem that Ward points us toward a nascent opportunity inherent within practical theology:

> If we view Practical Theology from their perspective we find that these students offer a particular hermeneutical and an epistemological viewpoint . . . This viewpoint has the merit of being rooted in the ordinary theology and lived practice of the Church.[42]

However, the legacy of post-Enlightenment education, as both a learning and socialization through scholarly activity, has left the epistemological position of theology as something of an amalgam between academic specialism and cultural adaptation. Tracing the roots of this fragmentation in contemporary theological education, Edward Farley's book *Theologia* is something of a primer, highlighting the impact of the "theological encyclopedia movement" in Germany, and the subsequent division of disciplines. Farley contends that the impoverished nature of this evolution is due to a loss of a praxis-oriented theological understanding (he calls it *theologia*, a reflexive theology). Echoing the cautions of Percy, he ascribes this disconnection to how theology is "experienced in seminaries as an exposure to a plurality of scholarly or skill-oriented disciplines."[43] He further contends that this "clerical paradigm"—whereby theological studies are instrumentalized toward the pragmatism of training "effective" clergy—is located within Schleiermacher's assertion that the church needs "educated leadership, as do medicine and law, and a university faculty which provides the cognitive foundations of that education."[44] As a corrective, and to restore *theologia* within training clergy, Farley proposes a recovery of the ancient Greek notion of *paideia* (training of virtue) as the necessary ecclesial counterpart. This resonates well within Percy's formational interests and offers a richer language than that of pedagogy.

Andrew Walker and Andrew Wright would seem to agree, articulating the potential of *paideia* as shaping "the formative task of transmitting a cultural heritage in order to school virtue and cultivate character."[45] Further to this, they point out that the early church had in fact appropriated this Hellenistic notion, altering it from one of self-discovery to an understanding that true virtue could only be founded in God as revealed in Christ. Hence virtues of love, faith, and knowledge could no longer be discovered from within fallen creation, but rather, that wisdom gained through lived experience (*phronesis*) was dependent upon reception to the Gospel

---

42. Ward, "Hermeneutical and Epistemological Significance," 56.

43. Farley, *Theologia*, 152.

44. Ibid., 86.

45. Walker and Wright, "A Christian University Imagined," 58.

and the work of the Spirit. This further resonates with Percy, who views the role of the institution as one of cultivating "pedagogies of love and spaces for spiritual discernment, wisdom and intuition."[46]

In order to revive this early Christian understanding of *paideia* in contemporary theological education, Walker and Wright propose a tripartite approach by recovering an ethos of learning suitable for Christian character formation. Firstly, they contend that recovering the interdisciplinary nature of theology is necessary to bridge between the existing fragmentations of academic disciplines. Second to this is an acquisition of knowledge grounded in spiritual growth. Such knowledge, they contend, flows from an understanding of reciprocity, whereby students are both recipients, and contributors to the scholarly life of the college. Then finally, and most significantly, *paideia,* as the distinct mode of Christian character formation, must begin and end in the worship of God.[47]

It is evident that recovery of theology from a marginal, academic subject, to one of grounded experience, offers enriching spiritual transformation. Yet as Joanna Collicutt points out, in order to cooperate with this transformation there needs to be an ethos of self-understanding at work, fostering the kind of cooperation where mutual consent becomes the norm: "Cooperation is a key aspect of the birthing that is formation. While there is no scope for meat to cooperate with the sausage machine or clay to cooperate with the Potter, the process of birthing is a different matter; it will go better if the mother works with the midwife."[48] If Collicutt is correct, then how might the "birthing" of a cooperative learning community exist in the life of a training institution? Etienne Wenger proposes a social theory of learning in the life of organizations whereby "communities of practice" evolve to build knowledge, transferring competencies through a blend of relations, identity, meaning, and shared practice. Rather than limit the concept of learning within set goals, activities, or subject matter, communities of practice remain open to ongoing possibilities and outcomes. As Wenger highlights:

> Their practice is not merely a context for learning something else. Engagement in practice—in its unfolding, multidimensional complexity—is both the stage and the object, the road and the destination. What they learn is not a static subject matter but the very process of being engaged in, and participating in developing, an ongoing practice.[49]

This process of mutual engagement is something that Wenger sees as having greater potential for being both "highly perturbable and highly resilient."[50] As a methodology

---

46. Percy, *The Ecclesial Canopy*, 156.

47. Walker and Wright, "A Christian University Imagined," 68–69.

48. Collicutt, *Christian Character Formation*, 6.

49. Wenger, *Communities of Practice*, 95.

50. Ibid., 96.

for education, this resonates with Percy's view of the continued and ongoing nature of formation, which "in pedagogical terms, this is more of an art than a science; a world for the reflective practitioner rather than the pure theorist."[51]

And whilst Wenger's proposal mainly focuses on the skills and knowledge of training, it holds the potential for offering the sorts of theological vignettes that Percy endorses; shaping and guiding formation, through the "tacit and intuitive knowledge" developed by the "very best kinds of 'reflective practitioner.'"[52] The opportunities for contribution and collegiality are also heightened through this approach; as Wenger points out, "people do not merely act individually or mechanically," but rather through "shared practice and their interlocked identities."[53]

If learning is to be understood as "the engine of practice," by implication, if learning stops, the engine seizes.[54] It is not, therefore, sufficient to say that clergy are trained and deployed, without an explicit expectation of, and preparation for, continued learning. On this basis, reflexive practice can be understood as the essential lifeblood of the church.

As we have seen throughout, Percy strongly advocates that all theology should be grounded in the praxis of the church; that fundamentally, theological education can only be recognized as being theological when it engages with the realities and challenges faced by the local congregation. Accordingly, "the church, in all its plurality as a culture, place, repository of beliefs and customs, is the primary location for theological education and formation."[55] The discipline of theology must not only teach, but also listen. This attentiveness to the learner locates Percy's philosophy more closely with an andragogical framework, anticipating prior knowledge and experience as constituent to the learning journey, rather than something to be overlooked, or merely appropriated. This Geertzian method of *deep listening* is also central to Percy's writing on practical theology more broadly as the kind of "non-directive attention" necessary to sustain fresh theological insight.[56] In characteristic style, this is more then rhetoric for Percy who concludes the following:

> A good practical theology of theological education will, in other words, seek the necessary transformations that might advance liberation and critical self reflection, helping the churches, individuals and colleges come to terms with the nature and tasks of theology in and relevant ways that might further enable social and human flourishing.[57]

51. Percy, *Anglicanism*, 35.

52. Ibid., 37.

53. Wenger, *Communities of Practice*, 97.

54. Ibid., 96.

55. Percy, *Engaging with Contemporary Culture*, 150.

56. Ibid., 7–9.

57. Percy, *Engaging with Contemporary Culture*, 150.

Practically Priests?

At this point we shall now draw some final conclusions. Our interest throughout this paper has been to explore Percy's educational philosophy in the context of vocations within the Anglican Communion. More specifically, attention has been given to the language of *pedagogy* as it relates to the shaping of character and virtue within the discourse of adult education. What we have seen is that, whilst Percy's use of the term "pedagogy" is economic, his language eliciting the formation and education of clergy is replete with deeply rich, illustrative language that reveals his educational philosophy. Namely, that "theological education needs to take seriously ecclesial communities as a primary *place* and *focus* of theological education."[58]

However, what has become clear through Percy's reading of theological education, across the Anglican Communion, is the endemic problem of "party-like" colleges with almost tribal tendencies. From their foundation, these institutions invariably sustain proclivities through theological (and by implication, pedagogical) convictions held by their various traditions. Thankfully, all is not lost, as we have also seen a glimmer of hope in the case of Cuddesdon, where Percy's theological convictions have been worked out through the institution. As both an Anglican priest, and an academic theologian, Percy does not abdicate himself from the context. His theology is effervescent, and apparent in the ethos and life of the college. Far from being subjective, or pragmatically orientated for the sake of quick results, it looks to the potential of the institution as a means of generously holding the convolution of traditions and identity. His vision of broad Anglicanism, concerned with the role of the church in the world today, can therefore only find its traction through a new educational paradigm: "This needs to begin with broadly conceived, open, generous, liberal theological education. It needs to be orientated toward wisdom, and the cultivation of character and virtue. It should not be concerned with 'missiological measurable results,' no matter how well intended this may be."[59] By continuously drawing our attention away from numbers and toward the nuanced life of the church, Percy calls for a deeper, more relational mode of learning, and one that is distinctly rooted in the person of Christ. Clearly church growth matters, but it is not a focus or an end in itself, but rather a reflection of our reflexive capacity, something that Dan Hardy gracefully calls a "dedicated attention to the intensity of God."[60]

In light of this attention toward character-virtue, the role and identity of the adult learner subsequently becomes increasingly prescient. To push this further, we find ourselves questioning the root of pedagogic praxis, asking the following question: where is the life experience of the adult located within this educational schema? Continuation of Percy's focus on formation reveals the essential nature of collegiality

58. Percy, *Anglicanism*, 43.

59. Percy, "Theological Education and Formation for an Uncommon Occupation," 242.

60. Hardy (et al.), *Wording a Radiance*, 2.

within the training process. With this in mind, we can conclude the semantics of pedagogy reasonably reaches its limit, and hence continued use clearly risks impoverishing this rich vision of formation. Following on from this we have seen that the learning theory of *andragogy*, tempered with a Christian reading of *paideia*, offers a potentially broader approach in keeping with Percy's practical theology. As such, this reading of andragogy conveys a particular telos: one that holds to an ecclesial moral vision of openness, through hospitality, service, and listening.[61] Ultimately, if the project is a broad Anglicanism, then Percy's andragogical vision of theological education seems to hold the key to unlocking a potential future of unity, beyond uniformity.

Bibliography

Briton, Derek. *The Modern Practice of Adult Education: A Postmodern Critique.* Albany: State University of New York Press, 1996.

Collicutt, Joanna. *The Psychology of Christian Character Formation.* London: SCM, 2015.

DeLashmutt, Michael. "Exploring Formation for Ministry in a Learning Church." *Discourse* 9:1 (2009) 211–36.

Farley, Edward. *Theologia: The Fragmentation and Unity of Theological Education.* Philadelphia: Fortress, 1983.

Fenwick, Tara, and Mark Tennant. "Understanding Adult Learners." In *Dimensions of Adult Learning Adult Education and Training in a Global Era*, edited by Griff Foley, 55–74. Berkshire, UK: Open University, 2004.

Foote, Laura S. "Re-Storying Life as a Means of Critical Reflection: The Power of Narrative Learning." *Christian Higher Education* 14:3 (2015) 116–26.

Ford, David. *Self and Salvation: Being Transformed.* Cambridge: Cambridge University Press, 2003.

Hardy, Daniel W., et al. *Wording a Radiance: Parting Conversations on God and the Church.* London: SCM, 2010.

HESA. "Summary of UK Performance Indicators 2014/15." https://www.hesa.ac.uk/data-and-analysis/performance-indicators/summary/2014-15.

Heywood, David. "Educating Ministers of Character: Building Character into the Learning Process in Ministerial Formation." *Journal of Adult Theological Education* 10:1 (2013) 4–24.

Lindeman, Eduard C. *The Meaning of Adult Education in the United States.* New York: Harvest House, 1926.

———. "The Meaning of Adult Learning." In *Learning Democracy: Eduard Lindeman on Adult Education and Social Change*, edited by S. Brookfield, 29–37. London: Croom Helm, 1929.

Merriam, Sharan B. "Andragogy and Self-Directed Learning: Pillars of Adult Learning Theory." *New Directions for Adult and Continuing Education.* Spring 2001 (89) 3–14.

Merriam, Sharan B., and Laura L. Bierema. *Adult Learning: Linking Theory and Practice.* San Francisco: Jossey-Bass, 2004.

O'Donovan, Oliver. *Finding and Seeking.* 3 vols. Grand Rapids, MI: Eerdmans, 2014.

61. Percy, *Anglicanism*, 38.

Percy, Martyn. *Anglicanism: Confidence, Commitment and Communion*. Ashgate: Routledge, 2013.

———. *Clergy: The Origin of the Species*. London: Continuum, 2006.

———. "Context, Character, and Challenges: The Shaping of Ordination Training." In *The Oxford Handbook of Anglican Studies*, edited by Mark Chapman et al., 490–502. Oxford: Oxford University Press, 2015.

———. *The Ecclesial Canopy: Faith, Hope, Charity*. Farnham, UK: Ashgate, 2012.

———. *Engaging with Contemporary Culture: Christianity, Theology and the Concrete Church*. Aldershot, UK: Ashgate, 2005.

———. *The Future Shapes of Anglicanism: Currents, Countors, Charts*. Abingdon, UK: Routledge, 2017.

———. "Theological Education and Formation for an Uncommon Occupation." In *Contemporary Issues in the Worldwide Anglican Communion: Powers and Pieties*, edited by Abby Day, 229–44. Farnham, UK: Ashgate Publishing, 2016.

Smith, Michael J. "The Role of the Pedagogue in Galatians." *Bibliotheca Sacra* 163:650 (2006) 197–214.

Walker, Andrew, and Andrew Wright. "A Christian University Imagined: Recovering Paideia in a Broken World." In *The Idea of A Christian University: Essays on Theology and Higher Education*, edited by Jeff Astley et al., 56–74. Milton Keynes, UK: Paternoster, 2004.

Ward, Pete. "The Hermeneutical and Epistemological Significance of Our Students: a Response to Bonnie Miller-McLemore." *International Journal of Practical Theology* 16:1 (2012) 55–65.

Wenger, Etienne. *Communities of Practice: Learning Meaning and Identity*. New York: Cambridge University Press, 2008.

14

Ministry as Occupation

The God Who Occupies Us

Samantha R. E. Gottlich

ANGLICANISM, IN SOME CIRCLES of thought, does not possess a singular theology or doctrine, but is instead in possession of a theological method.[1] The via media, at its finest, illumines the path of decision-making that leads to theological belief and doctrine. One need not believe what the church says just because the church says it, but one need not be left questioning all things without strong and loving guidance from the church, either.

While this might be altogether too bland for some, or too wildly liberal or open-ended for others, it is the essence of beauty for many Anglicans. The idea that many differences and alternatives can exist within one system of belief is, perhaps, the most Anglican idea there has ever been. As Martyn Percy would say, "We too easily confuse unity with uniformity."[2] This is the true essence of Anglican theology. We can stand united while we talk about and explore our differences in belief. And Percy believes it. His work in ecclesiology drives home the desire for an all-encompassing, all-loving church, as the volume of this book can attest to.

So rather than dwell further upon the church to which Percy aspires, it is my intent to peel back the layer of the church and investigate Percy's thoughts of the God whom the church serves. To put faith in the church and its work in the world, one must inevitably first put faith in the God who forms the church to gather as the Body of Christ. Perhaps, then, it is not a question of who or what is the church and how it is serving a changing world. Perhaps the more fruitful and fundamental question for Percy is: who is God?

Percy's published devotional writings are far less in number than his other works. They are, however, of the richest and most textured substance. The worry, of course, is

---

1. Percy, *Thirty Nine New Articles*, ix. Here we find a compelling argument for this statement, and well worth considering.

2. Percy et al., *The Bright Field,* 32

that for anyone in ministry, talk of God often returns to talk of the church. Percy once told a story of a principal of Ripon Cuddesdon that reserved Monday lunch hours for talking of God. The story revolved around the Principal's revelation that, more often than not, the hour passed in silence. The church has become so accustomed of talking around God, of moving to ecclesiology or polity, to doctrine or heresy, to the secular and commercialized world, that talking of God falls by the wayside. When the church stops to dwell upon God, not on God's actions or the state of the world that God has created, but just on God alone, there is often little to say. It is admirable, in light of this observation, that these reflections of Percy's begin to uncover the deep truths of God's nature, of God alone, for God's own sake. I think that this is because Percy believes ministry is occupation; first occupation with God fully, then occupation with what God is occupied with, and finally occupation with God's people. So now, finally, who is the God we are to dwell upon and be occupied by?

Through Percy's writing style, description, and self-reflection, we encounter a God of mystery but also of certainty. This nature of God displays itself in various forms, like being a God of heavenly unity but also of earthly flesh, and a God of complete inclusivity but also of consequences. Each contradiction is explored in various ways, some potentially unnoticed even to Percy himself.

The Great Paradox

It might be best to say that God is the Great Paradox. It surfaces again and again in Percy's content, and again and again in his own writing style. It's almost as if the paradoxical nature, of its own accord, refuses to be accurately or succinctly written. Percy's reflection on patience in the Christian life is one example. "Patience is always rewarded—because we always wait in hope, and because God is good. And if you can be hopeful, patient and good—all shall be well."[3] There is a tone of easiness which might catch the guarded reader askance. A simple answer to life's most complicated issues can seem demeaning. It seems to gloss over the antithesis of this—that if one loses hope, patience, or goodness at any point, chaos will reign and all previous effort at patience and goodness will go unvalued. So, entangled in the complex and paradoxical God that Percy dwells upon, there comes an impatience of his own. The evolution of his imagery is sometimes short-handed in a way that leaves readers at a dead end with no other roadmap to find the good God in moments of hardship or doubt. Paradoxical indeed.

3. Percy et al., *The Bright Field*, 13.

God in Heaven and on Earth

In one major vein of thought, Percy's various reflections on God in Christ are illustrative of this paradox. There are many. The argument over Christ's divinity and humanity is as old as the church itself. Division and condemnation have been the result of many such arguments over the course of time. Percy, to his credit, gives a nod to modern science and considers the implications of a God-made man. Does that mean God has DNA? How did the male chromosome come to be in a virgin birth? And yet, for Percy, it comes down to a rather humorous turn of phrase, "Perhaps Jesus, rather like atoms, isn't at his best when he is being split?"[4] Here the paradox of Percy's writing might be more powerful than his message. There is so much humor displayed with a topic that has split the church for millennia. Whether a lightness of touch or an intentional jab, the paradox of God is evident even in the structure of Percy's writing, itself. The more important point to Percy, and the one he drives home over the course of his devotional writing, is that God is enfleshed. The Word did not come to us in words, he came to us in flesh, an image, an object, a reality. A living, breathing thing that might better be represented by snapshots of his life rather than words.[5] Christ is the Word made flesh, not word. It is so important to Percy that God becomes man that he talks at length and in much detail about Christ's circumcision. His circumcision indicates, in a way that can only be hinted at through birth, that Jesus really is God in the flesh, in all of humanity, and foreshadows the bleeding he will do for us at the end of his life. The two wounds are tied together, the first and the last, taking on humanity and then saving all of it. A God who is beyond all things, incorporeal and vast, manifested only in light and sound before Christ's birth, purely divine, then becomes confined, finite, and encased in humanity. So the paradox continues.

Reflecting on Epiphany, Percy says, "Even beyond this, the stories point to the paradox that God is hidden and yet revealed. God is mystery and yet manifest. We can see God on our own yet discover him only when we are together. God is elusive, yet also the child next door or the visitor who turns up unannounced. We do not know God at all, and yet we do . . . That is the wonderful oxymoron that takes us to the heart of the Epiphany."[6] This gets to the heart of the paradox: a God revealed and yet unknown.

The greatest example of this comes with Percy's reflections on Christ's suffering. In *The Curse of God*, we find the speech-act explained.[7] Percy explores how cursing, slandering, or demeaning others can in action actually demeans or curses them. Then Christ, up on the cross, finds the ultimate curse, the silence of God. But if all the world's curses and slander are aimed at God in that moment, it becomes paradoxical that God's

---

4. Percy (et al.), *Darkness Yielding*, 4
5. Ibid., 19–21.
6. Ibid., 74.
7. Ibid., 83–86.

response is silence and then blessing. Jesus, in his last moments of life, offers forgiveness to those who slay him and a place in heaven for those who join him in death (i.e., the thief beside him). It is just another paradox, maybe the greatest paradox, that the sign of the cross transforms from curse to blessing because of God.

Inclusivity and Consequence

It might be the hardest contradiction of Percy's work to consider God both inclusive and consequential. But it is also, beyond Christ's life, the most heavily trafficked area of his devotions. His pure, unfiltered, unguarded belief in God's all-encompassing nature shines bright and clear. His reflection of the walls surrounding Jerusalem, and much of Israel and Palestine, are especially gripping in the twenty-first century, where the threat and reality of war and terror are always upon us.[8] Even here in the United States, the threat of walls that divide instead of include are heavy on people's hearts and lips. But in the midst of all the division, in the midst of fear and pain and suffering, in the midst of all the walls and gates that designate human rule and ownership, Percy, in simple words, utters the truth: "None of our walls reach to heaven; none of our boundaries and borders on earth, or in church, will be operational in God's Kingdom."[9] Here we find the notion of God as full inclusion, full embrace, full unity. Not even the divides between our churches can reach heaven. So, then, his further reflection on hope as the sustainer of all other virtues leads the readers to envision a time when the church is whole. Even in the divisions of the Anglican Communion, or the even larger split between Protestantism and Catholicism, or Eastern and Western Orthodoxy, or Islam and Judaism, there are no walls that reach heaven.

And yet he describes God in Christ as a discriminator. In a sermon he wrote on the healing of the Samaritan lepers, Percy writes, "In all of these healing encounters, the remarkable thing about Jesus' ministry is that it discriminates—for the unknown, the lost, the marginalized and the victimized. And almost nobody else . . . But the trouble with Christians is that we only regard ourselves as honorary sinners, and the church as a haven for the saved and secure. Yet it is for the lost and loveless . . . But the love of God is also free to those who don't say 'thanks', and seem not to deserve it."[10] How is it that God is free for all but also so costly? Again, Percy does not offer much in the way of explanation or excuse, only observation of the mystery of God. The greatest cost, that of one's life, comes in a few forms from Percy, but notably those in *Jonah and the Journey*.[11] This reflection on the entrance to Jerusalem at the start of Holy Week is a bit haunting. Equated to Bonhoeffer's return to Germany during the Third Reich, we encounter a Jesus who chooses always to face his destiny. As the

8. Percy et al., *The Bright Field*, 18–20.

9. Ibid., 19.

10. Ibid., 133–34.

11. Percy et al., *Darkness Yielding*, 79–82.

Gospel according to Luke would say, his face was always toward Jerusalem. Many of us, out of the instinct for self-preservation, turn and run at the knowledge of persecution or death due to our actions and beliefs, but Christ teaches us a new way. And because of Christ, it is with the hope of resurrection that we can turn and face danger and death ourselves. One of Percy's favorite quotes, mentioned more than a few times throughout his work, summarizes and concludes this well: "he does not ask too much of us—he only asks everything of us."[12]

Conclusion

There is an emotional, spiritual quality that enlivens Percy's text with sometimes flowing, sometimes halting, movement. It is his own experience and understanding of God and faith that drives his pen to the paper. It is clear that the God Percy is occupied with also occupies his writing. God, in a nutshell, is a paradox. God is known and unknown, heavenly and earthly, free to all and costly. Percy's writing, while clear in what he believes, leaves enough room for the reader to come to individual conclusions and beliefs about the nature of God. It is the Anglican theological method at its finest. In fact, it could be argued that the God who should occupy us, according to Percy, is quite a good Anglican.

While these reflections might offer some restlessness about the nature of God (they are, in fact, quite inconclusive in some regards), they also offer a measure of reassurance and confidence about the nature of God. The joy, the hope, the wonder to be found in God; these all rest in God as mystery and certainty. The observation of the dean of Ripon Cuddesdon bears out the truth. Eventually we must all fall into silence when we occupy ourselves with God. Perhaps Percy's writings reflect this more than they appear to. After all, for all the words he uses, he's only revolving around the reflection that God is the Great Paradox. What set of words could ever accurately describe that? Perhaps, then, that is the greatest paradox of all. For all the talking we want to do of God, it is only in the silence that God is found.[13]

Bibliography

Percy, Martyn. *Thirty Nine Articles: An Anglican Landscape of Faith*. Norwich, UK: Canterbury, 2010.

Percy, Martyn, et al. *The Bright Field: Meditations and Reflections for Ordinary Time*. Norwich: Canterbury, 2014.

———. *Darkness Yielding: Liturgies, Prayers and Reflections for Christmas, Holy Week and Easter*. Norwich: Canterbury, 2009.

12. Brother Roger of Taize, as found in various places throughout *Darkness Yielding* and *The Bright Field*.

13. 1 Kings 19:11–12 is the most poignant evidence for this, along with the observations made in this paper.

15

Response to Part III

Ecclesial Formation

Martyn Percy

F ORMATION SHAPES THE IDENTITY of the church—the extent to which it can adopt
a nature and character in its life after the example of Christ. Churches, congregations and those preparing for any kind of ministry—whether lay or ordained—seek
to live out the inner life of Christ that gestates within them. This is a calling rooted
in abiding and occupation. Just as God abided with us, and in Christ, made his home
amongst us, so are we called to form our churches into household and communities
which speak of the inhabitation of God. As God occupied the world, so are we called
to be occupied by the Spirit of God and the example of Christ.

This calls the church to a particular set of practices and virtues: patience, restraint, prophecy, and activism. The task of ministerial formation, much like ecclesial
formation, is to be shaped by the mind and heart of God: to become preoccupied with
what we think might be on God's mind and heart—the marginalized, and broken,
for example—and those on the very edges. The connections in this third section lie
hereabouts. Dan Warnke's essay examines and critiques the role of personal and pastoral formation in theological education, as men and women are incubated, educated,
and formed to become priests in God's church. This, in turn, has significant implications for wider ecclesial formation. Warnke notes the problems that there are with
"economic" models of the church, often driven by those who seek the church through
financial, managerial, or measurable criteria.[1]

This affects the mission and ministry of the church, and the ways in which it faces
outward to the challenges of contemporary culture (Samantha Gottlich). Correspondingly, the motif of jazz, explored by Monique Ingalls, illuminates the blends of freedom
and formality the church needs to fulfill its pastoral and prophetic tasks as much as

---

1. On this, see also Lough's unpublished paper, "The End of the Episcopal Seminary."

its inner life is a community of pragmatism and principle.[2] Much more could be said about the ways in which music, doctrine, and ecclesial identities feed off each other. Much of my work has explored the rise of new hymns and choruses in the worship of charismatic renewal. But in truth, one can see how the settings for an English-Anglican Eucharist are shaped by the musical setting. Thus, a modern rite states that the setting is to be sung "freely and flowingly"—yet also formally, much like the ecclesial polity it expresses. Likewise, the traditional setting expresses more formal, less fluid aspirations, and that the singing should sound more like "good public reading."[3]

Speaking of which, what of principles for the would-be pastoral-contextual theologian? In 1991, Bishop Peter Selby wrote an extremely important book called *BeLonging*.[4] It is a short, prescient, prophetic, and beguiling book, whose subtitle was "a challenge to a tribal church." In his book, Selby spoke of the kind of community the church is called to be, and contrasted it with the Church (of England) as it is often encountered. He wrote as a bishop and as a theologian. The book expresses some of the tensions that have coursed their way through my own writings on sexuality and the church.[5] These same tensions surface in studies on church polity and gender too,[6] and on worship and ecclesial polity.[7] The tensions are essentially the same throughout: between the local and the universal; the catholic and contextual; the church in the present, and the kingdom that is to come.[8]

Kate Blanchard's chapter neatly picks up on precisely this tension and trajectory in my writings on sexuality over a twenty-year period. That is, on the one hand, pushing the envelope, so to speak; and on the other hand, trying to hold to a catholic and collegial position that maintains unity. The same tension is there in writings on worship, and Monique Ingalls's chapter rightly sees this resolved—at least partially—in my use of the motif of jazz, blending together the formality of composition and freedom of improvisation. Precisely the same tensions are to be found in writings on theological education and formation. How is deep theological formation to take place if the learner is not free to critically explore tradition and revelation, and in so doing judiciously distance themselves from what, in the end, they must somehow embrace? And yet, there are some quite specific things—doctrines and articles of faith, for example—which are not up for negotiation, but rather for respectful assent.

The tension, then, is between the church as it is, and the church as it is surely called to become. The theologian, and indeed any who are charged with any kind of oversight

2. Percy, "Jazz and Anglican Spirituality"; Percy, *Words, Wonders and Power*. Bivins, *Spirits Rejoice!*.

3. See *The New English Hymnal*.

4. Selby, *BeLonging*.

5. See Percy, "Sex, Sense and Non-sense for Anglicans"; "Sexuality and the Citizenship of Heaven"; "Wheat and Tares and the Labourers in the Vineyard"; and "Beating the Bounds in States of Unfeeling."

6. See for example Percy, "Questions of Ambiguity and Integrity?"; "The Wisdom of Solomon."

7. Percy, *Words, Wonders and Power*.

8. Percy, *The Future of Shapes of Anglicanism*.

within the church, often walk a lonely road flanked by these two curbs. In Selby's chapter entitled "The Elders of the Tribe,"[9] he speaks about the bishops, reflecting on the moments when the ordination of women were discussed: "the House of Bishops on the issue show strong signs of having been diverted into accepting the agenda of those opposed to the change."[10] Selby interrogated the risks and dangers inherent in the idea that a bishop is called to be a focus of unity in the church, noting that "at the heart of that perception lies one of the most profoundly Christian of instincts, that we are called to bring together and not to divide, to seek and not to lose."[11] Profoundly Christian as this sentiment is, Selby also knew it to be only a half-truth. For the point he went on to make was that in the commitment to catholicity and collegiality—namely the act of standing together and speaking as one body—can unintentionally endanger and indeed exclude the possibility of prophetic dissent.

In one of his later essays for the *Church Times*, Selby noted that part of the cost of belonging to a church is "sacrificing a straight forward[sic] confidence in our own purity."[12] Communion is something that is necessarily shared, and correspondingly, we are all touched by one another's failures, and the necessary incompleteness of what constitutes church life. Selby's essay leaned on the parable of the wheat and tares and presents a characteristically systematic and passionate plea for living together in tension, rather than trying to pre-empt the refining fire of God by building a pure church on this side of the *parousia*. As he noted, situating the church in that context is not "a plea for flaccid tolerance, let alone indifference on the matters of profound importance."[13] It is, on the other hand, a plea to try to try to work together as much as possible for the widest common good.

All those who might claim to be more in the "Broad Church" camp and ethos, no longer occupy the central space in the Church of England. The debates on sexuality and gender in recent decades have pushed the church toward dilation and disagreement rather than any contracting consensus. The church has polarized. The center, as Yeats opined, might not hold. Even if it does, it has moved somewhere off to the right. We know that this is true, because all centrists now find themselves repositioned on the left, and it is very disorienting to be dislocated from the middle, without having done anything to move oneself.

Yet it is not in the character of those who are instinctive centerground moderates and committed to "Broad Church" polity to walk away from dialogue, or to behave in a sectarian manner. As Selby noted, "the structures of our church hold open the possibility of truth discovered in taking risks." Equally, on the other hand, they "hold open to us the possibility of shared decisions, or truth to be discovered when we take

9. Selby, *BeLonging*, 54–63.

10. Ibid., 61–62.

11. Ibid., 63.

12. Selby, "The Parable of the Wheat and the Tares," 11.

13. Ibid., 11.

risks with and for each other. The frustrations and tensions, and the loss of purity involved might turn out to be a price worth paying, despite all the apparent advantages of guarding our individual consciences."[14]

In this respect, Selby holds to a classic Anglican orthodox middle-way—one shared with committed centrists and "Broad Church" proponents. To paraphrase a writer from an earlier generation, Alec Vidler, the primary liberal-orthodox vocation, faithfully exercised, is not only humbling, but also *reconciling*.[15] It has the effect of showing that no party, or school of thought, or phase of orthodoxy, is ever as right as its protagonists are inclined to suppose, and that Christians of all persuasions have much more in common, both of frailty and strength, both of falsehood and truth, than the makers of systems and sects acknowledge. Here, Vidler prescribes a form of generous-orthodox liberalism and centrist moderation in the very act of preaching for it.

In Vidler's *Essays in Liberality* from 1970, he suggests that the patron saint of theologians ought to be the person who is tolerant. But not because they regard all opinions as doubtful or equal, but because they know that God alone is true. The person who is ready to learn from all people, not because he or she has no creed of their own, but because their creed assures them that God is teaching and chastening all people, the man who has plumbed the meaning for the human intellect of the great New Testament word about having nothing and yet possessing all things; that person who can at once rigorously doubt and sincerely believe epitomizes the true spirit of liberalism. I would go further here, and say that the spirit of Anglicanism lies with the "moderate majority"—tolerant, accommodating, open-minded, broad—but not flaccid or vapid.

For Vidler, this is the liberal, or perhaps moderate heart of Christianity. In some respects, these are the tensions in my writings that are surfaced so keenly, but quite differently, by Blanchard and Ingalls. It is not that I believe in liberal Christianity. Rather, I believe that Christianity is liberal. That is to say, humble: none of us have all the truth, and we need others, including those we don't agree with, to reach higher truths, together. It is reconciling too: in our divisions, we seek consensus and catholicity. It is questing: we all seek Jesus, Nicodemous-ly, so to speak.[16]

In terms of the wider church, we simply note that behind Vidler's ideas stands the deeper work of scholars such as Isaiah Berlin. Berlin is conscious of the tension between liberty and equality, which is frequently at the heart of many of our contemporary ecclesial dilemmas.[17] Equality may demand the restraint of liberty. Equally, liberty may prevent degrees of equality. In our churches, there is often a collision of values, which reflects the very essence of what we are as individual

14. Selby, *BeLonging,* 11
15. Vidler, *Essays in Liberality.*
16. I.e., Nicodemus, from the Gospel of John 3:1–21
17. Berlin, *The Crooked Timber of Humanity,* 12–18.

human beings, and as collective peoples or congregations and denominations—or as a global Anglican Communion.

Berlin is clear that the primary task of pursuing the ideal of an open society (or generous ecclesial polity) is to avoid intolerance and extremes, particularly extremes and intolerance that cause suffering and alienation. Yet in order to do that, Berlin states that it becomes necessary to live with tensions. Of course, one does not opt for intolerable choices, or choose to believe all opinions and behaviors are equally true and valid—they are not. But one is often left with a precarious equilibrium: "a certain humility in matters is very necessary," he writes, and then adds that "out of the crooked timber of humanity, no straight thing was ever made."[18]

The prophetic vocation, then—the radical, yet entirely reasonable challenge to the institution and its leaders—is sometimes to call it to straighten out. To speak out against the crookedness, so to speak. The irony is that far from being a choice between unity and catholicity, and justice and the prophetic, the church recovers its true self when it honours both, and heeds the critiques directed against it. The only issues here are truth, tone and time: how to speak the hard truths in love, and for how long.

The very idea of churches, congregations, denominations and a global Communion (such as Anglicanism) rests upon this. Churches are called to be places of education, among other things, where one can learn to live in fellowship and love with those we disagree with strongly, and yet still share in the life, joy, and liberty of the body of Christ. So are our seminaries and theological colleges. So are our clergy in their parishes, and congregations with their ministers. More unites and binds us in Christ than can ever divide us. Faith, hope, and love underpin this, supported by an ecology of deep and abiding charity toward one another, and directed toward the wider world.[19] It is the same charity and deep hospitality that God showed to the world in Jesus Christ. There can be no more profound witness than this to our world divided, as it is, and torn asunder by numerous alienating ideologies, divisive politics, oppression, inequality, and violence; namely, that despite our differences and disagreements as a body, love wins.

Bibliography

Berlin, Isaiah. *The Crooked Timber of Humanity*. London: HarperCollins, 1991.

Bivins, Jason C. *Spirits Rejoice! Jazz and American Religion*. Oxford: Oxford University Press, 2015.

Lough, Joseph W. H. "The End of the Episcopal Seminary." Unpublished manuscript, presented at the American Academy of Religion, 2014.

The New English Hymnal. Norwich, UK: Canterbury, 2005.

18. Berlin, *The Crooked Timber of Humanity*, 17.

19. See 1 Corinthians 13.

Percy, Martyn. "Beating the Bounds in States of Unfeeling." In *Intimate Affairs: Spirituality and Sexuality in Perspective*, edited by Martyn Percy. London: Darton, Longman and Todd, 1997.

———. *The Future of Shapes of Anglicanism: Currents, Contours, Charts*. London: Routledge, 2017.

———. "Jazz and Anglican Spirituality: Some Notes on Connections." In *Christian Congregational Music: Performance, Identity and Experience*, edited by Monique Ingalls, et al., 67–82. Farnham, UK: Ashgate, 2013.

———. "Questions of Ambiguity and Integrity?" *Modern Church* (March 2017). http://modernchurch.org.uk/downloads/send/32-articles/862-questions-of-ambiguity-and-integrity.

———. "Sex, Sense and Non-sense for Anglicans." *Modern Church* (January 2017). https://modernchurch.org.uk/downloads/send/32-articles/756-mpercy1215.

———. "Sexuality and the Citizenship of Heaven." *Modern Church* (January 2017). http://modernchurch.org.uk/january-2016/906-sexuality-and-the-citizenship-of-heaven.

———. "The Wisdom of Solomon." *Yorkshire Post*, March 9, 2017.

———. "Wheat and Tares and the Labourers in the Vineyard." *Modern Church* (January 2017). http://modernchurch.org.uk/january-2016/909-wheat-and-tares-and-labourers-in-vineyards.

———. *Words, Wonders and Power: Understanding Christian Fundamentalism and Revivalism*. London: SPCK, 1996.

Selby, Peter. *BeLonging: Challenge to a Tribal Church*. London: SPCK, 1991.

———. "The Parable of the Wheat and the Tares." *Church Times*, December 17, 1999.

Vidler, Alec R. *Essays in Liberality*. London: SCM, 1970.

Part IV

Selected Readings from the Works of Martyn Percy

16

Sampling

Martyn Percy's Essays
and Extracts

T HE WRITINGS IN THIS section are drawn from some of Martyn Percy's essays, journal articles, book chapters and shorter pieces (e.g., newspapers). They reflect his concerns with contextual theology, practical and pastoral theology, missiology and ecclesiology—and his wide-ranging writings that touch on subjects such as gender, sexuality, leadership, mission, congregational studies and Christianity in contemporary culture. Rather like Grace Davie's sociology, Percy invariably writes as someone who exhibits the very clear "traces of an Anglican mind" (as Timothy Jenkins puts it), and in so doing, much of his published material is irenic and temperate in tone, albeit seasoned with some sharp theological and ecclesiological critiques and interspersed with flecks of prophetic passion.

In the sample of writings that follows, we have opted for four groupings of writing. First, some very short extracts—shards, in effect—which offer some insight into the range of his writings. Second, three extracts from chapters and essays that address issues in ministry, such as formation, education, growth, management, and organization, but also attending to issues such as healing and prophetic social engagement. Third, three extracts from chapters and essays that address his concerns with congregational studies, including touching on his concerns with power and authority in congregational life, as well as fundamentalist and revivalist movements. Fourth, there are three extracts that address the concerns he has engaged with in the field of ecclesiology and missiology. Weaving in and out of each of these four sections are concerns with methodology, ethnography, the blend of elements that form contextual theology (e.g., pastoral, anthropological, etc.), as well as diverse threads and topics such as gender, music, authority, discipleship, the use of scripture, ecclesial organization, and institutional sustainability.

Percy's work often engages with contemporary crises and controversies in the church, as well as anxieties in mission and ministry. Percy's work also covers arenas such as theology, politics and public life, some work in doctrinal studies, and the study of religious conversion. The burden of his work, however, and the overall trajectory of his scholarship, has been centered on ecclesiology. Percy has emerged as arguably the key leader and developer of this field in Great Britain, through developing a blend of insights and methods drawn from the social sciences (especially anthropology and sociology) and theological studies. His overall "fit" within the field of contextual theology is dependent on understanding that Percy's work is primarily concerned with making sense of the church in society, and exploring the synergies that emerge in the interactions between Christianity and contemporary culture. As Harvey Cox noted, many decades ago,

> The theologian of culture cannot shift back and forth from his role as cultural analyst to his role as theological exegete as smoothly as Tillich could, or thought he could. The theologian of culture makes use of a variety of techniques—historical, social scientific, phenomenological—but his reading of a situation is informed at all times by his knowledge of theology. He writes quite self-consciously from a particular perspective and makes no false claims to sheer objectivity. His theological perspective colours everything from his selection of the topic, to his choice of sources, to his arrangement of the material and his decisions about emphasis and style. He tries to be conscious of his starting point and not to let his theology distort the picture. But he recognizes that no one writes without premises or a point of view. How to be aware of one's premises without being paralyzed by them remains one of the most persistent and fascinating problems with which any writer, theological or otherwise, must learn to contend.[1]

Readers will note how common motifs, themes, and issues emerge in Percy's work, as key-nodal points for interpretative insight. In attending to music, for example, Percy has directed our understanding of fundamentalism and revivalism away from explicitly articulated creeds and articles of faith, and more toward the tone and mood set by the worship songs that such groups sing, which to some extent are a more reliable indicator of the group's cherished theological proclivities. In the same way, musical orchestration and performance can be used as a motif for describing ministerial formation. Equally, the genre of jazz can be used interpretively with Anglican polity, helping us see how the blend of innovation and composition, the fluid and the fixed, fuse together in the repertoire of ecclesiological expression that typifies Episcopal congregations.

In the same vein, theories of power, authority, and charisma—and much of Percy's earliest work—continues to shape his understanding of leadership, ecclesial polity, governance, management, and mission in churches today. He has consistently developed frameworks here—applied and theoretical—that have been utilized by denominations across the ecclesial penumbra: Anglicanism, fundamentalism, revivalism, Pentecostalism, Methodism, Roman Catholicism, and more besides.

---

1. Cox, *The Feast of Fools*, 177.

At the heart of this enterprise lies a consistent academic vocation. Namely, how to read and interpret the church in the modern world; the contours and currents of contemporary culture, and how they shape and are shaped by Christianity; and the contours and calling of mission and ministry, as the church seeks to adapt to the complex and challenging environments in which it finds itself, and at the same time, continues to try and shape such contexts for the common good, and bearing in mind the deep calling of the church to enable the work of the Kingdom of God.

Bibliography

Cox, Harvey. *The Feast of Fools*. Cambridge, MA: Harvard University Press, 1969.

Jenkins, Timothy. *Religion in English Everyday Life: An Ethnographic Approach*. New York: Berghahn, 1999.

Part IV—Section 1

Short Extracts

17

Christianity and Contemporary Culture[1]

J ESUS INVOKES HIS DISCIPLES to be the "salt of the earth." Matthew 5:13 reads: "You are the salt of the earth; but if salt has lost its taste, how can its saltiness be restored? It is no longer good for anything, but is thrown out and trampled underfoot." In interpreting this text, most preachers and many Bible commentaries work with a single false assumption: that the "salt" in this text is the white granular chemical we know as sodium chloride, normally found in a condiment set or kitchen cupboard, where its purpose is to add flavor to foods, or occasionally to act as a purifier or preservative. Yet the fact that Jesus refers to "the salt *of the earth*" ought to immediately alert us to another meaning for the text. The "salt" (*halas*) mentioned in the text is hardly likely to be table salt, since it is a chemical and culinary improbability that sodium chloride will lose its flavor. Any salt that is extracted from food, water or any other substance remains "salty"; even if it loses its form, it retains its essence, as many a spoilt meal and frustrated chef can bear witness.

The substance of Jesus' words are, in Greek, *to halas tes ges*, "the salt *of the earth*," with the word for "earth" here not referring to the world at all, but rather to soil. In other words, the "salt" that Jesus is referring to here is probably a kind of salt-like material or mineral such as potash or phosphate. These *halas* elements were available in abundance in and around the Dead Sea area of Palestine, and were used for fertilizing the land and enriching the manure pile, which was then spread on the land.

There are further clues as to why our usual understanding of this text is, in some respects, flawed. The word "taste" that features in most English versions of this passage is actually a poor translation of the Greek word *moranthe*, which literally means "to become foolish." A number of translators render the word as "tainted," but "loses its strength" is probably the best way to translate the word: loss of strength and foolishness would have been synonymous in Jesus' age. Moreover, and ironically, although paved paths also have their uses; Jesus' salt is arguably never "useless."[2]

---

1. This chapter originally appeared in *The Salt of the Earth: Religious Resilience in a Secular Age* (Sheffield: Sheffield Academic Press, 2002), 16–18.

2. For a fuller discussion of this passage, see Shillington, "Salt of the Earth?"

The soil, of course, contains many different elements, all of which are intertwined. "Soil," then, is a kind of cipher for the particular cultural contexts (i.e., religious, cultural, ideological, social, etc.), in which Christians are to "be salt." The many soils of the world carry, in various degrees, qualities of empowerment and disempowerment within cultures. Moreover, in a post-modern world, we can now see that English culture is being increasingly homogenized through globalization, which has brought with it materialism, individualism, consumerism, and hedonism, with the undesirable result of suffocating the life-giving force of the earth.

The empowering mission of the church, like the salt of Jesus' parable, has a consistency of power. However, that power, enculturated into contexts, does not lead to uniformity. Rather, it leads to considerable diversity of expression, growth, and human flourishing. The salt must always respect the type of earth in which it is situated. Diverse cultural sensibilities have to be taken into account in the mission of the church. The soil may also be inhospitable; it may be rocky, thorny, and adversely affected by climatic conditions.

Under these circumstances, the task of being the salt of the earth is more demanding. A key to understanding the relationship between churches and their context rests on a tension. We might say that, on the one hand, churches are to be engaged in their communities and influence them, perhaps in ways that are not easily identified as specifically "Christian." The power of salt is that it is pervasive and nourishing. Here, ministry might accommodate culture; Christ is therefore, in some sense, *for* culture. On the other hand, Christianity also proclaims God's kingdom—a radically "other" culture that will sweep away the present order. This is the beacon of light set on the hill: it illuminates the present, but points to a new order. This is the Christ who is above or against culture. The ministry of the church seeks a kingdom that is to come, and it therefore resists the standards of the world.

Accommodation and resistance are, of course, closely related. What they share, in character, is resilience. We might say that accommodation is a "soft" form of resilience: flexible, pliable, adaptable, and so forth. Whilst resistance is a "hard" form of resilience: concrete, unyielding, and defiant. The true character of spiritual resilience—construed in almost any local church or ministerial context—will show that Christians simultaneously resist and accommodate culture. The church, albeit unconsciously for the most part, understands that it lives between two cultures.

This way of understanding the *halas* (salt) of Jesus' metaphor changes the sense of the text significantly. In fact, it completely undermines the most conventional translations and expositions. The "salt" is not to be kept apart from society, and neither is it to be used as a purifier or as an additive stabilizer. Ministers are not to be simply preservers of the good societies or institutions, and neither are they merely agreeable folk adding flavor to either an amoral or immoral context. More powerfully and positively, true religion, as salt, is a life-bringing force giving itself to an otherwise sterile culture. Thus, the "salt" of Jesus' metaphor is a mutating but coherent agent that is both distinct, yet diffusive, in its self-expenditure. As a result of individuals, communities, values, witness, and presence—the *halas*—being literally dug into society, the earth or soil will benefit, and many forms of life can then flourish. Correspondingly, salt that loses its strength (rather than its "flavor"—the more usual translation) is only suitable for making paths, as the biblical text confirms. Thus, the salt of Jesus' metaphor is not only counter-cultural; it enriches "the earth" and many more things besides, by being spread around and within it.

So there is an irony here. The "task" of the salt is not necessarily to maintain its own distinctiveness, but rather to enrich society through diffusiveness. There is teleology for this salt: what begins as being a distinct and separate substance—to be purposeful— has to give itself to the soil, and so ends up being absorbed and lost to the ground it nourishes. Of course, this reading of the metaphor makes sense of Jesus' own self-understanding, which in turn is reflected in his parables, teachings and other activities. So, if the church or the disciples of Jesus are the salt of the earth, they will begin by being a distinct yet essential component within society, but who will ultimately fulfill their vocation by engaging self-expenditure.

Bibliography

Shillington, V. G. "Salt of the Earth?" *The Expository Times* 112:4 (2001) 120-22.

18

Casual Ethnography[1]

ON A RECENT VISIT to a church that has spawned a large number of "cell churches" and "fresh expressions," I spied a map on the wall in the foyer that illustrated the issue starkly. Maps, of course, as any sociologist or anthropologist knows, are representations of reality. They require the reader to collude with scales, symbols, and other codes to develop a sense of what is on the ground. But the map is not reality; the same applies to any description of anything—it must also be interpretative. This particular map placed the church I was in right at the heart of the city it was ministering to. From this center, ribbons flowed out far and wide to the suburbs, which were then pinned in to a significant number of peripheral locations. It was a web-like image: a center, but reaching out far and wide with tentacles. The message of the map was clear: we touch every part of this city; we have it covered.

Yet I was well aware that a number of the identified locations for coverage were contentious. After all, I lived in this city. To be sure, there could be no question that small groups of Christians, who attended this church in the center, were meeting in these neighborhoods, week in and week out. They were praying for these localities too, "naming and claiming" the streets in passionate and concentrated extemporary prayer meetings. But I also knew where many of these gatherings were held. And that, with one or two rare exceptions, the vast majority of the inhabitants in the neighborhoods (including those that attended their own ordinary local or parish churches) were mostly ignorant of these other meetings. In other words, for the church identifying itself at the heart of the city center, there was a map and a story that spoke of widespread engagement with all these different neighborhoods. Yet on the ground, there was little evidence to support this.

In what way is such a map interesting? Simply, in the way that this city center church continued to feed off and promote its rhetoric of *extensity*. Whereas the actuality on the ground—in missiological terms—was that the church had confused extensity with *dispersed intensity*. The two are not, of course, the same. Dispersed intensity lacks the complex social engagement that can really only come about through dense

1. This chapter originally appeared in Peter Ward, ed., *The Wisdom of the Spirit: Gospel, Church & Culture* (Farnham: Ashgate, 2014), 16–21.

and reticulate institutional structures that emerge out of churches that are committed to deep local extensity. The map, in other words, told a story. And this is partly what the study of culture and Christianity needs to press on with. In so doing, we shall make some new maps. These maps will be of those who are themselves trying to navigate and chart the waters of how to be charismatic Christians, churches, and congregations amidst the challenges of contemporary culture in the twenty-first century.

19

On Women Bishops[1]

T HE FAILURE OF THE Church of England's General Synod to pass the Measure
   enabling women bishops will come as a heavy blow to many inside the church—
but also many outside the church, who will find the decision hard to fathom. Yet I
remain sure that it is only a question of time before the Church of England will take
this next step; it is just not now.

A concern for order and unity in the church is undoubtedly what drives many
of those opposing the ordination of women to the episcopate. But a concern for order
and unity in all creation—a no-less-Godly yearning—is just as vital for our church
and world. The church, meanwhile, must continue to wait prayerfully and hopefully,
and in a spirit of charity.

The church lives constantly in the tension between patience and faithful reform.
On the one hand, it is bound to remain true to its given nature. On the other hand,
it is bound to reform and change in each generation, as the Holy Spirit continually
renews the church. In a famous, if rather overlooked, essay written over sixty years
ago, Yves Congar (renowned French theologian) addressed the subject of true and
false reform in the church. Congar, a Roman Catholic, was attempting to reach out to
the Protestant denominations, and re-engage with the spirit that had given birth to the
Reformation. Like all Christians, Congar believed in unity. But he was also realistic
about the differences, diversity, and disagreements that caused division.

Congar starts with the virtue of patience. He moves on to exploring how impatient reform can lead to the reformers believing themselves to be persecuted. And
although the essay ends with a plea for unity, and for continued patience and dialogue,
Congar's revolutionary insight was that church leaders ultimately have a responsibility
to *not* be too patient. In other words, a moment comes when a decision must be made.
Hopeful patience may prove to be wise for some while. But pointless waiting is merely
prevarication posturing as discernment.

The church knows a great deal about waiting. It waits for the coming of the kingdom. In Advent, it waits for the coming of Christ. In Lent, the church waits for the

---

1. This chapter is adapted from an article that appeared in the *Daily Telegraph* (November 21,
2012).

radical transformation of Easter. Each of these periods of waiting is hard, yet anticipative; but is neither pointless nor endless.

The church waits in hope, because it believes that waiting, wisdom, discernment, and new insight will enable a purer and clearer leading of the Holy Spirit. All Christians know this can be difficult and demanding; but that for a flourishing church and the mature spiritual life of individuals, it is essential.

In respect of the ordination of women, there has already been much waiting. The earliest campaigners for women's ordination—those on the fringes of the suffragette movement, such as Maude Royden—could barely have imagined that it would have taken more than a century for women to receive equal treatment in the Church of England.

It was 1912 when Royden began editing *Common Cause*, the journal of the National Union of Women's Suffrage Societies. Five years later she became assistant preacher at the City Temple in London—the first woman to occupy this office. After the Great War ended, she founded the Society for the Ministry of Women, campaigning and speaking for the ordination of women well into the 1940s.

Royden did not live to see General Synod passing a motion in 1975 stating "this Synod considers that there are no fundamental objections to the ordination of women to the priesthood." And then General Synod, in 1978, asking the church to "prepare and bring forward legislation to remove the barriers to the ordination of women to the priesthood and their consecration to the episcopate."

The first women were ordained to the diaconate in England in 1987, twenty-five years ago. The first women ordained to the priesthood followed soon after in November 1994, with thirty-eight of our forty-four Diocesan Synods voting in favor. And for the recent debates on women in the episcopate, the numbers were even better, with forty-two out of forty-four dioceses voting in favor of women bishops. Maude Royden, you might think, would be rejoicing in heaven. She will have seen the celebrations of her American cousins taking place many years earlier. The Episcopal Church has had the pleasure and privilege of women bishops for many years.

But some will never move, and it is because of this that the duty of our church leaders to not be too patient now comes more sharply into focus. To place this in context, I have only to recall a conversation with a diocesan bishop opposed to the ordination of women. I asked him about the wider implications of already having women bishops in the Anglican Communion.

What would he do, say, with a male priest who had been faithfully offering priestly ministry overseas for many years, but was ordained by a woman bishop? And if that same priest now asked him for permission to officiate in his diocese when he returned home? Would he grant the license? No, he said. Would he insist on some sort of conditional re-ordination? No, he said. Then what, I asked? He replied, simply, that he would ordain. There was no question about this. The man was not a priest, and he never had been.

Herein lies the rub, I think. The legislation before Synod was already a "compromise," in the original sense of that word. That is to say, it was a co-promise: an agreement that together we would move forward mutually, not severally. It was this that the Synod had set its mind to. That the church lost sight, so early, of a simple one-clause measure, is a real tragedy. And it was this failure of leadership, ultimately, that led the church inexorably and slowly to the resulting failure of the legislation at General Synod.

How though, can the Church of England move forward? As a body, we seem to have been quite slow in learning that diversity, disagreement, and differences cannot simply be managed into consensus. The political, synodical, or managerial solutions that have been proffered so far have singularly failed to inspire and galvanize most of the debaters. And the public, understandably, have largely switched off in droves.

There needs be greater trust in the processes of Synod—for God meets us in meetings; and here we find truth too. But what is also needed, I think, is better and inspiring theological leadership (not just clearer or louder) that will lift the debate into a different dimension. This was lacking on the floor of the Synod debate. And its more general absence from the church quickly leads to a rather pedestrian debate about the rights of groups and individuals, how they compete and conflict, and how to find compromise.

The only sure result here is that everyone loses. Indeed, that was the result of the debate: nobody won. The church lost; the campaigners for women bishops lost; and the apparent victors lost too—but by a margin that gave them the strangest of pyrrhic victories. And the public lost too. They have lost confidence in a church that is supposed to serve the whole nation, and not just the qualms and proclivities of small squabbling interest groups.

What is not needed, I am sure, is for the debate to speedily descend and degenerate into a Left-Right divisiveness. Some are already eagerly talking about the Equality Act and relishing the prospect of political interference. Other are inferring that the principal problems are falling attendance, with further inferences and accusations of being out of touch with modern values. None of this will work, I fear.

At present, and in our attempts to organize the church and manage its diversity, we are often guilty of trying to "give unto thy servants that peace which the world cannot give" to ourselves.[2] But it is a gift of the Spirit, grafted through conversation, conflict and slow consensus that gradually builds us into communion. The genius of Christianity lies in its contestability; therein lies its richness too.

If diversity could have been easily managed, the New Testament would perhaps have given us some pointers; and the Apostles and Early Church Fathers might then have led the way. But alas, it is something of a conceit of modern times to suppose that the church is an organization in which diversity can be ironed out; difficulties managed; and the church homogenized into a discourse of uniform clarity for the media

2. Evensong, *The Book of Common Prayer* (1662).

and the public at large. The church is a body that seeks unity in the midst of diversity; it does not aspire to being an ecology of managed uniformity.

Munir Fasheh, the feminist Palestinian theologian, offers a telling insight into how the debate on women in the episcopate is now beginning to feel for all the women (and many men) who long and pray for women bishops in our church. Fasheh tells of how a woman in Beit Sahour (near Bethlehem) behaved when Israeli taxation officers came to town. When the army had already taken nearly everything from her house, she finally protested at the removal of her fridge—the last thing left in her kitchen. She said to the officer, "why don't you leave the fridge—I need it to feed my hungry children, and the food and milk will rot outside." Trying to tempt her, the officer said "OK—but pay $25, and you can have it." She said, "I am not bargaining with you; I am appealing to you as a human being who probably has children." He said, "alright, pay $5." She said, "you don't seem to understand." He said, "OK, pay just $1." She said, "take the fridge—it's yours."

From the outset, this debate has always been between those charged with a duty to compromise, and another group, who we are told, simply cannot move. But this dynamic has reduced the debate to some kind of plea-bargaining for women bishops. It is humiliating to have to barter and beg. Love, integrity, and dignity become diminished when having to bargain for something offered so begrudgingly.

This story from the Palestinian-Israeli conflict is, of course, not a comparable analogy for the debates that currently divide our church. Our saga is not about the oppressed and the oppressor. Yet the story from Beit Sahour more than does its job in conveying a deep and underlying dis-ease: that visceral sense of bewilderment and betrayal that many women now feel within the church. After all, pay a dollar, and you get the fridge: a bargain, surely? But as many have discovered before, power gained "at any price" (whether high, or seemingly very low), usually translates into ashes, not riches. So, that proverbial million-dollar question hangs in the balance: can the Women Bishops' legislation now get through? But Synod is not actually facing a million dollar question at all. This is a simple one-dollar question, straight from Beit Sahour. Should any gift that is not offered to the church—fully, freely, and graciously—really be bargained for?

So, the only way forward is for the church to be, as the Apostle once remarked, "transformed by the renewal of our minds" (Rom 12:2). Here, the word "renewal" can be taken in at least three senses: a recovery of something lost; improvement of what is in the present; or a complete exchange of the past and present for a new future. Just what kind of renewal the Church of England both seeks and needs is the key to the future of this debate. For this, we need outstanding theological leadership, and not a mere suite of managed compromises. And yes, more waiting: but perhaps in hope?

20

On Ministry[1]

PART OF THE PURPOSE of utilizing the analogy of evolution as an analytical and critical lens for the study of ministry has been to account not only for the differences, but also to map the commonality across the clerical species. It is at this point that something of the purposes of a Creator might be said to be manifest in the variegated patterning of clerical identity and roles. What, after all, are the clergy for? Whilst a variety of theologies of ministry may entertain romantic fantasies about their point of origin and purity, it is in the tasks and life of ministry that clergy—perhaps uniquely—begin to express something of the correspondence between the Creator and the created. The "set-apart-ness" that guarantees both centrality and marginality in any community is fundamental to the distinctiveness of the species and the particularity of the vocation. Moreover, it is frequently in the marginality of life and death that the office and the calling becomes grounded and apparent. It is here that the clergyperson connects with the enchantment of the Christian story, and, hopefully, becomes one who can in turn enchant with their ministry, by helping congregations find fresh meaning and substance in familiar materials.

One writer, a funeral director who constantly witnesses the ministry of clergy in death and bereavement, reflects upon this:

> I remember the priest I called to bury one of our town's indigents—a man without family or friends or finances. He, the grave-diggers, and I carried the casket to the grave. The priest incensed the body, blessed it with holy water, and read from the liturgy for twenty minutes, then sang *In Paradisum*—that gorgeous Latin for "May the angels lead you into Paradise"—as we lowered the poor man's body into the ground. When I asked him why he'd gone to such trouble, he said these are the most important funerals—even if only God is watching—because it affirms the agreement between "all God's children" that we will witness and remember and take care of each other.[2]

---

1. This chapter originally appeared in *Clergy: The Origin of Species* (London: Bloomsbury, 2006), 179–88.

2. Lynch, "Good Grief," and Lynch, *The Undertaking*.

This vignette, as if one needed reminding, illustrates how there is an emotional bond between the minister and those beyond the congregation. The bond, no matter how feint, is an expression of Christ's own for those who are beyond the immediate horizon of social or ecclesial communities. The calling of the clergy is, in other words, an extension of God's love that must surpass any interest in the protection or the interests of the species itself. It is inherently costly and sacrificial in its orientation, seeking not its own security, but rather expressing the continual risk of incarnation. The same writer notes how, even at apparently formulaic funerals, clergy frequently step across their own proscribed lines of denominational belief and liturgical behavior to form a bond with the deceased or the grieving, thereby expressing a commonality that is traceable throughout the clerical species. In so doing, ministers improvise and perform the love of God, holding souls and bodies in contested and ambiguous territory that is itself on the very edge of human existence and understanding:

> I remember the Presbyterian pastor, a woman of strength and compassion who assisted a young mother, whose baby had died, in placing the infant's body into a tiny casket. She held the young woman as she placed a cross in the baby's hands and a teddy bear at the baby's side and then; because the mother couldn't, the pastor carefully closed the casket lid. They stood and prayed together—"God grant us the serenity to accept the things we cannot change"—then drove with me to the crematory.
>
> Or the Baptist preacher called to preach [at] the funeral of one of our famously imperfect citizens who drank and smoked and ran a little wild, contrary to how his born-again parents had raised him. Instead of damnation and altar calls, the pastor turned the service into a lesson in God's love and mercy and forgiveness. After speaking about the man's Christian youth, he allowed as how he had "gone astray" after he'd left home and joined the army. "It seems he couldn't keep his body and his soul aligned," the young pastor said, and seemed a little lost for words until he left the pulpit, walked over and opened the casket, took out a harmonica, and began to play "Just As I Am" while everyone in the congregation nodded and wept and smiled, some of them mouthing the words of promise and comfort to themselves.

Whilst one can speculate on the ultimate origin of this type of ministry, most ministers will understand its purpose, and ultimately identify themselves within such stories. They will know that in this there is some spiritual comfort for one of the deepest human pains. They will understand they are expressing something of that divine balm for that most earthly of anguish. They will know that they have been called into a relationship with their environment that is flecked with certainties and ambiguities, coupled with insecurity and status. And in the midst of that, and perhaps pondering the origin of their own vocation, ministers will reflect on how they have been drawn into something deep and mysterious that can be lived, but seldom understood and articulated:

In each case these holy people treated the bodies of the dead neither as a bother or embarrassment, nor an idol or icon, nor just a shell. They treated the dead like one of our own, precious to the people who loved them, temples of the Holy Spirit, neighbours, family, fellow pilgrims. They stand—these local heroes, these saints and sinners, these men and women of God—in that difficult space between the living and the dead, between faith and fear, between humanity and Christianity and say out loud, "Behold, I show you a mystery."

In ending on this note, I am conscious that there is more than something of an irony here. We began these essays by noting Russell's observation (as well as those of others such as Bob Towler and Anthony Coxon[3]) that clergy had been facing a growing problem of marginalization since the Victorian era, and had through various means, not least the "invention" of professionalism, attempted to combat this in the nineteenth and twentieth centuries. However, this marginality is, it seems, part of the character and construct of being a minister. Clergy, to function as effective ministers, often discover their role and tasks to be about becoming central in the more marginal and ambiguous moments of life. Clergy occupy that strange hinterland between the secular and the sacred, the temporal and the eternal, acting as interpreters and mediators, embodying and signifying faith, hope and love. They are both distant and immediate, remote yet intimate. And in occupying this most marginal and transitory ground, and sometimes helping to close the gaps between these worlds, they become humanly and spiritually necessary even as they live out their (partly willed, partly imposed) social marginality. It is a unique, yet evolving, paradigm. It is nothing less than to follow the call of Jesus: to belong both to the wilderness, but also to the city. To be a citizen of some place; but also of heaven. To be of the people; but also for their sake, to be wholly other. And it is possible that even Darwin understood something of the complexity of this conundrum for the study of ministry, as he reflected on the role of the Creator, and the struggle for life within the environments he had studied. He concludes the sixth edition of *Origin* with these words:

> There is grandeur in this view of life, with its several powers, having been originally breathed by the Creator into a few forms or into one; and that, whilst this planet has gone circling on according to the fixed law of gravity, from so simple a beginning endless forms most beautiful and most wonderful have been, and are being evolved.

3. See Towlet and Coxon, *The Fate of Anglican Clergy*, and Anthony Russell, *The Clerical Profession*.

Bibliography

Lynch, Thomas. "Good Grief." *Christian Century*, July 26, 2003.

———. *The Undertaking: Life Studies from the Dismal Trade*. New York: Penguin, 1998.

Russell, Anthony. *The Clerical Profession*. London: SPCK, 1980.

Towlet, Robert, and Anthony Coxon. *The Fate of Anglican Clergy*. London: Macmillan, 1979.

21

Music, Theology, and Ecclesiology[1]

> I was watching (TV) one night, and they were interviewing a man about jazz music. He said jazz music was invented by the first generation out of slavery. I thought that was beautiful because, while it is music, it is very hard to put on paper; it is so much more a language of the soul. It is as if the soul is saying something, something about freedom. I think Christian spirituality is like jazz music. I think loving Jesus is something you feel. I think it is something very difficult to get on paper. But it is no less real, no less meaningful, no less beautiful."[2]

C ONNECTIONS BETWEEN MUSIC, THEOLOGY, and ecclesiology are not difficult to make. Historically, the rather raucous local musical ensembles that provided musical accompaniment to English church services in the early seventeenth century were gradually replaced by one single instrument—the pipe organ—in the eighteenth century. Were notes of harmony sounded by the accompanists, or was the noise made one of tuneful discord? Or was there another message? However one interprets the arrival of the pipe organ, the result was, invariably, an order and discipline applied to services that clergy themselves could not have orchestrated. The pipe organ, in other words, eventually provided a musical order and *discipline* to services that complemented the liturgy. This, in turn, was developed by the rise of hymnody in the late eighteenth and nineteenth centuries. Church services, from being times and occasions that could be contested, became far more coherent. Nowadays in the Church of England, one can occasionally catch a glimpse of what the local musical anarchy in churches might have sounded like three hundred years ago. Simply tune in to how the bells toll for services—and see if the bell-ringers stay for the service they have just announced.

This essay is, however, neither a historical or theological exploration of the connections between music and ecclesiology. Writers such as Jeremy Begbie (see *Theology,*

---

1. This article originally appeared in Monique Ingalls et al., *Christian Congregational Music: Performance, Identity and Experience* (Farnham: Ashgate, 2013), 67–80.

2. Miller, *Blue Like Jazz*, 239.

Music and Time, Cambridge: CUP, 2000; and *Resounding Truth: Christian Wisdom in the World of Music*, Grand Rapids: Baker Books, 2008) have contributed significantly to our understanding of the connections between theology and music. The work of many church historians—including Keith Thomas[3]—testify to the unusual and complex history of musical accompaniment down the ages in our English parish churches. That has tended to be more of a history of disconnections and reconnections. In contrast, the connections I want to explore in this essay are somewhat tendentious, and rooted in a kind of metaphorical reconstruction. And, more generally, the observations made in this essay are grounded in the principal concerns and approaches I take to the study of the church, and to Christianity and contemporary culture. Here, I am usually shaped by two intellectual genealogies. The fusion of the two is, in itself, a "jazz-like" combination: making space for improvisation, but also forming views, analysis and ideas through a tense synthesis of style and genre.

The first genealogical stream is broadly a fusion of sociology and anthropology. The legacy of Clifford Geertz, and indeed the more recent work of David Martin, for example, is constantly in the background. The second genealogical stream is theological, and shaped by writers such as James Hopewell, Jim Nieman, Denham Grierson, and Nicholas Healy—contextual theologians of varying hue and color. And these two intellectual genealogies produce a kind of "binocular" approach to the study of the church, with all that this metaphor implies. Some things, in the distance, come in to view; only a few things are focused upon, but in order to extrapolate a larger picture. So, as someone working with a framework of sociology and anthropology, I am naturally wary (some might say suspicious) of the ways in which structures and practices are legitimized by appeals to fundamentals—be they biblical or drawn from the "tradition." And one must be equally wary of the idea that the development of structures and practices can be further legitimized by appeals to the work of the Holy Spirit. That said, the theological element to the "binocular" is receptive to revelation, and to ways in which the body of Christ grows and develops in local contexts—denominations, places and times, and amongst people genuinely and truly seeking to live authentic and faithful Christian lives that correspond to God's revealed will for the world. It is has been my practice, in studying and writing on contemporary ecclesiology, fundamentalism, and revivalism, and together more generally with Christianity and contemporary culture, to deploy this "binocular" approach. I regard it as a complementary trajectory, and not a competitive impulse. And as I stated earlier, there is more than a hint of a "jazz-like" methodology in bringing the two together to create a harmony, rhythm, and sound from two streams or sources that usually, at first sight, do not appear as though they belong together.

This essay is a reconstructive enterprise, an attempt—tenuous in places, granted—to suggest some new and potentially illuminating connections between ecclesial polity and jazz music. And I must own up to a personal interest here—in jazz, generally,

---

3. Thomas, *Religion and Decline of Magic*.

and in *bossa nova* particularly—with which this essay is concerned. I am, of course, aware of some of the potential pitfalls in attempting such an essay. In characterizing jazz, I am aware that there can be a tendency to engage in "ethnic essentialism" (e.g., on rhythms) when trying to describe the origins of music.[4] Whilst I have tried to avoid this where possible, the purpose of this essay is, however, twofold. Namely, to make a general argument for jazz as a good metaphor for understanding Anglican ecclesial polity (or at least its ideal and caricatured forms of its English behaviorist proclivities); and from that, to infer something more particular about *bossa nova* in relation to Anglican polity. What I will be attempting to sketch, therefore, are the connections between a certain kind of jazz and the cadences and timbre of Anglican ecclesial polity, using jazz as a metaphor, to explore a kind of "morphological mood." In suggesting such a thing, I am mindful of the links that some authors—writing in the field of ministerial formation and spiritual development—have already made between music and ecclesiology; even though these are often more implicit than explicit.

Thirty years ago, two theologians, Daniel Hardy and David Ford, in their seminal collaborative work,[5] suggested that it might be fertile to think of the Trinity as music—and most especially as jazz. Their metaphor offers an insight into the Trinitarian nature of God: the composer-performer-listener linkage can resonate with the Father, Son, and Holy Spirit. Music is also created in time, and yet creates its own time. It also involves law and freedom, and its practice always reveals "more than there is." The authors also went on to suggest that ecclesial life has something of the "jazz factor" about it. Again, truth is comprehended through combinations. Hardy and Ford also suggested that, between order and disorder in worship, there is a third way: non-order. Non-order is, for Hardy and Ford, not a compromise between order and disorder, but rather a different way of seeing ecclesiology—something with an open, yet composed texture. They use the analogy of jazz to celebrate the freedom of worship (in effect, an orthodox, liberating theology of praise) by pointing out that jazz combines the two principal modes of musical expression in the West: composition and improvisation.

In jazz, they suggest, the two come together to create something that is fleeting, original, novel, harmonic, and spontaneous, and yet also recognizable and memorable. In using this analogy, Hardy and Ford find an expression of praise that is resonant with their doctrine of God: free and liberating, yet also known through specific types of agency, such as liturgy and sacraments. The theology that they articulate makes room for the novel and the innovative, whilst at the same time affirming the traditional and the concrete.

Hardy and Ford are therefore suggesting that music changes us, by wooing us into participation. Music is "a harmonic language" that is attentive to mood: sadness, celebration, reflection, and dynamism are "caught" in music. Moreover, music is a gift, and as we learn to read it, understand it and use it, we learn more about the God who

4. West, *Race Matters*, 150–151.

5. Hardy and Ford, *Jubilate*.

has given it. Gifts express the giver. In thinking about the Trinity metaphorically as jazz music, one becomes mindful of its combinations: its formal dimensions married to its innovative nature, and its capacity to cover a spectrum of needs from celebration to commiseration. Moreover, there are the many different sounds that make up *one* sound. Music is ultimately both purity and a blend; it is enriched by the singular and the symphonic. Like an ecclesial community, the distinctive and the different remain, even in the midst of diversity.

This might allow us to say that divine music is simultaneously scripted, yet improvised; formal, yet free. When the church (in all its breadth) corresponds to the Trinity in worship and appreciation, it becomes an *orchestra* of praise and participation. Likening the Trinity to jazz is perhaps not so strange. Jazz is a genre of music that is normally associated with both freedom of expression and a lesser degree of formality; where improvisation and composition meet. It is simultaneously transforming yet traditional; never predictable, and yet reliable. Order and freedom coexist, with passive listening turned into participation and communion. From an apparently tense synthesis of composition and improvisation, the fruits of inspiration, liberation, and dance can issue. To understand the Trinity through a jazz-like metaphorical lens is not to understand each note and sequence, nor is it to deconstruct the score: it is to listen, learn, and participate.

* * *

Ultimately, all we have attempted in this essay is to establish some playful connections between a certain kind of jazz and the cadences and timbre of Anglican ecclesial polity, and, using jazz as a metaphor, to explore a kind of "morphological mood." Perhaps as Burt Bacharach might have said, and so far as spirituality is concerned, it has "the look of love" about it. And so far as Anglicanism as a whole is concerned, it is a polity neither of order or disorder; it is an abductive faith, after all—composed, yet open. It has something of the *bossa nova* spirit; one that sees that improvisation and composition belonging together. True, this may be said of jazz more broadly, together with many other genres of music from around the world. But perhaps what is so distinctive about *bossa nova* specifically, and jazz more broadly (as opposed to other genres of music that combine improvisation and composition), and that is particularly helpful in this analogy, is the attention that it brings to mellowness and openness, which I hold to be deeply Anglican dynamics.

As George Herbert said of spirituality and prayer, in its ideal Anglican spiritual form, it is "softness, and peace, and love, and blisse . . . the milkie way; the bird of paradise." But let the last word go to Don Miller's homage to jazz and spirituality, and scripted toward the close of Steve Taylor's film (Lionsgate, 2012) of the book. Don, the subject of the book and film (and played by Marshall Allman in the film) sums it up like this:

Sometimes you just have to watch someone love something before you can love it yourself. Penny (my girlfriend) loves Jesus. My dad loves jazz. He told me jazz is like life because it doesn't resolve. And he gave me his record collection to prove it. And I have been listening to those records, over and over. But every time I put on John Coltrane's "A Love Supreme" [1964, Impulse Records] I swear I can hear something my father says isn't there. I hear a resolution. Resolution. A final end to the story? I know not everyone hears the universe this way. But what if Penny is right? What if God is trying to compose something? And what if all these stars (above us) are just notes on a page of music, swirling in the blue, like jazz?

Bibliography

Hardy, Daniel, and David Ford. *Jubilate: Theology in Praise*. London: Darton, Longman and Todd, 1984.

Ingalls, Monique, et al. *Christian Congregational Music: Performance, Identity and Experience*. Farnham, UK: Ashgate, 2013.

Miller, Don. *Blue Like Jazz*. Nashville: Thomas Nelson, 2003.

Thomas, Keith. *Religion and Decline of Magic*. London: Penguin, 1971.

West, Cornell. *Race Matters*. Boston: Beacon, 1993.

22

Peace-Building in the
Anglican Communion[1]

NORTHERN IRELAND HAS SEEN bitter civil strife and violence over the last century, and much of it predicated on religious difference. Yet somehow, the province has come together, and the violence abated, and the possibility of deep and lasting peace established. The "Balkanization" of the province—dividing the places and peoples into smaller autonomous self-governing entities—has been avoided. There are many, of course, who would seek exactly that future with the Anglican Communion: "virtual provinces,"[2] exclusions, and so forth; in effect, an attempt to create an array of small "safe" ecclesial homelands that no longer relate to neighbors. But the Communion, of course, is fiercely resistant to such Balkanization. It knows in its soul that the sum is greater than the part; that the catholic whole is to be preferred to an assemblage of parts that are each sure of their own individual righteousness. Northern Ireland has taught us that peace with our neighbor (so yes, our enemy) is worth struggling for, and that independence from each other is a lesser vision.

So how might a fusion of political, emotional, and ecclesial intelligence offer some kind of indicative pathway ahead for the Anglican Communion? Several things can be said. And in order to ground these brief ecclesial reflections more substantially, I am drawing upon the firsthand account of the peace-making process in Northern Ireland, written by Jonathan Powell. In *Great Hatred, Little Room*, Powell hints at several instructive, mediating, yet temporary paradigms that have implications for theology and ecclesiology.[3] Here again, and for illustrative purposes, our attention is drawn to current difficulties in Anglican polity.

First, Powell notes how the uses of "constructive ambiguity" can help establish conversation and rapport at the early stages of negotiation. In one sense, critics might say

1. This chapter originally appeared in *Anglicanism: Confidence, Commitment and Communion* (Farnham: Ashgate, 2013).

2. A "virtual province" refers to a non-geographic collation of congregations, bound together by theological proclivity or a specific dissenting (from the majority) position, serving under a designated archbishop.

3. Powell, *Great Hatred, Little Room*. The title of the book is taken from W. B. Yeats's poem, "Remorse for Intemperate Speech," 1931.

that this can mean two sides talking two slightly different languages. Speaking is taking place, but true listening is more limited than it may appear to be. Powell concedes that constructive ambiguity is fine for the beginning of a peace process, but not enough in the middle and end stages. Ambiguity has to be rejected in favor of clarity.

Second, Powell notes how consensus must be built from the center. Again, this is vital to begin with. But you have to reconcile opposites. So for Anglicans, the Archbishop of Canterbury—or other instruments of unity—may be able to hold together competing convictions for some while; effectively, to "manage diversity." But in the end, there is no substitute for the ultimacy of Peter Akinola shaking hands with Gene Robinson; or for Peter Jensen sitting down with Katherine Jefferts Schori. Whilst this may be hard to imagine, it is the kind of "peace" that is anticipated in God's kingdom; the end of rhetorical violence, and the ushering in of a community of blessing that transcends mere consensus.

Third, Powell's insights suggest that the fragmentation and "Balkanization" of polity be avoided at all costs, because it is difficult, if not impossible, to build consensus out of brokenness. In ecclesiological terms, if you have the choice between heresy and schism, choose heresy. You can correct the former; but it will always be difficult to ever heal the latter. This lays a particular burden on the identity and role for the so-called "instruments of unity": the Archbishop of Canterbury, the Primates, the Anglican Consultative Council, and the Lambeth Conference. The instruments will need to act lightly and precisely, lest they become part of the problem.

Fourth, these instruments of unity and peace may need to triangulate in times of crisis: it is not good hovering between passive/aggressive; liberal/conservative; traditional/progressive modes of behaviors. It will be necessary to get beyond these polarities; and for the instruments to become *facilitators of peace*, not mere persuaders for a temporary cessation in hostilities. The difference is crucial, clearly. But as Powell notes, bringing peace takes time, and necessarily involves setbacks. Underpinning this must be a resolute commitment to talking and listening—without which peace is impossible. And as the church is a community of peace, attentive listening to God, self and otherness is at the core of its very being.

Fifth, the exchange of peace is a central act of preparation and declaration in anticipation of receiving Christ in bread and wine. Communion is centered on companionship—literally, "those we break bread with." Because of this, compromise—literally to "promise together"—is something rooted in the heart of the Eucharist as we pledge ourselves to one another and to God. In accepting the consequential company that our ecclesial belief and behavior brings us, we commit to a form of unity that is predicated on peace and bound for unity. That form of Communion, of course, does not always mean agreement. Nor does it follow that there will never be anger and division. But because of God's economy of blessing, it remains the case that no "height or depth" (see Romans 8) can separate us from the love of God that is found in Jesus Christ. And because of this—God's ultimate purpose for creation—we cannot be separated from one another.

But the last word in this section belongs to Powell, as he reflects on the long and arduous road to peace in Northern Ireland. His reflections are instructive for all those who seek peace and unity in any context, including those wracked by the pain of ecclesial conflict, where there can often seem to be no hope of peaceful resolution, let alone unity:

> The ambiguity that had been essential at the beginning [of the process] began to undermine the Agreement and discredit the government—the referee for its implementation. We then had to drive ambiguity out of the process . . . and insist on deeds rather than words. This process of squeezing out the ambiguity and building trust was painful and it took time, but a durable peace cannot rest on an ambiguous understanding . . . .
>
> So if there is one lesson to be drawn from the Northern Ireland negotiations, it is that there is no reason to believe that efforts to find peace will fail just because they have failed before. You have to keep the wheels turning. The road to success in Northern Ireland was littered with failures. [But] there is every reason to think that the search for peace can succeed in other places where the process has encountered problems . . . if people are prepared to talk.[4]

But, what kind of talk? According to Peter Kevern, there is a reciprocal relationship between ecclesiology and practice in the Church of England. Logical arguments are invoked in support of a given course of action; conversely, pragmatic positions adopted by the church eventually find expression as ecclesiological arguments. The debate on women's ordination represents an anomalous instance of this process, because it has resulted in two parallel "integrities." Each integrity has separate beliefs about the wisdom of such ordinations, backed up in both cases by a range of internally coherent ecclesiological positions. Those of the opponents of women's ordination are on the whole, less widely noted, and less lucidly expressed.

Partly due to the fragile nature of the communion at present, and also to a rather odd enclave mentality, the practical beliefs of the two integrities are mutually exclusive. Of course, these ecclesiologies have far more in common than is immediately apparent. As I have argued before, Anglicanism is carried in a kind of kinship—a sort of familial morphology in which mutual recognition is often quickly discerned. There is initial evidence for this, in the fact that of those opposing the ordination of women, few have abandoned the Church of England, despite losing the debate. Oddly, both sides profess to share a structured way of thinking about the church, a meta-ecclesiology, in which both the wings and the center recognize something of the other, even if they are so far not giving formal expression to it. This all sounds very serious on one level, yet it perhaps pays to recall James Gordon Melton's sociological

---

4. Ibid., 315, 322.

treatment of churches in terms of "families." For all the protestations of Forward in Faith, or proponents of Third Provinces, it is simply not very easy for your average Anglo-Catholic to feel "at home" in Roman Catholicism.

Bibliography

Powell, Jonathan. *Great Hatred, Little Room: Making Peace in Northern Ireland.* New York: Vintage, 2008.

Mission and Ministry

The Formation of the Church

23

Restoration, Retrieval, and Renewal

Recovering Healing Ministry in the Church—Some Critical Reflections[1]

One of the Protestant Reformation's key contributions to the church was the recovery of the centrality of the Bible in the Christian life.... If we are serious about the Reformation doctrine—an idea found in the scripture—that the church reformed is always reforming, we must make room for practices like divine healing in the modern church. Divine healing undeniably was part of Christ's ministry and something that he expected the church to experience (today).[2]

T HIS ESSAY IS CONCERNED with a trinity of practical-pastoral theological questions. First, to what extent are the healing ministries—ones that are so prevalent in contemporary charismatic evangelicalism—different from those practiced in the gospels? Second, can the claims to have restored or retrieved the charism of healing ministry in the ministry of Jesus, and that of the early church, really be corroborated? Third, are the healings of the late twentieth century and early twenty-first century evangelicalism and revivalism really the same kind of phenomena that might have been witnessed in the eighteenth century?

One of the defining hallmarks of fundamentalist and revivalist communities is the claim to be "biblical." The reasoning runs simply and clearly, and as follows: things that were practiced and believed in the time of the apostles are now, once again, to be found amongst the "chosen" or the sanctified gathering of the faithful. Put another way, it has taken this new group of true believers to recover or retrieve a lost element or authentic practice from the early church—one that the wider church had either forgotten, neglected, or perhaps even repressed. Thus, the wider church, typically, is narrated as heterodox, distracted, or, at best, lacking in focus. But in the new community of the sanctified—the newly inaugurated biblical church—God's original intentions and blessing are restored.

---

1. This essay is a much shorter extract draws on material from *Words, Wonders and Power, Power and the Church*, and "Restoration, Retrieval and Renewal."

2. Wimber, *Power Healing*, 245.

Such reasoning found its purest expression in the United Kingdom within (so-called) Restorationism—a movement that gave birth to "House Churches" and other forms of communitarian Christianity from the 1960s. Restorationists believed that God no longer had much purpose for mainstream denominations. Instead, claimed those within the Restorationist movement, God was restoring his kingdom in these latter days, and new, purer forms of Christian discipleship would emerge, in preparation for and anticipation of Christ's imminent return. Restorationists stressed separatism (from other churches), and claimed to be restoring the original, true church that God had intended from the time of the apostles. The new House Churches emphasized charismatic epiphenomena such as healing, deliverance, and speaking in tongues. They also stressed the restoration of "original" patterns of church leadership, including apostles, prophets, and healers.[3]

Alongside the development of Restorationism in the United Kingdom, and from the post-war era onwards, the emergence of charismatic evangelicals also led to a renewed interest in prophecy, deliverance and healing ministries—in particular, there being some sense in which divine healing could be reclaimed as a fundamental charism of the true church. My doctoral study focused on fundamentalism and revivalism, and part of this work involved the habitual attending of healing meetings—as an observer, observing participant, participant observer, and sometimes just participant. I kept notes. I was absorbed by the dynamics of the gatherings, and the claims.

My purpose was never to ask if the claims to be healed were true or false—for theologians cannot know such things.[4] Rather, the question was: what do these healing encounters and stories mean to those who are gathered? I would listen to eloquent sermons and testimonies from healers, who would tell you that Jesus could heal anyone and anything. And I would then watch them take off their spectacles, put them carefully in their top pocket, and invite people to come to the front for ministry. I would puzzle over how illnesses were described, and addressed. Some of the things I saw and heard were profoundly moving. Some were troubling and disturbing. Others were risible; or just plain odd. Testimonies varied in scope, ranging from minor illnesses, diseases, or conditions cured; to stupendous claims of lost organs regrown (e.g., eyes, arms, etc.), cancers removed, and the dead raised.[5]

But I suppose what caused me to struggle was the refusal of most speakers and preachers to readily acknowledge the relationship between cause and effect, unless it could be tied to something personal and moral. Yet according to the World Health Organization, well over 90 percent of the illnesses and diseases on this planet have a single cause: poverty. We lose five million children a year, under the age of two,

---

3. On this, see Walker, *Restoring the Kingdom*.

4. There are studies that purport to "prove" miracles, and from the late twentieth century, sympathetic treatises that explore claims of healing have been undertaken by, amongst others, David Lewis (*Healing*) and Rex Gardner (*Healing Miracles?*).

5. See Cotton, *The Hallelujah Revolution*, ix–xiii.

to perfectly preventable malaria-related fever. Clean the nearby water supply, and you eradicate the breeding grounds for the mosquitoes that spread the disease. I sat through many healing meetings that described many individuals recovering instantly and miraculously from a fever. But inside I protested all the while, that even if that were true, it was *pointless* when the causes of fever were not addressed.

In the United Kingdom, obesity is now one of our biggest threats to health, and one of our biggest killers. Yet it is not a disease of the rich; but the poor. Maps of the United Kingdom spell out the demographics of obesity plainly. The concentrations of obesity lie in our poorest and most disadvantaged communities. I have been to many healing meetings that have been beautiful, pastoral, and powerful. But I have never been to one in which anyone returned to their home one hundred forty pounds lighter. (The dieting industry would be ruined if this happened). A recent map of Scotland, taken from September 2014,[6] showed that the concentrations of population voting "yes" to independence correlated precisely with earlier maps that chart concentrations of obesity (i.e., parts of Glasgow, Dundee, etc.).[7] In turn, those maps of obesity also correlated precisely with indices of poverty and unemployment. And the maps charting the related consequences—cancers, heart conditions and diabetes—follow in their wake. The areas in Scotland that voted "no" to independence were, unsurprisingly, the wealthiest and healthiest.

Re-Reading Healing in the Gospels:
Comparing and Contrasting

Contemporary charismatic renewal has witnessed a surge in specifically spiritual healing methods. A number of healers claimed that they were operating within a "revival tradition" that can be traced back to the New Testament, but point to specific periods of history when the church had retrieved its healing mandate. However, this account of history depends more than a little on literal and naive readings of the past. Although relatively little has been done in terms of intellectual evaluation of the revival, the field is wide open for a range of assessments.[8]

My purpose is not to examine whether or not modern Christian healing methods "work." Clearly, many people believe they do. What is perhaps of more importance is to enquire into the original purpose of miracles, particularly those in the gospels. I wish to argue that the task of miracles in the gospels primarily have more to do with social, political, and ethical considerations, rather than being naked demonstrations of divine power simply intervening in often tragic human

---

6. http://www.bbc.co.uk/news/uk-scotland-scotland-politics-29255449.

7. http://news.bbc.co.uk/1/hi/health/7584191.stm.

8. See Pattison, *Alive and Kicking*, 50.

situations—with consequent implications for their audiences and the disciples, and, therefore, for the church today.[9]

Jesus' healing ministry as recorded in the gospels appears to be extremely discriminating. On only four occasions is a healing recorded in a building used for religious purposes (see Mark 1:23–27, Mark 3:1–5, Matt 21:14, and Luke 13:10–13, and their Synoptic parallels). In two of these four cases, it is a woman who is healed, whose actual right to be there must be in question. In every other case, healings by Jesus take place outside any community of faith, except where "crowds" or the poor are deemed by an Evangelist to constitute a group of faithful people.[10] Jesus' friends or relatives are not usually the beneficiaries of his healing power either.[11] In fact, of those who are healed, we know little, not even a name, and certainly nothing of the long-term response of those who are healed.

In virtually every healing story—and there are over forty in the gospels—the person healed is politically, socially, or religiously disadvantaged—unloved or unnoticed by the majority of onlookers or witnesses. The gospel miracles, then, are a record of Christ reaching out to the marginalized, dispossessed, cast-out, and cursed in society and from faith communities. There is even a sense of urgency about this within the context of the Messianic mission. The woman healed of a crippling infirmity in Luke 13:10–17 is healed on the Sabbath: first century Rabbinism allowed for such healing, but only when there was danger of death, which the narrative strongly suggests was not the case. Fitzmyer describes this healing as "the welfare of a human being [taking] precedence over . . . religious obligations."[12] The thrust of the narrative is to contrast the jealousy or scepticism of the "leader of the synagogue" (v. 14) with the plight of the "daughter of Abraham" (v. 16): Jesus emerges as Lord of the synagogue and Sabbath in the space of seven verses—a healer whose responsiveness and urgency of ministry reflects his overall mission.

By way of comparison, much of what passes for charismatic healing movements in today's church is very different. Evangelists and healers who offer ministry usually do so in the context of a church or "faith-gathering." The ministry on offer is inward-looking, intended for those who join or become members. It largely leaves the dispossessed and marginalized of society alone. Where they are included, the terms are often

9. In saying "primarily," I would want to make it clear from the outset that I am not claiming to have constructed a complete scheme for interpreting miracles in the gospels; there will be exceptions to the rule. Equally, miracles in the Old Testament and in Acts have not been considered, which some readers may also find problematic.

10. On this, see Alkier and Weissenrieder, *Miracles Revisited*.

11. Exceptions to what I have stated above are few. Peter's mother-in-law is possibly a friend of Jesus, and is healed (Matt 8:14–15; Mark 1:30–31; Luke 4:38–39). However, she may have been a widow, and therefore her status as such may be more significant. Mary Magdalene is healed (Luke 8:2), but the precise nature of her affliction is unclear. Lazarus is raised to life (John 11:1–44), and is, according to John, "beloved" of Jesus.

12. Ibid., 101.

strictly defined, whereas those who were encompassed by Jesus' healing ministry had no obstacles placed in their way, at least by him. Frequently, those who claim to be healed already possess significant social, moral, or religious status, whereas the healings of Jesus seem to be directed at people who are exactly the opposite.[13]

In fact, Jesus, both in parable (e.g., Luke 15—the Prodigal Son) and activity (Luke 7—the woman at Simon's house) demonstrates the importance of the assurance of forgiveness being offered *before* the respondent can speak or confess their sin. The gospels seem to be saying that you can only truly confess once you have heard the words of absolution. In contrast, many exponents within contemporary charismatic healing movements would insist on confession of sin as a precondition to being offered healing ministry.

In saying this, I am not dismissing accounts where sin and sickness are bound up together. The social construction of reality concerning the relationship between sin and sickness in Jesus' day was complex, involving processes of hereditary curse, personal responsibility, third-party blaming, and psychosomatic causes. Jesus' attitude to the perceived cause and effect relationship between sin and sickness is, to say the least, ambiguous; he simultaneously rejects and accepts it, treating it almost playfully at times. It is not unfair to suggest that when he does appear to acknowledge it, agreement with the link is not necessarily implied.[14]

The disparities between the way in which Jesus conducted his healing ministry and the way in which modern healers usually proceed are numerous. However, what is perhaps more striking, as the table below shows, when compared to the subsequent list of healing miracles, are the *types* of people healed by Jesus, and the consequent implications for the church in "liberal" and "conservative" spheres.

Typologies of People and Groups Healed in The Gospels

1. The "demonized" (by society?), mentally ill, and therefore ostracized from society and faith community (1, 9, 17, 21, 22).

2. The handicapped—marginalized in society—due to inability to function or fit in "normally" (6, 7, 15, 16, 18, 40).

3. Lepers and other "untouchables"—banned from society (5, 11, 34).

4. Children and widows—little social status (10, 14, 17, 30, 38). Also single mothers (14, 30).

13. The question over the social status of people who are healed is a contentious one. Wimber's healing meetings seem to primarily cater for white American, European, and Commonwealth middle-class people. But other healers do operate in different racial and social contexts with equally dramatic effects. For a fuller discussion of this see my *Words, Wonders and Power*.

14. Alkier and Weissenrieder, *Miracles Revisited*, 103ff.

5. Women adjudged "unclean" through sin/sickness (11, 31, 32; see also Luke 7, John 4, and John 8).

6. Others judged to be ill through sin (40; but possibly the case with most sickness—see John 9).

7. People of other faiths (14, 19, 34, 38).

8. "Multitudes"—seemingly indiscriminate, except insofar as the gospel writers use the term "multitude" to refer to those excluded from "normal" religious activity and the poor in society. They are to be distinguished from the religious of the day such as the Pharisee and Saducee "denominations," as well as Elders, Scribes and Priests (3, 13, 23, 24, 25, 26, 27, 28, 36, 37).

An Overview of The Healing Ministry of Jesus

Description	Matt	Mark	Luke	John
1. Man with unclean spirit		1:21–28	4:31–37	
2. Peter's mother-in-law	8:14–15	1:30–31	4:38–39	
3. Multitudes	8:16–17	1:32–34	4:40–41	
4. Many demons		1:39		
5. Leper	8:2–4	1:40–42	5:12–13	
6. Man with palsy	9:2–8	2:3–12	5:17–26	
7. Man with withered hand	12:9–14	3:1–6	6:6–11	
8. Multitudes	12:15–16	3:10–11		
9. Gaderene demoniac	8:28–34	5:1–17	8:26–39	
10. Jairus's daughter	9:18–19,23–26	5:22–24, 35–43	8:40–42, 49–56	
11. Woman with bleeding	9:20–22	5:24b–34	8:42b–48	
12. A few sick people	13:58	6:5–6		
13. Multitudes	14:34–36	6:54–56		
14. Syrophoenician's daughter	15:21–28	7:24–30		
15. Deaf and dumb man		7:31–37		
16. Blind man		8:22–26		
17. Child with evil spirit	17:14–18	9:14–27	9:38–43	
18. Blind Bartemaeus	20:29–34	10:46–52	8:35–43	
19. Centurion's servant	8:5–13		7:1–10	
20. Two blind men	9:27–31			
21. Dumb demoniac	9:32–34			

Description	Matt	Mark	Luke	John
22. Blind and dumb demoniac	12:22		11:14	
23. Multitudes	4:23		6:17–19	
24. Multitudes	9:35			
25. Multitudes	11:4–5		7:21–22	
26. Multitudes	14:14		9:11	6:2
27. Great multitudes	15:30			
28. Great multitudes	19:2			
29. Blind and lame in temple	21:14			
30. Widow's son			7:11–17	
31. Mary Magdelene + others			8:2	
32. Woman bound by Satan			13:10–13	
33. Man with dropsy			14:1–4	
34. Ten lepers			17:11–19	
35. Malchus's ear			22:49–51	
36. Multitudes			5:15	
37. Various persons			13:52	
38. Nobleman's son				4:46–53
39. Invalid man				5:1–9
40. Man born blind				9:1–7

The types of people and groups listed in the table have their modern equivalents, and it is clear that the overwhelming focus of Jesus' ministry lay with the poor, unknown, and excluded of his day. So, the healings themselves can be seen as activity which characterizes the love of God for the forsaken and damned, especially those who are victims of religious, moral and societal exclusion. This love even extends to including those of other faiths, with no conditions attached; nobody becomes a Christian in the gospels, or is compelled to believe anything, because of a miracle. The activity therefore stands as a literal, as well as a symbolic, sign of God's love for the oppressed, and questions the role of religion and society in colluding with or instigating that oppression.

As Mary Grey says, the healings of Jesus are "characterised by a redemptive mutuality in which people come into their own."[15] This is endorsed in some of Jesus' encounters with others even where a physical healing does not take place. Therefore, to focus on repeating miracles as demonstrative acts and reifications of divine power

15. Grey, *Redeeming the Dream*, 51.

for today—trying to retrieve or restore the performance and practice of healing miracles—essentially misses the original context and target of Jesus' healings, which had radical political, social, and religious dynamics that were usually missed in their day, but should not be ignored for now.[16]

Healing as Taking on Affliction

There is a further dimension to the healings of Jesus that should be mentioned, which places his ministry in sharp contrast to much of today's charismatic healing movements. It is the notion that there is some sense in which Jesus takes on the suffering and affliction of the individuals he cures, such that it becomes part of him. This view would not have been strange to the early church Fathers, whose progressive move toward a richly incarnational theology required them to conclude that what was not assumed could not be redeemed. So, Jesus risks social ostracization when he dines with Zacchaeus, consorts with sinners, and receives women of dubious repute into his company, precisely in order to take on their brokenness, as well as take on the taboos of society that maintain structures that divorce the secular and sacred.

As Janet Soskice has pointed out, it is no different in the healing miracles themselves. Noting the story of the hemorrhaging woman in Luke 8:40–56 (c.f. Mark 5:21–43 and Matt 9:18–34), she points out that what is striking about it is Jesus' willingness to touch or be touched by an "impure" woman. Although modern readers of the text may find this aspect of the narrative difficult, the significance of Jesus' action should not be underestimated; "[she] defiled the teacher which, according to Levitical law, she would have done for she was in a state of permanent uncleanness, polluting everyone and everything with whom she came into contact."[17] Her poverty—"she had spent all she had"—is a direct result of her affliction. Yet Jesus, apart from healing her, also seems to challenge the social and religious forces that have rendered this woman "contagious." Jesus calls her "daughter" in all three accounts, and all three Evangelists stress the woman's faith. Interestingly, the Synoptic accounts of the hemorrhaging woman are all paired with the raising of Jairus's daughter. Again, the issues of impurity

16. On this point, we note Richard Hooker's critique of the Puritans, dated to the late sixteenth century. In the Preface to the *Lawes of Ecclesiastical Polity*, Hooker argues against the Puritan claim that church life should be based only on what is demonstrably proven by scriptural precedent. This endeavour, argued Hooker, is wrongly conceived and impossible to carry out:

> "What was used in the Apostles' times, the Scripture fully declareth not; so that making their times the rule and canon of church-polity, ye make a rule, which being not possible to be fully known, is as impossible to be kept . . . in this general proposing of the Apostolical times, there is no certainty which should be followed: especially seeing that ye give us great cause to doubt how far ye allow these times" (Preface IV.3–4—see Hooker, *Laws of Ecclesiastical Polity*, 77–146)

17. I am indebted to Dr. Janet Soskice for some of these insights, in her (unpublished) paper "Blood and Defilement," given at the Annual Society for the Study of Theology Conference, 1994.

(touching a corpse) and of menstruation occur: the girl is twelve, and her untimely death clearly prevents her from entering womanhood. Jesus declares her "not dead, but sleeping," and his touch, resulting in his defilement, raises the girl.

Frank Kermode's work has important resonances with the observations made by Soskice.[18] Kermode's discussion of the purity issues in Mark 5 picks up on the fact that the stories of the hemorrhaging woman and Jairus's daughter have been paired and conflated.[19] Kermode cites as evidence for this the undue prominence Mark gives to the narrative by the sharing of the number "twelve" (the girl is twelve, and the woman has also been ill for twelve years):

> This coincidence signifies a narrative relation of some kind between the woman and the girl . . . an older woman is cured of a menstrual disorder of twelve years' standing, and is sent back into society. A girl who has not yet reached puberty is reborn.[20]

Kermode presses his claim that the narrative is centered on gender-related taint with some force: "they take their complementary ways out of sickness into society, out of the unclean into the clean."[21] Jesus does not negate either of the women, nor does he "demonise" their afflictions, or imply that they are unclean—the healing comes from their being accepted by him as they are: their "defilement" is done away with.

Modern readers might well struggle with these texts, and wonder what all the fuss is about in relation to normal issues in "feminine hygiene." But contemporary society may not be quite as progressive as it imagines. The story of how the Samaritans began—the organization founded in 1953 by the Reverend Chad Varah—has some resonance with the story of Jairus's daughter. Varah's inspiration came from an experience he had had as a young curate in the city (and diocese) of Lincoln. Varah had taken a funeral for a girl of fourteen who had killed herself because she had begun menstruating, and was mortified that the girl had to be buried in un-consecrated ground, with parts of the burial liturgy redacted as it was a suicide. Varah became concerned about the state of sex education for teenagers in the city, and started to work with young people, especially listening to those who were contemplating suicide. Varah's Samaritan movement grew rapidly when he subsequently moved to London. Within ten years, the Samaritans were a sizeable charity, offering a supportive and empathetic listening service which is not political or religious.

So, the story of Jairus's daughter and that of the older woman (both women, note, are unnamed) are remarkable. The pairing of these two stories seems to turn everything around. A woman becomes a daughter, and a daughter becomes a woman. Moreover, we might also allow ourselves a little speculation. What precisely is the

18. See Kermode, *The Genesis of Secrecy*.
19. See also Myers, *Binding the Strong Man*.
20. Ibid., 132.
21. Ibid., 134.

relationship between Jairus and the bleeding woman? Remember, Jairus is the Synagogue Ruler, and would therefore have an instrumental role in policing its precincts, keeping the impure and undesirable out. So now we have a story about immediacy and patience. The woman has waited for twelve years—and probably been excluded from worship for the same period of time. One of the subtle yet blunt exercises of power is to make people wait, or be kept waiting.

If you are in power, people wait to see you—or you keep them waiting; it is the powerless who must wait. For that appointment, the letter, the news, the interview—waiting is a form of powerlessness. Jairus kept this woman waiting for years; but he wants Jesus, to heal his daughter, *now*. What does Jesus do? He gets distracted by an apparently pointless brush with a member of the crowd, and keeps Jairus waiting—and too long too. Where is the lesson in this? This is a miracle with a moral. So, we are now in a position to understand the significance of Jesus' encounter with the two women, and their "healing," or indeed, why Jesus bothered with lepers. When, in the midst of the dynamics of this particular understanding of the relationship between an "impure" body and the social body, Jesus reaches out and *touches* the unclean and declares them healed, he acts as an alternative boundary keeper in a way that is religiously and ritually subversive to the established procedures of his society. Jesus disrupts and undermines the social order that declares such people outcasts. So, Jesus makes possible a new community that now refuses to be founded upon the exclusion of the other.

Whilst these elements in the gospel accounts may be implicit in the text, or buried by "traditional" forms of exegesis, their uncovering raises serious issues for the contemporary church in its healing ministry. The taking on of another's affliction is not something many would contemplate, particularly if that requires the "healer" to then be regarded as also being "handicapped," "defiled," or "sinner."

So, my reading of this healing miracle in the gospels suggests three things. Firstly, that touching and embracing the afflicted, in the widest possible sense, is critical to Jesus' ministry. Secondly, that judging the cause of sickness, or naming it as "sin," has no place in Jesus' ministry. Thirdly, that (somehow) inculcating the sickness itself into the body of Jesus was important.

There is a fundamental sense then, in which the suffering God needs to be brought alongside the Jesus of healing miracles. The crucified Christ needs to be placed firmly in the center of any theology of healing, not because Jesus' death somehow negates sickness, but because the death itself is the ultimate fulfillment of those miracles. In death, Jesus becomes the man who is going nowhere, an emblem of hopelessness, betrayed, vilified, and cursed; he earns the scorn of society, for "he saved others, but he cannot save himself" (Matt 27:42). So, at the heart of the gospel, there is a profoundly broken person, who was prepared to be broken for others, and ended up paying the ultimate price. This vision of Jesus flies in the face of the usual portrayals one encounters in the majority of modern healing movements. The emphasis is usually on

Christ's strength and his ability to accomplish all things. Those who are afflicted must lose what afflicts them before they can join the company of the redeemed—that same company will certainly not be joining them, descending to their level. Yet at the heart of the Eucharist, it is the action of breaking bread that signifies Christ's solidarity with his people, and points to the salvation beyond.[22]

The Task of Miracles

The social, moral, religious and political impacts of Jesus' healing miracles are inescapable. Part of the value of these miracles in Jesus' ministry, besides healing individuals, seems to be in questioning society over its attitude to sickness itself. The sin of the individual as a cause is uniformly rejected by Jesus. Instead, he tends to challenge crowds and onlookers, questioning their implicit or explicit role in the person's misfortune. For Jesus, healing is never just an action for an individual; there are always wider, corporate implications.

This observation is particularly pertinent in the context of the changes taking place in health-care at present. Besides the radical shake-ups in the financing of the National Health Service (they are perennial), there is also a political and moral shift taking place. People are increasingly encouraged to relate to a system as individuals in their own right, competing for funds, care, and treatment. Increasingly, the causes of disease are portrayed as matters of individual choice: those who might have poor diets or smoke too much in, say urban priority or inner city areas, are "blamed" for their own bad health. The rhetoric of "choice" somehow implies that those who are ill, disabled, or marginalized have partly become that through their own free will. Even at its best, such rhetoric reduces the patient to the status of a unit of consumption, a figure whose only significance is their place on the balance sheet.

Contemporary charismatic healing movements, for the most part, are correctly diagnosed by Sobrino as being too "spiritualised" in its relation to the world.[23] There are, no doubt, many benefits in being part of the phenomenological escapism that many believe constitutes a revival.[24] But what I am arguing for is a "reading" of the healing stories that involves eschewing literal or demythologized paths, conservative or liberal slants, seeking instead a shared agenda for social, moral, and political praxis. There are implicit imperatives in the healing ministry of Jesus that the church needs to heed.[25]

22. See Hadley, *Bread for the World*, 87. I am grateful to the insights of Werner Kelber here, who originally set me thinking on this path. See Kelber, *The Passion in Mark*, especially chapters 2, 3, and 7.

23. See Sobrino, *Jesus the Liberator*. See also Cardenal, *The Gospel in Solentiname*. For a more devotional approach, see John, *The Meaning in the Miracles*.

24. See Percy, *Words, Wonders and Power*, 143–68.

25. See Pattison, 55–64. The theory that healing movements are a reflex response to secularisation and postmodernism remains unchallenged. I have been especially impressed with the work of Charles Davis in relation to some of these problems. See Charles Davis, *Religion and the Making of Society*,

The retrieval of healing ministries to the church, I would suggest, will only come when there is a serious theology of "touch" in relation to pain. Moreover, this cannot just be for individuals. To refract an old saying, "Jesus was not just tough on disease, but also tough on the causes of disease." When he heals a person, he also touches the social context and culture that frames the disorder and disease. Jesus hears the dumb; he speaks to the deaf; he sees the blind; and he touches the untouchable. The body of Christ is richly sensate.

So, can the church retrieve the healing ministry of the gospels, and restore it to the present church, so that renewal and revival will come? The answer must be "yes." But true revival will only come when the poor are accounted for and liberated. Renewal will only come when the culture that "blames" individuals for their sickness, along with the purchasing of "services" and "choices" in levels of treatment in health care, is subverted by a more corporate sense of responsibility and a spirit of true service. True gospel healing will always be about addressing the causes of illness and disease, and challenging the political and social forces that divide and demonize in our society. If the church wants to retrieve the healing miracles of Jesus, it can't just do this personally for individuals. It will have to engage with the more subversive political motivations that lie behind Jesus' healings.

Bibliography

Alkier, Stefan, and Annette Weissenrieder. *Miracles Revisited: New Testament Miracle Stories and Their Concept of Reality*. Berlin: De Gruyter, 2013.

Cardenal, Ernesto. *The Gospel in Soltiname*. Maryknoll, NY: Orbis, 2010.

Cotton, Ian. *The Hallelujah Revolution*, London: Little-Brown, 1995.

Davis, Charles. *Religion and the Making of Society: Essays in Social Religion*. Cambridge: Cambridge University Press, 1994.

Gardner, Rex. *Healing Miracles? A Doctor Investigates*. London: Darton, Longman and Todd, 1986.

Grey, Mary. *Redeeming the Dream*. London: SPCK, 1989.

Hadley, John. *Bread for the World*. London: DLT, 1989.

Hooker, Richard. *Laws of Ecclesiastical Polity*. Vol. 1. London: J. M. Dent, 1954.

John, Jeffrey. *The Meaning in the Miracles*. Norwich, UK: Canterbury, 2001.

Kelber, Werner. *The Passion in Mark*. Philadelphia: Fortress, 1976.

Kermode, Frank. *The Genesis of Secrecy: On the Interpretation of Narrative*. Harvard: Harvard University Press, 1979.

Lewis, David. *Healing: Fiction, Fantasy or Fact?* London: Hodder & Stoughton, 1986.

Myers, Ched. *Binding the Strong Man: A Political Reading of Mark's Story of Jesus*. Maryknoll, NY: Orbis, 2012.

Pattison, Stephen. *Alive and Kicking*. London: SCM, 1989.

Percy, Martyn. *Power and the Church: Ecclesiology in an Age of Transition*. London: Cassell, 1998.

199–201, on religious hope and praxis.

————. *Words, Wonders and Power: Understanding Contemporary Christian Fundamentalism and Revivalism*. London: SPCK, 1996.

Sobrino, Jon. *Jesus the Liberator: A Historical Theological Reading of Jesus of Nazareth*. Maryknoll, NY: Orbis Books, 1993.

Soskice, Janet. "Blood and Defilement." Unpublished paper, given at the Annual Society for the Study of Theology Conference, 1994.

Walker, Andrew. *Restoring the Kingdom*. London: Hodder & Stoughton, 1985.

Wimber, John. *Power Healing*. New York: HarperCollins, 1986.

24

Growth and Management in
the Church of England

Some Comments[1]

THE CHURCH OF ENGLAND, in every age, has faced fundamental challenges. Many would cite the challenge of secularization or consumerism in our time as one of the tougher trials the church has had to negotiate. I am less sure, however. But I do think there are two distinct challenges facing the church today. Or rather, it is one challenge, but with two faces. The single greatest challenge that the church faces today is that of distraction; and its two sides are mission and management. We appear to be preoccupied with both, and to such an extent that the Church of England now finds that its energies are consumed with perpetual drives toward efficiency and productivity.

Yet the church exists to glorify God and follow Jesus Christ, after which it may grow or it may not. Its performance may improve too, or it may not. But it is imperative that faithfulness is always put before any search for success. Indeed, for the vast majority of the population of England, church-talk of mission and numbers tends to drive away far more people than it ever draws near. Evelyn Underhill, writing to Archbishop Lang on the eve of the 1930 Lambeth Conference, reminded him that the world was not especially hungry for what the church was immediately preoccupied with. Underhill put it sharply in her letter: "may it please your Grace . . . I desire to humbly suggest that the interesting thing about religion is God; and the people are hungry for God."[2]

Preoccupied with Productivity?

As any student of early church history will know, the beguiling attraction of the very first heresies and heterodoxies lay in their simplicity. They presented the most

1. This chapter comes from two different sources: the *Church Times* (February 28, 2014) and *Modern Believing* 55:3 (2014) 257–70.
2. Percy, "More Than Tongues Can Tell."

attractive solution to any immediate and apparently unsolvable problems. For the first generations of Christians, these usually lay in the sphere of doctrine and praxis. For us as a church today, the problem appears to be declining numbers in our congregations. Ergo, an urgent emphasis on numerical church growth must be the answer. Right, surely? But wrong, actually. The first priority of the church is to follow Jesus Christ. This may be a costly calling, involving self-denial, depletion, and death. Following Jesus may not lead us to any numerical growth. The first priority of the church is to love the Lord with all our heart, mind, soul, and strength, and our neighbors as ourselves (Luke 10:25). There is no greater commandment. So the numerical growth of the church cannot be a greater priority than the foundational mandate set before us by Jesus.

It was Karl Barth who observed that the true growth of the church is not to be thought of in mainly extensive terms, but rather in those that are intensive. He argued that the vertical (or intensive) growth of the church—in both height and depth in relation to God—does not necessarily lead to any extensive numerical growth. He added that "we cannot, therefore, strive for vertical renewal merely to produce a wider audience." Barth concluded that, if the church and its mission were used only as a means of extensive growth, the inner life of the church loses its meaning and power: "the church can be fulfilled only for its own sake, and then—unplanned and unarranged—it will bear its own fruits."[3] That would seem to settle the matter. Moreover, many parish clergy, and those working in all kinds of sector ministries, already know this to be true. The church does not exist to grow exponentially. Mission is deeper than that. The church exists to be the body of Christ.

The pastoral theologian Eugene Petersen once commented that the one thing he had learned in mission and ministry is how complex measurable growth can be. Here, Petersen draws on the theologian, essayist, poet, and farmer, Wendell Berry. Petersen says that under Berry's tutelage he has learnt that "parish work is every bit as physical as farm work: it is about *these* people, at *this* time under *these* conditions."[4]

The pastoral turn toward an agrarian motif is arresting. Jesus told a number of parables about growth, and they are all striking for their simplicity and surprise, especially the allegory of the sower (Matthew 13:1–9, etc). This parable probably should be the template for all Diocesan Mission Action Plans. For what Jesus is saying to the church is this: have regard for your neighbor's context and conditions. So, you might work in a parish with the richest soil, where every seed planted springs to life. The seasons are kind; the vegetation lush; the harvest plentiful. But some places are stony ground, and faithful mission and ministry in those fields might be picking out the rocks for several generations. Others labor under conditions where the seeds are often destroyed before

3. Barth, *Church Dogmatics* IV/2, 648.

4. See Petersen, *Under the Unpredictable Plant*, and Bonzo and Stevens, *Wendell Berry and the Cultivation of Life*.

they can ever germinate. Or perhaps the weather is extreme in other places, and here we may find that although initial growth is quick, it seldom lasts.

The question the parable throws back to the church is this: what kind of growth can you expect from the ground and conditions you work with? And this is where our current unilateral emphasis on numerical church growth can be so demoralizing and disabling. Is it really the case that every leader of numerical church growth is a more spiritually faithful and technically gifted pastor than their less successful neighbor? The parable says "no" to this. It implies that some churches labor in harsh conditions, and some fairer. So be wise to the different contexts in which our individual and collective ministries take place.

I mention this for one very obvious reason. If we continue to place the heterodoxy of numerical growth at the heart of the church, we risk eroding our character and our morale. Some will argue, no doubt, that if you aim at nothing, you'll hit it every time. Better to have a target and a plan than just to keep plodding on. Maybe. But the Charge of the Light Brigade (1854) had vision, courage, objectives, and some strategy; these were not in short supply. But the rest, as they say, is history.

Factors producing numerical church growth and decline are always complex. But the church might need to do some basic work on maths. In the secular world, one plus one equals two. But counting and adding whole numbers in the church is fuzzy logic. Is a newly baptized infant "one unit" in terms of believers? Does the person who comes every week, but has more doubt than faith, count as "one" or a "half"? Is the regular, but not frequent churchgoer "one"—or less? Does the person who comes to everything in church, but has a heart of stone, count as one? Or less?

We know that God counts generously. The poor, the lame, the sick, the sinners; all are promised a place at God's table in his kingdom. That's why Jesus was seldom interested in *quantity*; the kingdom is about small numbers and enriching *quality*. Yet we live a culture that is obsessed by measuring things numerically, and judging success from this. Fortunately, God is loving enough to tell us lots of counter-cultural stories about numbers: going after one, and leaving the ninety-nine, for example. Or, dwelling on a single sparrow; or numbering the hairs left on your head.

God's maths is different to ours, and God does not easily concur with our cultural obsessions with "growth equals success." No one denies the urgency of mission, and of the church addressing numerical growth. But faithfulness must always be put before the search for success.

So, the key to understanding numerical church growth might be to engage in some deeper and more discerning readings of our contexts—the very soil we seek to nourish and bless, so the seeds can flourish. This will usually be a more complex piece of work than simply announcing another new vision or plan for mission. The pun is intended here: there is work to be done on the ground.

To be sure, we need leaders who can ride the cultural waves of our time. But we also need other leaders who can read the tides, and the deeper cultural currents of our age. Our recent emphasis on numerical church growth—borne largely from fear, not faith—has led to the unbalanced ascendancy of mission-minded middle managers.

It is hard to imagine a Michael Ramsey, William Temple, or Edward King receiving preferment in the current climate. If all leaders must now make obeisance before the altar of numerical church growth, we will erode our character and mute our mission. The veneration of growth squeezes out the space for broader gifts in leadership that can nourish the church and engage the world. As with all things Anglican, it is a question of balance. No one can or should say that an emphasis on numerical church growth is wrong. It isn't. The issue is one of proportion. There are no bad foods, only bad diets; and the continued over-emphasis of numerical growth skews the weight and measure in the body of our leadership.

This is a more subtle disproportion than it might at first appear. It was said of the late Cardinal Basil Hume that "he had the gift of being able to talk to the English about God without making them wish they were somewhere else." The value of this gift should not be underestimated. And for our national mission, this is precisely why we need a leadership that incorporates space for the holy and devout; the gentle pastor; the poet and the prophet; the teacher and theologian; and possibly a radical or two for good measure.

The church may not always draw near to such leaders. But the nation often does—especially those who don't usually go to church. For the first time since the Reformation, we now have no bishops who have held a university post in theology. The nation may not notice this explicitly, but at a subliminal level, it will certainly sense the lack. So for the sake of national mission, and our credibility, we may want to intentionally develop a broader range of leaders than the very singular objective of numerical church growth currently allows for.

But let us return to numbers. Some of the most recent figures for numerical church growth in the Church of England offer up some surprising anomalies. In the *Church Statistics 2010/11* (Church of England 2012), many dioceses that had well-developed mission strategies showed continuing numerical decline. Only a few did not. Perhaps the greatest surprise was to discover one diocese that had enjoyed significant numerical growth—a whopping 17 percent on average weekly and usual Sunday attendance. Ironically, this was led by a bishop who had seemingly little in the way of experience in mission and ministry. Like Basil Hume, the bishop had not been a parish priest, and could not tick any of the boxes that indicated he had led any congregation to numerical growth.

The diocese was Canterbury. And the bishop was someone who also had the gift of being able to talk about God in public. Having a knack for imaginative, reflective and refractive public theology and spirituality does indeed intrigue and draw in people, who might not otherwise pay attention to the rumor of God.

So by welcoming some teachers, poets and prophets amongst our leadership, who point us imaginatively and compellingly to Christ, we might yet discover an even richer, more effective purpose in our mission, and in so doing, find some other routes to numerical growth along the way.

Over-managed, Theologically Under-led?

What then, of management? Here, I do not propose to rehearse the extensive and helpful contributions of Richard Roberts to the debates on management and leadership in institutions such as universities and, by implication and extension, our churches. His recent work in this field is sublime and matchless.[5] Readers are also referred to Lewis-Anthony.[6] Instead, I want to begin with a story.

A few years ago, a guest of mine waited in the Common Room of Cuddesdon with a cup of tea until it was time to meet. She sat and read, but quickly found herself tuning in to a conversation some distance away between three ordinands, gathered around the fire. The subject was "how to get on in the church"—granted, a tiresome-though-typical conversation between students at any theological college. One said it was important to make sure you went to a high-profile parish as a curate. Another, that the key was connections—making the most of who you knew, not what. The third said that what was needed were intellectual qualifications—ideally, a doctorate in theology.

What my guest found strange was the way the first two ordinands rounded on the third. Being theologically well-qualified was fine if you wanted to specialize, they said. But as for getting on in the church, it was surely more of a hindrance than a help. Good management and good connections were the way forward. Good theology would most likely hold you back, and might even marginalize you as "a specialist."

My guest left at this point and headed over for our appointment. She reported the conversation with some bemusement. She asked whether or not I thought it was true. I said I hoped not, though I feared so. This is partly because our current appointments process serves a nest of core priorities: numerical church growth, management, and organization. Being a "teacher of the faith" or offering cogent public theology has now moved from "essential criteria" into the "desirable" column. Theologians amongst our leadership may be appealing, but are not actually necessary. We can manage without, apparently.

As a church, we are now management-led, albeit with an added emphasis on mission. We tend not to choose leaders with rough edges, or who might not fit the mold. The managerially led process delivers what the managers say the church wants: growth, organization, and management. So, predictability is preferred to prophecy. More alarmingly, consistency and compliance are mistaken for catholicity. As a church we have now

---

5. See Roberts, *Religion, Theology and the Human Sciences*, and "Contemplation and the 'Performative Absolute.'"

6. Lewis-Anthony, "Promising Much, Delivering Little."

confused management and leadership to such an extent that our system of preferment is geared up for the evisceration of truly creative theological leadership.

But there is a further problem here. The managers driving such processes believe and act as though they are leading the church. As Adrian Wooldridge and John Micklethwait claim, "managers have always fancied themselves in the officer class."[7] Most key policy areas in the church today are governed not by theological leadership and vision, but by management.

True, in some ways, leadership is a process similar to management. Leadership entails working with people; so does management. Leadership is concerned with effective goal accomplishment; so is management. But whereas the study of leadership can be traced back to Aristotle and Plato, management science only emerged around the turn of the twentieth century with the advent of advanced industrialized society. Management was created as a means of reducing chaos in organizations, to make them run more efficiently and effectively.

The primary functions of management—identified by Henri Fayol[8]—were planning, organizing, staffing, and controlling. These functions are still representative of management. Fayol worked for one of the largest producers of iron and steel in France. He became its managing director in 1888, when the mine company employed over ten thousand people. Fayol realized that the goal of management was to serve processes that produced predictable results. We make round pegs to fit round holes; square for square. Management eliminates rough edges. Any creative friction tolerated will have to be subordinate to the processes and their goals. So, management will not have a vision for an organic institution, where the wrong shapes might eventually meld together, or even ultimately make something better. As with management, so with the church, perhaps?

Comparing management with leadership, John Kotter's work argues that the two are contrary, but also connected.[9] The task of management is to provide order and consistency. The task of leadership, in contrast, is to produce change and movement. Management focuses on seeking order and stability, whereas leadership is about seeking adaption and constructive change. That's why management and leadership will always need each other, of course.

Abraham Zaleznik's work went one step further, however, and argued that managers and leaders are actually different *types* of people.[10] He maintained that managers are reactive, and prefer to work with people in order to solve problems—but tend to do so with "low emotional involvement." Essentially, they act to limit choices. In contrast, leaders are usually emotionally engaged. They try to increase the available

7. Wooldridge and Micklethwait, *The Company*, 11.

8. Fayol, *General and Industrial Management*.

9. Kotter, *A Force for Change*.

10. Zaleznik, "Managers and Leaders."

options in order to resolve problems. Leaders seek to shape ideas; managers just respond to them.

Whether or not one accepts this leadership–management distinction, it is my contention that the church today is primarily a *management-led* organization; which is why the relatively new procedure for selecting diocesan bishops is so interesting to reflect upon. It has become a management-led process.

The procedure is as follows. The Crown Nominations Commission (CNC) interviews are held in Lambeth Palace or at Bishopthorpe, so there is no opportunity for the candidate to see the place to which they might be called. Families and spouses—their needs (or indeed gifts)—are not part of the consideration process. There is little sense of this being a broader vocational discernment that involves a wide range of potential stakeholders. After a candidate has made a brief presentation, there is an interview lasting barely one hour. All candidates are asked the same questions. There is a nest of issues that all interviews focus on: the priority of numerical church growth, the need for management and clear organization. But there is no time for vocational dialogue or the development of shared wisdom. There is no space for serious discussion about public theology and national issues requiring theological reasoning, or questions on international issues.

There is no time to test the financial acumen of a candidate, despite diocesan budgets measured in millions of pounds. Questions on how candidates might approach divisive issues are mostly avoided. There are sixteen people present at the interview, but around two-thirds of the interviewers will sit in total silence—there is no time for them to ask questions, or engage in conversation. All candidates are processed identically, thereby ensuring fairness and organizational compliance. When voting takes place, the preferred candidate needs a two-thirds majority. Compromises are perhaps inevitable at this point. Yet everything remains subordinate to "the process."

Management-led processes tend to reproduce in their own image: more management. So the process cannot receive candidates, for example, who may be artful in the practice of "loyal dissent"—a charism often thought essential for the church, not least for its own good health and conscience. Instead, the premium is placed on managerial compliance.

The advent of women bishops will occlude this, but only briefly. The chance of a genuinely radical woman being appointed to a see remains remote. An emphasis on managerial amenability will, alas, see off any serious consideration of women who have prophetic or theological gifts. A one-hour interview for a position of major ecclesiastical responsibility will seem curious to most outsiders, especially since many clergy, when applying for an incumbency, might spend the best part of the day being interviewed by a very broad array of people. So, for a bishop who will have hundreds of "employees," and most likely sit in the House of Lords, a one-hour interview seems a rather slight process of discernment. At this point, some additional observations on the CNC interview process may provide further confirmation of the "management-led" dynamics with which this section is concerned. All the candidates (up to four) arriving for a CNC interview are "pre-processed"—required to fill in their DBS form (Disclosure and Barring Service check), and produce other relevant documentation before being seen by the panel. After all of the candidates have been interviewed and sent home, the panel discussion and voting takes place. The first and second names eventually forwarded to Downing Street each require a two-thirds majority. At present, an STV (Single Transferable Vote) system is in operation, by secret ballot.[11] Under STV, an elector has a single vote that is initially allocated to their preferred candidate, but as the count proceeds, and candidates are either selected or eliminated, that vote is transferred to other candidates according to the elector's stated second and third preferences.

However, this can produce some strange results. For example, it is possible for the panel to select a first-choice candidate (who has secured a two-thirds majority), but not reach agreement on a second name: in which case the whole process must be restarted from scratch. More generally, STV systems tend to eliminate the potentially more creative candidates, and coalesce around a compromise. So an STV system, on the face of it, might seem like a good "fit" for the Church of England. It can engage seriously with the kinds of tribalism that might be represented in the various wings and factions of the church, but the eventual outcome tends to lead to a compromise candidate. (This does, of course, help explain why poets, prophets and teachers are seldom selected). But the system has other flaws that can be exploited. There is some anecdotal evidence that in the past, local panel members may have run a "party whip" for their preferred candidate—effectively blocking the selection of any other nominee. So some tribalism can triumph in the process, after all.

Yet in all of this, the operation of such a complex system places managers, and managerial method, at the very heart and center of what should actually be a process of *spiritual discernment*. Ultimately, the whole process—and any discussion of it— tends to keep theology and theologians in a subordinate relationship to management; on a short lead, so to speak. But this situation is hardly unique in the church today. Similar tales could be told of theological courses, colleges, and programs being controlled and shaped by central management; or, by bishops, of pastoral and missional priorities being determined by executive managers. Some may ask, at this point, why doesn't the leadership of the church *do* something about this? The answer is simply that our current leadership is, largely, management-led.

By replacing older vocational processes for discerning diocesan bishops with a newer set of managerial procedures, there is a sense of subduing the work of the Spirit—of managing the transcendence of God. To be sure, management never intended this. But in the relentless pursuit of control, compliance, and consistency, the result is nearly always the same: predictability. The casualties are obvious: theological prescience and perceptiveness, both effectively eviscerated from the episcopacy.

11. See General Synod Standing Order 122, 2009, 11, amended in July 2013.

Conclusion

Last year marked the fiftieth anniversary of John Robinson's *Honest to God*. Half a century on, I sometimes wonder what he would make of the Church of England today. He would quickly realize he had few theological allies left amongst the bishops. But I also think he'd conclude that we are essentially over-managed and theologically under-led. He'd be alarmed at the weakening of theological acuity amongst our leadership, and the impact this now has on wider public theology. He'd be concerned about our attempts to cope with crises and debates (on sexuality and gender, for example) that present us with socio-moral issues which refuse to be managed—but do in fact require rich theological engagement and thoughtful directing.

This, in turn, leads to some additional problems for the church. It becomes hard to avoid a form of ecclesial narcolepsy if we have unintentionally muted theologians who have the necessary vision and urgency to cause the church to awaken. The revolutionary patience that Ched Myers speaks of, or the loyal dissent advocated by Gerald Arbuckle, can lose their place and value within a managerially shaped ecclesial body.[12] The possibility of radical theology—from the Latin, *radix*, meaning "root" (and that gets to the heart of a matter)—is quickly subsumed in cultures and agendas of conformity, management and productivity. Indeed, and to return to the parable of the sower, we can find that the forces of management and growth, weed-like, "choke" the rarer border plants that contribute differently and richly to our fields of life, vitality and abundance.

Leadership, it is often said, is doing the right thing; and management is about doing things right. The church needs both, of course. But it is perhaps not unfair to say that the church of the post-war years has moved from being over-led and under-managed to being over-managed and theologically under-led. Kenneth Thompson addresses this in his classic thesis, arguing that our post-war internal organizational reforms have been driven by two major external forces.[13]

The first, affecting the church in the late nineteenth and early twentieth centuries, was the differentiation of institutions as they became more specialized in their functions. The church, for example, ceased to run adoption services in the way that it once did—or hospitals, universities, and colleges, for that matter. The second to affect the church was an increased emphasis on rationality, accountability, and productivity—such that we are increasingly pre-occupied with immediate, empirical, and pragmatic ends. In other words, we try to justify our value through measuring success, and then driving that success by the criteria we chose to measure it by.

But what is often neglected by focusing on the measurable are more nebulous and extensive forms of engagement in public ministry. Prophetic engagement with issues of justice and peace, for example, may suffer: this can be time-consuming, and

---

12. Myers, *Binding the Strong Man*, and Arbuckle, *Refounding the Church*.

13. Thompson, *Bureaucracy and Church Reform*.

may not yield any immediate "measurable results." Pastoral work too, is hard to quantify and measure. In all of this, the organizational–managerial star tends to rise, whilst that of the institutional–leadership wanes.

Some years ago, John Milbank argued that the social sciences had little to contribute to our understanding of theology and religion.[14] He suggested that sociology or anthropology attempted to "police the sublime." Whilst I have always felt that social sciences and theology are rich in their complementarity, I am deeply concerned that the management sciences are now shaping our ecclesiology—and so yes, "policing the sublime." Certainly, managerialism is reining in the radical, patrolling our pastoralia, and taming the theological. Wisdom is pushed to the edges; "management strategy," masquerading as vision, has become central.

Some will doubtless opine that the church cannot wean itself off its absorption with management and mission—albeit one with such a narrow accent placed on efficiency and productivity. But as Wendell Berry has pointed out, the conviction that we cannot change, because we are dependent on what is wrong, is always the addict's excuse. Deep down, we know it will not do. We need be free of our distraction dependency, and of being satisfied with anything that sates the quantification of expectation, and our neuralgic yearning for conformity and control. We need more emphasis on wisdom and depth, and less dependency on orientating our life (and happiness?) by pursuing bigger and better numbers. Only when we are free, can we begin to reclaim our identity as an institution that radically speaks of and embodies God—rather than being consumed by shallower mission and management targets. To be sure, there is no doubt that the value of theological governance amongst our senior clergy has been steadily eclipsed by the current un-checked promotion of our own managerial culture, and by our absorption with numerical growth. I hope that the tide will turn. But in truth, I fear it is still rushing in, and fast. The time has surely come to stop, reflect, and radically review.

Bibliography

Arbuckle, Gerald A. *Refounding the Church: Dissent for Leadership*. London: Geoffrey Cahaman, 1993.

Barth, Karl. *Church Dogmatics*. Vol. IV/2. Edinburgh: T. & T. Clark, 1958.

Bonzo, J. Matthew, and Michael R. Stevens. *Wendell Berry and the Cultivation of Life: A Reader's Guide*. Grand Rapids, MI: Brazons, 2008.

Fayol, Henri. *General and Industrial Management*. London: Pitman, 1916.

Kotter, John P. *A Force for Change: How Leadership Differs from Management*. New York: Free Press, 1990.

Lewis-Anthony, Justin. "'Promising Much, Delivering Little': Ministry Development Review and Its Secular Critics." *Modern Believing*. 53:2 (2012) 140–51.

Milbank, John. *Theology and Social Theory: Beyond Secular Reason*. Oxford: Blackwell, 1993.

14. Milbank, *Theology and Social Theory*.

Myers, Ched. *Binding the Strong Man: A Political reading of Mark's Story of Jesus.* Maryknoll, NY: Orbis, 2012.

Percy, Martyn. "More Than Tongues Can Tell." Easter Sermon, 13 April 2013, delivered at Christchurch Cathedral, New Zealand. Reprinted in *Anglican Taonga* (May 2013).

Petersen, Eugene. *Under the Unpredictable Plant: An Exploration in Vocational Holiness.* Grand Rapids, MI: Eerdmans, 1992.

Roberts, Richard. "Contemplation and the 'Performative Absolute': Submission and Identity in Managerial Modernity." *Journal of Belief and Values* 34:3 (2013) 318–37.

———. *Religion, Theology and the Human Sciences.* Cambridge: Cambridge University Press, 2001.

Thompson, Kenneth. *Bureaucracy and Church Reform: The Organizational Response of the Church of England to Social Change, 1880–1965.* Oxford: Oxford University Press, 1970.

Wooldridge, Adrian, and John Micklethwait. *The Company: A Short History of a Revolutionary Idea.* London: Weidenfeld & Nicolson, 2003.

Zaleznik, Abraham. "Managers and Leaders: Are They Different?" *Harvard Business Review* 55 (1977) 67–78.

25

Sacred Sagacity

Formation and Training for Ministry[1]

I SUPPOSE THAT THE FIRST and most obvious thing to say about the purpose of ordination training—formation and education for ministry—is that it isn't immediately
obvious. What, after all, is one being prepared for? As Urban Holmes III presciently
observed more than thirty years ago, the roles and tasks of the clergy are not nearly as
palpable in the late twentieth century as they might have been one hundred years earlier.[2] It almost goes without saying that if the professional status of clergy is somewhat
ambivalent, then the training and formation that seminarians (or ordinands) receive
is also likely to reflect this.[3] Yet this is not quite so. Students preparing for ordained
ministry—in whatever institution they are being trained, formed and educated in—
can point to a curriculum (usually with a multiplicity of options, but also a "core");
some kind of disciplined approach to prayer and worship; an ecclesial tradition that
(at least) adds some kind of accent to the ethos of the institution; some practical assignments that continue to test the depth and trajectory of a vocation; and a continuous process of theological reflection that links the personal, social, intellectual, and
transcendent dynamics of formation.

Yet such a sketchy and skeletal outline of the priorities for theological education affords considerable licence to any ecclesial tradition and its training institutions.
What then, if anything, can be said about Anglican theological education? Is there
anything that might be said to unite the diversity of institutions one encounters within
the global Communion? Beyond the superficial obviousness of differences—in terms
of resources, history and ecclesial emphasis—is there some kind of trace or sense of
a common "genetic code" that might be said to be distinctive, especially in relation to
the rather nebulous concept of "formation"?

At the core of training and formation—and this will be true for almost all Anglican training institutions—is a commitment to interweaving theology with experience,

1. This chapter originally appeared in the *Anglican Theological Review* 90 (Winter 2008) 285–96.

2. See Holmes, *The Future Shape of Ministry*, and Percy, *Clergy*.

3. See Towler and Coxon, *The Fate of the Anglican Clergy*; Foster et al., *Educating Clergy*; Russell,
The Clerical Profession; Schillebeeckx, *Ministry*.

and usually in some kind of dynamic reflective practice. Often this is done through the exercise of ministry: observing, participating, leading, and then reflecting. In such a context, the experiences of ordinands can often be quite turbulent before they become fulfilling. They may undergo a process of "dis-memberment" before "re-membering," as they encounter a range of experiences and practices that can comfort and disturb in equal measure. The teaching underpinning this activity will most likely be constructive and edifying. Yet the very act of education (from *educare*—literally "to draw out") can be costly—but an essential prerequisite to the process of transformation that ministerial formation is concerned with. James Hopewell observes:

> Rather than assume that the primary task of ministry is to alter the congregation, church leaders should make a prior commitment to understand the given nature of the object they propose to improve. Many strategies for operating upon local churches are uninformed about the cultural constitution of the parish; many schemes are themselves exponents of the culture they seek to overcome.[4]

So the very nature of contemporary parochial ministry in England can place a demanding onus on institutions preparing individuals for the ministry of the church.[5] This might include, for example, instilling some sort of recognition that the (somewhat dubious) distinction between mission and maintenance is often a false dichotomy in the majority of parochial contexts, where the historic religious resonance of the church building will have a widespread (if sometimes unclear) spiritual significance. Thus, good maintenance of a building ("sermons in stone") is likely to be, *de facto*, good mission in any parochial context. The building may involve and affirm the neighborhood in a myriad of ways (beyond the merely functional operation of providing a place for meeting), thereby nourishing social and spiritual capital. The relationship between a church and its people in many parishes is essentially perichoretic—the "mutual indwelling" of various cultural and religious currents that blend and interpenetrate, producing new spiritual meanings, whilst also maintaining distinctive sodalities.[6]

These remarks are perhaps especially suggestive for parochial ministry, but also for formation and theological education more generally, whether in residential or non-residential contexts. Quality may need to be valued more than quantity; pace, solidarity, and connectedness more than haste, energy, and apparent achievement. It may be important to encourage ordinands to see that the worth of affirming the resonance of the past may have a higher spiritual value than the apparent obviousness of the need for relevance and progress. Presence and deep relational engagement may

---

4. Hopewell, *Congregation*, 11.

5. See Torry, *The Parish*, Markham and Percy, *Why Liberal Churches are Growing,* and Percy, *Engaging with Contemporary Culture.*

6. Although my comments mostly relate to preparation for parish ministry, the church increasingly recognizes that many engaged in training spend the majority of their ministry in a variety of sector ministries, or possibly new and innovative missiological initiatives that are non-parochial.

have a greater missiological impact than overt evangelistic schema and initiatives. And clearly, the ministerial "blend" of being and doing (i.e., the clergyperson as both contemplative and activist) may need to be adjusted in any transition from urban or suburban contexts to rural ministry. Context may have a direct bearing on theological output. In other words, theology can be a rather "slow" discipline; it takes time to accrue wisdom for the journey. Part of the process of formation is to comprehend the vision for theological reflection, which is attending patiently and deliberately to all kinds of material. This means helping ordinands to "loiter with intention" in issues and encounters; to consciously and purposefully dawdle in their deliberations, so that clarity and wisdom comes to fruition. Theology is not a discipline for hurrying.

Some Characteristics of Formation

That said, what might some of the common denominators in formation within Anglican theological education be? Here I want to confine my observations to residential and non-residential education and training within the context of an Anglican seminary in England, and make some remarks about the shape of formation as it particularly relates to such institutions, rather than to elucidate the principles of theological reflection more generally.[7] That said, I suspect that these observations will resonate with other parts of the Anglican Communion, and theologies of ministry in most mainline Protestant denominations. Here then, are several suggestions; a list that must be, clearly, far from exhaustive, and is perhaps quite personal. I have listed several characteristics that I would venture are relatively common to flourishing institutions, although they are clearly rooted in my own experiences and expectations.

First, the individual and the institution are set apart for deep and rich composition. There must be some understanding that the person in training, as a character formed within the Christian story and the demands of the gospel, has responded to a vocational call, and has in some sense now been set apart. Ordination is the process and event whereby this calling is recognized, and then established in office. Correspondingly, one of the primary tasks of education and formation for ministry is to integrate the individual character with the catholicity of the office. One of my predecessors at Cuddesdon articulated some of the dynamics within this process, in his inimitable manner:

> [A priest] will not depend on status, nor upon his own abilities, nor upon a system, but upon God. [The primary quality] required is a man's sincerity in prayer and faith and compassion. These may yet be hardly developed, but the relevant signs will consist in obstacles overcome, work voluntarily undertaken and thoroughly performed, and a general attitude of responsibility as a Christian man rather than an interest in the social and ornamental aspects of the

---

7. See for example Volf and Bass, *Practicing Theology*.

priesthood. Then they [the selectors] will look for something which can be described as a love of God's world and his people. Affectation and pretence are danger signs, and the sociability required of a priest consists in a spontaneity of interest in a world and a society of which he feels himself instinctively and naturally a part.[8]

* * *

Formation is a progressive and subtle journey. Whatever a theological college is, it is not an Ecclesiastical Boot Camp. There is no thirty-nine-buttoned-cassock Drill Sergeant to rouse the students to prayer. Yet most institutions, whether residential or non-residential, will speak quite naturally of "the discipline of prayer" as foundational. But it will invariably be something that is instilled rather than imposed. Similarly, despite all the assignments and other task to complete, institutions will require their students to pay attention to the condition of the heart as much as the head. In that sense, the process of formation requires students to adopt a sense of perspective and pace; to borrow an oft-quoted maxim from literature, "make haste slowly."[9] Discipleship is a marathon, not a sprint. Correspondingly, there has to be some trust in the continuing process of discernment, and less concern about the outcome: Christ is Lord of the Journey.

It therefore follows that ordinands should be encouraged to immerse themselves in the flow of what is happening; how they are becoming; and what they will be. Institutions invest much time and energy in trying to develop and cultivate a certain sagacity, shrewdness, and wisdom for the journey ahead, to say nothing of emotional and ecclesial intelligence. But in pedagogical terms, this is more of an art than a science; a world for the reflective practitioner rather than the pure theorist. One writer (John Paul Lederach) invites us to engage and trust in a process that is sometimes led by the heart as much as the head. His advice provides a good fit for any "recipe" in the field of theological education, reflection and formation:

> The more I wanted to intentionally produce a result, the more elusive it seemed to be; the more I let go and discovered the unexpected openings along the way, at the side of the journey, the more progress was made . . . [The] greatest contributions to peace building did not seem to be those that emerged from accumulated skill or intentional purpose. They were those that happened unexpectedly. At a certain time, I came to call this divine naivety . . . the practitioners' dilemma of learning more from mistakes than successes. But the reality was that they were not mistakes in the proper sense of the word; they were important things I learnt along the way that were not planned. I

8. Runcie, *Church Observer*, 11.

9. I.e., the Latin motto, *festina lente*. The maxim is alluded to in classical literature (Aesop's fable of "The Hare and the Tortoise" to Shakespeare's *Love's Labour's Lost*). See "Festina lente," https://en.wikipedia.org/wiki/Festina_lente, for more information.

needed a combination of [the] divine and naïve. [The] divine pointed to the transcendent and unexpected—but that led towards insight and better under-standing. To see that which is not readily planned or apparent, however, re-quires a peripheral type of vision, the willingness to move sideways—and even backward—in order to move forward . . . an innocence of expectation that watches carefully for the potential of building change in good and in difficult times . . . foster[ing] the art of the possible . . . the key is to [learn how] to build from the unexpected . . . to connect [the apparently] accidental with sagacity.[10]

Third, the type of knowledge acquired in formation is also at issue. Those charged with the ministry of oversight—in both sacred and secular spheres—often speak of *intuition* rather than extended calculation or analysis when dealing with "unique situ-ations to which they must respond under conditions of stress and limited time."[11] This "knack" or "wisdom" depends on "tacit knowing," where overseers seldom turn to theories or methods in managing situations, but instead realize that their own ef-fectiveness depends on having learned (and continuing to learn) through the "long and varied practice in the analysis of . . . problems, which builds up a generic, essen-tially un-analyzable capacity for problem-solving."[12] In other words, ordinands learn by experience in the field. Moreover, it is probably the case that Anglicanism is often easier to identify through persons rather than systems; *examples* of faith and polity rather than theories of it. Here, the management of a congregation within the context of the challenges of contemporary culture is much more like a "knack" than a skill. Organizing or shaping the church is about learned habits of wisdom more than it is about rules and theories.

Acknowledging the place of tacit and intuitive knowledge has important impli-cations for teaching those engaged in the task of Christian leadership. It is in shar-ing—sometimes quite deeply, I think, and at quite a personal level—how issues are addressed and resolved, and how individuals and organizations fare in this, and what reflections or analysis one may have about it, that "tacit knowledge" is built up—with-in relationships based on trust, such that the organization may then experience both stability and a degree of transcendence. There is a valuable repository of spiritual trea-sure in (dense, and occasionally tense) collegiality, and in the storied communion of shared wisdom. This is why the *character* of the theological college or non-residential course, as a community of fellow learners on the viaticum, is so important in forma-tion and training. Thus, how we teach ordinands to "hold" complex issues; the charac-ter that teachers and mentors exhibit under pressure; and how individuals continue to embody being the very best kinds of "reflective practitioner"—these are the skills that often make their deep mark in the formational process.

10. Lederach, *The Moral Imagination*, 115.
11. Schon, *The Reflective Practitioner*, 239.
12. Ibid., 241.

Fourth, openness and vulnerability have a role in learning. Thinking and practicing needs to be continually returned to the heart of the vocation, which is, of course, a mystery of risk. Unpacking it takes time and energy, but it also invites seminarians and ordinands to journey deeper into wisdom and wholeness. There is, therefore, a vested interest in encouraging students to engage with and encounter some of the things they might actually fear (e.g., issues, ideas, scenarios, etc.). This goes hand in hand with sounding the depths of the complexities of all kinds of encounters, and developing the habit of deep listening, of imagining beyond what is seen, and what presents on the surface. Risking vulnerability is part of the price we pay for love; and this kind of openness belongs to the economy of vocations. In this sense, every truly self-conscious theological college will know, somewhere, that all the members of its community are beginners.

To complement this, there must be the possibility of failure. However, it is also recognized that institutions are often best-judged not by how many stellar scholars they produce, but by how they care for and mentor the weak and the vulnerable. Mistakes happen, and I think the best thing that those charged with teaching and mentoring can try to do is encourage seminarians to learn from these things when they happen. Failure is not the worst thing; letting it utterly defeat you is. It takes a special kind of wisdom and courage to face failure and defeat, and then to try and move on from this. But this kind of maturity should perhaps especially be cultivated, in order to help cope with the reality of life's miscibility.[13]

Fifth, the relationships between embodiment, power, and wisdom need continual exploration. There is arguably something to be said for a formational process that probes and loosens any relationships with power and privilege. It is perhaps good to be reminded that the gospel is about eternal rewards, not the temporal baubles of the church. Our eyes are to be fixed on Jesus, not on achievement. God is interested in "much more than a set of competencies. No accumulation of skills impresses God. God is interested in the heart of the priest, more than how impressive his or her curriculum vitae appears to be."[14] Yet there is no substitute for the cultivation of holy wisdom. All of us, I think, encounter projects and persons in ministry that either fail to turn out to be all that we hoped, or can even become arenas of defeat. It is reminiscent of what Graham Greene has to say in *The Power and the Glory*, namely that hatred is the failure of the imagination. Holy wisdom, then, is something related to, but "other" than, conventional wisdom. It is an embodied form of spiritual intelligence that is more than mere shrewdness. It is interpretative, lived, and transformative; and those who encounter it will more often speak of an epiphany than mere insight.

13. See Freire, *Pedagogy of the Heart*.
14. Pritchard, *The Life and Work of a Priest*, 4.

An Analogical Coda

In summary, there may be something to be said for theological institutions—of whatever tradition, and whether residential or non-residential—placing a stress on the great Benedictine virtues of hospitality, service, and listening. Each of these is vital to the flourishing of the community of learning and the individual in formation. Being open to God, paying attention to others, and deep listening—these are the profound spiritual exercises that allow individuals and communities (whether gathered or dispersed) to attend to the cadence, timbre, and rhythm of what they are about. So how can we understand the dynamics that take place during ministerial training and formation? Mere description, I think, does not do justice to the depth and richness of the process that takes place. The language we need to capture the journey often comes to fruition by being framed in paradox;[15] in this case, that of the heart and the soul. And this is where the analogical imagination can be helpful. Thus, one aspect of what takes place in formation is that seminarians learn to find ourselves in what one writer describes as "God's orchestra." John Pritchard puts it like this:

> Christian leaders are like conductors of God's local orchestra. Our task is multi-layered. We have to interpret the music of the gospel to bring out all its richness and textures and glorious melodies. We have ourselves to be students of the music, always learning, and sharing, with the orchestra what both we and they have learned about this beautiful music. We have to help members of the orchestra to hear each other, and to be aware of each other as they play their "instrument" or use their gift. Without that sensitivity to each other both an orchestra and a church descend into a cacophony of conflicting noises.[16]

To continue with this analogy, and to apply it more directly to theological institutions, three key observations seem to be particularly pertinent. First, whatever part one plays in the orchestra, institutions have to try and pay attention to the bass-line, and to not get overly distracted by the melody. The bass-line is all about patience, depth and pace. It may also contain the givens of theological discourse. It is about developing sustainable rhythms for the entire symphony—not just the short movements in which one part of orchestra might mainly feature.

Second, teachers and mentors have the task of coaching and conducting. There may be some new scores to teach as well; and the performance of these helps to form the necessary skills in theological and pastoral discernment. In turn, this enables ordinands to develop intuition in relation to knowledge; to become reflexive, yet also sure-footed. Thus, institutions carry the responsibility for developing the natural and given talents,

15. On this, see Dykstra, *Images of Pastoral Care*. Paradoxical images include "wise fool," "servant-leader," "wounded healer," and "intimate stranger." These images help frame the pastoral nature of ordained ministry, alongside the classic biblical models ("shepherd") and those drawn from contemporary life (e.g., coach or manager).

16. Pritchard, *The Life and Work of a Priest*, 109ff.

rather than simply replacing them with new instructions. Education is both input and drawing out, to enable spiritual, pastoral and intellectual flourishing.

Third, just as scripture is symphonic in character—many different sounds making a single, complex, but beautiful melody—so it is with God's church, and the institutions that equip ministers for the communities in which they serve. The task of the teacher and mentor is, then, not just to help students understand and critique the scores they read and perform, but also to try and help each seminarian play beautifully and function faithfully—and all within the context of the diversity of the many different sounds and notes that God gives an institution to make.

Bibliography

Church of England. *Church Statistics 2010/11*. London: Church House, 2012.

Dykstra, Robert, ed. *Images of Pastoral Care: Classic Readings*. St. Louis: Chalice, 2005.

"Festina lente." https://en.wikipedia.org/wiki/Festina_lente.

Foster, Charles, et al. *Educating Clergy: Teaching Practices and Pastoral Imagination*. San Francisco: Jossey-Bass, 2006.

Freire, Paulo. *Pedagogy of the Heart*. New York: Continuum, 2006.

Gardner, Rex. *Healing Miracles? A Doctor Investigates*. London: Darton, Longman and Todd, 1986.

Grey, Mary. *Redeeming the Dream*. London: SPCK, 1989.

Holmes, Urban T., III. *The Future Shape of Ministry: A Theological Projection*. New York: Seabury, 1971.

Hopewell, James. *Congregation: Stories and Structures*. Philadelphia: Fortress, 1987.

Lederach, John Paul. *The Moral Imagination: The Art and Soul of Building Peace*. Oxford: Oxford University Press, 2005.

Markham, Ian, and Martyn Percy, eds. *Why Liberal Churches are Growing*. London: Continuum, 2005.

Percy, Martyn. *Clergy: The Origin of Species*. London: T. & T. Clark, 2006.

―――. *Engaging with Contemporary Culture: Christianity, Theology and the Concrete Church*. Burlington, VT: Ashgate, 2005.

―――. "More Than Tongues Can Tell." Easter Sermon, 13 April 2013, delivered at Christchurch Cathedral, New Zealand. Reprinted in *Anglican Taonga* (May 2013).

―――. *Power and the Church: Ecclesiology in an Age of Transition*. London: Cassell, 1998.

―――. "Restoration, Retrieval and Renewal: Recovering Healing Ministry in the Church—Some Critical Reflections." In *Theologies of Retrieval: Practices and Perspectives*, edited by Darren Sarisky, 333–50. London: T. & T. Clark, 2017.

―――. *Words, Wonders and Power: Understanding Contemporary Christian Fundamentalism and Revivalism*. London: SPCK, 1996.

Pritchard, John. *The Life and Work of a Priest*. London: SPCK, 2007.

Robinson, John. *Honest to God*. London: SCM Press, 1963.

Runcie, Robert. *Church Observer*, 1964.

Russell, Anthony. *The Clerical Profession*. London: SPCK, 1980.

Schillebeeckx, Edward. *Ministry: Leadership in the Community of Jesus Christ*. New York: Crossroads, 1985.

Schon, Donald. *The Reflective Practitioner: How Professionals Think in Action*. London: Ashgate, 1991.

Torry, Malcolm, ed. *The Parish: A Theological and Practical Exploration*. London: Canterbury, 2004.

Towler, Robert, and Anthony Coxon, *The Fate of the Anglican Clergy: A Sociological Study*. London: Macmillan, 1979.

Volf, Miroslav, and Dorothy C. Bass, eds. *Practicing Theology: Beliefs and Practices in Christian Life*. Grand Rapids, MI: Eerdmanns, 2002.

Comprehending Congregations

Power and Polity

26

Power in the Local Church

Locating the Implicit[1]

G ENERALLY, ONE PROBLEM THAT faces many theological colleges is the unspoken assumption that most of the churches in which clergy will serve are essentially similar in character, and only different in form. Thus, principles, ideas, and visions are taught and offered as though what might work in one place can be easily transferred to another context. Formulae for church growth particularly comes to mind. Yet, as one educationalist cautions,

> The "church" so talked about in seminary is neat, tidy, and generally civilised. A particular congregation is never neat, sometimes barely Christian and only rarely civilised. Part of the "culture shock" is due to the changed status of the student. There is a world of difference between being a member of a congregation, and carrying the weight of its symbolic meaning in the institutionalised role of "priest," whether that word is understood in a high or low sense. In addition, the student emerging from theological college is a different person from the one who entered.
>
> Again what appears to be the case upon the surface is not necessarily the case. In one parish a prolonged conflict occurred over the practice of the ladies' guild of placing a vase of flowers on the communion table. The new minister on the basis of sound theological principles and an impeccable liturgical viewpoint well supported in theological college, made strenuous efforts to remove them.
>
> The conflict proved to be an illustration of two world views[sic] passing each other. The practice had arisen in the particular congregation positively as a confession of God's grace in renewing the world daily, and negatively because of the attempt of a former minister to close the women's group down. A vase of flowers was to the women's group, a symbol both of their identity as a group and a confession of their faith as Christians. The new minister saw only a custom he could not affirm with integrity. That was all he saw, and before

---

1. This chapter originally appeared in Jeff Astley and Leslie Francis's *Exploring Ordinary Theology: Everyday Christian Believing and the Church* (Farnham: Ashgate, 2013), 55–64.

his outlook had become informed much damage had been done to the life of the parish. Similar stories can be told about attempts to remove national flags from churches, or to change the arrangement of church furniture bearing brass plates in honour of deceased parents and grandparents.[2]

Power in religious institutions can be as inevitable and ubiquitous as anywhere else. It can be the power of virtue or vice. Equally, it can be a power that drives a morally ambiguous potency, or the naked assertion of a particular fecundity. Power can be seen gorgeously vested; splendidly arrayed in ritual, material, and organization. But it can also be disguised in the apparently ordinary and insignificant, only erupting as problematic when a synergy of events causes the hidden face of power to be revealed.

An understanding of power, then, is a crucial hermeneutical key for arriving at an understanding of the local church, and in specific congregations. To understand the nature of power in churches, it is not necessary to be engaged in a reductive sociological or psychological task. It is, rather, to recognize that any social body (and this includes churches) can benefit from a form of "deep literacy"[3] that readily faces up to the myriad of ways in which power is present, distributed, wielded, and transformative. Furthermore, and perhaps inevitably, attention to the phenomenon of power as a primary motif within congregations can provide a degree of illumination that leads to transformative self-critical praxis within a congregation. In seeking to understand the local church, attention to the dynamics of power can go some considerable way to providing some causal explanations related to organization, mission, identity, and worship.

Because the nature of power is essentially contested—either within any one individual discipline, or in dialogue between the disciplines—there is no common analytic or explanatory language that uniquely commends itself to the study of congregations or the local church. Theologically, it is commonplace to speak of the power of God. In turn, most denominations will have a conceptualization of how that power typically is expressed or reified (i.e., materially manifested) in the midst of a congregation. Put another way, the "pure" power of God is known through particular and given "agents" which (or who) are deemed to most faithfully express that power, and the nature of the Giver (God). Thus, for some denominations, the power of God is made known in the celebration of the Mass; or in a particular individual; or in the exposition of an inerrant Bible; or in the faithful gathering that witnesses miracles, signs, and wonders; or in debate and dialogue, where fresh vistas of perception are reached through new patterns of communion.

What is interesting about "mapping" theological conceptualizations of power in this way, is noting how conflated the Giver and the gift become. Critics of the traditions mentioned above will often remark upon how the Mass is raised to a level of

---

2. Grierson, *Transforming a People of God,* 18.

3. To coin a phrase from Freire, *Pedagogy of the Oppressed,* and Freire, *Education for Critical Consciousness.*

apotheosis; or how the Bible is almost worshipped; or comment upon the exalted status given to ministers who are gifted in thaumaturgy; or on how democracy can sometimes be paraded as the eleventh commandment. These preliminary critiques are all linked, insofar as they have identified one of the most pressing problems in expressions of theological and ecclesiological power: the problem of conflation. In other words, the inability to distinguish between the power of God, and then again, on the other hand, the power of the agencies or channels through which such power is deemed to flow. This is an acute issue in the study of congregations, and in coming to terms with implicit and explicit theologies in churches.

Until recently, sociologists have perhaps been more alert to these issues than theologians. Writers such as Max Weber, developing theories of charisma, have been able to point to dynamics of power that explain the functioning of complex organizations such as local churches.[4] For Weber, charisma is a mysterious and extraordinary quality that can confer authority upon a person, movement, or situation. Charismatic authority governs through a combination of mystique, sublime quality, and ultimate efficiency (i.e., there are "results" from this leadership). Thus, the advent of a charismatic leader within a church typically inspires new patterns of believing and belonging, which inevitably tend to be more demanding. In order to witness or receive greater power (sociologists explain, especially in exchange theory), adherents are likely to be schooled into greater acts of submission and sacrifice. This, in turn, can make intense charismatic situations highly volatile, since the most exciting religious leaders will normally tend to be the most demanding. This leads to a form of power exchange, in which those hoping to receive greater power or spiritual fulfillment will, most likely, have given their self even more fully to the situation or person.

Typically, attention to power in local congregations focuses on abuse and the problematic. High profile cases are often reported in the media: clergy who sexually abuse adults or minors; arguments over money and trust; disputes about promises made, and then broken. But it is a pity to become fixated on the pitfalls of power and to overly problematize it, since a deeper appreciation of the dynamics of power can reveal the hidden governance, resources, and untapped potential in a congregation. Too often, it is the fear of power and its potential for harm that prevents many congregations from coming to a more assured appreciation of how they (as a body) might symbolize that power to the wider community. Understanding power is essential for mission, organization, and transformation; its dynamics need ownership, not shunning.

Conventional Thoughts on Power

In paying attention to the reality of power in the local church, it is virtually inevitable that a whole set of social and material relations will become subject to scrutiny. In

4. Weber, *Charisma and Institution Building*.

turn, some of the theological rationales that support those relations will also need to be assessed. For example, the defense of a particular tradition or custom is not "simply" a group of people protecting what they know to be the truth. It is also a statement about a way of being; a preference for one type of tradition over another; a formula that affirms one pattern of behavior, but at the same time resists others. Power, therefore, is not one "thing" to be discovered and studied. It is, rather, a more general term that covers a range of ideas and behavior that constitute the fundamental life of the local church.[5]

To help us think a little more about the study of power in the local church, it can be helpful to begin by focusing on different types of leadership, which in turn tend to embody different views of power. Consider, for example, three different caricatures of how Church of England bishops might operate within a diocese. One may see their role and task as primarily *executive*: being a hands-on manager, making key strategic decisions on a day-to-day basis. This view of pastoral power thrusts the bishop into the contentious realm of management, efficiency, and rationalization, where they operate as a kind of chief executive officer in a large organization. This is a form of *rationalized* authority, and it will typically empathize with reviews, strategies, and appraisals.

Another may take a different approach, and see their power in primarily *monarchical* terms. There are two faces to monarchical power. One is to rule by divine right: like a monarch, the bishop's word is law. But the second and more common manifestation of monarchical law is manifested in aloofness. Like most monarchs, bishops seldom intervene in any dispute decisively, and choose to remain "neutral" and "above" any divisive opinions or decisions. This is not an abrogation of power; rather, the adoption of the second type of monarchical model proceeds from an understanding that others ("subjects") invest mystique and meaning in the power of the ruler, which in turn leads many monarchs and bishops to be "officially silent" on most issues that have any immediacy, or are potentially divisive. Their symbolic power is maintained through mystique, and ultimately reticence. This is a form of *traditional* authority, where the power is primarily constituted in the office rather than in the individual charisms of the person holding it.

Another model is more *distributive*, and is concerned with facilitation and amplification. In this vision for embodying power in any office, the bishop becomes an enabler, helping to generate various kinds of powers (i.e., independent, related, etc.) within an organization. He or she will simply see to it that the growth of power is directed toward common goals, and is ultimately for the common good. But in this case, power is valued for its enabling capacities and its generative reticulation (i.e., the energy derived from and through networking, making connections, etc.); it is primarily verified through its connecting and non-directional capacities. To a point, such leadership requires a degree of *charismatic* authority, since the organization constantly requires a form of leadership that is connectional and innovative.

5. Percy, *Power in the Church*.

To be sure, most bishops will move between these models of power (and their associated types of authority), according to each case, and with each situation dictating which mode of power is deployed. But most bishops will naturally favor one kind of model over another. The advantage of looking at power through models of leadership, though, is that it illuminates other issues. For example, how is power conceptualized in this situation or place? Who is said to have any ownership of power? How is power shared or dispersed in a congregation or denomination?

These issues are important when one considers the perpetual puzzling that often persists in relation to the status of charismatic leaders. For power is at its most obvious when it is at its most concentrated, and is intensely experienced. For this reason, an understanding of the complexities of power in relation to the local church is an essential element within the study of congregations. There are at last three ways of "mapping" the power as it is encountered.

In one sense,[6] power can be understood as *dispositional*. This refers to the habits and worldview of a congregation, and will closely correspond to their normative "grammar of assent." Appeals to an almighty God and Lord will have direct social consequences in terms of the expectations set upon obedience and compliance. On the other hand, *facilitative* power describes the agents or points of access through which such power is accessed. Here, the status of those agencies will normally match the power that they are connected to. Then again, *episodic* power, however, refers to those events or moments in the life of a congregation that produce surges of energy, challenge, or opportunity.

Putting this together—with a charismatic congregation serving as an example—one could say that the worship is dispositional, the leaders are facilitative, and the invocation of the Holy Spirit is a cue for episodic manifestations of power that are unleashed. This sequence, of course, quickly becomes a dynamic cycle: the episodic confirms the validity of the facilitative and dispositional, and in so doing, creates further expectations of episodic manifestations of power, and the strengthening of other kinds. There is a real sense in which the local church is a "circuit of power," replete with connections, adaptors, converters, and charges of energy. The local church is a complex ecology of power, where energy of various types can flow in different ways, be subject to increase and decrease, and be converted and adapted for a variety of purposes.

Closely related to power is the question of authority. All Christian denominations evolve over time, and their patterning of power and arrangements for agreeing on normative sources of authority are also subject to change. Again, given proper scrutiny, excavating models of authority and power can reveal much about the structure of a church or congregation. Following Paula Nesbitt's sociological observations, we might note that in the first evolutionary phase of denominationalism, or in specific

---

6. As theorists of power in organizations argue; see Percy, *Power in the Church* and Percy, *Engaging with Contemporary Culture.*

congregational evolution (which can currently be seen in the early history of new house churches), institutional relations usually can be governed through obedience, and, if necessary, punishment. We might describe this as the exercise of *traditional* authority, where power over another can be nakedly asserted.

However, in the second phase, interpersonal contracts emerge between congregations, regions, and individuals. Here "ecclesial citizenship" is born, and law and order develop into agreed rather than imposed rule. We might call this *rational* authority: it has to be argued for and defended in the face of disputes and questioning. Again, a number of new churches are now at the point where their power and authority needs explaining in relation to their context and other relations. In the third phase (postmodern, etc.), more complex social contracts emerge between parties, which require a deeper articulation of a shared ethos and an agreement about the nature of a shared moral community. To retain unity and cohesive power, authority must be *negotiated*. It is here that the denomination effectively crosses the bridge from childhood to adulthood. Congregations learn to live with the differences between themselves.

Finally, there is *symbolic* authority. This states that authority and power are constituted in ways of being or dogma that are not easily apprehensible. Networks of congregations may choose a particular office ("chief pastor"), event ("synod"), artifact of tradition ("Bible"), or position as having supreme governance. However, the weakness of symbolic authority is often comparable to the dilemma faced by those who prefer monarchical power. By positing power in an office that seldom intervenes in a decisive way, symbolic authority normally has to justify its substance. If it can't, it loses its power and authority. And now amount of assertion can make up for the imprecision which people vest in symbolic or monarchical power. Attempts to compensate for this dilemma often end with accusations of capriciousness.

Unconventional Thoughts on Power

Locating instances of power and abuse is a fairly obvious way of studying the shape and cadence of a congregation. However, some attention to apparently "neutral" phenomena is also useful when trying to sketch or map the power dynamics of the local church. At least one of Paulo Freire's aspirations was to help people achieve "deep literacy"—to be aware of the far-from-innocent forces which can shape lives and institutions. Freire argued that deep literacy came through dialogue.[7] It is in conversation and reflection that we become aware of how we are *determined* by our cultural inheritance and the powers within them. For example, the power of a building, and the mystique invested in its capacity to mold and inspire, is a form of power that may operate restrictively in a certain context.

---

7. Freire, *Pedagogy of the Oppressed*.

Equally, one must also pay attention to the numerous instances of power relations that continually construct and reconstruct power relations in a congregation. Silence on the part of individuals or groups within a congregation, and in the midst of a dispute or debate, can be interpreted in a variety of ways: as defeat (they have nothing more to say in this argument); as withdrawal (a refusal to participate); as "wisdom" (they are waiting for you to see their point of view); as an act of defiance or disapproval; or as a spiritual rejoinder to too much discussion. Silence, then—even in its informal guise—is seldom innocent. It is a form of power that needs to be "read," understood and interpreted.

Another example of what educationalists term the "hidden curriculum" in relation to power can also be detected in apparently ordinary phenomena, such as dress codes and manners. I have often remarked that an important hermeneutical key for understanding Anglican congregations is to appreciate that, at a deeper level, Anglicanism could be said to be a sacralized system of manners. In other words, any disagreements must be moderated by a quality of civility. The means usually matter more than the ends; better to chair a good, but ultimately inconclusive, discussion, than to arrive prematurely at a (correct) decision.

Similarly, codes of dress in church can also carry theological meaning that is related to dynamics of power. For some, dressing in a relaxed style connotes disrespect, a lack of formality, and, ultimately, is unacceptable. It is not that a congregation will necessarily have any hard or written rules about how to dress (e.g., gentlemen must wear ties and jackets, etc.). The codes and expectations evolve over a period of time, and in their own way, act as a sieve within the congregation. Conformity in uniformity indicates a degree of acquiescence in the pattern of belonging. To "not dress right" is to not only rebel against the prevailing code; it is also to question the formal or informal ascriptions of God that are symbolized in those dress codes. Thus, in the relaxed gathering of a house church, where God is deemed to be immediate, friendly, and even neighborly, relaxed dress codes will tend to "fit" and symbolise the theological outlook. Where God is deemed to be more formal and distant, with worship to compliment this, it is likely that, like the worship itself, the dress code will be much more "buttoned up."

To be sure, one would have to exercise considerable caution in pushing these observations too far. But my point is that by paying simple and close attention to what the laity chooses to wear when they come to church, one can begin to gain some understanding of how power relations and expectations are constructed locally, and how they, in turn, reflect upon the congregation's (often unarticulated) theological priorities. Furthermore, this is an area that can be rich with conflict.

For example, in a North American church that I was briefly involved with some years ago, the pastor presented the following problem. One of the newest additions to the team of twelve elders, and elected by the congregation, was refusing to wear a suit and tie for Sunday worship as the others did. (The Elders were all male by custom rather than rule.) The new elder was also late for weekly meetings, and sometimes failed to turn up at all. The eleven elders petitioned their pastor to have the errant elder removed or "brought into line," claiming that the casual mode of dress signified disrespect (to God), and was mirrored in "sloppy attendance habits." The pastor made inquiries of the dissenter, and discovered that he had his reasons for "dressing down." He wanted the church to be more relaxed and less stuffy; he thought that formal attire inhibited worship, and also suggested a stern, somewhat formal God. The dissenting elder added that he thought that God was more mellow and relaxed, and he was merely expressing this. It was to this God that he was committed—or at least thinking about being committed to. So he did not miss meetings to be rude, or to make an obvious point; he simply didn't think it that it mattered that much, *theologically*, and in the wider scheme of things. And that, of course, is itself theologically significant.

This story leads me to conclude this brief section by underlining the importance of reflecting on stories. James Hopewell, in his alert and prescient study of congregations, discusses the extent to which congregations are "storied dwellings." By this, Hopewell means that congregations are frequently in the grip of myths and narratives that reflect world-views, which in turn determine theological priorities. Congregations seldom understand that they are often owned or "performed" by these "dramatic scripts," but the stories do shape a congregation, nonetheless. His book is too rich and complex to be discussed further here, but the agenda he sets is a teasing one for the subject that we are concerned with. More often than not, what makes a congregation are the powerful narratives and stories it collects, which then go on to construct and constitute its inner life. These may be heroic stories, or they may be tales of triumph over adversity. Equally, however, the preferred stories can be centered on struggle, or on the value of coping.

But in focusing on stories, Hopewell has understood that power in the local church is more than a matter of studying the obvious or official lines of authority, or the authorized power constructions and relations. True, there is value in paying proper attention to what we might term "formal" religious structures and apparatus. Who is pastor or vicar, and how does their style mediate their authority and power? In what ways do people regard the clergy? And how do the laity perceive themselves—as passive receptors of power, or as generators of empowerment? This is important, to be sure.

But there is also value in paying attention to the less formal and "operant" faith of a congregation. What is the scale of the gap between the "official" teaching of a church, and the actual "concrete" discipleship of a congregation and its individuals? What does that gap tell us about power relations between the macro denomination and the micro congregation? Quite independent of what congregations are supposed to affirm, what kinds of stories of faith do they commonly tell? Where does the congregation think power lies? With the clergyperson? Or perhaps with a committee or governing body? Or perhaps with named individuals who wield different kinds of power—e.g., "a pillar of the church"—perhaps through patronage, age, skill, charisma, or experience? Or perhaps because an individual has an alternative theological and spiritual agenda that attracts a significant part of the congregation?

Ultimately, stories have power because they give us a kind of knowledge that abstract reasoning usually cannot deliver. One of the advantages of "story knowledge," as a conveyor of power, lies in its sheer concreteness and specificity. Stories give us individualized people in specific times and places doing actual things: so they speak to congregations with a force and a power that dogma sometimes lacks. Rationality and theological formulae can tend to sidestep the messy particulars of life; stories, however, immerse us in life. So, if Hopewell is right, it is the narratives we tell each other that build and make the church what it is, and determine its sense of power. In imagining that the local church is a "storied dwelling," to borrow a memorable phrase from Jim Hopewell, we are invited to contemplate the many different ways in which we become what we speak, as churches.[8] It is the stories that churches tell—much like personal testimonies—that turn out to be reliable reservoirs of power and authority. Such vignettes can be midrash—creeds-in-waiting.

Conclusion

Whilst it is commonplace to pay attention to abuses or collapses of power in churches, the purpose of this section has been to show that there are deeper reasons why a focus on power is important for the study of the local church. First, the contested nature of power means that its study is essential if one is to clarify the culture, theology, or anatomy of the local church. Second, there are conventional understandings of power that can illuminate ecclesiological analysis. Third, there are unconventional ways of understanding the identity and location of power that also merit attention. To simply study "official" authority in the church is to only undertake half the task, since there are hundreds of subtle and unofficial forms of power and authority that are no less significant. Ultimately, it is only by immersing oneself in a local church that one can begin to understand the complex range of implicit dynamics that make and shape a congregation. And in the act of immersion, the scholar needs to develop a deeper literacy that is attentive to the multifarious dynamics of power.

8. Hopewell, *Congregation*.

Bibliography

Freire, Paulo. *Education for Critical Consciousness*, New York: Seabury, 1973.

———. *Pedagogy of the Oppressed.* Harmondsworth, UK: Penguin, 1972.

Grierson, Denham. *Transforming a People of God.* Melbourne, Australia: Joint Board of Christian Education of Australia and New Zealand, 1985.

Hopewell, James. *Congregation: Stories and Structure.* Philadelphia: Fortress, 1987.

Percy, Martyn. *Engaging with Contemporary Culture: Christianity and the Concrete Church.* Aldershot, UK: Ashgate, 2006.

———. *Power in the Church: Ecclesiology in an Age of Transition.* London: Cassell, 1996.

Weber, Max. *Charisma and Institution Building.* Chicago: Chicago University Press, 1968.

27

Rules, Recipes, Rubrics

A Theological Anatomy of Contemporary
Christian Fundamentalism[1]

T HE SHEER BREADTH OF Christian fundamentalism makes it a difficult movement to characterize. Indeed, because it is not one movement, but rather a term that describes diverse forms of behavior, belief, and practice that are widespread, extreme caution should be observed in using the word at all. Nevertheless, the Fundamentalism Project argues that there are nine characteristics that typify fundamentalism. Five of these are ideological in outlook: a reaction to the perceived marginalization of religion; selectivity of religious essentials and issues; moral dualism; a commitment to an inerrant scripture and a tendency toward absolutism; and millennialism and "messianic" interests. The remaining four characteristics are organizational: an "elect" membership (i.e., an elite, whose identity is clear); sharp delineation of boundaries (e.g., "saved" and "unsaved," "church" and "world," etc.); authoritarian and charismatic leadership (i.e., anointed leader, guru, etc.); and behavioral requirements (e.g., abstinence, etc.). The vast majority of the expressions of fundamentalism from within the "Abrahamic" faiths (i.e., Christian, Jewish, and Muslim) exhibit these characteristics. Many expressions of fundamentalism that fall outside this category (e.g., Sikh, Hindu, Buddhist, etc.) also share most if not all of these characteristics. In a slightly different vein, Martin Marty sees fundamentalism almost entirely as a matter of "fighting"— against the world and the devil, for a theocracy, with righteousness, and so forth. He also notes how the "mindset" is reliant on control and authority, echoing the work of James Barr's critiques, amongst others.[2]

A common misconception about fundamentalism is that it is simplistic. On the contrary, the structure of fundamentalistic thinking is, far from being simple and clear, highly complex, differentiated, accommodating, and fluid. Exegesis (i.e., reading meaning out of a text), eisegesis (i.e. reading meaning into a text), interpretation, and exposition abound. The Bible can function almost totemically in some communities,

---

1. This chapter originally appeared in James D. G. Dunn, ed., *Fundamentalisms: Threats and Ideologies in the Modern World* (London: I. B. Tauris, 2016), 47–68.

2. Percy and Jones, *Fundamentalism, Church and Society.*

whilst in others it provides illumination, inspiration, and canonicity—but is rarely read or regarded as wholly inerrant. There is, in short, no *precise* agreement on the nature of the Bible and what it determines of itself for fundamentalists. Some have "high" views of inspiration, but have abandoned inerrancy. Others qualify inerrancy, insisting that the doctrine only applies to original autographs, excludes grammatical errors or misspellings, and is exempted from lack of precision in certain matters, or apparent contradictions.

This leads scholars to identify at least five different versions of the doctrine of inerrancy: *propositional* (absolute); *pietistic* (i.e., a kind of spiritual biblicism); *nuanced* (some portions of scripture weigh more than others); *critical* (identifies non-essential errors); and *functional* (limited inerrancy, or particular infallibility). Each of these versions will produce a distinct kind of spiritual harvest. The freedom to interpret some parts of the Bible analogically instead of historically will open up particular vistas of meaning for the reader. Even in the most tightly defined fundamentalistic communities, there is considerable divergence on what constitutes an inerrant Bible. And bearing in mind that, for such communities, authority flows *from* the inerrancy of scripture (which is to say that ecclesial and ministerial authority is regarded as being *under* the Word), the patterns of authority and teaching in such communities will vary widely. Where there are similarities between them, they may be morphological rather than doctrinal (in other words a matter of style, not substance).

The role of women in faiths and society is an arena where fundamentalistic views can be tested and studied comparatively. In Protestant Christian fundamentalism, the majority of churches and movements will not regard women holding spiritual authority or office to be either appropriate or biblical. But there are will be some notable exceptions to this. For example, a small number of house churches will recognize women as having an Apostolic ministry of oversight and leadership, although this is still a relatively rare feature in the house church movement.

In Christianity, a more fundamentalistic outlook tends to assign an apparently "traditional" role to women—as wife, mother, and homemaker[3]—which some women may experience as "empowering." In certain religious traditions, women will be barred from certain ritual activities such as public prayer, or will be required to carry out worship in a segregated arena. But at the same time, there are some scholars who take the view that women can be spiritually empowered by what is apparently manifest oppression. Ironically, the spirituality of women in fundamentalist communities can have a powerful leavening effect upon the overall polity of a movement, and several studies have shown that women can feel liberated and empowered by particular expressions of fundamentalism.

Invariably, the roles assigned to women are traced back to (apparent) scriptural norms, but this can lead to some peculiar anomalies. For example, in college and university Christian Unions (Inter-Varsity Fellowship in the United States, and Universities

3. Bendroth, *Fundamentalism and Gender*.

and Colleges Christian Fellowships in the United Kingdom), women are often not allowed to hold authority at particular levels, and some will forbid women from addressing main meetings. This tradition is observed in spite of the fact that Christian Unions are not churches, and the scriptural injunctions pertaining to women holding authority only seem to be applicable in ecclesial contexts. Suffice to say, debate on the issue within any Christian Union would normally be seen as divisive. But Christian Unions are by no means unique in holding to a literalist or fundamentalistic interpretation on the role of women. Within mainstream Christian denominations, some will assert that Jesus' choice of male apostles has always implied that women should not hold authority in churches. Some will go further, and argue that the maleness of Christ reveals an absolute truth about appropriate priestly representation.

Thus, a review of the authority of the Bible in different denominations would reveal a similarly significant range of diversity. Some treat the sacred text as a rule book"(instructions to be carefully followed), others as a guidebook (a few rules, many recommendations, warnings, suggestions, etc.), and most interchanging between the two. (But is it not the case that the parabolic tradition of Jesus gives the church precisely this permission to act so fluidly?) Ecclesial communities and fundamentalistic movements are unavoidably hermeneutical rather than (vapidly) receptive. They are *within* the (ultimate) parable of Jesus Christ—experiencing God's story of incarnation, redemption and resurrection as it continues to unfold within them and around them: the Word made flesh. This makes them responsive and reflexive in character; their only difference, arguably, lies in the degrees to which differences and diversity are tolerated. It is a common misconception of Christian fundamentalism to imagine that it is merely concerned with rules. It is usually a more subtle blend of beseeching: rules, recipes, and rubrics that share a common thread, namely protecting or removing the believer from the world, and at the same time offering them an alternative theological construction of reality which enables them to survive, and perhaps flourish.

So, in talking about fundamentalism in this way, it is important to remember that although (allegedly) inerrant texts frequently play a major part in defining the movement and constituting its identity, other "agents" may operate just as effectively as fundaments. A Pope or guru, a type of experience, or even a moral code, can all function just as programmatically. Fundamentalism remains a broad umbrella term for a cluster of movements that are habitually restless within the world. Fundamentalism seeks clarity in the midst of ambiguity. It strives to locate and celebrate certainty in the midst of doubt. It anticipates and expects faith to triumph over secular reason.

At the same time, it cannot be said that fundamentalism absolutely and necessarily resists modernity. Fundamentalists are remarkably adept at accommodating the world in order to achieve their higher religious, political, and social purposes. Thus, while some may decry the influence of the media or the internet, it is precisely in such arenas that fundamentalists are also to be found at their most active. Fundamentalism, in other words, does not simply resist modernity; it also engages with it—radically—in order to achieve the restoration of a "purer" form of faith that will provide a credible alternative to secularity. Fundamentalism therefore continues to be a diverse but pervasive spiritual force within most developed and developing societies at the beginning of the twenty-first century.

Pursuing this question of terminology is important here, because it is an acute difficulty for many of its subjects, and with good reason. Fundamentalist attitudes can be found in a wide variety of individuals and communities, and yet few wish to own a title with such pejorative connotations. However, from our brief survey so far, the term "fundamentalism" can at least be used to describe a set of common social, theological, and ecclesiological outlooks, shared between traditional fundamentalists (i.e., Anti-Pentecostal), some evangelicals, and those from the charismatic movement or Pentecostalism. A good analogy might be to describe the "movement" as a (dysfunctional?) family tree—all are connected and related, even if some members sometimes wish this were not so. What, then, unites these disparate family members? Five hallmarks suggest themselves.

Firstly, contemporary fundamentalism is a "backward-looking legitimation" for present form of ministry and belief. Present patterns of operation are justified in legalistic and historicist fashion via a claim on an exclusive validity for one line (or a very small core) of developments from Scripture, one that refuses to recognize the diversity and development of others. In other words, an absolute authority must be established. This in turn affords participants a viable perception of reality in the modern world, a template through which experience can be processed. Some of these experiences themselves—as in the case of charismatics or Pentecostal—can then become actual fundaments, although the validating line of interpretation—usually an interpretation of a text or texts, or possibly a written creed or articles of faith—often remains the supreme authority. This backward-looking legitimation is subsequently represented by a myth or constellation of myths that are "at home" in the modern age. The metaphor "home" is not meant to connote an impression of happiness or comfort. Instead, it suggests that these mythic constructs provide a perception of reality that is more usually opposed to many aspects of Western culture. It is "at home" however, because it eclectically "maps" traditional Christian mythologies and symbols onto the modern situation, thus forming a basic comprehensive cognitive picture of how the world is, how it should be, and how it will be. This cognitive picture is comprehensive enough to influence, amongst other things, family life, the role of women,[4] attitudes to politics, other faiths, ethics, and questions about life after death.

Secondly, fundamentalism is dialectical: it exists in relation to and opposition to trends in society that it perceives as modernist (i.e., where the authority of the existing tradition is challenged), pluralist (i.e., the dissipation of "common beliefs" and moral values related to religion, giving rise to competition in society between competing convictions; what was once implicit must now become explicit in order to survive), or

4. Bendroth, *Fundamentalism and Gender.*

compromised. Thus, it is programmatic; it aims at reversing certain traits and establishing a new type of order or perceptions of reality. This is most commonly expressed in the controlling symbol of "Holy War" that is variously employed. It is a primary perceptual and conceptual lens through which the past, present, and future are processed. Fundamentalists see their enterprise as a struggle, in which the order they seek to advance must overcome the present (ungodly) order. The trends of modernity that fundamentalists oppose are to be resisted precisely because they represent a threat to the authority that they place themselves under. Therefore, we can speak of fundamentalism being non-dialogical. It has nothing to receive from the world, since the world must receive the trends first, wholesale. Some sociologists of religion (such as Bryan Wilson) identify this phenomenon as sectarianism, which is usually quite correct. However, caution needs to be exercised in using that term, since it might indicate that fundamentalists are somehow retreating from the world. In fact the opposite is true; they are engaging with it most forcefully, yet with a faith that is committed to addressing a monologue to the world that arises out of their authoritarian dogma.

Thirdly, although fundamentalism now enjoys considerable breadth of expression, including its own competing sectarian factions that deny each other the right to own the title, I nevertheless hold that there is a traceable phenomenon that we can call "fundamentalism." By viewing it as a discrete set of cultural conventions or tendencies, a habit of mind, rather than a single movement or body, it is possible to discern a phenomenon that is widespread, yet with common features. It is an attitude, sometimes selective on subjects (e.g., sexuality) and found within traditions that are otherwise quite catholic or plural. These features generally include a hostile reaction to the mixed offerings of modernity, and in order to combat it, a set of "fundamentals," such as a "core doctrine," an absolute source of authority, a specific program that is to be imposed rather than shared, and clear patterns for mediating authority and power. It might also be said to be a language, replete with authenticating procedures (e.g., "Have you been born again?" or "Are you saved?") that validates and recognizes existing members, and sifts potential recruits. To respond to such questions quizzically or sarcastically is to speak a different language—one of inquisition and doubt. For the believers who ask such questions, only certain types of answers, phrased in a range of quite particular ways, will suffice. In that sense, the questions asked by fundamentalists are not, strictly speaking, "open" in texture. They are, rather, modes of speech that are intended to construct a rapport between the questioner and the responder.

Fourthly, fundamentalism, like liberalism, is not just a theological perspective localized to a particular denomination, (or even religion, although I am only concerned with Christian fundamentalism for the moment). It is a trans-denominational phenomenon that denotes standpoints, attitudes, patterns of behavior, and theological methods. Although it has its origins in the emerging evangelicalism of the eighteenth century and in the "historic fundamentalism" of the early twentieth century, contemporary fundamentalism's chief nemesis is theological and ethical liberalism, which it opposes in varying degrees. In fact, what distinguishes fundamentalism from other similar faith perspectives is its opposition to liberalism; where opposition to liberalism is lacking, I hold that one cannot speak of true fundamentalism, but only of an analog or close relative. At first sight, this might appear to rule out many charismatic or Pentecostal groups, but not so. These groups are just as anti-liberal; they simply construct their remedial program differently. A good example of this is the British Evangelical Alliance, an umbrella organization incorporating many different fundamentalist groups from different denominations, in order to bring a greater degree of pressure to bear on certain issues.

Fifth and last, fundamentalism is a cultural-linguistic phenomenon. All of the studies discussed regard fundamentalism as a primarily noetic phenomenon, concerned with certain beliefs and doctrines, and propagating informational propositions. We have already noted this problematic aspect in some scholarly treatments of fundamentalism, namely the habit of treating fundamentalism as a (primarily) credal phenomenon. For example, the doctrine of inerrancy does not just exist to counter the excesses of form-criticism and Darwinist ideas about the origin of humanity. It is more subtle than that. The cognitive approach does not do justice to the rich intricacy of the fundamentalist universe; it fails to attend to how a doctrine such as inerrancy helps constitute a habit of mind, viable perceptions of reality—in short, a whole world. Stories also help constitute communities, not just propositions; it is often the group's own narrative that shapes its theology, as for example, in the case of fundamentalist Afrikaaners. Equally, fundamentalism cannot be regarded as just a matter of expressing experience. There is more to fundamentalism than a primordial religious feeling, which, when articulated, becomes thematized into a type of determinate "mystical" language. For example, Methodists do not all seek to have their hearts "strangely warmed" as Wesley did. It is the telling of the story, with its message of intervention and immanent change, the hope of transformation, and the renewal of inner beings, that helps place that story centrally in the Methodist tradition. The point of expressing experience belongs in a wider context.

So, fundamentalism should probably be best read (or decoded) as a comprehensive interpretative schema, employing myths or narratives that structure human experience and understanding of the self and the world. This view recognizes the power of language to shape, mold, and delimit human experience, to the extent that it may be said that the way language itself is used can give rise to certain experiences. If fundamentalism can be seen as a cultural-linguistic system, the operating scaffold of symbolism within can be shown to be, in part, the idiom that describes realities, formulates beliefs, and the experiencing of inner attitudes, feelings, and sentiments—in short, a complete interpretative framework.

Moreover, like a culture or language, fundamentalism as a tendency is a communal phenomenon that shapes the subjective of individuals and the objectives of communities, rather than being a manifestation of them. It comprises a vocabulary of discursive and non-discursive symbols, together with a distinctive logic or grammar in terms of which this vocabulary can be deployed. It is a form of life, with cognitive and behavioral dimensions; its doctrines, cosmic understandings, myths, and ethics relating to the ritual practices, the sentiments and experiences evoked, the actions recommended, and the subsequent institutional form that develops. All this is suggested in comparing fundamentalism to a "cultural-linguistic system."

* * *

The irony in the emergence of the fundamentalism "movement" is that it remains a peculiarly modernist construction of reality. It is a kind of pseudo-science and quasi-rationality that abrogates its own self-consciousness. Despite its claims to purity, it is self-evidently a byproduct of hybridity. It imagines itself to be amongst the purest expressions of faith; but in so doing, often substitutes a narrow heterodoxy for a broad orthodoxy. Thus, and in the case of Christian fundamentalism, it often refuses to recognize that the Bible is a consequence of Christianity, and not its major cause. In seeking to uphold the "plain meaning" of scripture, there has to be some kind of denial that Christians do not disagree so much about what the Bible says as what it means, and what kind of weight to attach to the different passages, and their many nuances.

The emergence of fundamentalism as a major force within world religion is now well into its second century. The term "fundamentalism" has successfully migrated and evolved from referring to a specific group of Christians in the early twentieth century, to defining more generic behavioral and ideological positions within other established religious traditions. Invariably, such positions involve hostility toward secular modernity, and to any (allegedly) compromised religious tradition. The term fundamentalism has now become an indicator of fury, resistance, power, and theocracy. Its detractors still cast it as an oppressive and simplistic form of religiosity. But its resilience, vibrancy, and adaptability suggest that scholars need to take its cultural complexity and directive sagacity ever more seriously. There is no sign that modernity will gradually dissolve emergent fundamentalisms. Indeed, some indications seem to point in the opposite direction.

Bibliography

Barr, James. *Fundamentalism*. London: SCM, 1978.

Bendroth, Margaret. *Fundamentalism and Gender: 1875 to the Present*. New Haven, CT: Yale University Press, 1993.

Berger, Peter. *Between Relativism and Fundamentalism*. Grand Rapids, MI: Eerdmans, 2010.

Bramadat, Paul. *The Church on the World's Turf*. New York: Oxford University Press, 2000.

Bruce, Steve. *Fundamentalism*. Oxford: Blackwell, 2000.

Harris, Harriet. *Fundamentalism and Evangelicals*. Oxford: Clarendon, 1998.

Hodge, A. A., and B. B. Warfield. "Inspiration." *The Presbyterian Review* 2 (1881).

Kepel, Gilles. *The Revenge of God*. Oxford: Polity Press, 1994.

Malley, Brian. *How the Bible Works: An Anthropological Study of Evangelical Biblicism.* New York: Altamira, 2004.

Marty, Martin. *Religion and Republic.* Boston: Beacon, 1987.

Marty, Martin, and Scott Appleby. *Fundamentalisms Observed.* Chicago: Chicago University Press, 1992.

Murphy, Nancey. *Beyond Fundamentalism and Liberalism.* Valley Forge, PA: Trinity Press International, 1996.

Nesbitt, Paula. *Religion and Social Policy.* New York: Rowman & Littlefield, 2001.

Packer, J. I. *Fundamentalism and the Word of God.* London: IVP, 1958.

———. "The Fundamentalism Controversy: Retrospect and Prospect." *Faith and Thought* 90:1 (1958).

Percy, Martyn, *Words, Wonders and Power: Understanding Contemporary Christian Fundamentalism and Revivalism,* London, SPCK, 1996.

Percy, Martyn, and Ian Jones, *Fundamentalism, Church and Society.* London, SPCK, 2002.

Stott, John. "Are Evangelicals Fundamentalists?" *Christianity Today,* September 8, 1978.

Watt, David Harrington. *Bible-Carrying Christians.* New York: Oxford University Press, 2002.

28

Adventure and Atrophy in a Charismatic Movement

Returning to the "Toronto Blessing"[1]

D ATING FROM 1994, "THE Toronto Blessing" is the name for a phenomenon that is associated with the Toronto Airport Christian Fellowship. From its very foundation, the Vineyard Christian Church in Toronto had experienced many of the things that would be typical for Christians within the fundamentalistic-revivalist tradition: miracles, healings, an emphasis on deliverance, speaking in tongues, and a sense of the believers being in the vanguard of the Holy Spirit's movement as the millennium neared. However, what marked out the "Toronto Blessing" for special consideration were the more unusual phenomena that occurred. A number of followers trace the initial outpouring back to Father's Day, the result being that some prefer to call the movement "the Father's Blessing."[2] There was an unusually high reportage of people being "slain in the Spirit." A number would laugh uncontrollably, writhing on the floor (the leaders of the movement dubbed this "carpet time with God"), make animal-like noises, barking, growling, or groaning as the "Spirit fell on them." Others reported that this particular experience of God was more highly-charged than anything that had preceded it.[3]

Thus, the "blessing" became known by the place where it was deemed to be most concentrated. To date, around two million visitors or "pilgrims" have journeyed to Toronto to experience the blessing for themselves. Many of these pilgrims report dramatic miracles, supernatural interventions, or substantial changes in their lives,

1. This chapter originally appeared in Martin Lindhardt, ed., *Practicing the Faith: The Ritual Life of Pentecostal-Charismatic Christians* (Berghahn Books, 2011), 152–78; it was partially funded by a Research Grant in 2002 from the American Academy of Religion.

2. Chevreau, *Catch the Fire*. Ironically, and according to the late John Wimber, a founder member of the Vineyard Church, the seminal moment in the formation of Vineyard ministry (the parent movement for the Toronto Blessing) is traced to Mother's Day, 1980.

3. See Hunt et al., *Charismatic Christianity*; Poloma, *A Preliminary Sociological Assessment of the Toronto Blessing*; Percy, *Words, Wonders and Power*; Percy, *The Toronto Blessing*; Percy, "The Morphology of Pilgrimage"; Richter and Porter, *The Toronto Blessing—Or Is it?*; Walker et al., *Charismatic Renewal*.

and greater empowerment for Christian ministry. More unusual claims have included tooth cavities being miraculously filled with gold, and "dustings" of gold on the hair and shoulders of believers, indicating a specific spiritual anointing. Some have even claimed that children born to believers will have supernatural resurrection bodies. A small number of other women of child-bearing age claimed to have had spiritual pseudo-psychotic experiences.

In spite of the extraordinary success of the church, John Wimber (1934-1997), founding pastor of the Vineyard network, excommunicated the Toronto fellowship for "(alleged) cult-like and manipulative practices." Some evangelical critics of the "Toronto Blessing Movement" cited the influence of the Rhema or "Health and Wealth" movement, through the Toronto Fellowship's own connections with Benny Hinn and Rodney Howard-Browne, as another reason for Vineyard-led secession.[4] In January 1996, the Toronto Vineyard became independent. But under the leadership of its pastor, John Arnott, it has flourished, and continues to exercise an international ministry in the fundamentalist-revivalist tradition.

The Toronto Airport Christian Fellowship still meets in a converted trade center on an industrial estate that is less than a mile away from the main city airport. Contextually, it is conveniently located in a matrix of highways that criss-cross downtown Toronto. There are no residential areas remotely near the fellowship, and members or visitors need a car to travel to meetings—but this is not unusual in North American church-going. Local hotels that are linked to the airport and conference economy also enjoy a good reciprocal relationship with the fellowship and its "pilgrims." The fellowship building is functional, compromising between offices and meeting rooms, and a large sanctuary area for celebrations. It is a spacious, adaptive building. For example, there was once a large area at the back of the church that was segregated into track lanes. This is where worshipers, at the end of a service, could stand waiting for individual ministry to take place. A minister stood in front of the worshiper, and a "catcher" at the back. When or if a worshiper fell to the ground—"slain in the Spirit"—they were caught, and the minister moved on to the next worshiper on their track, leaving the previous one on the floor to "marinade in the Spirit." Worship or revival meetings can last several hours, but pilgrims can also avail themselves of café facilities if they need physical rather than spiritual refreshment. Yet, as a cultural creature of its time, the "Toronto Blessing"—in spite of its claims to represent a pre-eminent type of pneumatological power—ironically seemed to place *less* emphasis on aggressively reified spiritual power (a particular feature of John Wimber's teaching in the 1980s—e.g., "power evangelism"), and through its distinctive grammar of worship, put more accent on concepts such as the "softness" and "gentle touch" of God, and the desirability of acquiescence in the believer. The popular worship song "Eternity"[5] perhaps captures this best, sung many times over by followers, and set to a soft melody:

4. Hillborn, *Toronto in Perspective*, 4–10.

5. By Brian Doerksen, Vineyard/Mercy Publishing (1994).

I will be yours, you will be mine.

Together in eternity

Our hearts of love will be entwined.

Together in eternity,

Forever in eternity.

No more tears of pain in our eyes;

No more fear or shame.

For we will be with you,

Yes, we will be with you,

We will worship,

We will worship you forever.

It is through this distinctive grammar of assent that the fellowship continues to configure its life. The motto of the fellowship is "to walk in God's love and give it away," and the life of the congregation emphasizes this in its ministerial distinctiveness. Thus, there are programs for single parents (e.g., "*Just Me and the Kids*—Building Healthy Single Parent Families: a Twelve Week Program for Single Parents and Their Kids," etc), a conference entitled *Imparting the Father's Heart* ("Are you called to minister the Father Heart of God? This course will take you deeper into the Father's love . . . giving you the tools to give it away . . . topics include the need to be fathered, hindrances to receiving the Father's love, shame, Father issues, prodigal issues, orphan heart," etc.), and various schools of ministry or programs that center on spiritual-therapeutic approaches to brokenness, abuse, neglect, and failure.[6] There are also some social and welfare programs that reach out to the poor and homeless.

More generally, we should also note that the "Toronto Blessing" was one of the first revivalist movements to be promoted through the internet, and to a lesser extent on television networks such as CNN. (Indeed, I debated with John Arnott live on television on the BBC 2 *Newsnight* program in 1996.) Through skillful marketing and public relations, the "Toronto Blessing" spread its message and testimonies quickly and easily; it developed speedily into becoming an "international" movement. But with the benefit of hindsight, the net result of the "blessing" seems to have been individual and atomized in its beneficence, rather than galvanizing for the world of revivalism. Indeed, the epiphenomena associated with the "Toronto Blessing" succeeded in dividing many constituents within the world of charismatic renewal, with some declaring that the manifestations of spiritual outpouring (e.g., laughter, howling, animal noises, etc.) were Satanic, whilst others proclaimed them to be a pre-eminent

---

6. Information source: leaflets on display at the Toronto Airport Fellowship.

sign that this was the prelude to the greatest revival ever. In retrospect, neither side—promoter or detractor—could claim an interpretative victory.[7]

Perhaps all that now can be said is that the experiences of those attending Toronto Blessing meetings since 1994 seem to have been primarily cathartic; one could almost describe the effect of the "blessing" upon worshipers as having been something like a cleansing spiritual enema. However, the influence of the Toronto Blessing has steadily waned since the late 1990s, and its position and prominence within global revivalism and the charismatic marketplace have been quickly forgotten. The movement, after a period of intense etiolation, has been subject to some serious atrophy. There are now comparatively few visitors to the fellowship in Toronto, and the phenomenon is now rarely mentioned in revivalist circles.[8] Scholars such as Festinger might see this as a simple matter of cognitive dissonance—the process whereby a belief or expectation, having been disconfirmed, is nonetheless adhered to (and perhaps even more strongly).[9] In this scenario, the much anticipated fruits and blessings of revival are usually deemed to have arrived as promised and predicted, but just not widely perceived and reified. Margaret Poloma pays some attention to this perception in her analysis of the Toronto Blessing.[10] However, the majority of churches that were initially supportive of the Toronto Blessing seemed to have moved on quickly, redeveloping their focus, and also their interpretation of the Blessing. For some, the promised revival is deemed to be "manifest" in the phenomenal success and growth of Alpha courses.[11] Only a few Christian fellowships and churches have persisted with a focus on exotic spiritual ephiphenomena and healings, including missing body parts and organs regrown, the power of some to predict the future, or to detect people's secret thoughts. (Suffice to say, and in spite of the claims made for these miracles on various websites, the evidence for such miracles remains circumstantial and uncorroborated.) We should also note that a small number of Vineyard churches have become more liturgically-orientated in the wake of the Blessing: spiritual experience has led to an embracing of tradition and order.

Interpreting Toronto: A Methodological Sketch

In my return to the Toronto Airport Christian Fellowship, I wanted to see how the fellowship was dealing with the decline in demand for its conferences, and how it

7. See Hilborn, *Toronto in Perspective*.

8. Visitor figures are hard to procure. The Fellowship claimed—with some justice—that up to two million had visited between 1994 and 2000. The visitor figures are now harder to calculate, as the fellowship runs so many commercial conferences, so that delegates are indistinguishable from pilgrims. My own estimation is that the combined numbers of delegates and pilgrims visiting annually is between fifty to seventy-five thousand.

9. Festinger, *A Theory of Cognitive Dissonance*.

10. Poloma, *Preliminary Sociological Assessment*.

11. Hunt, *Anyone for Alpha?*

was coping in a post-millennial climate—in which the rhetoric of a much-anticipated global charismatic revival had patently receded. The added grist for such a study was that, strictly speaking, many scholars for the past twenty-five years have only been predicting uniform growth for conservative churches, especially those with a charismatic flavor.[12] Only a small minority of scholars have predicted the very opposite of this in relation to charismatic renewal and revivalism, especially in relation to the "Toronto Blessing."[13] In this micro-study, I wanted to explore how participants now understood the movement of which they were still a part—one that had witnessed stunning but ultimately unsustainable growth, followed by "wilting"; a process that biologists know as etiolation. Or, and put more colloquially in the rhetoric of the 1980s and 1990s that partly constructed the language and vistas of "power evangelism" and "power healing" programs, adherents have lived through the "boom and bust" years. So how did they now interpret the apparent atrophy of revivalism? Of course, pilgrims and members tend not to construct their self-understanding in these terms, and this immediately raises some sensitive questions about appropriate methodological approaches within the field, and participant observation. Yet there can be no substitute for being there. As James Hopewell notes:

> The fullest and most satisfying way to study the culture of a congregation is to live within its fellowship and learn directly how it interprets its experiences and generates its behaviour . . . participant observation . . . as the term suggests [involves the analyst] in the activity of the group to be studied [whilst] also maintaining a degree of detachment.[14]

As a general guide, three distinctive, but closely related, tactical trajectories have conditioned my reading and re-appraisal of the "Toronto Blessin g" some six years after my first visit. The first is drawn broadly from anthropology, the second from ethnography, and the third from "congregational studies." Each focus their attention upon first-hand accounts of local practices and beliefs, rather than solely being concerned with "official" texts.[15] In this regard, the disciplines are more "behaviorist" than "functionalist." The distinction is important, for it moves research away from concentrating on the primary claims of "pure" or "central" religion (or its analysis) toward the grounded reality of praxis (e.g., it might assess a number of Roman Catholic congregations and their practices, and not ask the Vatican or theologians what

12. See Kelley, *Why Conservative Churches are Growing*; Tamney, *The Resilience of Conservative Religion*; Cox, *Fire From Heaven*; Miller, *Re-inventing American Protestantism*; Weber, "The Social Psychology of the World Religions," 295.

13. See Walker, *Restoring the Kingdom*, 313–15; and Hunt et al., *Charismatic Christianity*.

14. Hopewell, *Congregation*, 86.

15. See Geertz, *The Interpretation of Cultures*; Geertz, *Local Knowledge*; Dey, *Qualitative Data Analysis*; Maykut and Morehouse, *Beginning Qualitative Research*; Hammersly and Atkinson, *Ethnography*; Atkinson, *The Ethnographic Imagination*; Mishler, *Research Interviewing*; Burgess, *In the Field*, etc.

such churches should be doing or believing). Or, put another way, the focus shifts from "blueprints" about the way the church or congregation could be or should be to that of "grounded ecclesiology"—discovering how and why Christian communities are put actually together in their localized context.[16] It is through a matrix of conversation, interviews, observation, and the savoring of representative vignettes, that one can begin to piece together a more coherent picture of what it is like to belong to a group, to be a pilgrim, and to believe.[17]

For the purposes of this study, the work of Clifford Geertz has proved to be most illuminating. Geertz is an anthropologist of religion, and his two principal works are *The Interpretation of Cultures* and *Local Knowledge*. Both these works argue for research that consists of ethnography and theoretical approaches. In my own research, I have tended to treat religion as a complex cultural system. That is not to say that I in any way ignore or reject any idea of revelation, divinity or "genuine" religious experience. Theologically, I expect such things to be treated seriously, and I expect their reality to have some sort of impact upon any empirical study. But I do not think that "religion" is only the repository for revelation. I regard it as a complex system of meaning; a mixture of description and ascription; of deduction and induction.

For Geertz, a cultural system is a collection of symbols—objects, gestures, words, events, etc—which all have meanings attached to them and exist outside of individuals, and yet work inwardly to shape attitudes and guide actions. Referring to Max Weber, Geertz takes the view that [man] is "an animal suspended in webs of significance he himself has spun." Furthermore, to explain cultures, Geertz takes the view that analysts and interpreters have to engage in "thick descriptions," not thin ones. It is important to understand what people *meant* by a word or gesture, so that we can understand its *significance*. An obvious example is two boys—one with a twitch of the eye, the other who winks. A "thin" description would say they made the same movement. A "thick" description unpacks the significance of the wink, and what the gesture means and infers, why it is unspoken language, and so forth. That said, the study of culture is not just about meanings, as though the currency of behavior was agreed. People often do things that are counter-cultural. This means that anthropologists can often do little more than faithfully re-construct what people did and meant, and then interpret this. Cultural analysis is "guessing at meanings, assessing the guesses, and drawing explanatory conclusions."[18] Geertz regards his interpretative anthropology as being constituted through "ethnographic miniatures"—small studies that paint a bigger picture of society, a tribe or culture.

This means that Geertz tends to not be in favor of "general" theories. He sees anthropology not as "an experimental science in search of a law, but an interpretative one

16. See Healy, *Church, World and Christian Life*.

17. See Watt, *Ethnography*; Bramadat, *The Church on the World's Turf*; Dempsey, "The Religioning of Anthropology."

18. Geertz, *The Interpretation of Cultures*, 20.

in search of a meaning."[19] Thus, an anthropologist, like a doctor, cannot predict what will happen—say, that a child will develop flu—but an anthropologist can *anticipate* what might happen, based on patterns they have observed, studied, and interpreted. At this point, anthropologists have a variety of ideas at their disposal: ritual, structure, identity, worldview, and ethos, to name but a few. Thus, Geertz is primarily interested in religion as a cultural system, or the "cultural dimensions" of religion, because he sees culture as a pattern of meanings or ideas, carried by symbols, by which people pass on knowledge and express their attitudes to knowledge. "Common sense" can be a system as much as any political ideology. So, for Geertz, religion is:

> [1] a system of symbols which acts to [2] establish powerful, pervasive, and long-lasting moods and motivations in men by [3] formulating conceptions of a general order of existence and [4] clothing these conceptions with such an aura of factuality that [5] the moods and motivations seem uniquely realistic.[20]

Geertz adds to this definition by reminding his readers that religions distinguish between worldviews and ethos. A worldview is the way things could be or should be: "blessed are the poor, for theirs is the kingdom of heaven" (Matt 5:3). An ethos, however, is the way things are: "they gave alms to the poor" (Matt 6:2). In ritual and belief, ethos and worldview are often fused together; religion expresses both. The moods and motivations created within an ethos reach toward a worldview—the ways things could be or should be. To be sure, there are limits on what can be done with Geertz's work. Many scholars regard him as a functionalist. But this may be more of a compliment than an insult. Like many anthropologists, he is compressing complex data into a system of agreed symbols and contours—not unlike a cartographer. And as with cartography, there is no map that is a one-to-one scale which records what the observer sees. A good map is a *guide* to a field or an area; the chosen symbols help us to look on unfamiliar terrain with some agreement—churches with spires, a pub, a post office, an incline, and a forest of deciduous trees. Insofar as it goes, Geertz offers us a reasonable, accurate, and creative way of navigating through complex data, and making some judgments about the shape of the subject. And as with maps, each is *specific*, but uses general ideas to help us create an accurate impression.

As a discipline, ethnography (or second tactical trajectory) comes in all shapes and sizes: some are mainly quantitative, whilst other kinds can be mostly qualitative; some depend on formal questionnaires and clearly proscribed methods; other kinds are more like "participant observation" and accept the partiality of the observer/interpreter as a given. As Wuthnow points out, ethnography is "a highly diverse set of techniques and practices." It can be closely related to anthropology: the direct observation of social events, and reflections on firsthand accounts, drawn from the field.

19. Ibid., 5.
20. Ibid., 90.

Equally, however, ethnography can also be a matter of data collection: church records, interviews, and other kinds of primary data are brought together to help construct an assemblage of resemblance.[21] But fundamentally, as Courtney Bender notes, ethnography is also always

> about human relationships: it is built (or broken) through trust and through barter and exchange of various kinds. Although [we] focus on fieldwork relationships, ethnographers carry on simultaneous dialogue and exchange (and human relations) with the scholarly community and other texts as well. These concurrent dialogues make ethnographic research unique amongst investigative journeys.[22]

Bender describes the delicate balance between stepping into "streams" of events and conversations, and the need to stay just outside them. There is an ambiguity in making "their" talk "our" talk, in order to bridge the gap between the gaze of the ethnographer and the lives that are being lived. Inevitably, the ethnographer is not simply a passive listener, but is an active agent in conversations, and becomes a reflective partner in dialogue. This requires a degree of self-awareness in the ethnographer; they must not only be attentive to the words and moods they study, but also conscious of their own vocabulary and emotions in a given situation.

Bender recognizes that her ethnography does not "reproduce" the voices of others. Those events that are recorded are inevitably shaped by the particularity of the ethnographer—what strikes them will not necessarily be what strikes another. As Foucault famously quipped of his own ethnography, "I am not a pipe": there is no neutral conduit through which "pure" information flows from source to receptor. (This seems to me to be more of a commonsensical observation than anything particularly post-modern.) This means, as Bender notes (quoting James Clifford), that dialogue occurs as ethnographers "try on" different languages and perspectives: "Dialogic[al] textual production goes well beyond the more or less artful presentation of "actual" encounters. It locates cultural interpretations in many sorts of reciprocal contexts, and it obliges writers to find diverse ways of rendering negotiated realities as mini-subjective, power-laden and incongruent."[23] Put more succinctly, the expression of dialogue in the text of an ethnographer will inevitably contain more than the author could intend. Granted, the text will convey what the author wants to say, and the recorded dialogue will "fit" their interpretative framework. But there will also be, as Bender says, enough "surplus" to question these interpretations. This admission is important, for it alludes to the limits of explanation, but without implying a necessary equality between speakers and the ethnographer. The ethnographer is therefore free to identify those common "stories" and "typical" events that they deem to occur most

21. Wuthnow in Becker and Eiesland, *Contemporary American Religion*, 246.
22. Bender, *Heaven's Kitchen*, 148.
23. Geetz, *Local Knowledge*, 14–15.

frequently, or to be of most significance for a community. This, in turn, can allow such communities to be "read" for "deep meanings." But the door is always open for others to listen to the community under investigation in quite different ways, and offer a different interpretation.[24] However, the keys to good ethnography remain constant: immersion in a community; many hours of patient and deep listening; conversation and rapport; not jumping to premature conclusions; not adopting interpretative matrices too early on in an investigation; faithful (or verbatim) recording of narratives and voices; shaping the material coherently; being attentive to the fact that nothing can be studied without being changed—either the material or the investigator.

As Bender quips, there are, in the end, really only two kinds of (intellectual) books: (1) the stranger that comes to town, and (2) someone who goes on a journey. In ethnography, she notes, one always finds oneself in the second category, but always with some sympathy for the first:

> the ethnographer is always in some sense a pilgrim . . . a seeker . . . we go on trips to undiscovered countries or, armed with notepads and a "critical eye," we make our own countries strange . . . [but] fieldwork [also] compels us to circle back on ourselves, our ideas, and our worlds, just as it also compels us to keep moving toward answers to our questions about the worlds of those around us.[25]

The third methodological trail draws upon—appropriately enough—the burgeoning field of congregational studies,[26] but with a special focus upon the interpretative framework provided by James Hopewell.[27] In many ways, the discipline is a natural complement to anthropology and ethnography, since practitioners of congregational studies pay particular attention to the local or "concrete" church rather than to the "ideal" constructions; it stresses the value of uncovering "operant" rather than "official" religion. Put another way:

> As slight and predictable as the language of a congregation might seem on casual inspection, it actually reflects a complex process of human imagination. Each is a negotiation of metaphors, a field of tales and histories and meanings that identify its life, its world, and God. Word, gesture, and artefact form local language—a system of construable signs that Clifford Geertz, following Weber, calls a "web of significance." Even a plain church on a pale day catches one in a deep current of narrative interpretation and representation by which people give sense and order to their lives. Most of this creative stream is unconscious and involuntary, drawing in part upon images lodged long ago

---

24. Bender, *Heaven's Kitchen*, 150.

25. Ibid., 151.

26. See Ammerman, *Congregation and Community*; Williams, *Community in a Black Pentecostal Church*; Eiesland, *A Particular Place*; Dorsey, *Congregation*, etc.

27. Hopewell, *Congregation*; Ammerman et al., *Studying Congregations*, 91–104.

in the human struggle for meaning. Thus, a congregation is held together by much more than creeds, governing structures and programs. At a deeper level, it is implicated in the symbols and signals of the world, gathering and sur-rounding them in the congregation's own idiom.[28]

Hopewell, rather like certain anthropologists (he was heavily influenced by Geertz) and ethnographers in the field, takes the many and multifaceted *stories* of faith seri-ously. Rather than simply attending to the credal statements and articles of faith that are said to provide ecclesial coherence, ethnography, and congregational studies, he probes deeper, and listens to (and observes) the expressive narratives of belief that make up the practice of a community. It is by attending to the apparently *trivial*—tes-timonies, sayings, folk wisdom, stories, songs, and so forth—that one can begin to understand the truer theological construction of reality under which believers shelter. But what exactly emerges from this "narrative trawl"? As we shall see, there are many rhetorical shards that speak of heroism, romance, adventure, risk, and reward, and whilst these may lie scattered on the surface of congregational story telling, their ori-gin comes from deep within the movement. As Wade Clark Roof notes, the beliefs of churches cannot be construed entirely in terms of their credal statements:

> Theological doctrines are always filtered through people's social and cultural experiences. What emerges in a given situation is "operant religion" will differ considerably from the "formal religion" of the historic creeds, and more con-cern with the former is essential to understanding how belief systems function in people's daily lives.[29]

So, in telling the story of the congregation, we unravel its plot: "church culture is not reduced to a series of propositions that a credal checklist adequately probes. The con-gregation takes part in the nuance and narrative of full human discourse. It persists as a recognizable storied dwelling within the whole horizon of human interpretation."[30] This observation is important, for it would be a mistake to read or judge the "Toronto Blessing" movement by its formal declarations of belief. (Most adherents are, in any case, unaware of these, and would regard them as unimportant.) So, although the To-ronto Airport Christian Fellowship does have a Statement of Faith, and also adheres to certain formal credal articles, their main purpose is to position the fellowship as a mainstream (Evangelical) ecclesial organization. To focus on these as constituting the core identity of the fellowship would be to entirely miss the point. It is the combina-tion of divine dramaturgy (i.e., healings, miracles, etc.) and the distinctive romantic grammar of assent that attracts believers by the thousands, and then enriches their lives. Phrases such as "you will be lead into greater intimacy [with God] and personal renewal" are abundantly present in literature and teaching, peppering pamphlets

28. Hopewell, *Congregation*, 11.

29. Roof, *Community and Commitment*, 178–79.

30. Hopewell, *Congregations*, 201.

and "pep talks" alike. Similarly, worship songs such as "I Can Feel the Touch of Your Presence" and "Dancing in Daddy's Arms" are manifestly more important for the constituent contouring of belief and practice within the fellowship than any creed. The operant stress is on tactile, almost romantic-somatic encounters with God, which lead to deep cathartic spiritual moments, which then provide liberating and generative possibilities for individual spiritual renewal and further empowerment.

Bibliography

Ammerman, Nancy. *Congregation and Community.* New Brunswick, NJ: Rutgers, University Press, 1997.

Ammerman, Nancy, et al. *Studying Congregations.* Nashville: Abingdon, 1998.

Atkinson, Paul. *The Ethnographic Imagination: Textual Constructions of Reality.* London: Routledge. 1990

Becker, Penny Edgall, and Nancey Eiesland, eds. *Contemporary American Religion: An Ethnographic Reader.* Walnut Creek, CA: AltaMira, 1997.

Bender, Courtney. *Heaven's Kitchen: Living Religion at God's Love We Deliver.* Chicago: University of Chicago Press, 2003.

Bramadat, Paul. *The Church on the World's Turf.* New York: Oxford University Press, 2000.

Burgess, Robert. *In the Field: An introduction to Field Research.* London: Routledge, 1984.

Chevreau, Guy. *Catch the Fire.* London: HarperCollins, 1994.

Cox, Harvey. *Fire From Heaven.* New York: Addison-Wesley, 1994.

Dempsey, Corinne. "The Religioning of Anthropology: New Directions of the Ethnographer-Pilgrim." *Religion and Culture* 1:2 (2002).

Dey, Ian. *Qualitative Data Analysis: A User-Friendly Guide for Social Scientists.* London: Routledge, 1993.

Dorsey, Gary. *Congregation: The Journey Back to Church.* New York: Viking, 1995.

Eiesland, Nancy. *A Particular Place.* New Brunswick, NJ: Rutgers University Press, 1998.

Festinger, Leon. *A Theory of Cognitive Dissonance.* Stanford: Stanford University Press, 1957.

Geertz, Clifford. *The Interpretation of Cultures.* New York: Basic Books, 1973.

———. *Local Knowledge.* New York: Basic Books, 1983.

Hammersley, Martyn, and Paul Atkinson. *Ethnography: Principles in Practice.* 2nd ed. London: Routledge, 1995.

Healy, Nicholas. *Church, World and Christian Life: Practical-Prophetic Ecclesiology.* Cambridge: Cambridge University Press, 2000.

Heather, Noel. "Modern Believing and Postmodern Reading." *Modern Believing* 43:1 (January 2002) 28-38.

Hilborn, David, ed. *Toronto in Perspective.* Carlisle, UK: Paternoster, 2001.

Hopewell, James. *Congregation: Stories and Structures.* London: SCM, 1987.

Hunt, Stephen. *Anyone for Alpha?* London: Darton, Longman and Todd, 2000.

———. "The Toronto Blessing—A Rumour of Angels?" *Journal of Contemporary Religion* 10:3 (1995) 257-72.

Hunt, Stephen, et al. *Charismatic Christianity: Sociological Perspectives.* London: Macmillan, 1997.

Kelley, Dean. *Why Conservative Churches are Growing.* New York: HarperCollins, 1972/1986.

Levine, Donal, ed. *Georg Simmel: Selected Writings on Individual and Social Forms.* Chicago: Chicago University Press, 1971.

Maykut, Pamela, and Richard Morehouse. *Beginning Qualitative Research: A Philosophic and Practical Guide.* London: The Falmer, 1994.

Miller, Donald. *Re-inventing American Protestantism.* Berkeley: University of California Press, 1997.

Mishler, Elliot. *Research Interviewing: Context and Narrative.* Cambridge: Harvard University Press, 1991.

Percy, Martyn. "The Morphology of Pilgrimage in the Toronto Blessing." *Religion* 28:3 (1998) 281–89.

———. "Sweet Rapture: Subliminal Eroticism in Contemporary Charismatic Worship." *Journal of Theology and Sexuality* 6 (1997) 71–106.

———. "The Toronto Blessing." *Oxford Latimer Studies* 53–54 (1996).

———. *Words, Wonders and Power: Understanding Contemporary Christian Fundamentalism and Revivalism.* London: SPCK, 1996.

Poloma, Margaret. *A Preliminary Sociological Assessment of the Toronto Blessing.* Bradford-upon-Avon, UK: Terra Nova, 1996.

Richter, Philip, and Stanley Porter, eds. *The Toronto Blessing—Or Is it?* London: DLT, 1995.

Roof, Wade Clark. *Community and Commitment.* Philadelphia: Fortress, 1985.

Stott, John. "Are Evangelicals Fundamentalists?" *Christianity Today,* September 8, 1978.

Tamney, Joseph. *The Resilience of Conservative Religion.* Cambridge: Cambridge University Press, 2002.

Walker, Andrew. *Restoring the Kingdom.* Guilford, UK: Hodder and Stoughton, 1998.

Walker, Andrew, et al. *Charismatic Renewal.* London: SPCK, 1995.

Watt, David Harrington. *Bible-Carrying Christians.* New York: Oxford University Press, 2002.

Weber, Max. *Economy and Society.* Vol. 1, edited by Guenther Roth and Claus Wittich. New York: Bedminster, 1925.

———. "The Social Psychology of the World Religions." In *From Max Weber,* edited by H. Gerth and C. Wright Mills, 267–301. New York: Oxford University Press, 1946.

Williams, Melvin. *Community in a Black Pentecostal Church.* Pittsburgh: University of Pittsburgh Press, 1974.

Part IV—Section 4

Church and World

Challenges in Contemporary Culture

29

Sex, Sense, and Non-Sense
for Anglicans[1]

FOR ONE GROUP OF Christians, at least, sex has become really rather boring: Anglicans. Not for individuals, necessarily. But rather, for the worldwide Anglican Communion. It is weary of the topic, and dog-tired of debating sex and sexuality—continuously wracked by insoluble disagreement and divisive dialogues it cannot seem to resolve.

To be sure, Anglicanism is not the only denomination trying to find a way through the mire and myriad of conversations on sexuality. But as a global church, Anglicans would quite like to change the subject, please. The Anglican Communion knows that its public mission and ministry is perpetually blighted by the issue, and will remain so until it can draw a line under this debate, and finally move on.

The Anglican Primates from around the world gather from January 11th–16th, 2016, at the behest of the Archbishop of Canterbury. This is, we are told, a last-ditch attempt to stop the Communion either imploding or exploding—a steady, solid, prominent planet in the ecclesial universe, and that might be about to morph into a burning star. Brightly shining, but nonetheless burning—frictionally breaking apart.

Yet other churches have faced the divisive issue of sexuality with a bit more nuance. The Church of Scotland, for example, deemed that same-sex relationships were a "matter of liberty of conscience, guaranteed by the Church, on matters that do not enter into the substance of faith." Here, the question of same-sex relationships was left to the liberty of conscience of individuals, congregations, and their ministers.

Thus, a few might say that they cannot support same-sex relationships, and never will. But a quieter majority of others might think otherwise, and therefore affirm such relationships. The liberty of conscience applied here is still a matter of beliefs and practice, but not one that ultimately divides members of the church, who are all mutually affirmed as still ascribing to the core substance of Christian faith.

That carefully worded phrase, which was supposed to bring peace to the Church of Scotland, almost succeeded. Almost. The intention in the drafting of the "liberty of

---

1. This chapter originally appeared in *Modern Church* (December 2015), https://modernchurch.org.uk/downloads/send/32-articles/756-mpercy1215.

conscience" clause was to accommodate revisionists and traditionalists alike, liberals and conservatives. In many ways, it aped that beloved Anglican ideal—an "ecclesial DNA" of inclusive dynamic conservatism that characterises the polity of the church.

Unfortunately for the Kirk, however, when the debate on sexuality took place at the General Assembly in 2014, the "traditionalist" line was reaffirmed as the normative-default position, although the Kirk subsequently permitted congregations and ministers to opt out if they wanted to affirm civil partnerships. This was done to "keep the peace of the church," of course—and avoid an unholy row.

That was a pity, because there are two problems with this compromise, and they are ones that the Archbishop of Canterbury, and the Anglican Primates, would do well to avoid next month. First, the concession maintains discrimination and perpetuates an injustice against lesbian, gay, and bisexual people, and so runs contrary to the spirit of the 2010 Equality Act in the United Kingdom. Second, and despite initial appearances, the two interpretations of "liberty of conscience" are not in fact symmetrical. They appear to be chiral, so to speak; but there is one crucial difference to note.

And here, an allegory may be helpful. There is a world of difference between going to an ordinary restaurant and requesting a vegetarian option, and going to a vegetarian restaurant and asking for a steak, medium-rare. The first scenario is fine and has sense—no decent restaurant menu is without vegetarian options. But we would rightly regard the second scenario as non-sense; indeed, potentially rather offensive to vegetarians, and entirely against the spirit of the restaurant.

Yet by making heterosexual relationships the exclusive and traditional default position, the Kirk effectively chose this second scenario. The relatively small numbers of traditionalists and conservatives who reject same-sex unions and gay marriage in churches, are, in effect, dictating the menu for everyone else.

In this allegory, gay people are fully part of the mainstream of the population. The majority are usually quite happy to eat vegetarian food; just not all the time. But that same majority would not think of insisting vegetarians occasionally ate meat. That would be non-sense.

Living with Diversity

One key ecclesial question flows simply from this allegory: how might churches manage to live well with constrained differences and minorities? Moreover, in a way that does not stigmatize minorities, and caters for them in a non-discriminatory way?

Is this a recipe for diversity of practice that inexorably leads to irreparable disunity? Not really. The Church of England already knows how to live with this kind of reality. Some of the more catholic-inclined clergy and congregations already exercise their liberty of conscience on women priests and women bishops. They've opted out, and reasonable (some would say overly generous) provision is made for them. Some of the more evangelically-inclined clergy and congregations don't always hold services that technically conform to stricter interpretations of canon law on robing or liturgy; they also exercise a liberty of conscience.

In neither case are these clergy or congregations cast out. They are catered for; or even permitted to self-cater. And although both these groups might claim to hold more firmly to the truth than others, no one is asked to dine elsewhere, so to speak. No established church can afford to de-nationalize itself on an issue that is now treated as a matter of equality and justice by the state. Civil partnerships and same-sex marriages, and those entering into these unions, enjoy the full protection of the law, and majority affirmation by the population as a whole. For any national church to turn its face away from those who are full and equal citizens, and have their unions and marriages recognized as such, effectively augments a process of de-nationalization and privatization. It is a route-march toward a tribal church.

The church becomes, in effect, a sad and unwelcoming restaurant with a rationed menu, where the diners who tried to order a meat dish were made to feel terribly guilty. Or more likely, quietly asked by the sullen owner, or embarrassed waiter, to take their custom elsewhere. The diners duly leave.

In effect, this is the adopted position of the Church of England by the current Archbishop. But a national church must cater for the whole palate of the population. That is what a broad church does.

So, what about the rest of the Anglican Communion? Here, it might be time for some home truths. In forty-one of the fifty-three countries within the British Commonwealth, homosexual conduct is still regarded as a serious crime. This categorization and legal stigmatization of homosexuality was largely "made in England" in the nineteenth century, and imposed on cultures and emerging countries and that had not been, hitherto, homophobic. This is one of England's less wholesome exports. The Archbishop of Canterbury could begin the Primates' meeting by accepting responsibility for the part the Church of England has played in perpetrating this discrimination and the subsequent injustices—and publicly repenting of them.

There is also widespread myth in the Anglican Communion, that the dioceses and congregations of the global south now form the majority, and are the only ones growing numerically. Moreover, this myth has some leverage. It prompts reactionary post-colonial guilt in Anglican churches, and those in the United States, Canada, and New Zealand. So when it comes to divisive debates, more moral ground is ceded to African churches, amongst others, than might be judicious.

But a new study by the Spanish Anglican academic, Daniel Munoz, suggests that in the geography of worldwide Anglicanism, the evidence claimed for the number of Anglicans is questionable. The Church of England counts twenty-five million members; in Nigeria, the figure is eighteen million. But in both cases, actual numbers attending every Sunday are a small fraction of this. The claimed numbers are unreliable—perhaps deliberately exaggerated to acquire leverage in debates.

The actual asserted "core membership" of Anglicans in many African countries may be no more dependable than it is for the Church of England. In contrast, figures for the United States and Canada may be more robust. So the received wisdom—that the future lies with the majority, growing, surging churches of the global south—may not be as trustworthy as some assume. The Church of England has plenty of recent cause to be suspicious of spurious statistics that are used to shape policy and polity. Conservative Christianity is not the only brand of faith capable of withstanding the onslaught of modernity.

The Communion might therefore want to think harder about poise, proportionality, and perspective in relation to its moral reasoning, geographies, membership, and guilt-tinged post-colonial identities. The Primates cannot simply align themselves with those proffering inflated claims to represent the largest, growing churches. The right treatment of homosexual people is not a conditional concern to put to a vote of argumentative Archbishops. Remember, this is a fundamental issue of truth and justice.

Nor should post-colonial guilt be allowed to be converted into spiritual capital that then becomes a tool of oppression. And who, exactly, are the oppressed? Not the surging, strident churches of the global south. Those needing protection and care are still lesbian, gay, and bisexual Christians; or women in violent, abusive relationships. The reconciliation required is between, note, *inequalities of power*. Conservatives are not oppressed or criminalized for their opposition to lesbian, gay, and bisexual people—ever, anywhere.

For some Christians, the issue will continue to be non-negotiable. Conservative Christians argue that relationships between the sexes are prescribed and proscribed in the Bible. God has willed heterosexual union as a natural given, and any deviation from this is to be regarded as an illness, other form of disorder (i.e., fall), or a willful act of disobedience (i.e., a sin).

But if equal rights for lesbian, gay and bisexual people seeking to have their faithful and life-long relationships recognized and blessed is seen as matter of justice and equality, then we have a different Christian perspective to contemplate. At the heart of this is a debate over what is "natural" and "normal," and therefore part of God's created order.

Sinful and intentionally disobedient humans are not hard to imagine. Yet as any zoologist will confirm—and this is awkward for some Christians to face up to—same-sex unions and acts do seem to be, in fact, quite normal and natural, and commonly occur across the mammalian genus. What exactly are we to say about same-sex acts between apes, or llamas? As Oliver Reed's opening line as the character Proximo in *Gladiator* has it: "those giraffes you sold me were queer." Maybe. But were those giraffes sinful, fallen, or just plain dumb animals? Or, perhaps, normal—but a minority?

Facing the Future

On the surface, a businessman-turned-Archbishop, with skills in negotiation, may seem like an ideal person to resolve this for the church. But we should be wary, and probe deeper. Negotiating and achieving results in business is often based upon intrinsic and extrinsic inequalities in power relations. The new company seeking to buy the larger, older, but now weaker competitor may be in a much stronger position than others. In business, risk, aggression, and decisiveness are often rewarded—handsomely.

But these are not necessarily the characteristics one wants to the fore in ecclesial contexts. Especially now. Moreover, the Archbishop can do little to re-narrate his background—as a privileged white male; Etonian; upper-class; and related to titled people, who has little experience of powerlessness. Indeed, in terms of powerlessness, it is hard to see how he can enter into it, let alone comprehend it. His negotiations as a businessman in sensitive areas of Nigeria, whilst winning plaudits in the media, are not the same as the work of reconciliation, and arguably not the right "fit" for the church, where first-hand experiences of powerlessness are often important for shaping episcopal ministry. Indeed, any ordained ministry.

What the Archbishop must not do, I think, is use the Primates Conference to affirm dissonant voices from the global south, in order to uphold an oppressive conservative coalition that is determined to denigrate those of a more liberal persuasion. It may be important for the Archbishop to remember that the Scottish, Welsh, and Irish Anglican churches have all been far more positive and open-minded on the issue of same-sex marriage and civil partnerships. Meanwhile, the Church of England—alone in Britain—has continued to travel in the opposite direction. This puts the Church of England in an alliance with developing nations, but is out of kilter with the rest of the United Kingdom.

The Archbishop knows full well that this is a problem, and here he is caught between a rock and hard place. A theologically conservative church is not an attractive proposition to the emerging generation. The Church of England's stance on sexuality is deeply alienating and quite incomprehensible for most young people in the United Kingdom. It confirms their view of religion as being backward-looking and bigoted. Justin Welby knows that he won't make much headway on evangelism and mission with a church that saddles him with an inherently homophobic polity. A non-inclusive church is an evangelistic dead duck.

The recent employment tribunal finding for Jeremy Pemberton—a priest who has married his male partner—gave the Church of England the worst kind of Pyrrhic victory. The Tribunal ruled that the Church of England was allowed to discriminate against Pemberton, because the church had exempted itself from the Government's equality legislation of 2010.

To add to the problems, the Church of England has recently decided that it can also lawfully discriminate against those being considered for future high office in the church. So a selection panel may now take into account the content and manner of any statements previously made by *any* candidate on same-sex relations. The Church of England is, in other words, not only enshrining, but also perpetuating its own discrimination.

To be sure, the church can be quite slow when it comes to a change of mind. It can take a century or more. United, it can fiercely resist change for twenty-five years. It can bicker about that change internally for another twenty-five years, then quietly drop any resistance to change for another twenty-five years, and then spend another twenty-five years trying to convince the world that the change now being embraced and promoted was what the church really thought all along. Whilst this may be depressing news for many, the pace of change is now noticeably quicker in churches—partly due to advances in media and communication.

Some recent studies carried out by Gallup in the United States highlight the extent of the social and moral changes, and cultural shifts on sexuality. For example, in 1977, 56 percent of Americans thought that homosexual people should have equal rights in the workplace; the figure for 2004 was 89 percent. Support for gay clergy moved in the same period from 27 percent to 56 percent. Some 60 percent of Americans in the eighteen-to-twenty-nine age bracket now support same-sex marriage, compared to only 25 percent of those who are over the age of sixty-five.

Statistical surveys of churchgoers repeatedly show that there is growing toleration for same-sex unions in congregations and amongst clergy, across the ecclesial and theological spectra. All of which suggests a church that will adapt and evolve in relation to its changing cultural context.[2] The world only spins in one direction. It doesn't stand still. And it doesn't spin backwards.

Discernment and Difference in a Global Communion

So, can the Bible help the churches resolve their differences on the matter of human sexuality? To some extent, perhaps, but not as easily as some suppose. It is important to remember that as the churches divided over the issue of slavery, the remarriage of divorcees, and the role of women—all on the basis of sound or literal interpretations of scripture—so the churches are here again on the issue of sexuality. Some Christians claimed that the Bible is pro-slavery, against the remarriage of divorcees, and not especially happy about women in leadership roles—at least in the church. Many more Christians have dissented, and have worked over the centuries for a different interpretative framework, cast in a different, more generous light.

Though some say this is mere liberalism, and not *Mere Christianity*, the Bible has to be read intelligently, and with compassion on matters of sexuality. "Same-sex attraction," for example, is not a phrase that appears in scripture. It is all too easy for

2. Myers and Scanzoni, *What God Has Joined Together?*, 140–46.

conservatives to claim that they alone uphold to the "traditional" biblical teaching on homosexuality. Those same conservatives forget, perhaps, that the concept of "homosexuality" is a modern one. Indeed the "normal range" of sexual behavior we now take for granted was something the Early Church knew little of.

The Primates need to grasp that lesbian, gay, and bisexual Christians are now an inescapable part of the Anglican Communion. In many countries across the world, they enjoy full and equal citizenship under the law. So, the Primates need to turn their critical attention to those countries in which they have influence where this is not yet so. Lesbian, gay, and bisexual Christians will not suffer discrimination in heaven. In the kingdom of God, as faithful Christians, all enjoy a full and equal citizenship.

Exploring what "liberty of conscience" means for the global Anglican Communion will therefore be a fruitful pathway for the Primates to explore as they meet next month. Liberty of conscience recognizes that that there will be some disagreement on some practices. But such diversity is not part of the substance of faith that ultimately unites Anglicans. Anglicans have always varied in their practices—they continue to manage this on women priests and bishops. But they remain as one on the creeds, doctrine, and the essentials of faith. They always have.

So, over the coming weeks, Archbishop Justin has a real opportunity to succeed where Pope Francis has recently failed in his Synod. This gathering of Archbishops ought to be an easy win for Justin Welby—an open goal for the taking. Simply put, no matter what his fellow Archbishops think about the right way to talk about homosexuality, there is no case for oppressing lesbian, gay and bisexual people under criminal law. In any country, anywhere.

As the head of the Anglican Communion, and with forty-one Commonwealth countries still criminalizing homosexuality, the Archbishop could take a simple moral lead, call his fellow Primates to repent, and in so doing remind them that people of different sexualities should neither be oppressed or criminalized. Nor should they be unwelcome in our churches. As fellow believers, they should be received as such in Anglican churches across the globe.

The church needs to get past its judgmental and nonsensical mantra, "love the sinner, hate the sin." This simply won't do. To be sure, the Archbishop of Canterbury has some difficult choices ahead. The task is to appease conservative voices in the developing south of the Communion, yet at the same time not lose a whole generation of young people to the Church of England. He has to find a way forward—of squaring the circle, so to speak—such that progressive, traditional, conservative, and liberal voices all have some sense that this beloved Communion can remain united, as one.

In all this, there are some pitfalls to avoid. One is for the Church of England, led by the Archbishop, and out of some sense of misplaced post-colonial guilt, to align with a majority of African stances on sexuality, and against the rest of the British Isles and North America. But Africa, note, does not speak with one voice on same-sex relations. South Africa, for example, already models inclusiveness and toleration at a constitutional level that is highly advanced.

Equally, the Archbishop might be tempted to try and avoid the subject of same-sex relations altogether when the Primates gather, and simply try and develop organizational and pastoral solutions to profound theological differences. This would be a shame, but it would fit the pattern and paradigm of Archbishop Welby's executive-managerial style of leadership. This is one that places process far above content, leaving awkward theological disputes to one side, and simply seeks a managerial and organizational solution.

Indeed, one organizational model hinted at from Lambeth Palace is for the Anglican Communion to become more like the Orthodox churches—one where the member patriarchies may not get on with each other (e.g., Russian and Greek), but all agree on a kind of titular head. So Anglicans in North America may not see eye-to-eye with Nigerian Anglicans, and may never settle their differences. Indeed, they could individuate further. But they would nonetheless remain in communion with each other *through* the Archbishop of Canterbury, who would be a focus of unity in the Sees (and seas) of diversity.

But to try and strive for such a model would be to ignore the complexity of Orthodoxy, and its tentative unity. For example, most outsiders will not be able to tell the difference between the Romanian Orthodox Episcopate of America—a Diocese of the Orthodox Church in America (headquarters in Jackson, Michigan) and the Romanian Orthodox Archdiocese of America and Canada (headquarters in Chicago, Illinois). These two expressions of Romanian Orthodoxy are quite separate churches, overseen by different archbishops. But they cover and compete over similar territory, whilst basically sharing a common faith. The Archbishop needs to understand that there is a theology of Communion: a delicate relationship between geography, catholicity, ontology, theology, authority, and pastoral oversight. Pushing the Anglican Communion to a more dispersed "Orthodox" paradigm would cause irreparable damage to Anglicanism, licensing schismatic-churches in all but name.

Anglicans in Sydney, for example, are content for a layman (note, not a person—I do mean a lay "man" here) to celebrate Holy Communion, because they don't have much time for women; and no time at all for women priests. If there are to be more relaxed approaches to territorial oversight, what is there to stop Sydney Anglicans planting a congregation in London? Or conservative evangelicals opting out, and coming under the control of the Archbishop of Sydney? Or, for that matter, a more liberal bishop from North America, overseeing an Anglican LGBT mega-church in Manchester? Bishops need to exercise a degree of local control in the areas they preside over. This is important for pastoral care, teaching, and authority. A bishop trying to exercise such control from another continent (a model that could potentially emerge from the Primates' Meeting) would be ill-equipped to offer the oversight that most local congregations require.

Giving churches and individuals who disagree with each other even greater degrees of separateness, with even more room to individuate, merely presents Anglicans with an organizational paradigm that licences schism. Such a move would privilege organizational process, but would avoid the deeper issue of theological content: that shared vocation of finding a theological way forward—together.

To turn the Communion into a cheap replica of Orthodoxy—were such a feat even possible—would be to sell the very soul of Anglicanism. We need wisdom from the Archbishop that will help Anglicans find new unity; not more space to express greater individualisms.

Here, the Archbishop could make a thoughtful and opening conciliatory personal gesture, and that would sound the right note for the gathering. Welby's invitation to Archbishop Foley Beach of the Anglican Church in North America (ACNA) to attend the Primates' meeting seems to some to be a brave, even entrepreneurial move toward some sort of rapprochement. Archbishop Foley will apparently attend the meeting in Canterbury, for a limited period.

But Archbishop Foley heads a breakaway Anglican church in the United States and Canada. ACNA is not in communion with Canterbury, or the official Episcopal churches of the United States and Canada. Yet Welby invited Archbishop Foley without consulting either the Presiding Bishop of the United States, or the Archbishop of Canada. In much the same way, indeed, that Welby also invited the Revd Dr Tory Baucum to be one of Canterbury Cathedral's Six Preachers—without consulting America or Canada. Baucum is Rector of Truro Church in Fairfax, Virginia, and part of ACNA. Yet this initiative from Welby, in 2014, was badged as helping to promote "reconciliation and unity."

Now, you could read Welby's gesture as innovative and brave. But it is also *offensive* to those who fought to keep these Anglican provinces together. Far from being reconciling, it is, *de facto*, alienating to the majority. One wonders how Welby might respond if the North American Archbishops invited the Free Church of England (originating from 1844) to the January gathering? Or perhaps members of the Ordinariate (established in 2009)? Could these rifts not be addressed as well? The Archbishop of Canterbury has a track record in announcing apparently bold, eye-catching initiatives. For example, announcing in July 2013 that he intended the Church of England to "compete" Wonga, the payday lender, "out of business," and replace the company with church-based credit-unions. But little reflection was offered on the future for Wonga's several hundred employees, or their hundreds of thousands of customers.

So the Archbishop of Canterbury could begin proceedings in January by offering an apology to American and Canadian Anglicans for his intemperate gestures toward ACNA, and his lack of consultation, which has undermined them. He should further apologize for dealing in territories and spheres of authority that are simply not his to meddle with.

Conclusion

So, how will the January 2016 meeting pan out for the Primates? I hope and pray there will be much poise, prayer, patience, perspective—and poetry. Yes, poetry. One of the key problems the church currently faces is our lack of poets, and those prophetic theologians who often accompany them. Our lexis on the "issues of human sexuality" debate is far too shallow; the words and phrases at hand simply lack requisite depth.

It was the spiritual writer Bill Vanstone who once remarked that the Church of England is like a swimming pool—all the noise comes from the shallow end. On any issue of gravity, the commotion tends to come from shrill reactionary voices that crave attention. Fathomless profundity goes unheard; depth-words that need to be received and discerned are drowned out by all the noisy splashing and shouting.

There will undoubtedly be valiant attempts to construct some much-needed rapprochement for the Anglican Communion at the Primates' gathering. At the forefront—or at least facilitating—is Canon David Porter, the Archbishop of Canterbury's appointee for reconciliation. Porter is an Irish Presbyterian by background, and an Evangelical-Anabaptist by conviction. But he will have his work cut out to fashion some theological unity, in what is essentially an Anglican-catholic problem of polity.

Much has been made of Porter's credentials, and of the Archbishop of Canterbury's knack of fashioning results when a stalemate looked a more likely result. To be sure, process-led approaches to ecclesial problems can be helpful. But pastoral and pragmatic solutions don't tend to resolve deep theological divisions, any more than vitamin pills can cure a patient of serious disease. The divisive theological issues across the Anglican Communion will require deep work, no matter what short-term organizational structures are put in place to somehow hold together a range of competing convictions.

It is possible that the Commonwealth, rather than the Orthodox Church, might serve as a better model for the future of global Anglicanism. But the Archbishop of Canterbury will need to understand that the governance of the church—provinces and dioceses—is a *theological* matter, not just a debate about how to organize territories.

If diversity of belief and practice in the church could be so easily managed, we might have expected the New Testament to say so. It doesn't. It is the vanity of our age to suppose the Church is just like an organization in which diversity can be smoothed over; the faithful warily kettled into some false compliance manufactured by its leaders; difficulties managed and controlled; and the Church pasteurized so as to become a body of utterly consistent clarity. All for the benefit of some imagined public relations exercise.

So what's to be done with all this? I think that we badly need our poets right now—people who understand how simple words can take Anglicans to new spaces and places as a Communion. Poems are just words, of course. But words so woven that they express a truth more compactly and subtly than if the words were left to their own devices.

Poetry takes a seemingly simple word, term, or expression—like "sex," "gay," "issues in sexuality," or even "church"—and turns this into a quite different language. Poems are tongues of desire; of longing, lament, and laughter. Poetry transforms ordinary words into new shapes and ideas that enhance our existences. It creates something new out of seemingly nothing. It finds wisdom and words of resolution where texts and tongues have failed before.

Just like an ecclesiastical Communion, a poem is greater than the sum of its parts. So as the Anglican Primates gather, may God grant them—and the church that I love and long to see swell and intensify—exactly what it needs right now: the true non-sense of poetry.

Bibliography

Myers, David, and Letha Scanzoni. *What God Has Joined Together?* San Francisco: Harper, 2005.

30

Mind the Gap

Generational Change and Its
Implications for Mission[1]

> Young people are important members of the Church today, and they
> also hold the future in its hands. This future is by no means certain.
> To quote just one statistic, churches lost 155,000 teenagers between
> 15 and 19, from 1979 to 1989, a loss far greater than the decline of 15
> to 19 year olds in the general population . . . .[2]

T HERE ARE GOOD REASONS for these types of anxieties being expressed, to be sure.
Concerns about young people and the church are perfectly legitimate missiological issues that need to be addressed. But having said that, one might note that the work
of the church with the young has a curiously brief history. True, in the "golden age" of
pastoral ministry (from the Reformation through to the beginning of the Industrial
Revolution), many parish priests catechized the young as part of their priestly duties,
although there was no particular or specialized outreach to young people worthy of
note. George Herbert (1593–1633), for example, advises that children be admitted
to Holy Communion as soon as they can distinguish between ordinary bread and
consecrated bread, and when they can recite the Lord's Prayer; he estimates the age at
which these things come together to be at around seven. Similarly, Parson Woodforde
(1740–1803), whilst clearly showing an awareness of young people in his parish, has
nothing remarkable to offer them in his ministry.

But lest this sound too complacent, the advent of the Industrial Revolution
caused many parents to begin to dread Sundays. As the only day that was free of
the toil of the factories (in which the children also worked a six-day week), church
services became increasingly rowdy. With traditional village and rural ties broken,
the "new generations" of children were also less likely to be inducted into any kind
of religious instruction or church custom, and there was general concern about the

1. This chapter originally appeared in Paul Davis, *Public Faith? The State of Religious Belief and
Practice in Britain* (London: SPCK, 2003), 106–22.

2. Collins, "Spirituality and Youth," in Percy, *Calling Time*, 221.

lapse of the young into crime and delinquency. In Gloucester, England, Robert Raikes (1735–1811), the owner and printer of the *Gloucester Journal*, decided to establish a "Sunday School" for the children of chimney sweeps, housed in Sooty Alley, opposite the city gaol. The School began in 1780, and was immediate success, offering general and religious education to children from the working classes. The idea of the schools spread with astonishing rapidity. By 1785 a national Sunday School Organization had been established, and many thousands of children were attending in most major cities.[3] In 1788 John Wesley wrote that: "verily I think these Sunday Schools are one of the noblest specimens of charity which have been set on foot in England since William the Conqueror."

Sunday Schools continued to spread and develop throughout the nineteenth century, with their aims and objectives altering in the course of their evolution. By 1851, three-quarters of working class children were in attendance, and many adults too.[4] In Raike's original scheme, social action and evangelization had been the primary motivation in the formation of the schools. Yet by the mid-1800s, some scholars assert that the primary focus of the Sunday School had become a means of expressing emergent working class values (e.g., thrift, communalism, self-discipline, industry, etc.). In other words, the Sunday Schools had become a means of providing some generational continuity and identity. Moreover, the "associational" character of the Sunday Schools also provided a significant social environment in which young and old, male and female, could meet and interact. Thus, Joseph Lawson, writing in the 1890s, notes:

> Chapels are now more inviting—have better music—service of song—which cannot help being attractive to the young as well as beneficial to all. They have sewing classes, bazaars, concerts, and the drama; cricket and football clubs, and harriers; societies for mutual improvement and excursions to the seaside.[5]

Lawson's observations from over a century ago are illuminating because they draw our attention to the fecund associational nature of Victorian religion. Indeed, this lasted, in all probability, well into the twentieth century, with religious bodies providing significant social capital, the means whereby malevolent and anti-social forces were overcome by the purposeful encouragement of "mutual support, cooperation, trust, institutional effectiveness."[6] Religion, in its many and varied associational forms and offshoots, provided social capital that was both bridging (inclusive across different social groups, trans-generational, gender-encompassing, etc) and bonding (exclusive clubs and societies for particular groups, boys clubs, girls clubs, etc.), and

3. Kelly, *A History of Adult Education in Liverpool*, 74–76.

4. Laqueur, *Religion and Respectability*, 44.

5. Cunningham, *Leisure in the Industrial Revolution*, 181.

6. Putnam, *Bowling Alone*, 22.

was therefore part of that new social culture which now obviated the generational gaps that had first awoken the reformers of the early nineteenth century. But the mid-twentieth century was to mark further changes for the churches. As Putnam notes of North America, in the 1950s roughly one in every four Americans reported membership with a church-related group, but by the 1990s that figure was cut in half, to one in eight. Americans now devote two-thirds less of their time to religion than they did in the 1960s.[7]

What has led to this change? There are a variety of theories that offer "generational change" in religious affiliation as a way of framing the causes and trajectories, and the insights, although of a fairly general nature, are useful. Putnam, for example, states that:

> The decline in religious participation, like many of the changes in political and community life, is attributable largely to generational differences. Any given cohort of Americans seems not to have reduced religious observance over the years, but more recent generations are less observant than their parents. The slow but inexorable replacement of one generation by the next has gradually but inevitably lowered our national involvement in religious activities.[8]

For Wade Clark Roof and William McKinney, the transition is marked by movement from formal religious observance and membership to "surfing" from congregation to congregation, not belonging strongly to any one particular body of believers, and an increased appetite for spirituality:

> Large numbers of young, well-educated middle-class youth[s] . . . defected from the churches in the late sixties and seventies . . . Some joined new religious movements, others sought personal enlightenment through various spiritual therapies and disciplines, but most simply "dropped out" of organized religion altogether . . . [there was a] tendency toward highly individualised [religion] . . . greater personal fulfilment and the quest for the ideal self . . . religion [became] "privatised" or more anchored to the personal realms.[9]

We might add to these observations a remark from Margaret Mead, that "the young cannot learn in the old ways" and that "the old are outmoded rapidly" in the speedily advancing and saturated world of media, science, questing and consumerist cultures.[10]

Speaking of culture, we might also mention Callum Brown's *The Death of Christian Britain*, in which he argues that the very core of the nation's religious culture has been irrevocably eroded. More unusually, however, he argues that the process known as "secularization," whilst gradual and endemic, is not the industrial revolution or the enlightenment. Rather he argues that it is the catastrophic and abrupt cultural

---

7. Ibid., 72.

8. Ibid., 72.

9. Roof and McKinney, *American Mainline Religion*, 7–8, 18–19, 32–33.

10. Mead, *Culture and Commitment*, 78.

revolutions of the post-war years, and most especially those trends and movements that began in the 1960s.

Charting the growth of institutional religion in Britain from 1945 to the early 1960s, Brown contends that it is the change in the role of women that has done for Christianity, rather than scientific rationalism. The apparent feminization of religion in the Victorian led to a resurgence of family values in post-war Britain, in which various bourgeois standards rose to the surface, and were equated with "religion" (e.g., Sabbath observance, drinking in moderation, etc). What undid this cultural trajectory was a combination of liberalism and feminism—Brown cites The Beatles and the end of the ban on *Lady Chatterley's Lover* as examples. Brown's book is full of insight, and his appeal to cultural forces of late modernity as a corrosive influence on religious adherence, have far more nuance than those that are normally to be found amongst the pages of secularization theorists:

> It took several centuries (in what historians used to call the Dark Ages) to convert Britain to Christianity, but it has taken less than forty years for the country to forsake it. For a thousand years, Christianity penetrated deeply into the lives of the people, enduring Reformation, Enlightenment and the industrial revolution by adapting to each new social and cultural context that arose. Then really, quite suddenly in 1963, something very profound ruptured the character of the nation and its people, sending organized Christianity on a downward spiral to the margins of social significance. In unprecedented numbers, the British people have stopped going to church . . . The cycle of intergenerational renewal of Christian affiliation, a cycle which had for so many centuries tied the people however closely or loosely to the churches and to Christian moral benchmarks, was permanently disrupted in the "swinging sixties." Since then, a formerly religious people have entirely forsaken organised Christianity in a sudden plunge into a truly secular condition.[11]

Brown's assertions appear to confirm the underlying thesis that we have so far been sketching in this opening section, namely that large-scale disaffection with organized religion is primarily a post-war phenomenon in both Britain and America. Furthermore, the changes are due to broader cultural streams that the churches have no direct control over. These cultural changes might include the rise of the "post-associational" society, consumerism, individualism, an accentuation of generational identity and familial atomization. However, it is important not to allow such descriptions to become the only frames of reference for determining reality. To this end, some problems with the historical narrative are worth pointing out.

First, it needs to be remembered that our ways of talking about generations—especially childhood—do not have fixed points of meaning. Historians of childhood often quip that a child over the age of seven in medieval times did not exist. The term

---

11. Brown, *The Death of Christian Britain*, 1.

"teenager" and the very idea of adolescence are comparatively recent "discoveries." The emergence of a "buffer zone" of development between childhood and adulthood is something that is mostly attributable to economic and social conditions that can afford such space for maturity and advancement. The cultivation of such a zone as an arena for further specific forms of consumerism only serves to concretize and consecrate such identities. (Today, in many developing countries, a "child" of ten can be the main "breadwinner".) Before the onset of the Industrial revolution in Western Europe, it should be recalled that the churches could not claim to be doing any special work with children. As Heywood points out, prior to 1800, there was "an absence of an established sequence for starting work, leaving home and setting up an independent household."[12] Indeed, it is only the child labor laws and schooling that provide "age-graded" structures for social ordering at this level, and such provisions are less than two hundred years old. Often, the work of churches went hand in hand with educationalists, and a newly perceived need to provide "nurseries of Christian character" at every "stage" of childhood, from infancy through to the age of twenty, in order to advance civilization and good social ordering.[13]

Second, generational change in religious adherence does not necessarily mean the rise of secularization. Brown, for example, cites 1963 as the beginning of the end for the churches. So how long will it be before Britain becomes "truly" and wholly secular? Brown does not say, but the teasing question draws our attention to his rhetoric, which contain built-in vectors of decline: "ruptured," "downward spiral," "disrupted," "forsaken," and "sudden plunge" suggest a mind already made up. Whilst it may be true that the sixties, with its revolutions of popular culture, social liberalism, and political upheaval did more to question and shake the foundations of institutions than in previous generations, it would appear that Brown is also guilty of shaping his facts around his thesis. Whilst it is clearly helpful to assess religious adherence down the ages through the lens of generational change, it simply does not follow that if the present generation are uninterested in religion or spirituality, then the next will be even less so. Moreover, is it not the case that many religious movements began in the 1960s? Ecumenism, charismatic renewal, the New Age movement, and a variety of sects, cults and new religious movements were part and parcel of culture of experimentation that dominated the 1960s. Would it not be fairer to say that, far from turning off religion, people were rather turned on by it, and tuned into it in new ways (e.g., spirituality) that simply reflected the emerging post-institutional and post-associational patterns of post-war Britain?

Third, far from seeing generational change as a threat to the churches, the cultural forces that shape debates should be seen in the wider context of general social change. In a capitalist and consumerist culture, it is probably reasonable to go along

12. Heywood, *A History of Childhood*, 171; see also Goldscheider and Goldscheider, *Leaving Home Before Marriage*.

13. Kett, *Rites of Passage*.

with Putnam's hypothesis that the late twentieth century has seen a dramatic collapse in many forms of civic association, and a corresponding rise in individualism. However, churches have tended to hold up rather well under this pressure when compared to their non-religious counterparts. That said, changes in the way people spend "free" time does appear to have had a deleterious effect on associational forms, and in all probability no agent of change has been more influential than the television. Initially, the creation of the "electronic hearth" was a family-bonding and generation-bridging experience. But as consumerism and individualism has steadily increased, this phenomenon has changed. In the United States, the average adult now watches almost four hours of TV per day. As the number of television sets per household multiplies, watching programs together has become more rare. Television has evolved into an example of "negative social capital"; it is the new public space through which the world speaks to us, but it means that we no longer talk to one another. Putnam points out that "husbands and wives spend three or four times as much time watching television as they spend talking."[14] Similarly, Putnam points out that "unlike those who rely on newspapers, radio and television for news . . . Americans who rely *primarily* on the internet for news are actually *less* likely than their fellow citizens to be civically involved."[15] But of course, this does not mean that technology spells the end for civic life, associations, and religious adherence. Rather, it suggests a new mutation of social and religious values, and it is to the discussion of this that we now turn.

Generations and Mission

Every generation that has ever lived has done so within its own modernity. Each new generation that faces its past, present, and future does so with a sense of being on the cusp of time. Continuity between generations may be valued; but it is also evaluated as it is appreciated, and then perhaps subjected to alteration. But how true is it that the cultural and social forces being addressed at the present are more problematic than those faced in the past? Can it really be said that the transformations of the late twentieth century are more disruptive than those experienced in the Industrial Revolution, or in the wake of the economic and social re-ordering that followed the Black Death in medieval England? In general, it would be imprudent to argue (historically) that one generation has struggled more than another, and that the forces shaping religion and society are now more or less inimical than in another period. It is important that in any sociological and cultural analysis, proper attention is paid to (proper) history, before engaging in any kind of speculative futurology. There is a well-known aphorism that needs heeding by every would-be cultural commentator: "sociology is history, but with the hard work taken out." To avoid the endemic sociological habit of generalizing, it is important that any discussion of the generations is rooted in a sound grasp

14. Putnam, *Bowling Alone*, 224.
15. Ibid., 221.

of historical enquiry, and, where possible, married to data, ethnography, and other forms of intellectual garnering that are rooted in methodological rigor. Two examples are offered here that paint slightly different pictures. The first is a Roman Catholic and North American perspective, and the second is a British one.

Roman Catholics are a diverse body of believers in the Third Millennium, and the relationship between "official" and "operant" in American Catholic religion is under increasing academic scrutiny:

> Most observers agree that there is a great deal of diversity among American Catholics. . . . While there was a certain amount of diversity in the 1940s and 1950s . . . the beliefs and practices of American Catholics have become increasingly varied since then. Studies done during the 1950s and 1960s indicated that there was more uniformity among Catholics than among mainstream Protestant groups . . . More recent research, however, suggests that American Catholics' beliefs and practices are now more diverse than they were prior to the Second Vatican Council.[16]

Williams and Davidson, in their study of American Catholicism, offer a generational explanation for the seismic shifts of the last fifty years. The pre-Vatican II generation (born in the 1930s and 1940s) viewed the church as an important mediating force in their relationship with God. When asked why they were Catholic, many participants in the Williams and Davidson study replied that it was because "it was the one true church." The Vatican II generation (born in the 1950s and 1960s), however, were more circumspect about the nature of the church and its absolutist claims. Interviewees were more inclined to see their priest as representing "official" religion, which, in turn, was only one religious source that fed and nurtured their private and individual spirituality. In this sense, the Vatican II generation is pivotal, since the post-Vatican II generation (born in the 1970s and 1980s) has tended to be even more liberal and open. For this generation, Mass attendance is not a priority; being a good person is more important than being a good Catholic; faith is individualistic and private— "what really counts is what is in your heart." Williams and Davidson conclude their study with these words:

> One thing is certain: the hands of time cannot be turned back. Societal changes, as well as changes occurring within the church, leave no doubt that tomorrow's Catholics will be very different from previous generations. The children of post-Vatican II Catholics will receive their religious education from those who never read the *Baltimore Catechism*, and are likely to know little about the changes brought about by Vatican II. The conceptions of faith post-Vatican II Catholics are apt to pass on to the next generation will look decidedly individualistic in nature.[17]

16. Williams and Davidson, "Catholic Conceptions of Faith," 70.

17. Ibid., 75.

In a similar vein, Sylvia Collins bases her assessment about the future shape of spirituality and youth on just such foundations. Her research is not motivated by confessional or denominational anxiety, but is rather located in the quest to discover how young people are changing in their attitudes to belief. Contrasting "baby boomers" (those born between 1945 and 1960) and "baby busters" (those born after 1960), Collins skilfully notes and narrates the changes between the generations. On balance, "boomers" tended toward radicalizing religious traditions in the wake of post-war settlement. This was to include an emphasis on liberation, justice, and political involvement, but was also coupled to an increasing tendency to experiment with religion (e.g., innovative "sects," New Religious Movements, Communitarianism, etc.). Thus, the

> baby boomer generation . . . saw spirituality among young people move in line with social change from its location in one main tradition associated with the old established order, through to a new spirituality that sought to break the bonds of establishment and set the self free to reach its new potential. Even more widespread, however, was a growing apathy and indifference towards the spiritual realm altogether in favour of materialistic self-orientation in terms of hedonistic consumption."[18]

Collins argues that "baby busters" followed up and extended these changes. She notes, in common with other sociologists such as Hervieu-Leger,[19] Walker,[20] and Francis and Kay,[21] that the late twentieth century has seen "a thorough-going fragmentation in lineage of Christian memory," that "gospel amnesia" has set in, as society has come to observe the fragmentation of belief and decontextualisation of spirituality. But lest this sound too pessimistic already, Collins points out that religion has merely mutated rather than disappeared:

> Spirituality . . . has moved from the self-spirituality of the boomer generation to a more aesthetic spirituality, a spirituality which is focused on pleasure and experience in and of itself. . . . Successful churches, it seems, offer an atmosphere and intimate experience of God over and above doctrine . . . the spirituality of intimacy of the millennial generation will be deeply bound up with the consumerism that has increasingly concerned youth throughout the post-war period.[22]

Collins analysis is persuasive on many levels; her descriptive arguments appear to be a good "fit" for young people and spirituality at the dawn of a third millennium. However, one important caveat should be mentioned, namely that of change. Interest in, or even a passion for "an intimate experience of God over and above doctrine" is not

18. Collins, "Spirituality and Youth," 229.

19. Hervieu-Leger, *Religion as a Chain of Memory*.

20. Walker, *Telling the Story*.

21. Francis and Kay, *Teenage Religion and Values*.

22. Collins, "Spirituality and Youth," 233–35.

necessarily sustainable over a period of time. It does not follow that those things that are valued and cherished in teenage years or one's early twenties will even be regarded in one's thirties or forties. For example, many young people are enchanted by the discipline, fellowship, and spiritual atmosphere of a Christian Union (UCCF) whilst at college or university. But large numbers of students will quietly forsake this type of commitment for a different *attitude* to belief in later years: something altogether more mellow, temperate, open, ambiguous—a faith that can live with doubt.

This transition from the early twenties into "young adulthood" raises some intriguing issues for the consideration of generations. Wade Clark Roof notes that "in times of social upheaval and cultural discontinuity especially, generations tend to become more sharply set off from one another."[23] The added power of consumerism in late modernity reinforces this sense: niche marketing to almost every age group for every stage of life is not only prevalent, but also highly successful. And in the early years of adulthood, the desires appear to be less clustered around fulfillment and more around authenticity. As Parks notes, there is a "hunger for authenticity, for correspondence between one's outer and inner lives . . . a desire to break through into a more spacious and nourishing conception of the common life we all share."[24] Parks work is one of the few treatments of faith and belief in the "twenty-something" age group, and her work is a prescient consideration of how generational change evolves within itself, even to the point of questioning the contemporary bewitchments of consumerism and self-fulfillment.

The idea that changes take place *within* generations, and not simply between them, is an important one to grasp in the consideration of the future of religion, spirituality, and the churches. Personal and communal beliefs have to be sufficiently robust to cope with all stages of life (if they are to last), and they also need the capacity to be able to negotiate the standard ruptures in mundane reality that raise questions about meaning and value. Such occurrences are typically located in the traditional turning points, moments of life such as birth, death, and marriage.[25] And of course, as we have been inferring throughout this essay, cultures themselves can undergo rapid changes that make adaptation essential, particularly for institutions, with which we are also concerned.

The idea of churches adapting to culture is as old as the hills. There is no expression of ecclesiology that is not, in some rich and variegated sense, a reaction against, a response toward, or the attempted redemption of its contextual environment. Churches may choose to regard themselves as being primarily for or against culture (following Niebuhr), but as I have recently argued,[26] what mainly characterizes ecclesial responses to culture is their *resilience*, either in the form of resistance or accommodation, but, more usually, by combining both its strategic survival and mission within late modernity. This

---

23. Roof, *A Generation of Seekers*, 3.

24. Parks, *Big Questions, Worthy Dreams*, 9–16.

25. See Goldscheider and Goldscheider, *Leaving Home Before Marriage*, and Kett, *Rites of Passage*.

26. Percy, *Salt of the Earth*.

observation is important here, for it reminds us that religion is both deeply a part of and also totally apart from culture. Its sheer alterity is what gives it its power, as much as it is wholly incarnated within space, time, and sociality. In other words, religion is that material which generations will attempt to fashion and shape around their needs and desires. But the power of religion will also fashion and shape its "users," causing them to question, reflect, and wonder. Religion evokes awe; the numinous inspires; the spiritual invites a quest of ceaseless wandering.

That said, many theological, ministerial and ecclesial responses to the rapid cultural changes of late modernity, coupled to the apparently dynamic differentiation between generations, has caused the spilling of much ink. Christian bookshops are awash with literature on how to reach the young, how to engage with secular culture, and how to reach those who are "spiritual but not religious." Typically, the character of these works is conditioned by a general sense of panic and fear, with churches engaging in ever-more neuralgic responses to the perceived crisis: flight, fright, and fight would not be too far off the mark. This is especially true in the arena of popular culture, where, ironically, spiritual motifs, symbols, and ideas are plentiful; one trips over such "cultural furniture" all the time in the somewhat haphazard assemblage of late modern life. There are, of course, more sophisticated attempts to read "the signs of the times," and come up with compelling and thoughtful responses to the apparent generation gap.

Paul Albrecht, for example, offers a serious theological and ecclesiological program for the churches that was pregnant with prescience for its time—the crucible of the early 1960s.[27] More tangentially, Milton Rokeach provides a way of understanding how human values are translated and learned from one generation to the next, and from group to group within institutions.[28] Indeed, there is now an abundance of works that could be at the service of the churches, helping them to read cultural and generational change.[29] But overall, most theologians ignore such tasks, leaving the arena free for smaller confessional voices to shout and narrower tribal interests to be developed.

So far, I have deliberately avoided mentioning postmodernity—the "name" for the "condition" that many of the present generation are supposed to be laboring under. I have chosen this path because I do not think it is especially useful to add further characterization to the present debate. Of course, I am prepared to concede that there are aspects to postmodern reflection that are appropriate and analytically-descriptive for our purposes here. For example, I find that Lyotard's quip that postmodernity is essentially "incredulity at metanarratives" to be an apt encapsulation of our political, social, and civic times. It is true that attitudes toward truth have shifted too, but this does not appear to mean that Western Civilization is about to collapse, or that

27. Albrecht, *The Churches and Rapid Social Change*.

28. Rokeach, *Understanding Human Values*.

29. See for example Hall and Neitz, *Culture*; Strinati, *Popular Culture*; Thompson, *Cultural Theory*; Zaltman, *Processes and Phenomena*, etc.

my grandparent's generation will have proven to be more truthful than that of my children's. It is also true that many belief systems—for individuals and institutions—more often than not resemble a new assemblage and collage than any strict continuity with tradition. But at the same time, no one can convincingly prove that this situation for society is new, namely a morass of competing convictions, and that pluralism is particular to late modernity. It isn't. From earliest times, Christians have carved out their faith in a pluralist world, settled churches in alien cultures, and adopted their practices and customs that have eventually become "tradition."

I suspect that the litmus test for assessing the extent of generational change and its implications for mission can probably be best understood by speculating about death and memorialization in the future. If our cultural commentators—who speak of "gospel amnesia" and "a thorough-going fragmentation in lineage of Christian memory"—are right, then what will a funeral visit look like in fifty years time? At present, many ministers conducting funerals can be confident that, unless otherwise requested, there will be Christian hymns and prayers at the ceremony. The Lord's Prayer may be said (and is still mumbled) by many in traditional language. Some hymns—a number of which were learned at school—can be sung, and it is just possible that certain passages of scripture and collects will be familiar to a number of the mourners. But what of the future, where prayers, collects, and hymns are not likely to have been part of the schooling for the vast majority of mourners? What types of religious sentiment will be uttered by the generation that is, in all probability, non-conversant in the language of formal religion, but fluent in the many dialects of spirituality?

To partly answer my own question, I turn to an analogy drawn from the world of art history. Restorers of paintings sometimes talk about the "pentimento," the original sketch that is underneath an oil painting beginning to show through as the painting ages. The pentimento is a kind of skeletal plan (the first lines drawn on canvas): where paint falls or peels off, the earliest ideas for the picture are sometimes revealed. The analogy allows us to pose a question: what will the spiritual pentimento of millennial children look like when it comes to their funeral? It will, I suspect, at least at a church funeral, be primarily Christian, provided we understand the term "Christian" broadly. It will be a kind of vernacular, operant (rather than formal), folk Christianity, not that dissimilar from what many ministers already encounter. But it will also be a more spirituality open and evocative affair, with perhaps readings from other traditions. It will be more therapeutic, centered less on grief and more on celebration. In all likelihood, the funeral of the future will be able to tell us just how much change there has been between the generations. There will be gaps, to be sure, but they are unlikely to be unbridgeable. Previous generations have always found a way through to the next; there is no reason to suppose that this generation will lack the wisdom and the tenacity to do likewise. After all, the original etymology of religion comes from two Latin words, meaning "to bind together."

Bibliography

Abrecht, Paul. *The Churches and Rapid Social Change.* London: SCM, 1961.

Brown, Callum G. *The Death of Christian Britain: Understanding Secularisation 1800-2000.* London: Routledge, 2000.

Collins, Sylvia. "Spirituality and Youth." In *Calling Time: Religion and Change at the Turn of the Millennium*, edited by Martyn Percy, 221-37. Sheffield: Sheffield Academic Press, 2000.

Cunningham, Hugh. *Leisure in the Industrial Revolution.* Beckenham: Croom Helm, 1980.

Francis, Leslie, and W. Kay. *Teenage Religion and Values.* Leominster, UK: Gracewing, 1995.

Goldscheider, Frances K. and Calvin Goldscheider. *Leaving Home Before Marriage: Ethnicity, Familism and Generational Relationships.* Wisconsin: University of Wisconsin, 1993.

Hall, John, and Mary Jo Neitz. *Culture: Sociological Perspectives.* Upper Saddle River, NJ: Prentice Hall, 1993.

Hervieu-Leger, Daniel. *Religion as a Chain of Memory.* Cambridge: Polity, 2000.

Heywood, Colin. *A History of Childhood: Children and Childhood in the West from Medieval to Modern Times.* Cambridge: Polity, 2001.

Hopewell, James. *Congregation: Stories and Structures.* London: SCM, 1987.

Kelly, Thomas. *A History of Adult Education in Liverpool.* Liverpool: Liverpool University Press, 1970.

Kett, Joseph F. *Rites of Passage: Adolescence in America, 1790 to the Present.* New York: Basic Books, 1977.

Laqueur, Thomas W. *Religion and Respectability: Sunday Schools and Working Class Culture.* New Haven: Yale University Press, 1976.

McLeod, Hugh. *Secularisation in Western Europe 1848-1914.* London: Macmillan, 2000.

Mead, Margaret. *Culture and Commitment: The New Relationships Between the Generations in the 1970s.* New York: Doubleday, 1978.

Parks, Sharon D. *Big Questions, Worthy Dreams: Young Adults in Their Search for Meaning, Purpose and Faith.* San Francisco: Jossey-Bass, 2000.

Percy, Martyn. *Calling Time: Religion and Change at the Turn of the Millennium.* Sheffield: Sheffield Academic, 2000.

———. *Salt of the Earth: Religious Resilience in a Secular Age.* Sheffield: Sheffield Academic Press, 2002.

Putnam, Robert. *Bowling Alone: The Collapse and Revival of American Community.* New York: Simon & Schuster, 2000.

Rokeach, Milton. *Understanding Human Values: Individual and Societal.* New York: Free Press, 1979.

Roof, Wade C. *A Generation of Seekers: The Spiritual Journeys of the Baby Boom Generation.* San Francisco: HarperCollins, 1993.

Roof, Wade C., and William McKinney. *American Mainline Religion: Its Changing Shape and Form.* Rutgers, NJ: Rutgers University Press, 1987.

Strinati, Dominic. *Popular Culture: An Introduction to Theories.* New York: Routledge, 1995.

Thompson, Michael, et al. *Cultural Theory.* Boulder, CO: Westview, 1990.

Walker, Andrew. *Telling the Story.* London: SPCK, 1996.

Williams, Andrea S., and James D. Davidson. "Catholic Conceptions of Faith: A Generational Analysis." *Sociology of Religion* 57:3 (1996).

Zoltman, Gerald. *Processes and Phenomena of Social Change.* New York: Wiley, 1973.

31

The Anglican Communion
as Ecclesial Vocation

Faith, Hope, and Charity[1]

O NE OF THE MORE subtle temptations for the church—faced with pluralism, yet equally resisting a resort to fundamentalism or relativism—is to find solace in privatization and specialization; to become so bound up in itself that its language, practices, and rubrics begin to take on the air of a body that unintentionally excludes the very people and communities it is for. Some years ago I was asked to fill in a questionnaire for a survey organized by some local schoolchildren. One question was this: "what is the church?" My answer was as follows:

Partly a building

Partly people

Partly an ideal

Partly complete

The idea of partiality to describe the church is intriguing—as though we need reminding that we, as a church, remain incomplete. We await the fullness promised: "when we shall no longer know in part, but full . . . and see face to face" (1 Cor 13:12). Neither is our church ever the finished product. And yet God accepts us, and continually beckons us to his house—the heavenly place where there is room for all.

Equally, Philip Sheldrake states that a "theology of place must maintain a balance between God's revelation in the particular and a sense that God's place ultimately escapes the boundaries of the localised[sic]."[2] He argues that God in Jesus becomes committed to and redeems all humanity, including the places that are marginal, excluded, and unacceptably "other" to humanity. The very idea of the body of Christ is about God remaining—dwelling with us—such that we are always in,

---

1. This chapter originally appeared in *The Ecclesial Canopy: Faith, Hope, Charity* (Farnham, UK: Ashgate, 2012), 165–82.

2. Sheldrake, *Spaces for the Sacred*, 30.

under, and surrounded by the grace of God, and there is no space and place that God is not in and over.

It is in precisely this vein that Daniel Izuzquiza[3] sets out to shape a spirituality of ecclesiology rooted in a more contemporary catholic theology. Engaging with the Radical Orthodox School of theology and writers such as Milbank,[4] Izuzquiza acknowledges that the church has suffered much in contemporary culture through secular reasoning, becoming, in effect, a private, marginal, and compressed space within an over-arching secularist sphere. A social construction of reality, if you will, in which the secular domain is an imagined meta-space, into which religion falls as a mere "sub-product"—a private set of beliefs and practices that are merely part of a larger set of values and more convincing, shared meta-narratives. Milbank, of course, rejects this construction of reality, and proposes a theology that is rooted in creation and providence, which then relocates the secular within the paradigm of theology, rather than being an emancipation from it.

Izuzquiza, whilst critical of aspects of Milbank's theological approach (and especially his *style* of argument)[5], clearly shares some common concerns. Izuzquiza finds Milbank's interpretation of secularization problematic; his critique of positivism (and especially the status of the social sciences) overbearing; and the political implications of his theology imperialist, noting here the powerful reassertion of a superior premodern Christianity in a postmodern context. Izuzquiza rightly identifies Milbank's ecclesiology as a delicate fusion of conservatism and socialism, and of nouveau-Anabaptist communitarian polity flecked with strong high-church and Anglo-Catholic accents. He does not find this adequate, and suggests that it remains strangely abstract and disembodied as a vision. Instead, Izuzquiza proposes a radical ecclesiology that is rooted in a theology of the body of Christ:

> The body of Christ speaks about communion, inclusive relations, unconditional welcoming, union-in-difference, incorporation in a common reality. The body of Christ talks about the Eucharist, about our Lord Jesus and his healings, the cosmic Christ and the final recapitulation of every body, caress, hug, and tear of human history. The body of Christ builds up the church as a real and visible alternative to the system. The body of Christ shows that another world is actually possible.[6]

Thus, and in this broad, capacious ecclesial ecology, there will be cooperatives, credit unions, houses of hospitality, farming communes, and shelters for the homeless. This place, in other words, will be the specific practice of Christian space—the kingdom of God in action. Not a utopia, of course; but quite possibly a monastery, convent, church,

---

3. Izuzquiza, *Rooted in Jesus Christ.*

4. See especially Milbank, *Theology and Social Theory.*

5. Izuzquiza, *Rooted in Jesus Christ,* 46–47.

6. Ibid., 109.

or faithful gathering that is rooted and grounded in the Christian story, and knows that under the sacred canopy, God sees all. No sparrow falls to the ground without God seeing; the hairs of our head are numbered; all desires known, the thoughts of our hearts weighed, and no secrets hidden.

There is some sense, then, in which Izuzquiza is articulating a vision that is resonant with the *Rule of St Benedict*—the ordering of community life as a school for the Lord's service, promoting hospitality, hope, faith, and charity. Izuzquiza roots his ecclesial vision in a rich reading of Paul's notion of the body of Christ, which, he argues, consists of four interrelated ideas: the bread, Christ's body, the church, and the body of the Christian. The personal and communitarian aspects are therefore richly related, and irreducible. For Paul, therefore, there is no distinction between private and public, or corporate and individual. The term, like the vision, is comprehensive.[7] Closely related to these four interrelated ideas are four models of the church. First, it is a purity system (anthropological), in which differences and defilement are named, challenged, and overcome. Second, it is a physical space (archaeological), in which the physical plant becomes the site of practice for God's kingdom, with a focus on celebration and sharing. Third, it is an economic program, including acts of hospitality, alms-giving, and the redistribution of wealth. Fourth, it is a political alternative to the prevailing powers and authorities, in which Jews, gentiles, men and women, slave and free can co-exist in mutual love and interdependence.

For Izuzquiza, the key to understanding the body of Christ is rooted in the interrelationships that now form a new social reality. Indeed, the social-sacramental life of the church is formed in the bread, Christ's body, the church and the body of the Christian. A deep experience of the body of Christ will be one without division (though it may have much diversity); one of unity (though this is not the same as uniformity) and of common purpose (though there are varieties of gifts), which leads to a truly deep social transformation. When this occurs, the body of Christ cannot be broken (by which we mean atomized), nor can Christ's power be limited, since a life rooted in Jesus Christ will have powerful and radical consequences in all areas of reality.[8] This is the body of Christ in both its corporeal reality and its mystical state: "the ecclesiology of the church as (a) radical sacrament."[9] As Izuzquiza says,

> Ecclesial communion generates social communion. A life rooted in Jesus Christ means a radical transformation of all reality. Eucharistic dynamism embraces each Christian's personal life. It embraces ecclesial life. It embraces the world's life. United to Jesus Christ, we believers are called to be the body of Christ, to be a sacrament of communion and liberation for the life of the world.[10]

7. Ibid., 139.
8. Ibid., 138–52.
9. Ibid., 160.
10. Ibid., 165.

But what might this mean more practically? Now, in our final section we turn to work this through the context of Anglican belief and practice.

Anglicanism: Communion as Breadth and Charity

The idea of the Anglican Communion as a Big Tent, or as a capacious space which all may inhabit, has a long and august history in the practice of polity, ecclesiology, and the spirituality of the church. Yet in times of crisis, that sense of space can quickly evaporate. What was previously experienced as gracious and capacious can quickly become licence and disconnectedness. Atomization follows, accompanied by a sense of compression and alienation. Yet the recovery of this sense of God-given space and grace lies at the heart of the Communion, and having the wisdom and patience to wait for its re-emergence will undoubtedly serve the church well. Oliver O'Donovan contends that waiting and striving for this moment will ultimately serve the church, and the gospel, well:

> There are no guarantees. There never are in the Christian life. But that is not a reason not to try. And seriously trying means being seriously patient. Anyone who thinks that resolutions can be reached in one leap without mutual long exploration, probing, challenge, and clarification has not yet understood the nature of the riddle that the ironic fairy of history has posed for us in our time.[11]

If the Lambeth Communion can be said to have passed off relatively peacefully in 2008, the years since then (not many of them, granted), seem to have been a little less kind to the Communion. Debates on sexuality have returned to haunt the Instruments of Unity and the Provinces, and the Church of England has had some turbulent debates on women bishops. Moreover, there seems to be no sign of these difficulties disappearing. The fractious nature of the debates appears to be as polarizing as before, and the Communion is under some strain and duress.

Whilst acknowledging these cultural shifts and tensions, and their impact on the wider Communion, I nonetheless see no reason to despair at this juncture. Our hope, after all, is not rooted in political compromise, but in the gospel. It is grounded in the virtues and character that all Christians are called to. Which is why, I suspect, we shall rediscover as a Communion something deeper in our calling to develop bonds of affection, and in the kind of story-swapping and listening that is encouraged through the ongoing Indaba process.[12] The content of the stories and experiences exchanged and reflected upon in the Indaba process is, arguably, not the issue for Anglicans.

---

11. O'Donovan, *The Church in Crisis*, 119.

12. "Indaba" is a concept used in contemporary Anglican ecclesiology, and is derived from a Zulu or Xhosa (South Africa) term that describes a meeting to resolve differences and achieve reconciliation and harmony when faced with complex, competing convictions.

Rather, the key questions are, can we listen to one another attentively and patiently, mindful that this is God's time, God's church, and God's future and not ours to possess and shape to suit our own requirements and proclivities? Can we, as a mature Communion, develop levels of intellectual and emotional composure, fashioning a deeper kind of ecclesial intelligence that comprehends the subtle relationships between content and mood, style and substance, the now and the not-yet? Can we, as a Communion, place our trust in God for each other, and commit to acting together for the sake of the gospel and God's kingdom, even if we know we cannot be like-minded? I strongly suspect that the Anglican Communion will, through patience, forbearance, courage (and perhaps a little fear), rediscover its bonds and unity, even amidst its differences.

This will also mean a more charitable understanding of conflict in the life of the Communion. Too often, we assume that conflict is a sign of weakness, that difficult arguments point to eventual fragmentation. Yet it need not be so. The history of the Christian church rests in contending for creeds, articles of faith, the canon of scripture and actual doctrines that began their life in the most acrimonious of debates. Luis Bermejo SJ argues that there are four stages to a cyclical process in ecclesial life: communication, conflict, consensus, and finally Communion.[13] Issues in the Anglican Communion tend to get refracted through this four-fold process. Bermejo argues that this is how the Holy Spirit moves the church—it is not the case that only the last of these stages is "spiritual." The Holy Spirit can also be manifested in gifts and fruits: tested, pruned, and refined in conflict. Yet the problem remains; the catholicity of Anglicanism is more geographical than theological. That said, Anglicans need not fear the arguments that appear to divide, or their causes and consequences. Rather, they should see that conflict is a phase of life in the church in which the Holy Spirit moves. Indeed, the Spirit is present in the conflict; it is part of the gestation of the church. And, indeed, its vibrancy, with occasional ruptures, may in fact be a sign of maturity, rather than problematic.

Correspondingly, this can point us to the imperative of continuous scriptural reasoning for the church—a process of reading the Bible together, recognizing that the diversity of scriptures (note the plural) is where we discover both our unity and diversity, and our plurality and commonality. This means waiting upon the Lord together, sitting under the word of God together, and continuing to share in the common sacramental life that God has given us:

> The Bible reveals the self-revealing God along with the way the world is, the way life is, the way we are. We need to know the lay of the land that we are living in. We need to know what is involved in this Country of the Trinity, the world of God's creating and salvation and blessing. . . . The text is not words to be studied in a library but a voice to be believed, love and adored in workplace

13. Bermejo, *The Spirit of Life*.

and playground, on the streets and in the kitchen. Receptivity is required. . . .
Spiritual theology, using Scripture as text, does not present us with a moral
code and tell us to "live up to this"; nor does it set out a system of doctrine and
say "think like this and you will live well." The biblical way is to tell a story and
invite us to live like this.[14]

The Anglican Communion manifestly lives under the scriptures; they are what help
shape and form the ecclesial ecology. By continuing to enter into and under the word
that God has given us, the body of Christ is nourished and transformed by new understandings. Yet even when these do not immediately emerge, the mode and manners
of sharing and being together have a deep impact on the formation of our common
life. Sometimes, living righteously is more important than being right; being good and
charitable more important than having our perspective vindicated. Embodying faith,
hope, and love is more of a witness to the truth than winning a debate.

Charity, then—as an ecclesiological characteristic—is both a value and a virtue.
In contemporary culture, we are often tempted to view charity with mild pity; it comprises gifts and donations that mend gaps that should otherwise not be there. Giving to
charity is, all too often, an exercise which prompts either parting with loose change; or
perhaps something more planned and systematic. Yet charity, properly understood, is
something much richer and deeper than this, and should form one of the well-springs
that sustains the church; or constellations that guide it. The word has roots in the
Latin term "caritas," and means "costly esteem and affection"—there is a warmth and
tenderness to charity. It is a word that resonates with "cherishing" and "benevolence";
the one who is charitable is the one who sees the other as dear and valued—esteeming
highly, and loving. There is diligence and duty here, to be sure; but also a deep and
compassionate love for the other that is Christianity at its best. Wycliffe used the word
"charity" in his translation of 1 Corinthians 13 in order to (slightly) draw out the
contrast with love; charity is active, and it also has a mood—a cadence and timbre, if
you will. It is not just an act, but a tone of engagement.

In the same vein, hope is a leap[15] in expectation; it is a wish, dream, and anticipation of what is to come, just as faith is trust, confidence, and reliance, and the living
out of what is believed. To be charitable, ultimately, and to live charitably, is to both
imagine and see the world benevolently and mercifully—as God might see it. This
not, I must stress, a new vision for pastoral theology. The idea of faith, hope, and
charity being the very foundations for an attentive, loving, compassionate pastoral
theology should not surprise us. And that such love and compassion have political
implications—for society and ecclesial polity—will hardly be news. William Paley, in
a treatise on morality from 1785, states that

14. Peterson, *Eat this Book*, 113.

15. Some etymologists suggest that hoping is indeed connected to hopping: leaping forward.

> I use the term Charity neither in the common sense of bounty to the poor, nor in St Paul's sense of benevolence to all mankind: but I apply it at present, in a sense more commodious to my purpose . . . charity [is] promoting the happiness of our inferiors. Charity, in this sense I take to be the principal province of virtue and religion: for, whilst worldly prudence will direct our behavior towards our superiors and politeness to our equals, there is little to set beside the consideration of duty, or an habitual humanity which comes into the place of consideration, to produce conduct towards those who are beneath us, and dependent on us. [16]

But here, charity is not a gift, as we have been describing it. It is a duty, and conferred on those "who are beneath us." Yet true charity would be a form of gift. It would be the giving of something that could be kept or, in turn, given away—so the gift is significant in scale and scope. And the gift should also, to be a true gift, raise the status of the recipient—otherwise it is merely a distraction or some sort of sop. Charity should ultimately dissolve social barriers and boundaries, not perpetuate them, or merely try to negotiate difference, without challenging divisive diversities rooted in class, wealth, and other forms of discrimination.

Lest this sound too abstract, we may do well to remember that the ministry of Jesus is rooted in God's charity—a radical commitment to challenging divisions, and bringing about forms of equality that amounted to a nascent form of politically-led pastoral theology. The early Christian church took this to heart, and extended the articulation and practice of the body of Christ to include the widows and orphans, gentiles, slaves, women, children, and foreigners. The call was for universal brotherhood. The reason for driving out the money-changers in the temple was a fundamental expression of his rejection of a "gifts-for-God" spiritual economy. Charity, for Jesus, was freedom from any kind of bondage—and all with equal access to his Heavenly Father. Later, Christians in the Middle Ages, like Bernard of Clairvaux, would take this message to heart, and practice the richness of their relationship with God through a deep solidarity with the poor.

Alms were there to empower and enable, not merely to provide additional help and support but with no prospect of deliverance from economic or social bondage. Martin of Tours (died 397 AD) is one of the early saints who is defined by a charity that is both politically radical and also daring in its implication for ecclesial polity. Martin, a serving solider in the Imperial Roman army, had a vision of a cold and naked beggar. In his vision, he cuts his cloak in half, and gives half to the beggar. In a subsequent vision, he sees Christ wearing the same cloak, rejoicing in the gift. Martin, in serving the beggar, has served God. His charity is one that Christ recognizes and affirms. At the same time, it appears that Martin has understood from the outset that charity is not simply being moved to act through pity. It is also passion—dear and costly love for, and passion for, the other. Charity is a fusion of pity, passion, and compassion. It

16. Paley, *The Principles of Moral and Political Philosophy*, 12.

is something well beyond filling in the gaps; it is an extravagant, excessive passion for equality. It is a practice, not a theory.

The concept of practice has recently received significant interest in organizational circles through the work of Etienne Wenger. Wenger analyzed workplace habits, and then attempted to develop a social theory of learning. It is this that gave birth to the concept of communities of practice, which Wenger defines as "groups of people who share a concern or a passion for something they do and learn how to do it better as they interact regularly."[17] Even if participants in such communities are innocent of their membership and unaware of their practices, the very idea of

> a concept of practice includes both the explicit and tacit. It includes what is said and what is left unsaid: but is represented and what is assumed. It includes the language, tools, documents, images, symbols, well-defined roles, specified criteria, codified procedures, regulations, and contracts that various practices make explicit for a variety of purposes. But it also includes all the implicit relations, tacit conventions, subtle cues, untold rules of thumb, recognisable institutions, specific perceptions, well-tuned sensitivities, embodied under-standings, underlying assumptions, and shared worldviews. Most of these may never be articulated, yet their unmistakable signs of membership in com-munities of practice are crucial to the success of the enterprises.[18]

Wenger sees one of the primary functions of communities of practice as the formation of identity. And identity, according to Wenger, is negotiated through the shared mem-bership of social communities; he says that "practice defines a community through three dimensions: mutual engagement, a joint enterprise, and a shared repertoire."[19] His approach remains realistic throughout—identity is not something we construct in our heads intellectually or in our imagination, but rather something that is con-structed by our day-to-day practices.

In terms of the practice and identity of the church, the trinity of faith, hope, and charity is complex. The disciples do not easily "read" the nuance of what is being asked of the church by Christ. Identity and practice are bound up in complex gestures, sym-bols and inferences. Perhaps an obvious example of this is when Jesus begins to pre-pare his body for crucifixion and burial, and is anointed with precious oil by a woman. John 12: 1–8 names the woman as Mary, and the text assumes her to be Mary, a sister to Lazarus, as the text also identifies her sister as Martha. However, the iconography of the woman's act has traditionally been associated with Mary Magdalene, even though there is no biblical text identifying her as such. According to Mark 14:3, the perfume in his account was pure and expensive. Many biblical commentators assume that this story occurs only a few days before the crucifixion, due to the numerous events that

---

17. Wenger, *Communities of Practice*. See also Wenger et al., *Cultivating Communities of Practice.*
18. Wenger, *Communities of Practice*, 47.
19. Ibid., 152.

followed in Luke's gospel. This seems the most logical timing to me, not least because of the discourse that follows the complaint from the disciples that the oil could have been sold, and the money put to better use to feed the poor (charity?). Jesus, however, replies that "the poor you have with you always . . . but I am only with you a little while" (faith?). And Lewis Hyde says of the issue of hope in the story,

> As usual, they [the disciples] have been a little slow to catch on. They are thinking of the price of oil as they sit before a man preparing to treat his body as a gift and atonement. We might take Jesus' reply to mean that poverty (or scarcity) is alive and well and inside their question, that rich and poor will live among them so long as they cannot feel the spirit when it is alive amongst them.[20]

This is, I am sure, a subtle and sound reading of the story. The implication is that faith, hope and charity cannot be understood apart. It is only when they are brought together in conversation, structures, constructions of reality and theology, and in the church and under God's supreme love, that the wisdom of their intra-dependence can be fully appreciated and understood.

Faith, Hope, and Charity: Applied Anglican Polity

Education is what is left—the residue—after we have forgotten all the things we learnt. The challenge for Anglicans, then, and in their polity, is to recover some real sense of and actual practice of *charity* in relation to faith and hope, and under love. To develop a charitable imagination that is not rooted in pity and perceived need, but rather in a rich and generative appreciation for the other—valuing them as dear, cherished, and beloved. To "live in love and charity with your neighbour," as the *Book of Common Prayer* puts it. Such a way of living requires both warmth and coolness; acts of faith; and the practice of hope. This may seem just too liberal and unspecific for some, but I think the tone of the church matters very much, not just for Christians in their churches, but also because it is part of the wider and deeper way in which ecclesial polity shapes society. As Will Hutton remarked on the eve of the 2008 Lambeth Conference:

> Anglicanism is a liberal tradition central to the very conception of Englishness, but it finds itself under mounting threat. . . . The genius of the Church of England is that because it is the official church it has to include the universe of all the English—Christian, agnostic and atheist, of whatever sexual orientation. It represents the cultural heartbeat of the country, and as the country has become more progressive so has it. . . . This is not just a precious institution at individual moments of crisis. Anglican priests are bulwarks for a cluster of values—tolerance, mutual respect, kindness, altruism, redemption—wherever they go in the

20. Hyde, *The Gift*, 119.

communities they serve. I've never met one I did not respect enormously. In some social housing estates they are the only decent non-official figures people encounter. And even if God is only a hypothesis, it is crucially important that the country's leading religious institution is liberal.

[Rowan] Williams understands this. The popular view is that he is an ineffectual hand-wringer who is risking the break-up of the Church of England. I disagree. He obviously has a responsibility to try to keep the worldwide Anglican church together if he can. But he has a greater responsibility to the genius of Anglicanism—its capacity to reconcile Christian faith with the lived lives of the English and in so doing transmute religion into a powerful liberal, rather than reactionary, force.[21]

One of the characteristics that marked out early Christianity is that it understood faith to be an expression of passion and deeply held convictions. Faith, in terms of discipleship, is often not reasoned coolness. As we reflected in the previous chapter, faith is passion that spills over; the love that is stronger than death. Yet excessive, passionate faith is not the same as extreme faith. The former is intemperate and im-modest; but it abounds in energy because it springs from the liberty of God. It is released as a kind of raw energy, precisely because it breaks the chains of inhibition, and springs forth from spiritual encounters that can border on ecstasy. But this is not, as I say, extremism. It is merely passion resulting from encounter, conversion, conviction, resurrection, and transformation.

Yet our passion and energy as a Communion is also to be linked to our call to temperance and self-control—the kinds of virtues listed by Paul in Galatians. But temperance and self-control are not about control from without. The modeling of such virtue is, rather, the deep spiritual exercise of restraint for the sake of the self and the other. It is a spiritual discipline and a character that can only be exercised in proportion to the energy and passion that wells up from the same source. It is a steely and willed act of moderation or self-control that emerges out of passionate convictions, grace, and love. That's why the list of the fruits of the Holy Spirit from Galatians is so important. Love, joy, peace, patience, kindness, self-control, humility, gentleness and faithfulness are all rooted in the passion of Christ—a putting-to-death of our desires, and seeing them reconfigured through the Holy Spirit into the heart of God. So excess and abundance are of God; extremism, however, is of the flesh. As one theologian puts it, living like this would mean that, in the church:

> We have a gift to share which will enlarge any culture because without a scriptural vision of covenant and justice, mercy and fidelity, generosity in personal relations and political structures alike, we shall find ourselves and our cultures becoming less and less human, less and less sustainable, less and less liveable.

---

21. Hutton, "Rebel Anglican Bishops Threaten the Very Heart of our Liberal Traditions," 25.

This is a vision of a gospel that seeks to be at home in the human world, yet reshapes it more radically than we could have imagined.[22]

Bibliography

Bermejo, Luis M. *The Spirit of Life: The Holy Spirit in the Life of the Christian*. Chicago: Loyola University Press, 1989.

Hutton, Will. "Rebel Anglican Bishops Threaten the Very Heart of our Liberal Traditions." *The Guardian*, July 6, 2008.

Hyde, Lewis. *The Gift: Creativity and the Artist in the Modern World*. New York: Random House, 1983.

Izuzquiza, Daniel. *Rooted in Jesus Christ: Toward a Radical Ecclesiology*. Grand Rapids, MI: Eerdmans, 2009.

Milbank, John. *Theology and Social Theory: Beyond Secular Reason*. Oxford: Blackwell, 1990.

O'Donovan, Oliver. *The Church in Crisis: the Gay Controversy and the Anglican Communion*. Eugene, OR: Cascade, 2008.

Paley, William. *The Principles of Moral and Political Philosophy*. Indianapolis: Liberty Fund, 2002.

Peterson, Eugene H. *Eat this Book: A Conversation in the Art of Spiritual Reading*. London: Hodder and Stoughton, 2006.

Sheldrake, Philip. *Spaces for the Sacred*. London: SCM, 2001.

Wenger, Etienne. *Communities of Practice: Learning, Meaning and Identity*. Cambridge: Cambridge University Press, 1998.

Wenger, Etienne, et al. *Cultivating Communities of Practice*. Boston: Harvard University Press, 2002.

---

22. Archbishop Rowan Williams, *Sermon*, Service to celebrate the Bicentenary of the British and Foreign Bible Society, St Paul's Cathedral, March 8, 2004.

Afterword

32

Confessions: Tone and Content in a Reasonable Radical

—A Self-Critical Retrospect

Martyn Percy

W HAT DOES IT MEAN to be a reasonable radical? It was often quipped of Robert Runcie that during his tenure as Archbishop of Canterbury, he was adept at "nailing his colours to the fence." Implied in this quip is a stinging critique—and arguably of one the great Archbishops of Canterbury in the twentieth century. Runcie was committed to the broad, middle-way of Anglican polity.

Runcie could see that, in describing Anglicanism as a matter of "passionate coolness," one was carefully advocating a measured, reasonable, and temperate ecclesial polity. In fact, Runcie often used the phrase to refer to ideal forms of English Anglicanism. The phrase is as striking as it is oxymoronic. Runcie believed that Anglican polity was essentially gentle, mild, and cool, by which he meant temperamentally measured and reflective, even rational. Just the same, it was passionate about this coolness, and passionate in its aesthetics expressed in the measured intensity of its dramatic liturgy; the beauty of its architecture, music, poetry; and its spiritual piety, whether high, low, or broad.

This passionate coolness, crucially, *gathered* people—but did not force, compel, or corral them. Much like a great work of art, passionate coolness gathers people around, and draws them in. But it still leaves spaces for God to be present in deep experiences of the numinous, and for themselves to be individuals too, while still providing ample space to be together. Passionate coolness, then, is typically an Anglican phrase, framing ecclesial identity within an apparent paradox. Anglicanism is a kind of practical and mystical idea that embodies how people might be together. Anglicanism is a social vision before it is an ecclesiology, and not a confessional church in which membership is conditional upon precise agreement with articles or statements.

In spite of the internal difficulties that global Anglicanism encounters, its strength may still lie in its apparent paradoxes: its unity in its diversity, its coherence in its difference, its shape in its diffusiveness, its hope in a degree of faithful doubt, its energy in passionate coolness. As a polity, it embodies feint conviction; it is Protestant and Catholic; it is Synodical and Episcopal; it allows for troubled commitment. As I have often remarked, in its own deliberations, it can't easily resist the pairing of two three-letter words: "yes, but . . . ."

I was immensely touched—overwhelmed, indeed—to receive an invitation from the Dean of Virginia Theological Seminary, The Very Revd Professor Doctor Ian Markham—to come and engage with a range of scholars over the course of three days in 2016, and discuss the corpus of my writings. The papers and conversations that followed and flowed in Alexandria, Virginia, were profoundly stimulating, and I was on many occasions simply awestruck by the depth and range of critiques, interpretations, and applications that had emerged. Alternately humbling and affirming, inspiring and chastening, the papers ranged over the body and trajectory of my writings from the last twenty-five years. And in the preceding pages, the contributors have engaged with a variety of topics, including issues in contemporary ecclesiology, pastoral theology, theological education, and formation.

The essays also pick up on my long-standing commitment to "binocular" ways of reading issues: frequently reading theology with sociology, or ecclesiology with anthropology, or congregational studies with musicology. I have always maintained that this approach to theological studies is good for the discipline, as well as being rooted in the conviction that the study of the church—ecclesiology—is the study of how congregations manifest their theological convictions. Every denomination is, to some extent (to borrow a phrase from John Caputo), an attempt to express the "mood of God."[1] Ecclesial life is, inevitably, the social reification of any group's theological priorities and spiritual proclivities. Class, ethnicity, gender, and various contextual factors all have a bearing on the shaping of denominational character and congregational life. The mood of a denomination or congregation essentially captures and communicates what it thinks is the heart, mind, and nature of God.

My journey in ecclesiology began with a study of the theme of power in contemporary fundamentalism and revivalism. The study sought to achieve some illumination into how congregations and movements could be better understood, and so blended theological insights with anthropological and sociological lenses. The book drew on the insights of Clifford Geertz and his notion of "religion as culture." The result was *Words, Wonders and Power*[2]; and this book, I later discovered, became the subject of conferences from Copenhagen to California, with anthropologists of religion constituting the main readership. Even at the time of publication, I had begun

1. See Gutting, "Deconstructing God," in an interview with John Caputo discussing his book, *The Prayers and Tears of Jacques Derrida*.
2. Percy, *Words, Wonders and Power*.

to realize that the study of the church—its self-understanding, issues, travails, virtues, vices, character, mood, and proclivities—had become a lifelong commitment.

Further studies followed. I was fortunate to be able to do some fieldwork on the "Toronto Blessing." I began to write about Anglican ecclesiology and polity, touching on issues of governance and leadership, gender, justice and sexuality, and pastoral praxis and political engagement.[3] I also began a series of engagements in the Christianity-Culture arena, which offered revisionist and fresh readings of topics such as religion and consumerism, secularization, and contextual theology.[4] Some of these engagements have been practical, and applied. I have taken on roles in public that have been at the sensitive intersection of media and consumer affairs, and the weighing of values and ethics in contemporary culture. I have been a Director of the Advertising Standards Authority, a Commissioner for the Direct Marketing Authority, an Adjudicator for the Portman Group (the self-regulating body for the alcoholic drinks industry in the UK), and an Advisor to the British Board of Film Classification.

When I moved to Cuddesdon in 2004 in order to take up the post of Principal of Ripon College and the Oxford Ministry Course, I was drawn into writing and reflecting on the dynamics of theological education, formation, and theory and practice in ordained ministry.[5] And this period also marked a more intentional program of devotional writing and radio broadcasting, which continues to nourish me—and, I dare to hope, readers and listeners alike.

As the Dean of Christ Church, Oxford, one is afforded a very particular opportunity to reflect on how institutions tend to cohere, and the implicit values, character, and behavior that marks out such a body as distinctive and flavored. As with my former colleagues at Cuddesdon, I am continually enabled and enriched by the many conversations that take place in "The House" (as it is colloquially known), and by the blend of college and cathedral life that constitutes the unique foundation that is Christ Church.

In some respects, my academic outlook is entirely comprehensible and cognizant with the consistent manner in which I seek to approach the task of exercising oversight within those institutions I have been fortunate enough to serve in. There is a five-fold staging to this, one that respects the subjects or institutions being addressed. Both subject and institution are manifestly particular, "living" as distinctive material realities (albeit within wider contexts). They are also incomplete, and so are constantly evolving, which therefore requires both humble and dynamic approaches to their study and analysis. Moreover, the student of either will be changed as they engage in interpretation and analysis.

3. See, for example, Percy, "The Holy Spirit in the Church of England Today." See Percy, *Intimate Affairs* and Percy, *Managing the Church?*; Percy, "Falling Far Short" and Percy, "The Anatomy of Fundamentalism."

4. See Percy, *Salt of the Earth*. See also Percy, *Engaging with Contemporary Culture*.

5. Percy, *Clergy*.

The five-fold process can be summarized in comparatively simple terms. First, there is *noticing*. That is to say, identifying and dwelling upon phenomena that may be odd, familiar, unusual, taken-for-granted, or unnoticed. Quite often, such things may be "hiding in plain sight."[6] The skill of the academic, or the leader of an institution for that matter, should be able to see the forest, the trees, and the individual species and grain of wood, so to speak. It is about seeing the detail, and also understanding the bigger picture.

Second, there is *reading*. That is to say, finding a method or lens that makes particularly *good* sense of what has been observed, intuited, or recognized. Some readings will be, qualitatively, better than others. Some will be alien to the material, but nonetheless illuminating. Some experiments in reading can, therefore, be constructive; there is an element, inevitably, of trial and error. A lot of work in social sciences is predicated on good guesswork, before it can start to become a "thick(er) description," as Clifford Geertz would say.

Third, the process of reading moves into *interpreting*. Here, some more intentional methods and lenses can be brought to bear upon the subject or issue. Sometimes the phenomena under scrutiny will struggle under the weight of the method. Equally, some issues will struggle to support the weight of a complex nexus of problems, where the signs, symbols, and phenomena may point in contrary ways. For this reason alone, "binocular" approaches to interpretation can be advantageous when trying to read and interpret ecclesial life, as there is, unavoidably, social behavior to comprehend, as well as an inner theological construction of reality to take account of.

Fourth, there is *reframing*—beginning to crystallize new understandings and frames of reference for what is being studied and analyzed. This, let me stress, requires a degree of openness and humility. Most things are capable of being read and understood in countless ways. Something as simple as being in love, or having a religious experience, does not have one explanation, nor does it have one meaning. And the explanations and meanings will change over time, as the actors evolve, and as contexts alter. Reframing is a considered, temperate, modest exercise, involving a blend of caution and risk.

Fifth, and finally, there is *returning*—taking the analysis and any tentative conclusions back to what was first observed, and testing its wisdom, efficacy, and appropriateness. It is at this point that the process, far from being complete, may require refinements and review. For example, one may need some further negotiations with the issues in hand, or for that matter, the people and groups being studied. And over time, the insights may be vindicated, or may need adjustment. For example, in my work on the "Toronto Blessing," I identified romantic tropes and ideologies that fed the expectations of the movement in terms of its social bonding, worship, and the anticipated eschatology. Such analysis has been largely affirmed over time, although it was difficult for enthusiasts of the movement to comprehend this when

6. On this, see for example Percy, *Shaping the Church*.

the movement was still at its peak.[7] As C. Wright Mills puts it, there is a vocational aspect to this: "The sociological imagination enables its processor to understand the larger historical scene in terms of its meaning for the inner life and the external career of a variety of individuals."[8]

In a similar vein, Peter Berger makes a similar case for the five-fold process I have consistently advocated, namely noticing, reading, interpreting, reframing, and if possible, returning to the beginning:

> To ask sociological questions, then, presupposes that one is interested in look-
> ing some distance beyond the commonly accepted or officially denied goals
> of human actions. It presupposes a certain awareness that human events have
> different levels of meaning, some of which are hidden from the consciousness
> of everyday life...we will not be far off if we see sociological thought as part of
> what Nietzsche called "the art of mistrust."[9]

So let me to say something brief about the methodological horizon that has helped to shape my writing. Theologians are divided on the use of social sciences in terms of providing an account of the churches and their practices of Christian life. However, I maintain that

> All forms of social science are useful, perhaps even necessary for ecclesiology,
> including those that are thoroughly antagonistic to the church or to religious
> bodies generally. However, since they examine religious bodies in a variety of
> ways, they cannot be useful in quite the same way, and none of them is ever
> normative.[10]

The fact that some social scientists are now prepared to acknowledge their disciplines as interpretative rather than complete descriptors and analyses of religion affords an opportunity for theology and the social sciences to collaborate more richly in their readings of church and society.[11] In turn, this permits some degree of honesty in naming the underlying presuppositions of methodological approach to the study of religion. Instead of pretending that the methodology being used is "neutral," Clarke and Byrne suggest that there are four stances to consider when studying religion: atheistic, agnostic, religious, and theological. The stance I adopt is primarily religious and theological in character, not atheistic or agnostic.[12] This more self-conscious methodological syncretism can lead to what Nicholas Healy calls "a church-wide social practice of

---

7. See Percy, "The City on a Beach"; Percy, "A Place at High Table?"; Percy, "Adventure and Atrophy"; and Percy, *Power and the Church*.

8. Mills, *The Sociological Imagination*, 5.

9. Berger, *Invitation to Sociology*, 41.

10. Healy, *Church, World and the Christian Life*, 155.

11. For further discussion see Percy, "Label or Libel," 82–92.

12. Clarke and Byrne, *Religion Defined and Explained*.

communal self-critical analysis [bearing] upon the issue of Christian formation."[13] In turn, this might lead to what he describes as "practical-prophetic" ecclesiology, which arises out of particular ways of reflecting on the church in the world:

> Ecclesiological forms of history, sociology and ethnography, in debate with parallel non-theological disciplines, may help the church live more truthfully by drawing critical attention back to the confusions and complexities of life within the pilgrim church. Practical-prophetic ecclesiology acknowledges that Christian existence is never stable or resolvable in terms of purely theoretical constructions, but is ever-moving, always struggling along with the theo-drama. It acknowledges too that the church must engage with other traditions of enquiry not only for their sake, but for its own, in order that it may on occasion hear the Spirit of the Lord in their midst.[14]

I hold that the benefits of such reflection for the churches should help lead to a new kind of confidence in the resilience of faith, and in the shaping and future of religious institutions. While such confidence is not without its caveats, the primary burden of my work nevertheless remains constant; namely to argue for interrogative and empathetic theological engagements in the field of ecclesiology.

There is also some teleology to disclose in all this. In his ground-breaking and magisterial book *The Clerical Profession*,[15] Anthony Russell combines history, sociology, and theology to explore how ordained ministry moved from being an "occupation" to understanding itself as some kind of "profession." In the book, he writes of three possible ways of imagining the future of the church.

The first is *traditionalist*, in which the past and present is largely retained for the future. Dwindling numbers in congregations, secularization, consumerism, or pluralism, or other crises or issues that require a dynamic and responsive engagement, are simply met by the advocacy of an unchanging tradition.

The second is *adaptionist* in character. Promoters of this approach recognize that elements of the tradition have become redundant and cannot be rehabilitated. The church adapts and changes, as much as any living organism or institution does in response to its changing environment. Adaptionists maintain as much coherence with the past as is possible, but adopt a faithful-pragmatic outlook for the present, as they look to the future.

The third is *reformist* in character, and this is typically the most radical of the three. (That said, one often encounters many individuals and groups in the study of contemporary ecclesiology, who also claim the "radical" crown for being traditionalists or adaptionists. In some ways, it is like small conservative groups claiming to be "radical" solely because they constitute an unfashionable minority.) Reformers

---

13. Healy, *Church, World and the Christian Life*, 178.

14. Ibid., 185.

15. Russell, *The Clerical Profession*.

typically tend to make and drive deliberate changes, and will be the most likely group to conceive of radical possibilities for the institutions and organizations they are part of. That said, many who narrate themselves as "radical" in the church will transpire to be closet-adaptionists.

In outlining this methodological approach—tempered and moderate in tone, as well as open and circumspect—I take seriously the counsel of Catherine Bell: "that we construct "religion" and "science" is not the main problem: that we forget we have constructed them in our own image—that is a problem."[16] I am also mindful of the vocation ascribed to social scientists, and for that matter, to anyone embarking on the study of ecclesiology, from Raymond Aron:

> At the risk of shocking sociologists, I should be inclined to say that it is their job to render sociological or historical content more intelligible than it was in the experience of those who lived it. All sociology is a reconstruction that aspires to confer intelligibility on human existence, which, like all human existences, are confused and obscure.[17]

Naturally, there is no doubt that faith communities, churches, and congregations do look to formal theological propositions, creeds, articles of faith, and the like to order their inner life, establish their identity, and maintain their distinctiveness in the world. Yet it is also true that music, moods, and manners, informal beliefs and learned (and therefore valued) behavior, apparently innocuous and innocent practices and patterns of polity, performance, dance, and dramaturgy, together with aesthetics and applied theological thinking, are no less constitutive for the shaping of the church. Attention to the role and vitality of the implicit is therefore vital if one wishes to comprehend the depth, density, identity, and shaping of faith communities.

That said, it does not follow that all differences are rooted in proclivity or context. All that can be said here is that such factors, whilst significant and worthy of theological evaluation, are not necessarily determinative. Although variable ecclesial accents (e.g., Baptist, Anglican, Methodist, etc.) sometimes accentuate differences, ecclesial communities cannot evade their intrinsic and extrinsic unity. As Kathryn Tanner observes,

> Religious beliefs are a form of culture, inextricably implicated in the material practices of daily social living on the part of those who hold them . . . in the concrete circumstances in which beliefs are lived . . . actions, attitudes, and interests are likely to be as much infiltrated and informed by the beliefs one holds as beliefs are to be influenced by actions, attitudes and interests.[18]

---

16. Bell, "Modernism and Postmodernism in the Study of Religion," 179–90.

17. Aron, *Main Currents in Sociological Thought*, 207.

18. Tanner, *The Politics of God*, 9.

This is why the interlocutors that I have tended to prefer using in my own ecclesial frameworks of reference have been characteristically open; circumspect; innovative (but reasonably so); and above all, inter-, intra-, and multi-disciplinary. I have eschewed "pedigree" and "purist" approaches to subjects and issues, preferring instead the cross-breeding and blending that produces a certain kind of interpretive individuality.

The usual name for this, in ordinary idiom, is "mongrel": an animal or plant that results from various kinds of inter-breeding. Used most often of canines, the word is also sometimes coined as a term of offense. But a mongrel is simply something that is a mixture or combination of elements. Indeed, purists may object that Bordeaux wine is a mongrel, because it mixes two (or sometimes several) grape varieties. But Claret, undoubtedly one of the best wines in the world, is nonetheless the result.[19]

This might also explain my more natural métier as an essayist. For the most part, I have not sought to write singularly-focused monographs. Rather, my work has tended to consist of essays, compositions, treatises, and trials. These are often reflections, refractions, and reviews that are tested in reception, before being further refined. Contextual theology is dialogical discipline. It is not a matter of making definitive and declamatory statements that drown out the subject. Contextual theology listens, receives and revises itself in the very acts of speaking and writing: it understands that the circumstances it writes on and in are subject to change.

One can quibble about labels here. If this is theology, exactly what *kind* of theology is it? Is it pastoral, practical, systematic, confessional—or even pragmatic? The labels don't easily work here, though "contextual" would be the broadest christening here, largely due to the intentional and consistent binocular approach, namely reading and interpreting the church-world, Christianity-culture, theology-society and politics-religion axes, each of which depends of a measure of seasoning from the realms of social scientific theory in the field of ecclesiology. The art is in the blend. I am ever-mindful of Rowan Williams's understated confession that "the theologian is always beginning in the middle of things."[20]

So my work simply highlights the fact that purist approaches to subjects and issues, whilst highly-prized—and rightly so—can sometimes be restrictive in the narrower, single lens they afford us. There is a difference between a telescope and binoculars. And the blended theological-social science approach I bring to ecclesiology recognizes the social reality of churches, as well as respecting their spiritual claims and experiences. So the work of Nicholas Healy, James Hopewell, Urban Holmes III, Daniel W. Hardy, Mady Thung, and others, all enable us to gain some kind of illumination through the blend of disciplines, methods, and insights they bring together. Those looking for other theological interlocutors who have served as signposts for my work, in some respects, will recognize David Tracy's approach to theology as constitutive. Tracy had dual commitments and his own binocular approach to theology. He was

19. But if I may permit personal confession here: I am teetotal.
20. Williams, *On Christian Theology*, xii.

a committed member of the church, and of the academy, and he wrestled with the conflict of interests and moralities this sometimes posed. Tracy was also clear, as am I, that the theologian has a vocation to address three publics: the church, the academy, and society. These frequently overlap, and cause us to fuse our perspectives in order to sustain the richest possible theological insight and reading of texts, situations, and possibilities. In a similar vein, George Lindbeck's approach to theology—constructing conversations across disciplines and issues in the interests of wider ecclesial and ecumenical illumination—also shapes my thinking. There is some recognition here (perhaps following Peter Berger's notion of the "heretical imperative") that no single theological method on its own is ever sound or sufficient. The art of theology lies in the blending of recipes, methods, and ingredients. So for Berger, the deductive, reductive, and inductive theological strategies, though separable, are always in fact intra- and interdependent. Kathryn Tanner expresses the nature of the work like this:

> The basic operations that theologians perform have a twofold character. First, theologians show an artisan-like inventiveness in the way they work on a variety of materials that do not dictate of themselves what theologians should do with them. Second, theologians exhibit a tactical cleverness with respect to other interpretations and organizations of such materials that are already on the ground. . . . The materials theologians work on are incredibly diverse . . . theologians use a kind of tact requiring numerous ad hoc and situation-specific adjustments. In contrast to what the values of clarity, consistency and systematicity might suggest of themselves, even academic theologians do not simply follow logical deductions where they lead or the dictates of abstract principles when arriving at their conclusions. They do not construct their theological positions by applying generalities to particular cases, or emend them by trying to reproduce the same clear meanings in the terms of a new day, so as to convey them across putatively accidental differences in circumstances and vocabulary. Instead, they operate by tying things together—the Latin meaning of *religare*, after all, is to bind.[21]

In much of what I have described above, in terms of the five-fold process, one can easily imagine getting lost in the detail, and lost in space—the space of research, and perhaps the fieldwork. I am mindful of the counsel of Berger and Luckmann: "It is important to keep in mind that the objectivity of the institutional world, however massive it may appear to the individual, is a humanly produced, constructed objectivity."[22] The key to orientation is perspective: wisdom is born from humility, and it is crucial to respect the material under consideration.

It is a work of "deep listening," as one commentator puts it;[23] "sounding the depths" of ecclesial life is how James Hopewell has described it. This approach has at

21. Tanner, *Theories of Culture*, 87–92.

22. Berger and Luckmann, *The Social Construction of Reality*, 78.

23. An article in the academic journal *Theology*, by Nigel Rooms, states that Martyn Percy is

least one practical application for churches. Much of my work has explored ecclesial *adiaphora*—the term for those issues that are *not* fundamental to the faith, so can be classed as "second order." Sexuality and gender might be examples; as might be governance and polity. Richard Hooker's Laws of Ecclesiastical Polity consistently argued that adiaphora should not be allowed to affect the unity of the church. Indeed, there might be a case for adopting elements of *eudiaphora* in today's church—literally, "good difference." Hooker also wrote of "harmonious dissimilitude"—agreeing to disagree, but agreeing to still walk together into (God's) future.

For our time, this "good difference" may be a profound vision. It is striking that Hooker wrote four hundred years ago, and before the outbreak of a deeply divisive civil war that lasted from 1642 until beyond 1649. The religious and political passions and opinions divided families down the middle, young from old, kith from kin, neighbors from friends. Even the death of Charles I did not heal these wounds. Neither did the Restoration of his son, Charles II, in 1660.

So in these difficult and demanding times for the Anglican Communion, as well as religion and public life more generally, I have sought to advocate a "peaceable, polite and restrained" approach whilst "making peace between competing communities of conviction.[24] My viewpoints typically argue for the "middle ground" between evangelical and catholic positions, and appeal to Anglican comprehensiveness, the tradition of respecting theological differences.[25] A proponent of "generous orthodoxy," I consistently argue for a theological approach that copes with serious forms of dispute and threats of schism, and addresses emerging or manifest power inequalities building up in the church, such that certain proposed reforms can be experienced as alienating, and even oppressive.

So for all my advocacy of moderate, temperate, and mild ecclesiology, there must also be a place for passion, and even for some "prophetic anger." The blend is, perhaps, unavoidable. And here one thinks of family life, which one hopes will be mostly peaceable, and develop a functioning home for the nourishing and flourishing of those who dwell therein. But that same home—the household of faith—also has to reserve a place and have respect for the expression of ire, which can signal a range of possibilities: injustice, alarm, concern, love, and censure are just some of the reasons why anger can be good and appropriate.

As I sat down to write this, I could not help but note that the set lectionary reading for our service of Sung Evensong in the cathedral tonight features John's account of Jesus cleansing the temple (John 2:13-22). Jesus is supposed to be a peaceable and wise teacher. But he creates mayhem in the temple, and upsets all the people going about their lawful trading in dubious "religious tat" and offerings. He goes the whole

---

the British theologian who is the closest to being a "missionary anthropologist." See Rooms, "Deep Listening."

24. Cornwell, "Quiet, Please."

25. See Percy, *Anglicanism*; *Thirty Nine New Articles*; and *The Future Shapes of Anglicanism*.

hog too, driving them out with a whip that he made himself. That must have taken time; so this is a planned attack.

The story in John's gospel is a meditation on Jesus' manifesting wisdom, and also his alleged foolishness; Jesus spends much of his ministry being cast, not as a hero, but as something of a loose cannon; and possibly even a deranged prophet. His words and works are prejudged by his critics, because even in first century Palestine, the social and theological construction of reality seem to prejudice many people's perceptions of Jesus.

To casual onlookers, turning out the traders from the Temple is a foolish thing to do: they don't mean any harm, do they? True, we all know that the price of pigeons will be double what you'd pay outside the Temple. We all accept this. Jesus, in contrast, does not; and as in other cases, behaves "rather badly." Behold! He eats and drinks with a bad crowd; he finds himself narrated as a glutton and a drunkard. So Jesus says, somewhat cryptically, that "wisdom is vindicated by her deeds."

Wisdom is key. Because the second part of the gospel story outlines how the seemingly wise and righteous appear not to be able to see what is front of their noses, whilst the apparently foolish and unrighteous seem to have perceived. So Jesus' action in the Temple—reckless, violent, and apparently intemperate—contains quite a radical, strong message. It conveys wisdom: sometimes, breaking our frames of reference with such sharpness and anger is the only way to get people to see how foolish they have been.

This is the key to understanding the incident: it is about breaking paradigms, and disrupting prevailing frames of reference. So, Jesus is acting something out in this narrative: there was really no point at all in trading up from a pigeon to a dove. Neither sacrifice would bring you closer to God; you are wasting your money. There was no point in going for the "three-for-two" offer on goats; or the "buy-one-get-one-free" offer on lambs.

Much of the gospel of John is all about being reconciled to what has been hidden, and looking deeper into what has been revealed, and to seeing beyond the apparently obvious: to find the wisdom in apparent folly. This is why Jesus' anger in the gospel is so interesting in this story; for it seems not to be a hot, quick, irrational "snap", but rather a cold and calculating anger; inspirational ire, indeed.

There is a difference between hot anger and cold, perhaps righteous, anger. Jesus actually went away and *made* the whip of cords he used on the hapless traders. This is a cold premeditated attack; not a rush of blood to the head. He has, as the Epistle to James puts it, "been slow to anger"—but he's got there. And now he's meting out some discipline. Rather like Arnie (a robot from the future) in the film *The Terminator*, he's seen the Temple, and said to his audience: "I'll be back." As Harvey Cox noted in *On Not Leaving it to the Snake* (1968), the first and original sin is not disobedience. It is, rather, indifference.[26] We can no longer ignore the pain and alienation that others in

26. Cox, *Not Leaving It to the Snake* (SCM Press, 1968).

the church experience—and especially when this is *because* of the church. Indifference is pitiful, and it is the enemy of compassion.

So there are three things to say in relation to Jesus' emotional temperament here. First, what is Jesus so upset about in the Temple? It seems to me that it lies in assumptions: about the "natural order of things"; about status and privilege; about possessions; about prevailing wisdom. This is, in other words, un-examined lives and practices lived in unexamined contexts. Everyone is blind. Jesus' action forces us to confront the futile sight before us. His anger forces us to look again. (On this, see Lytta Bassett's excellent *Holy Anger*—which offers a profound theological excavation of these themes.)[27]

Second, the story chides us all for that most simple of venial sins: overlooking. The trading has been happening down the ages. It is simply part of the furniture; it barely merits a look, let alone comment. Jesus, of course, always looks deeper. But the lesson of the story is that, having looked into us with such penetration, his gaze then often shifts to those who are below us, and unseen. That is, those with less wealth, health, intelligence, conversation and social skills; or just less life.

Third, the besetting sin is that the Temple traders appear to accept the status quo. The story has one thing to say about this, and one only: *don't*. Don't accept that a simple small gesture cannot ripple out and begin to change things. Don't accept, wearily, that you can't make a difference. You can. Sometimes the change may be radical; but more often than not, the change comes about through small degrees. Reform can be glacial, and it can be adaptionist. We need to be ready to do both.

So, what of our unity, maturity, and stability in a church that makes space for radical gestures such as Jesus, and even for a measure of righteous, prophetic, prescient anger? Specifically in Anglican terms, it is perhaps worth pointing out that Anglican polity is, first and foremost, a social vision that has ecclesial consequences. It is not an ecclesial polity with (accidental) social consequences. The Elizabethan Settlement was a social vision for mildness, breadth, inclusiveness, charity, generosity, diversity—and it produced the *Prayer Book*. The *Prayer Book* did not produce that society. The *Prayer Book* is not the cause of settlement: it is just one result of that settlement.

Settlement is a small seed, to be sure. But Anglicanism is not alone in being a social vision first, and a church second. I think of Methodists, and in particular, a word used of their polity in governance: that word is "Moderator." It is not the only church to be governed by a Moderator. But the word implies that "moderation"—the practice and virtue of being intentionally and dispositionally "moderate"—might be incredibly important for social and ecclesial life.

The word was originally used of weather and other physical conditions. But the one who moderates is the one who works within peaceable bounds, and practices restraint. The Moderator regulates, mitigates, restrains, tempers; is one who "abates excessiveness" and gently but firmly "presides" over potentially divisive debates.

27. Bassett, *Holy Anger*.

In his recent book, *Faces of Moderation*,[28] Aurelian Craiutu argues that moderation is not an ideology, but rather a disposition. It is a composite of character and virtues that does not divide the world into light and dark, true and false, good and bad. At the same time, moderation does not accept everything as equal and valid. It does not, for example, split the difference between racism and inclusion. It accepts that some opinions and ideologies are irredeemable, and should be rejected. Rather, moderation works at unity and harmony. And it accepts that on our own, we cannot be entirely right or good. We need each other, and we need to value and cherish our differences—and sometimes our disagreements—if we are to progress.

In his earlier book, Craiutu argued that moderation was a virtue for courageous minds. Tacitus mourned the lost virtue of moderation—calling moderation "the most difficult lesson of wisdom." I think that being a moderate, rather like being ecumenical, is not weak-willed or sloppily liberal; rather, it is about being charitable, generous, and tough-minded, and committed to holding the center as a place of civil convening. In other words, this is a difficult blend to achieve.

We live in uncertain times: an age of austerity, anxiety, assertion, and anger.[29] It can all feel a bit unstable at times. Institutions such as our universities, seminaries, galleries, museums, and most especially our churches, are called in such times to be stable, public bodies that transcend epochs like this. They are to be places of inclusive learning and profound reflection. They are here for human and social flourishing, nourishing, and learning. These places are called to be oases of moral agency and social capital. We will need this in the future. In the here and now, therefore, we are here to create citizens and cultivate citizenship; and yes, continue the work of building civilization.

These are some of the reasons why I am so committed to the mild, temperate, and middle ground so beloved on Anglican polity, and to the virtue of moderation. I believe that to be honed in the manner of Christ is to become gentle, meek and mild. But without foregoing the capacity to be radical when needed, and when necessary, using passions, energies and anger creatively, because they are signs of love and commitment, not envy, malice, or vengeance. In all this, and if we can create a mild cultural climate, we will discover that freedom flourishes in temperate zones. It does not survive the burning faith of our demagogues, prophets, and crowds, as Raymond Aaron once remarked.

But we know too, as Isaiah Berlin reflected, that the middle ground is a notoriously exposed place; a dangerous and difficult position to inhabit. But it is the place for governing and shaping society. As Michael Oakeshott once opined, the business of government is not to inflame the passions of the people and give them new subjects to feed off; but rather, to inject into the activities of an already too-passionate people an ingredient of moderation.

28. Craiutu, *Faces of Moderation*; see also Craiutu, *A Virtue for Common Minds*.

29. Mishra, *Age of Anger*.

Now, moderation may seem like a tiny seed. In some ways it is. So we do well to remember that what Jesus inaugurated was eternal: "the just and gentle rule of the Kingdom of God"—inclusive, prophetic, pastoral, kind, wise, and foolish. And to live and practice this most taxing of blends, we need to become seeds of moderation, and God's most generous moderators, to settle and establish his kingdom. The call of our Christian faith is to be a people of unity, maturity, and stability. But this also incites us to be a people of fervent faith and calm temperament; a people of moderation and passionate commitment; and we are invited to be agents of its inauguration.

That said, and taking account of Gerard Mannion's earlier chapter (seven), I note that Pope Francis's ecclesial vision calls for "prophetic obedience" to the gospel. This prophetic obedience is faithful to the word of God, and to Christian tradition. But it is also faithful to the prompting of the Holy Spirit in the here and now. The prophetic obedience requires the church and believers to listen to what the Spirit is saying to the church through LGBTQ agendas, through the marginalized (on grounds of race, age, or gender), through the poor and suffering, through the damage being done to our natural environment and climate. All of this requires personal and communal discernment. The task of the church is not only to be faithful to the past, and to the inherited treasures of its tradition, but also to listen attentively to what the Spirit is saying now to the churches. It was just the same in the early church—who soon embraced Gentiles, and many kinds of minorities—recognizing that the prayer "thy kingdom come" is an utterance that requires the church to listen and receive from the world, as much as it might proclaim its message. The Spirit of God is already abroad in the world: that is the *Mission Dei*.[30]

In all this, I am mindful of the counsel of one of my colleagues, the Reverend Canon Professor Nigel Biggar, the Regius Professor of Social, Moral and Pastoral Theology here at the University of Oxford—one of the four Professorial Canons' posts here at Christ Church, Oxford. Nigel writes that:

> True prophets are ones who don't much enjoy playing prophet. They don't enjoy alienating people, as speakers of uncomfortable truths tend to do. They don't enjoy the sound of their own solitary righteousness and they don't enjoy being in a minority of one. True prophets tend to find the whole business irksome and painful. They want to wriggle out of it, and they only take to it with reluctance. So beware of those who take to prophesy like a duck to water, and who revel in the role. They probably aren't the real thing.[31]

I find myself agreeing with these sentiments, and as I now reflect, realize that my favorite book of scripture was always *Jonah*: short, simple—and a decisive vindication of God's unquenchable love and inexhaustible mercy. Prophets are innately cautious creatures. Caricatures of raging firestorm preachers should be set aside. True prophets are

---

30. See Hinze, Prophetic Obedience.
31. Biggar, "On Judgment, Repentance and Restoration."

more emotionally integrated. Their anger, if they have it, is born in deep love, not hate. They are pastoral, contextual, and political theologians. They care about people and places. They have virtues such as compassion, care, kindness, self-control, humility, and gentleness. They are peace-builders, rooted in hope. Their preaching seeks the same world envisioned by Isaiah: "the wolf shall dwell with the lamb, and the leopard shall lie down with the kid; and the calf and the young lion and the fatling together; and a little child shall lead them" (Isa 11:6). But prophets have anger too; albeit only reluctantly expressed. So the passion to protest advocated and the vocation of resistance against prevailing powers by the likes of Una Kroll, Ched Myers, or Gerald Arbuckle[32]—all can play their part in shaping the world and the church. A thorough radical/contextual/ pastoral theology—from the Latin word *radix* (literally, "root")—gets to the heart of the matter, as Christ frequently does in his teachings and ministry.

All this needs to be blended with the pure and peaceable wisdom of God and the virtue of moderation that is no less of the Holy Spirit, and which seeks to bring us together—through certain conflicts—to a place of truer communion. This, in turn, needs to be rooted in the hope of the kingdom of God that is to come, and in the generosity and pastoral-patience of God with us all in the here and now. The tension all Christians labor with frequently lies in the gaps: between the values, hopes, and deep desire for the Kingdom of God to come; and the church here on earth, in all its miscibility, muddling, and machinations. Becoming a reasonable radical, or a radical-moderate, or even an avowed advocate of passionate coolness is, I think, not so much a question of a person's character, personal outlook, or even their encultured worldview. It might actually be our vocation—as a church, and as Christian disciples—to embrace and follow.

Bibliography

Arbuckle, Gerald. *Refounding the Church: Dissent for Leadership.* London: Geoffrey Chapman, 1993.

Aron, Raymond. *Main Currents in Sociological Thought.* No. 2. London: Penguin, 1970.

Bassett, Lytta. *Holy Anger: Jacob, Job, Jesus.* London: Continuum, 2007.

Bell, Catherine. "Modernism and Postmodernism in the Study of Religion." *Religious Studies Review* (July 1996).

Berger, Peter. *Invitation to Sociology.* New York: Doubleday, 1963.

Berger, Peter L., and Thomas Luckmann. *The Social Construction of Reality.* London: Penguin, 1967.

Biggar, Nigel. "On Judgment, Repentance and Restoration." Unpublished sermon preached at Christ Church Cathedral, March 5, 2017. Quoted in *Untamed Gospel: Protests, Poems, Prose*, edited by Martyn Percy (London: Canterbury, 2017).

Caputo, John. *The Prayers and Tears of Jacques Derrida: Religion without Religion.* Bloomington: Indiana University Press, 1997.

32. See Myers, *Binding the Strong Man*, and Arbuckle, *Refounding the Church*. See Kroll, *Vocation to Resistance*.

Clarke, Peter, and Peter Byrne. *Religion Defined and Explained*. New York: St Martin's, 1993.

Cornwell, Peter. "Quiet, Please." *Times Literary Supplement*, October 25, 2013.

Craiutu, Aurelian. *Faces of Moderation: The Art of Balance in Age of Extremes*. Philadelphia: University of Pennsylvania Press, 2017.

———. *A Virtue for Common Minds: Moderation in French Political Thought, 1748–1830*. Princeton: Princeton University Press, 2012.

Gutting, Gary. "Deconstructing God." *The New York Times*, March 9, 2014. http://opinionator. blogs.nytimes.com/2014/03/09/deconstructing-god/?_r=0.

Healy, Nicholas. *Church, World and the Christian Life: Practical-Prophetic Ecclesiology*. Cambridge: Cambridge University Press, 2002.

Hinze, Bradford. *Prophetic Obedience: Ecclesiology for a Dialogical Church*. New York: Orbis, 2016.

Kroll, Una. *Vocation to Resistance: Contemplation and Change*. London: DLT, 1995.

Mills, C. Wright. *The Sociological Imagination*. New York: Oxford University Press, 1959.

Mishra, Pankaj. *Age of Anger: A History of the Present*. London: Allen Lane, 2017.

Myers, Ched. *Binding the Strong Man: A Political Reading of Mark's Story of Jesus*. Maryknoll, NY: Orbis, 1970.

Percy, Martyn. "Adventure and Atrophy in a Charismatic Movement: Returning to the 'Toronto Blessing.'" In *Practicing the Faith: The Ritual Life of Pentecostal-Charismatic Christians*, edited by M. Lindhardt, 152–78. Oxford: Berghahn, 2011.

———. "The Anatomy of Fundamentalism." In *Fundamentalisms: Threats and Ideologies in the Modern World*, edited by James Dunn, 47–68. London: I. B. Tauris, 2015.

———. *Anglicanism: Confidence, Commitment and Communion*. Farnham: Ashgate, 2013.

———. "The City on a Beach: Future Prospects for Charismatic Movements at the End of the Twentieth Century." In *Charismatic Christianity: Sociological Perspectives*, edited by S. Hunt, M. Hamilton, and T. Walter, 205–28. London: Macmillan, 1997.

———. *Clergy: The Origin of Species*. London: T. & T. Clark International, 2006.

———. *Engaging with Contemporary Culture: Christianity, Theology and the Concrete Church*. Farnham: Ashgate, 2005.

———. "Falling Far Short: Taking Sin Seriously." In *Reinhold Niebuhr and Contemporary Politics*, edited by R. Harries and S. Platten, 116–28. Oxford: Oxford University Press, 2010.

———. *The Future Shapes of Anglicanism: Charts, Currents, Contours*. London: Routledge, 2017.

———. "The Holy Spirit in the Church of England Today: Some Factors in Occlusion." In *The Holy Spirit and the Church: Economic Reflections with a Pastoral Perspective*, edited by T. Hughson. London: Routledge, 2016.

———. "Label or Libel." In *Sociology, Theology and the Curriculum*, edited by L. Francis, 82–92. London: Cassell, 1999.

———. "A Place at High Table? Assessing the Future of Charismatic Christianity." In *Predicting Religion: Christian, Secular and Alternative Futures*, edited by G. Davie, P. Heelas, and L. Woodhead, 95–108. Farnham, UK: Ashgate, 2003.

———. *Power and the Church: Ecclesiology in an Age of Transition*. London: Cassell, 1998.

———. *Salt of the Earth: Religious Resilience in a Secular Age*. Sheffield: Bloomsbury Academic Collection, 2016.

———. *Shaping the Church: The Promise of Implicit Theology*. Farnham: Ashgate, 2010.

————. *Thirty Nine New Articles: An Anglican Landscape of Faith.* London: Canterbury, 2013.

————. *Words, Wonders and Power: Understanding Contemporary Christian Fundamentalism and Revivalism.* London: SPCK, 1996.

Percy, Martyn, ed. *Intimate Affairs: Spirituality & Sexuality in Perspective.* London: DLT, 1997.

Percy, Martyn, and G. R. Evans, eds. *Managing the Church? Order and Organisation in a Secular Age.* Sheffield: Sheffield Academic, 2000.

Rooms, Nigel. "Deep Listening: A Call for Missionary Anthropology." *Theology* 115:2 (2012) 99–108.

Russell, Anthony. *The Clerical Profession.* London: SPCK, 1980.

Tanner, Kathryn. *The Politics of God: Christian Theologies and Social Justice.* Augsburg: Fortress, 1992.

————. *Theories of Culture: A New Agenda for Theology.* Minneapolis: Fortress, 1997.

Williams, Rowan. *On Christian Theology.* Oxford: Blackwell, 2000.

Martyn Percy: Selected Publications

Authored Books:

1996   *Words, Wonders and Power: Understanding Contemporary Christian Fundamentalism and Revivalism*, SPCK

1998   *Power and the Church: Ecclesiology in an Age of Transition*, Cassell

2002   *Salt of the Earth: Religious Resilience in a Secular Age*, Sheffield Academic Press and T&T Clark (reissued in Bloomsbury Academic Collection, 2016)

2005   *Engaging with Contemporary Culture: Christianity, Theology and the Concrete Church*, Ashgate

2006   *Clergy: The Origins of the Species*, T&T Clark International

2010   *Shaping the Church: The Promise of Implicit Theology*, Ashgate

2012   *The Ecclesial Canopy: Faith, Hope, Charity*, Ashgate

2013   *Anglicanism: Confidence, Commitment and Communion*, Ashgate

2013   *Thirty-Nine New Articles: An Anglican Landscape of Faith*, Canterbury Press

2017   *The Future Shapes of Anglicanism: Charts, Currents, Contours*, Routledge

Edited and Co-Authored Books:

1997   *Intimate Affairs: Spirituality & Sexuality in Perspective*, Darton, Longman & Todd

2000   *Previous Convictions: Studies in Religious Conversion*, SPCK

2000   *Managing the Church? Order and Organisation in a Secular Age* (with G. R. Evans), Sheffield Academic Press/T&T Clark International

2000   *Calling Time: Religion, Society and Change at the Turn of the Millennium*, Sheffield Academic Press/T&T Clark International (reissued in Bloomsbury Academic Collection, 2016)

2001   *Restoring the Image: Essays in Honour of David Martin* (with A. Walker), Sheffield Academic Press/T&T Clark International

2001   *Darkness Yielding* (with Rowan Williams et al.), Cairns Publishing

2009   *Darkness Yielding* (Third Edition, Revised), Canterbury Press

2002   *Fundamentalism, Church and Society* (with Ian Jones), SPCK

2004   *The Character of Wisdom: Essays for Wesley Carr* (with Stephen Lowe), Ashgate

2005   *Why Liberal Churches are Growing* (with Ian Markham), T&T Clark,

2008   *Evaluating Fresh Expressions* (with Louis Nelstrop), Canterbury Press

2010   *Christ and Culture: Essays After Lambeth* (with Ian Markham et al.), Canterbury Press

2010   *Transfiguring Episcope: Women, Church, Leadership* (with Christian Rees), Canterbury Press

2012   *A Point of Balance* (with Robert Slocum), Canterbury Press

2014   *The Bright Field* (with Rowan Williams, Sam Wells, et al.), Canterbury Press

2014   *The Wisdom of the Spirit: Gospel, Church & Culture* (with Peter Ward), Ashgate

2015   *The Curate's Survival Guide* (with Matthew Caminer and Beau Stevenson), SPCK

2015   *Oxford Handbook of Anglican Studies* (edited with Mark Chapman and Sathi Clarke), Oxford University Press

2017   *SPCK Handbook (Study of Ministry)* (edited with Ian Markham & Emma Percy), SPCK

2017   *Untamed Gospel: Poems, Prose and Protests* (title TBC; with Jim Cotter et al.), Canterbury Press

2017   *Clergy, Culture and Ministry The Dynamics of Roles and Relations in Church and Society* (by Ian Tomlinson), SCM Press

Edited Works:

- "Falling Far Short: Taking Sin Seriously" in *Reinhold Niebuhr and Contemporary Politics*, eds. R. Harries and S. Platten, Oxford University Press, 2010

- (from "Adventure and Atrophy in a Charismatic Movement" in *Practicing the Faith: The Ritual Life of Pentecostal-Charismatic Christians*, ed. Martin Lindhardt, Berghahn Books, 2011

- "The Future of Religion" (with Grace Davie) in the *Oxford Textbook of Spirituality in Healthcare*, eds. M. Cobb, C. Puchalski & B. Rumbold, Oxford University Press, 2012

- "Jazz and Anglican Spirituality: Some Notes on Connections" in *Christian Congregational Music: Performance, Identity and Experience*, eds. M. Ingalls, C. Landau, and T. Wagner, Ashgate, 2013

- "The Anatomy of Fundamentalism" in *Fundamentalisms: Threats and Ideologies in the Modern World*, ed. James Dunn, I. B. Tauris, 2015

- "Identity, Character and Practices in Rural Anglican Congregation" in *Theologically-Engaged Anthropology*, ed. Derrick Lemmons, Oxford University Press, 2017

- "Class, Ethnicity and Education: Leadership, Congregations and the Sociology of Anglicanism" in *Oxford History of the Anglican Church in the Twentieth Century*, ed. Jeremy Morris, Oxford University Press, 2017

- "The Household of Faith: Anglican Obliquity and the Lambeth Conference" in *The Lambeth Conference and the Anglican Communion*, ed. Paul Avis, Bloomsbury T&T Clark, 2017

- "Restoration, Retrieval and Renewal: Recovering Healing Ministry in the Church—Some Critical Reflections" in *Theologies of Retrieval: Practices and Perspectives*, ed. Darren Sarisky, Bloomsbury T&T Clark, 2017

Author Index

Subject Index

ACNA, 299

bishops, 10, 12, 69, 92, 94, 99, 109–10, 119, 144–
45, 148–49, 171, 186–87, 205, 217n2,
218, 236, 239, 242–44, 262–63, 292–95,
297–300, 323n21, 327
bishops, women, 12, 143, 144n46, 147, 149n76,
204–7, 242, 292, 317
Body of Christ, 10, 100, 103–6, 109–10, 112–13,
180, 189, 213, 234, 237, 314–16, 319–20

charismatic, x, 5, 7–8, 11, 16n2, 20n15, 23–25,
39–41, 46–50, 52–55, 56n46, 57n49, 87,
138, 154–60, 167, 186, 203, 223–27, 230,
233, 261–63, 269, 272, 274, 277, 279–81,
306, 346

demon (demonic, Satan), 3, 17, 38, 227n1, 228–
29, 231, 234, 279

ecclesiology, xi, xv, xvii, 10, 14n38, 18, 20, 23, 47,
59, 61–63, 80–88, 91–97, 104, 117, 120–
24, 127, 130–31, 154n4, 158, 169, 173,
180–81, 193–94, 212–14, 217, 219, 245,
282, 310, 315–17, 327–29, 331–36, 345
ecclesiology, liberation, 92–94
ethnography, xvii, 23, 62n11, 63, 123, 193, 202,
281–86, 308, 332

feminism, xv, 19n8, 207, 305
formation, 62n9, 67, 70n16, 100–103, 106,
114–15, 130n5, 148n73, 153–56, 165–71,
173–78, 185–86, 193–94, 214, 247–53,
277n2, 303, 319, 321, 328–29, 332
Fundamentalism, 3, 21–22, 25, 47, 56–57, 117–
18, 121–23, 194, 213, 224, 269–75, 314,
328, 329n3, 345–47

healing, 48, 50, 74–75, 110, 141, 183, 193, 223–
34, 277, 280–81, 286, 315, 347
homosexuality, 12, 114, 293–94, 296–97

LGBT, 11–12, 59, 125, 139, 141, 144, 147, 292,
294, 296–97, 301, 324

marriage, 12, 68, 76, 120, 125, 138, 141, 144–46,
149, 292–93, 295–96, 306n12, 310
music, xv, 7, 9, 11, 72, 77, 152–62, 186, 193–94,
212–16, 253, 303, 327–28, 333

Pedagogy, 91, 124, 164, 166–74, 177–78, 252n13,
260n3, 264n7
politics, 18, 22, 29, 64, 107n35, 112n54, 114n62,
115, 116, 189, 193, 272, 333n18, 334,
342–43, 346
prayer, 8, 40, 50–52, 54–55, 57, 70–71, 74–75,
112, 171, 202, 204, 206n2, 215, 247,
249–50, 270, 300, 302, 312, 322, 328n1,
338, 340

radical orthodoxy, xvi, 3, 13–14, 19–21

sacraments, 67, 70–72, 79, 94n53, 104–5, 109–
11, 214
sex, 12, 22–23, 29, 32, 40, 74, 90, 117, 119–26,
137–49, 186–87, 193, 231, 244, 261, 273,
291–98, 300–301, 317, 322, 329, 336, 345
symbol(s), 4, 6, 10, 20, 50, 53, 67–68, 70, 72,
74, 76–79, 92, 104, 115, 129, 131, 142,
202, 229, 259, 261–62, 264–65, 272–75,
282–83, 286, 311, 321, 330

theology, x, xv-xviii, 3–4, 6–10, 14n38, 18–19,
21–25, 27, 32, 40, 47–48, 59–63, 67–72,
76–77, 82–86, 91–94, 101, 104, 117–18,
120–21, 123–25, 131–32, 138, 140, 141,
142n33, 148–49, 153, 160–62, 165,
167–72, 173–78, 180, 193–94, 212–14,
217, 230, 232, 234, 239–40, 242–45, 247,
249, 267, 274, 298, 314–15, 319–20, 322,
328–29, 331–32, 334–35, 341

353